THE ANNALS OF ST-B

Manchester Medieval Sources series

series adviser   Janet L. Nelson

This series aims to meet a growing need amongst students and teachers of medieval history for translations of key sources that are directly usable in students' own work. The series will provide texts central to medieval studies courses and will focus upon the diverse cultural, social as well as political conditions that affected the functioning of all levels of medieval society. Each volume will include a comprehensive guide to the sources' interpretation, including discussion of critical linguistic problems and an assessment of the most recent research on the topics being covered.

forthcoming titles in the series will include

Donald Bullough   *The Vikings in Paris*

John Edwards   *The Jews in western Europe, 1400–1600*

Chris Given-Wilson   *Chronicles of the Revolution, 1397–1400*

Rosemary Horrox   *The aftermath of the Black Death*

Simon Lloyd   *The impact of the crusades: the experience of England, 1095–1274*

Tim Reuter   *The Annals of Fulda: ninth-century histories, volume II*

Richard Smith   *Sources for the population history of England, 1000–1540*

Robert Swanson   *Catholic England: religion, faith and observance before the Reformation*

J. A. Watt   *The origins of anti-semitism in Europe*

THE ANNALS OF ST-BERTIN

NINTH-CENTURY HISTORIES, VOLUME I

translated and annotated by   Janet L. Nelson

 Manchester University Press
Manchester and New York

distributed exclusively in the USA and Canada by St. Martin's Press

Copyright © Janet L. Nelson 1991

Published by Manchester University Press
Oxford Road, Manchester M13 9PL, England
and Room 400, 175 Fifth Avenue, New York, NY 10010, USA

Distributed exclusively in the USA and Canada
by St. Martin's Press, Inc., 175 Fifth Avenue, New York, NY 10010, USA

A catalogue record for this book is available from the British Library

Library of Congress cataloging in publication data
Annales Bertiniani, English.
      The annals of St-Bertin : translated from the edition of Léon Levillain
(1951) and Félix Grat (1940) / translated and edited by Janet L. Nelson.
            p. cm. — (Ninth-century histories : v. 1) (Manchester medieval sources
series)
      Translation of: Annales Bertiniani.
      Includes bibliographical references and index.
      ISBN 0-7190-3425-6. — ISBN 0-7190-3426-4 (pbk.)
            1. France—History—To 987—Sources. I. Nelson, Janet (Janet L.)
II. Saint-Bertin (Monastery : Saint-Omer, Pas-de-Calais, France)
III. Title. IV. Series. V. Series: Manchester medieval sources series.
DC70. A2A713 1981
944—dc20   91-4030

ISBN 0 7190 3425-6 *hardback*
ISBN 0 7190 3426-4 *paperback*

Printed in Great Britain
by Bell & Bain Ltd, Glasgow

CONTENTS

PREFACE

This book began as a rough translation for the use of history students taking the 'Charles the Bald and Alfred' special subject in the University of London. Over the past twelve years the translation has been much revised, and the notes gradually supplied, in response to continuing student demand. I am extremely grateful to all those undergraduates and postgraduates whose suggestions and questions have helped to improve and clarify the text, and whose keen interest in ninth-century history has been a constant inspiration. It is entirely appropriate that this should be the first of a new series of annotated translations of medieval texts. My own teaching experience has convinced me over the years that students well supplied with primary sources can find the study of the Middle Ages particularly satisfying: it offers, as more recent periods seldom can, direct experience of working with a sizeable proportion, sometimes all, of the raw materials available on major historical problems. What is needed, therefore, is to make available in (as King Alfred put it) 'a language we can all understand' the 'tools' of our craft. And just as tools come supplied with 'instructions for use', our translations need introductions and extensive notes to enable students to make the most of them.

The project of translating, and explaining, a wide range of sources for Continental as well as British history is especially timely, as the prospect of a wider and more united Europe evokes growing interest in a shared, and crucially formative, European past. Here, medievalists look forward to making a large contribution. From its inception, the present series has drawn strength from the positive response and practical help of many colleagues in polytechnics (where the teaching of medieval history ought surely to retain its place) as well as in universities. I welcome the opportunity to thank them here, and to acknowledge in particular the support of Margaret Gibson and Edward James, whose pioneering work in translating the sources of a rather earlier period has provided a model for a medieval series, and of David Rollason, whose farsightedness smoothed our path. The onlie begetter of the present series is Richard Purslow of MUP: he and his colleague Jane Carpenter (both with fairly recent first-hand experience of studying medieval history) have worked like Trojans (or Franks) to research potential topics and recruit author-translators. I greatly appreciate their professionalism and enthusiasm.

In preparing the present volume, I have incurred particular debts of gratitude. The most longstanding is to Silvia Blumer, who typed *The Annals of St-Bertin* from my original draft translation and responded with characteristic efficiency and good humour to this unexpected extension of her *au pair* job. The second, almost as longstanding, is to Tim Reuter, whose labours on the *Annals of Fulda* have paralleled and inspired mine on the *AB*, and whose advice and friendship have sustained this enterprise from first to last. I am very grateful to Simon Coupland, John Gillingham and Ian Wood for critical comment on the translation and for many helpful suggestions. My special thanks go to my husband Howard for long-term encouragement and, more recently, for providing an ideal working environment in Aquitaine. Finally, this book's dedication acknowledges the achievement of the editors of the Latin text of the *Annals of St-Bertin*: Félix Grat, finest of textual scholars, *mort pour la patrie* in 1940,[1] and Léon Levillain, tireless student and still unrivalled connoisseur of the Carolingian world.[2]

1 See the *mémoires* in *Mélanges dédiés à la mémoire de Félix Grat*, vol. i (Paris 1946).
2 See the obituary in *Le Moyen Âge*, 58, 1952: 213-19.

LIST OF ABBREVIATIONS

AAng — *Annals of Angoulême*

AB — *Annals of St-Bertin*

AF — *Annals of Fulda*

AFont — *Annals of Fontenelle (St-Wandrille)*

AM — *Annales du Midi*

ASC — *Anglo-Saxon Chronicle*

AX — *Annals of Xanten*

AV — *Annals of St-Vaast*

BEC — *Bibliothèque de l'École des Chartes*

BISI — *Bollettino dell'Istituto Storico Italiano per il medioevo*

CCM — *Cahiers de Civilisation médiévale*

CMH — *Cambridge Medieval History*

DA — *Deutsches Archiv für die Erforschung des Mittelalters*

EHR — *English Historical Review*

FMS — *Frühmittelalterliche Studien*

GC — *Gallia Christiana*

HZ — *Historische Zeitschrift*

JEccH — *Journal of Ecclesiastical History*

L. — L. Levillain ed., *Actes de Pépin I et Pépin II, rois d'Aquitaine*

L/G — *Les Annales de Saint-Bertin*

LM — *Lexikon des Mittelalters*

MA — *Le Moyen Âge*

Mansi — J.-D. Mansi, ed., *Sacrorum Conciliorum Nova et Amplissima Collectio*

MGH — *Monumenta Germaniae Historica*
  Capit. — *Capitularia regum Francorum*
  Conc. — *Concilia*
  Epp. — *Epistolae*
  Fontes — *Fontes Iuris Germanici Antiquae*
  SRG — *Scriptores rerum germanicarum in usum scholarum*
  SSRL — *Scriptores rerum Langobardorum*
  SSRM — *Scriptores rerum Merovingicarum*
  SS — *Scriptores*

NCE — *New Catholic Encyclopedia*

PL — *Patrologia Latina*

RB — *Revue Bénédictine*

RFA — *Royal Frankish Annals (Annales regni Francorum)*

RH — *Revue Historique*

RHE — *Revue d'Histoire Ecclésiastique*

SCH — *Studies in Church History*

SS Spoleto — *Settimane di Studio di Centro Italiano di Studi sull'alto medioevo*

T. — *G.* Tessier ed., *Receuil des Actes de Charles II le Chauve*

WaG — *Die Welt als Geschichte*

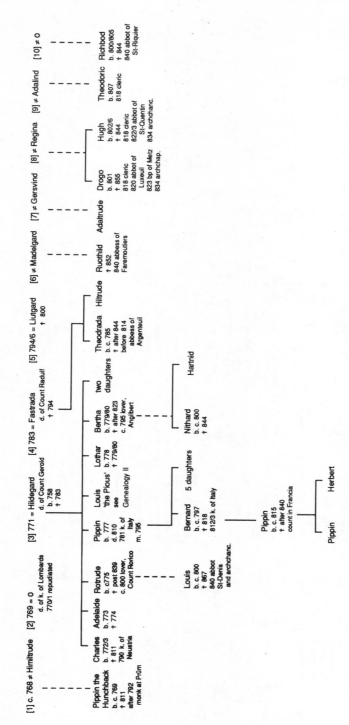

Genealogy I   The descendants of Charlemagne

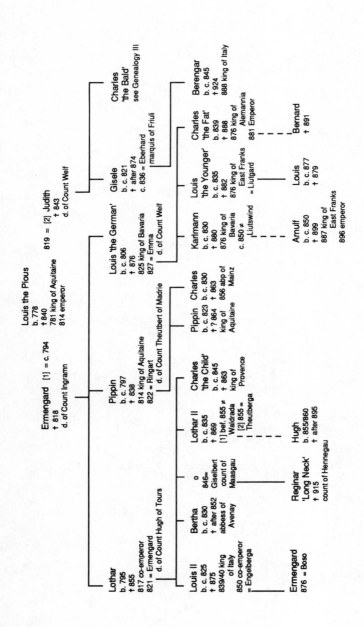

Genealogy II   The descendants of Louis the Pious

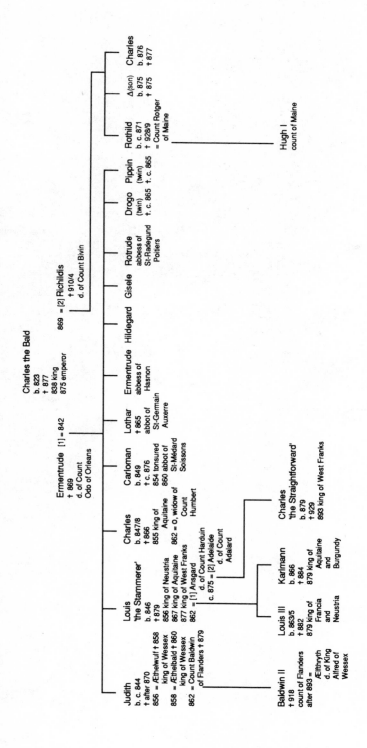

Genealogy III   The descendants of Charles the Bald

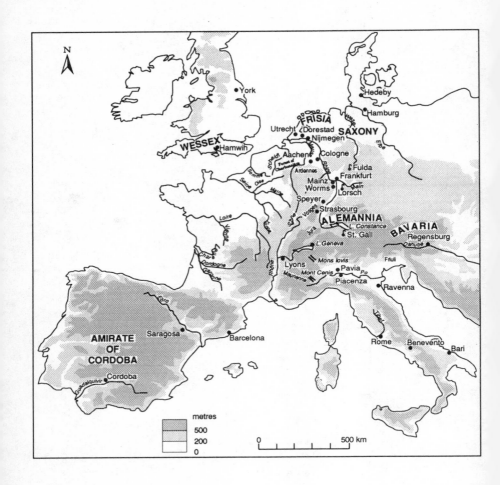

Map I   The Carolingian world

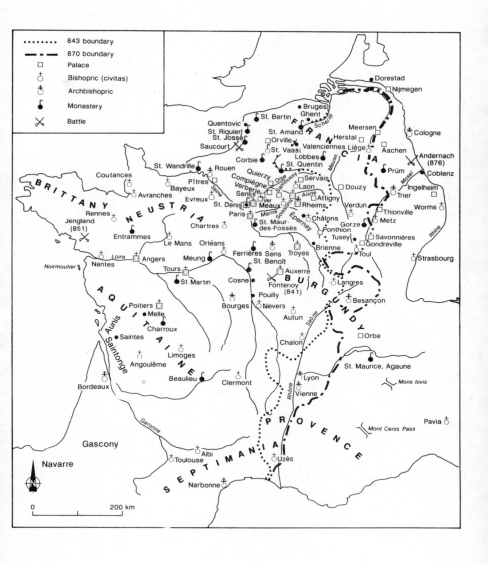

Legend

⋯⋯⋯⋯	843 boundary
▬ ▬ ▬	870 boundary
□	Palace
⚲	Bishopric (civitas)
⚱	Archbishopric
●	Monastery
✕	Battle

Dorestad
Nijmegen
FRANCIA
Bruges
Ghent
St. Bertin
Meersen
Quentovic
St. Riquier
St. Josse
Saucourt
Corbie
St. Amand
Orville
St. Vaast
Valenciennes Liège
Lobbes
St. Quentin
Herstal
Cologne
Aachen
Andernach (876)
Prüm
Coblenz
St. Wandrille
Rouen
Pîtres
Quierzy
Compiègne
Verberie
Ver
Senlis
St. Denis
Paris
Meaux
Laon
Servais
Soissons
Aisne
Rheims
Attigny
Douzy
Verdun
Ingelheim
Trier
Worms
Thionville
Metz
Savonnières
Gondreville
Strasbourg
Coutances
Bayeux
Avranches
Evreux
Chartres
BRITTANY
NEUSTRIA
Rennes
Jengland (851)
Entrammes
Le Mans
Orléans
Ferrières
Sens
St. Benoît
Troyes
Épernay
Châlons
Ponthion
Gorze
Tusey
Brienne
Toul
Langres
Besançon
Meung
Tours
St. Martin
Cosne
Auxerre
Fontenoy (841)
Pouilly
Nevers
Autun
Angers
Nantes
Noirmoutier
Loire
Poitiers
Melle
Charroux
Saintes
Aunis
Saintonge
AQUITAINE
Limoges
Angoulême
Beaulieu
Clermont
Bordeaux
Garonne
Gascony
Navarre
BURGUNDY
Chalon
Orbe
St. Maurice, Agaune
Mons Iovis
Lyon
Vienne
Rhône
Saône
Rhine
Mosel
Seine
Marne
Meuse
Scheldt
PROVENCE
Mont Cenis Pass
Pavia
SEPTIMANIA
Albi
Toulouse
Uzès
Narbonne

0   200 km

Map II   The kingdom of Charles the Bald

To the memory of Félix Grat (1898–1940)
and Léon Levillain (1870–1952)

INTRODUCTION

1. The importance of the text

The *Annals of St-Bertin* give a detailed record of events in the Carolingian world, covering the years 830-82. They constitute the most substantial piece of contemporary historical writing of their time[1] – a time that was, on any reckoning, a critical one in western European history. As on most major issues, modern historians' interpretations have diverged widely. Some see the period as a catastrophic one, when the Carolingian Empire declined and fell, the western economy re-entered a deep recession, and Christendom reeled under the blows of pagan Viking attacks. Others see this as a period of creativity and growth, when new political communities, a new and dynamic western economy, and a self-conscious Latin Christendom first took distinctive forms.[2] The debate offers a challenge. For anyone concerned to make a judgement of their own, the *AB* more than any other single text supply essential evidence.

The *AB* contain, for instance, uniquely extensive information about Viking activities, constructive as well as destructive, and also about the variety of responses to those activities. There is plenty of blood and guts, but there is also evidence of the everyday: of money, markets and diplomacy, of ships and sealing-wax. The *AB* throw sometimes lurid light on Carolingian politics: on deep structures as well as on changing surfaces, on local (rather than national) sentiment refracted through the authors' sense of the persisting unity of the Carolingian Empire, on the clash of ideals with realities but also of competing ideals, on rulers trapped (like Wotan in the *Ring* story) by their own treaties, on nobles caught between conflicting loyalties and jarring short- and long-term interests, on peasants driven to self-defence as well as to flight, on women who as queens and concubines and

---

1 Levillain 1964: 15-16; Löwe 1967: 9-10; Ganshof 1970: 679-82.

2 For mainly pessimistic views of the ninth century, see Bloch 1961: 39-42. 52-6; Le Goff 1969: 11-14; Fossier 1981 and Fossier 1986. Compare the more positive views of Duby 1974: 77-139; McKitterick 1989; Verhulst 1989; Hodges 1990a, 1990b; Nelson 1992: ch. 2.

heiresses sometimes wrote their own scripts as well as acting out roles assigned them. Through the *AB* can be glimpsed a Christendom in uneasy yet intimate relationships with pagan neighbours, from Muslim Spain to the Scandinavian North, a Christendom bound by multiple contacts, political and cultural, yet divided in its attempts at mission work, divided too between Greek East and Latin West, and within the West, between papal and episcopal authority, and between opposed conceptions of predestination and free will. In the *AB*'s reporting, both style and content are extremely varied: from the near-'tabloid' (racism and sexism are here) and the anecdotal (there is the earliest description known to me of the ironing of a shirt) to 'quality' passages of high seriousness and official protocol (no comparable text offers more to students of medieval political ideas). Readers with preconceptions about 'dry-as-dust' annals will find *these* annals a revelation.

After all this, it may come as no surprise that these annals have nothing whatsoever to do with the monastery of St-Bertin. The name was given simply because the text's first published (and only complete) manuscript, written out in the eleventh century, was preserved at St-Bertin thereafter.[3] The *AB* are not, then, monastic annals, with all that that genre implies of restricted vision. The scope of the *AB* embraces a realm, and beyond that a world that stretches from Constantinople to Cordoba, from Sicily to Sweden. Its authors' perspective is that of palace clergy and bishops rather than monks, and their primary concern is with the deeds of secular rulers and prelates. Yet the *AB* were not produced at any ruler's behest: they are not 'official history', still less propaganda. Though their concern is with public events, they represent, for the most part, individual responses.[4] This is the paradox to be explored. But first, the writing of annals as a genre in the Carolingian world needs a little explanation.

2. Annals: the conditions of production

The keeping of chronological records, widely practised in the Roman world, survived as a slim but tenacious tradition in the early medieval

---

3 See below: 16, for the St-Bertin manuscript 'O'.

4 Nelson 1990b. The *AB* thus flout the generalisation of Van Caenegem and Ganshof 1978: 34: 'The positive point about annals is their precise matter of fact style, trustworthiness and care about chronology. On the negative side they are extremely brief and attempt nothing more than to give an unconnected enumeration of political, military, ecclesiastical and meteorological facts.'

west. In the fourth century, Eusebius had chronicled the peoples and rulers of antiquity and their superseding by the single Empire of Rome: translated into Latin by Jerome in 380, Eusebius's firm chronological framework provided a model which early medieval chroniclers could imitate and/or continue.[5] Thus, in the mid-seventh century, in the lands ruled by the Frankish Merovingian dynasty, Eusebius–Jerome inspired Fredegar to produce a world-chronicle that became a history of the Franks.[6] The entering of notes on historical events in the margins of Easter Tables (used to calculate for successive years the changing dates on which fell the greatest day in the liturgical calendar) was another route by which chronological works came to be compiled. Annals, literally a 'year-by-year' record, were a characteristic product of early medieval monastic culture: a genre came of age when margins were outgrown, and one-line notes expanded into snatches of narrative.[7] Both concerns – to extend Christian world-history forwards into a new age of 'gentile' kingdoms (that is, kingdoms constructed by the peoples, *gentes*, of the post-Roman west) and to establish a framework of Christian chronology – merged in the early eighth century in the work of Bede: his *Reckoning of Time* had a large impact on the Continent in the historical output of the Carolingian Renaissance.[8]

For it was in the early eighth century that a new dynasty rose to power in the kingdom of the Franks. This, the longest-lived and most dynamic of the successor-states to the Western Roman Empire, had tended to split into warring parts, Austrasia (around the valleys of the lower Meuse and Rhine) and Neustria (the Seine basin). The man who reunited the two parts, and gave his name to the new Carolingian dynasty (though he himself remained for most of his life the mayor of the palace to the last scions of the Merovingians) was the Austrasian magnate Charles Martel. By the time of his death in 741, the keeping of annals had been resumed when an Austrasian writer in the 730s produced a Continuation of Fredegar's seventh-century Chronicle. Then Martel's own half-brother sponsored a second Continuation which was in effect a set of annals of the Frankish realm from 736 until 751.[9]

5 Hay 1977: 23; Van Caenegem and Ganshof 1978: 18–25, 30–4; Goffart 1988: 3–19.

6 Wallace-Hadrill 1960.

7 Ganshof 1970: 669–74.

8 Goffart 1988: 240–7.

9 Wallace-Hadrill 1960: xxv–xxvi.

The year 751 was the year in which Martel's family became a royal family, with the consecration of Martel's son Pippin as king of the Franks (and the consigning of the last Merovingian to monastic retirement). A third Continuation of Fredegar's Chronicle carried the story on down to Pippin's death, and the accession of his two sons, in 768.[10] At monastic houses protected and exploited by the new dynasty, annalistic writing revived, often fuelled by Bedan concerns.[11] In the reign of Pippin's son Charlemagne (sole ruler from 771, died 814), with the organising of a royal chapel staffed by a small team of palace clergy, and with the ruler's increasingly frequent stays at Aachen from 794 onwards, the royal household seems to have become also a home for the production of annals. The deeds and diplomacy of Charlemagne and of the Frankish nobles who sustained his power were noted down, year by year, in the *Royal Frankish Annals (Annales Regni Francorum)*.[12] There is no evidence that Charlemagne ever sought to influence the annals' content, or to exploit the annals for what would nowadays be termed 'public relations' purposes. His biographer does not mention historical writing as among Charlemagne's scholarly interests, not does he list the sponsorship of an 'official record' as among Charlemagne's concerns after he became emperor on Christmas Day 800.[13] If the annals for the eighth century were revised and amplified late in Charlemagne's reign, the initiative may have lain with the revisers rather than the ruler himself. The *RFA* are less evidently dynastic in focus than the so-called *Prior Metz Annals (Annales Mettenses Priores)*, compiled (making heavy use of the *RFA*) probably at the convent of Chelles under the auspices of Abbess Gisèle, Charlemagne's sister, in the early ninth century;[14] and they are less overtly propagandistic than the annals produced c.890 very probably in the circle of King Alfred of Wessex – the *Anglo-Saxon Chronicle*[15].

In the reign of Louis the Pious, the *RFA* continued to be produced down to 829, with successive archchaplains, it seems, taking responsibility for their contents.[16] Louis himself is nowhere credited with any involvement with what his chaplains were recording. There is little

10 Wallace-Hadrill 1960: xxvi-vii, xlv.

11 Löwe 1953 (Wattenbach, Levison and Löwe 1952-73) 180-92; Hoffmann 1958; Werner 1975.

12 Kurze 1895; Scholz 1970.

13 Einhard c. 29.

14 Nelson l990e: 80-2.

15 Wormald 1982: 158-9.

16 Malbos 1966.

sign of any central interest in disseminating an 'official' view of the recent past, or of local concern to acquire 'up-to-date' copies of the ongoing work. (The manuscripts are nearly all of the complete text down to 829, and were written out, at a single go, considerably after the events described.)[17] The authors' working conditions cannot have been easy. When the ruler moved, his household, including chaplain-annalists, moved with him, as did the royal archive (sometimes called 'the cupboard', which is probably just what it was). Louis in his early years moved about a good deal; and from 822 Aachen was less often favoured as a winter residence than Ingelheim and Compiègne. Under such conditions, the annalists would hardly envisage the collection of written material and its incorporation in their work; instead they used the evidence of their own eyes and ears, or others' oral testimony. The palace was the centre to which information flowed and politically important informants were drawn. But the flow of information was uncertain. Rumours could not always be checked and were often false. Messages might be delayed, letters lost. Even a courier with regular changes of horses at his disposal, and in summertime, took two weeks to convey the most urgent of messages from Lombardy to northern France (a travel-rate of approximately 60 km. per day).[18]

The year 830 marks a break in annalistic activity in the chapel of Louis the Pious. Most manuscripts of the *RFA* stop at 829. This implies that there was some diffusion of an existing set of annals at that point in time. The explanation is clear: the rebellion of 830 caused a dispersal of Louis's entourage, and in particular the removal of the archchaplain Hilduin who had sided with the rebels.[19] But the work of annal-keeping was soon resumed within the old milieu: the *Annals of St-Bertin* started as a continuation of the *RFA*, thus remained the work of palace chaplains and archchaplains. The manuscripts show no break, offer no new heading. The story is taken up where the *RFA* left off. The 'he' in the opening sentence of the 830 annal is the subject of the last sentence of the *RFA* for 829: namely, Louis the Pious.[20] But the *AB* did not remain a palace product. To explain how and when they ceased to be so, and what they then became, we must ask who wrote them.

---

17 Kurze 1895: ix-xv.

18 *AB* 869, below: 157. Cf Brühl 1968: 66; Prinz 1977.

19 Malbos 1966; Brown 1989: 29-33. Hilduin was abbot of St-Denis.

20 Below: 21; Nelson 1990b: 24. Contrast *AF* and *AX*, which carry on the Frankish annalistic tradition, but do not literally continue the *RFA*. Translations of the *AF* by T. Reuter (1991) and of the *AX* by S. Coupland are forthcoming from MUP.

3. The authors of the *AB*

(i) The early years

Successive editors, first Pertz, then Waitz, and finally Levillain, looked for successive single authors of the *AB*. The first author was thought to have been responsible for the annals from 830 to part-way through the annal for 835, when a first break in authorship was detected.[21] Though there was no break in any manuscript, no explicit statement in the text, the modern editors found stylistic clues to authorial change: in general, the annals from 830 up to this point were allegedly written in language that was 'awkward, sometimes obscure'; in particular, Louis the Pious was 'consistently' referred to as *domnus imperator*, Judith as *domna imperatrix*. The 'new author', from mid-835 onwards, referred to Louis simply as 'imperator', Judith as 'augusta'. Further, a difference was observed in the forms in which place-names were given: the 'first author' used names current in the ninth century, but the 'second author' preferred more elaborate classical forms. Levillain identified 'the first author' as Fulco, a royal chaplain who had been trained under Hilduin in the 820s, but remained loyal to Louis the Pious in the rebellion of 830 and succeeded Hilduin as archchaplain. Fulco stayed loyal too in the second rebellion against Louis in 833-34, and in 835 received his reward: when Archbishop Ebbo of Rheims was made the rebels' fall-guy, removed from office and consigned to a monastic prison, Fulco became administrator of the see of Rheims (though not archbishop, since doubt remained about the canonical validity of Ebbo's removal). For Levillain, Ebbo's 'confession' and 'resignation' thus aptly formed the last great set-piece of Fulco's annals, and a new author took over at this point. A clinching argument was the reference to Drogo of Metz as 'bishop' immediately before the alleged break, and 'archbishop' immediately after it: this was 'precisely the point' at which Drogo succeeded Fulco as archchaplain.[22]

Levillain's argument, though seductive, is not totally convincing. It is true that the annals for 830 and 833-34 consistently present Louis the Pious in a sympathetic way. Further, they appear to be contemporary, written up at the end of each year (or early in the next) from notes presumably kept as information was received. In 832, Louis is described acting mercifully 'as is his usual way'.[23] The fullness and

21 Waitz 1883: v-viii; Levillain 1964: vi.
22 Levillain 1964: viii-xii; below: 835. n. 1.
23 Below: 25.

continuity of the annals for 833 and 834 testify to the short-lived impact of the rebellion against Louis: it lasted a mere seven months, and the threads of the annalistic record were easily picked up. The assumption of a single author (and hence his identification as Fulco) can be quest-ioned, however. The stylistic traits are in part a matter of subjective judgement, and in any case do not point quite un-equivocally to a break in mid-835: Louis the Pious is called *religiosissimus* (not *domnus*) *imper-ator* just before the alleged break; and after as before it, the rendering of place-names is not wholly consistent, with Aachen appearing as both *Aquae* and *Aquisgrani* in the last sentence of the 835 annal, for instance. The fact that one manuscript, 'M', contains the annals from 830 to part-way through 837 perhaps points to an alternative, or additional, break, and might tell against the hypothesis of single authorship of the work at this stage.[24] If the archchaplain had general oversight of the annals' production, team-authorship remains a possibility for as long as the palace remained the environment in which the *AB* were written: that is, for the rest of Louis the Pious's reign.

(ii) Prudentius

In a letter of September 866, Archbishop Hincmar of Rheims quoted from the 859 annal of the *AB*, and stated explicitly that the work's author was Prudentius. Of Spanish origin (his given name was Galindo), Prudentius was probably the son of refugee parents who had moved north of the Pyrenees early in Louis the Pious's reign. The boy was apparently sent to the palace *c.* 820 to serve in due course in Louis's chapel. He may have had some input into the *RFA*, and then the *AB*, before 835. After that date, if manuscript 'M' perhaps reflects the continuing interest of Drogo, as archchaplain, in the *AB*'s pro-duction, Prudentius, resident in the imperial household, remained well placed to participate in the ongoing task of annal-keeping. The annals for 836 to 839 are impressive in their fullness. The focus on the palace is clearer than ever: only there could much of the information entered in the *AB* have been amassed.[25] Thanks to the *AB* more than any other single source, the years 835-40 can be seen in terms of a genuine Restoration of Louis the Pious's regime.[26]

Louis's death on 20 June 840 meant a break in the activity of the

24 Below: 15.
25 See further Nelson 1990b: 26-7.
26 Nelson 1990c.

palace, and of palace-clerks: a break faithfully reflected in the annalistic record. The succession was disputed, with most of the old emperor's entourage transferring their loyalty to his eldest son Lothar. The *AB* have little information for the year 840 after the death of Louis, and something like the earlier density of reporting is resumed only with the battle of Fontenoy (25 June 841).[27] Former annal-keepers prudently lay low until the battle's outcome was clear. Once Lothar's two younger brothers, Louis the German and Charles the Bald, had emerged the victors, there was the prospect of peace and a more or less stable royal household to provide, once again, the traditional environment for royal annalists to resume work. It was in the entourage of Charles, a youth well known to former members of his father's household (and perhaps hopefully looked to by them as a promising patron of learned men), that the resumption occurred.[28] From 841 on, the *AB* were based in the western part of the old empire, in what became, with the Treaty of Verdun in 843, the kingdom of Charles the Bald. Thus the division of Verdun is, again, faithfully reflected in the *AB*'s record. From time to time, information was received from Lothar's Middle Kingdom, and from Louis the German's East Frankish kingdom; but the *AB*'s main focus after 843 was on events in the West and on the doings of Charles the Bald (840-77).

A second, equally significant change in the nature of the *AB* came very soon after the first. From late 843, the *AB* ceased to be a palace product. Instead, the record was being maintained by someone working for the most part at a distance from the royal household. It is at this point (if not before) that the assumption of Prudentius's sole authorship seems to fit the evidence. For the change in the *AB* coincides with a change in Prudentius's personal life. He was appointed bishop of Troyes in the ecclesiastical province of Sens.[29] This sort of promotion was what a loyal chaplain hoped for as the reward for long service. It meant that Prudentius left Charles's palace. He seems to have taken with him the sole working manuscript of the *AB*. There is no evidence that the annals were continued at the palace thereafter, or that Charles himself took any interest in their continu-

27 Below: 50.

28 For Charles's education and tastes. McKitterick 1980, 1990; Nelson 1992: ch. 4.

29 Probably in late 843 or 844; Nelson 1990b: 28.

30 There is no necessary link between learned tastes and patronage of historians. Perhaps Charles had had his fingers burned by Nithard who, having been commissioned by Charles to write propagandistic 'public *Histories*,' then turned his work into a 'private history'; Nelson 1986a (1985): 195-233.

ance there.[30] In other words, the *AB* from 843 were no longer in any sense an 'official' record. This is evident from the partial and spasmodic quality of the information Prudentius was now able to acquire (or thought fit to record), and from the jerkiness of his narrative. Further, as the years went by, Prudentius's work acquired a more personal and 'private' tone. In the 850s, he voiced in his annals criticisms of Charles, making it clear that the *AB* were in no sense a court product any more, and that the author did not foresee the king or his entourage as potential readers. If Prudentius's personal situation at Troyes imposed this distancing from the palace, his personal views reinforced it. In the theological debate over predestination which racked the scholarly world of the 850s, Prudentius took a line sympathetic to the theologian Gottschalk whom Charles and his court condemned.[31] Charles's chief adviser on this issue, and a major source of political support, was Archbishop Hincmar of Rheims. Hincmar and Prudentius had other grounds for disagreement: the see of Rheims held some proprietory churches in the diocese of Troyes, and Prudentius had caused difficulties for Hincmar as landlord.[32] During the years 850 to 858, a powerful faction based in the Loire valley became increasingly alienated from the king. In 858, that faction was joined by Prudentius's metropolitan Archbishop Wenilo of Sens and by the count of Troyes. They were among the leading men involved in a conspiracy to invite Louis the German to take over the kingdom of his brother Charles. It is hardly surprising that the record of these events in the *AB* shows certain peculiarities and reticences.[33] Prudentius the annalist withdrew increasingly into his own world, yet he stuck to his self-imposed task of keeping up the historical record. He died in 861, 'still scribbling things that were mutually contradictory and contrary to Faith'. The waspish epitaph was supplied by Hincmar of Rheims, leading spirit in the condemnation of Gottschalk, and faithful supporter of Charles the Bald in 858. The epitaph was entered in the *AB*.[34]

(iii) Hincmar of Rheims

Hincmar clearly took over the writing of the *AB* after Prudentius's death. But exactly when did the new author start work? The answer

31 Below 849: 67; 853:76-7.
32 Below, 861: 94 with n. 3.
33 Below 858: 85-9; Nelson 1990b: 30-1.
34 Below: 94.

can be reconstructed from the letter (referred to above) which Hincmar wrote in 866 to Archbishop Eigil of Sens. It seems clear that in accordance with customary practice, the movable goods of the recently deceased bishop of Troyes had passed into the hands of the king in 861. Prudentius's papers included the *AB*: hence 'a number of people' at the court now, for the first time, could read Prudentius's annals.[35] Hincmar took the initiative in asking the king to loan him the single manuscript, which he then copied, and continued from the point where Prudentius had left off. Hincmar had known of the earlier, 'palace' section of the *AB*, for he referred in 860, in his *Third Treatise on Predestination*, to the account of Ebbo's deposition in the 835 entry of 'the Annals of the Lord Emperor Louis'.[36] The date at which Hincmar, having learned of the existence of Prudentius's continuation, borrowed the manuscript from the king, has been suggested as 865, on the grounds that this was the year when Eigil became archbishop, and Hincmar in his letter of 866 reminded Eigil that the loan had been made in his presence.[37] But in fact Eigil left Prüm in the Middle Kingdom, and was granted the abbacy of Flavigny by Charles in 861[38]; so the occasion when the king handed over Prudentius's annals could have happened at any date between 861 and late 866, by which time Hincmar had returned the manuscript to Charles.

In the seventeenth century there survived at Antwerp in the library of the great Jesuit scholar Jean Bolland a manuscript containing part of the *AB*. A copy of the annals from part-way through 839 to near the close of 863 made on Bolland's orders in 1638 was rediscovered by René Poupardin in 1905. [39] Bolland's now lost early-medieval manuscript was closer to Hincmar's own than any of the other copies extant. It may even have been Hincmar's manuscript. The vital clue is the presence of a marginal note, according to Bolland in the same hand as that of the main text, beside the passage in the annal for 859 where Prudentius had attributed to Pope Nicholas I views on predestination that accorded with his own. The annotator had written: 'Here Bishop

---

35 *MGH Epp.* VIII, no. 187, pp. 194–5. Cf. Nelson 1990b: 32–3.

36 *PL* 125, col. 391. Cf. Levillain 1964: xvi–xvii; below: n. 43.

37 Nelson 1990b: 32.

38 Löwe 1973 (Wattenbach, Levison and Löwe 1952–73): 628.

39 For manuscript 'C', see below: 16. The fact that the annals stopped part-way through 863 could imply that Hincmar's discovery of Prudentius's manuscript, and initial continuing of it, occurred in that year.

40 Ganshof 1949: 163; Levillain 1964: xviii–xxi.

Prudentius wrote concerning Nicholas what he (Prudentius) wished
was the case; but in saying that it *was* so, he said what was not true.'
The annotator, and hence the writer of the *AB* copy, and its continuation, can plausibly be identified as Hincmar himself.[40] His interest in
Prudentius's work clearly had much to do with his theological
concerns: he needed to know what Prudentius had alleged about Pope
Nicholas's views. He also needed to see how Prudentius had presented
the preceding quarter-century of history; for, in Hincmar's mind,
theology and history were interlinked, and faulty theology would give
rise to a misrepresentation of the past.[41] Having seen Prudentius's
annals, Hincmar not only copied, but decided to continue them. He
would record 'The Deeds of Kings' as seen through his own eyes.[42]
Perhaps he wanted to carry on the work for which Hilduin had once
been responsible. As a young member of the community of St-Denis in
the 820s, Hincmar had frequented the palace in Hilduin's entourage:
continuing the annals may have been a way of paying an old debt of
loyalty.[43] Like Prudentius, Hincmar persisted with his self-imposed
task until his death in 882.

Hincmar's annals resemble Prudentius's in two further crucial respects. They are a record of events written away from the palace, from
the perspective of an ecclesiastical magnate; and they represent a
personal, often idiosyncratic view, not intended for the public gaze,
still less for the king's. What distinguishes Hincmar's work from his
predecessor's is a much more significant involvement in high politics
and much closer (if intermittent) contacts with the king and the court.
For Hincmar's position among the Frankish elite was unlike
Prudentius's. The Spaniard had been an outsider, lucky to receive a
bishopric of the second rank. Hincmar was born a Frankish noble, and
numbered counts among his kinsmen.[44] As archbishop of Rheims he
was also among the greatest magnates in Charles the Bald's kingdom.
Furthermore, Hincmar was one of the most prolific writers of the

41 Wallace-Hadrill 1981.

42 *MGH Epp.* VIII, no. 187, p. 194.

43 Hincmar remained loyal to Hilduin in 830, but in 833 preferred loyalty to the
emperor; Flodoard III, c. 1, p. 475. After 834, however, Hilduin was restored
to imperial favour and he and Hincmar were again close; Devisse 1976: 1094–
5; Wallace-Hadrill 1981: 45–7. In the early years of Charles's reign, Hincmar
seems to have been a priest in his household; Flodoard II, p. 178. T. 57, dated
12 August 844, a grant of lands to 'the venerable man, the priest Hincmar',
suggests that Hincmar had accompanied Charles on campaign in Aquitaine.

44 Flodoard III, c. 26, pp. 543 (Bernard count of Toulouse) and 545 (Bertram
count of Tardenois).

Carolingian period, and in a variety of genres. Thanks to his management of a scriptorium and an archive at Rheims, he could ensure that many of his works were preserved. He also ensured the preservation of official documents, capitularies, which he himself had either written or helped draft. Perhaps most important of all for modern historians, his letters (or at least abbreviated versions of them) have survived.[45] Thanks to this wealth of documentation, we can not only read Hincmar's annals for what they have to tell, but we can sometimes see what Hincmar has chosen *not* to tell. Hincmar could be inconsistent, and he was often economical with the truth. True, such is the practice of politics in any period. But what is unusual for the ninth century is that, thanks in large measure to his own voluminous writings, we can not only suspect Hincmar but catch him in the act.[46] When Charles the Bald's nephew Lothar II attempted to divorce his wife, Hincmar upheld the indissolubility of marriage; yet when Charles the Bald himself wanted his son's remarriage, Hincmar connived at, and in the *AB* was silent over, the repudiation of a royal bride.[47] In his annalistic record, we can find repeated instances of suppression of vital evidence. Who was Hincmar attempting to mislead? The answer (beyond a measure of self-deception) seems to be: his own circle at Rheims; and posterity. For he could never have intended his work for a wide contemporary audience. When relations between him and the king were cool, as in 866, and positively icy in 874–77, Hincmar confided his criticisms and resentments to the annals.[48] Charles was known for his fiery temper, and his harshness to those he suspected of disloyalty. Hincmar wrote for his own entourage what he could never have said or written for a wider public. And yet he was not disloyal: his complaints were those of a jilted favourite, ousted by other, younger men at court. Hincmar remained a would-be confidant of the king, and did in fact recover something of his influence during the brief reign of Charles's son.[49] The special value of Hincmar's annals as a historical record is the result of precisely this combination of closeness to royal

---

45 Schieffer 1986: 355–60.

46 E.g. below 865:121, n. 1; 868:150, n. 15; 870:167, 168, 171, nn. 8, 13, 21; 875: 188, n. 9; 876:189, 190, nn. 2, 5.

47 Nelson 1990b: 38–9.

48 Below: 133, 136, 141, 192, 197.

49 *Instructio ad Ludovicum Balbum regem, PL* 125, 983–90; cf. below 877:203, n. 19. For the content of Hincmar's political advice here, see Devisse 1976: 966–79, with the comment at 969: 'l'analyse nous paraît singulièrement forte chez un homme de 70 ans qui n'a pas lu Marx!'

power (with all that that meant in terms of access to documents and to information), and frankness in expressing his own changing reactions to its exercise. The flood of light thrown by the sheer fullness of Hincmar's record on the 860s and 870s makes the reader painfully aware of how much of the rest of the Carolingian period remains a closed book. Yet Hincmar's evident bias should warn against taking his judgements at face value or allowing them to determine ours.

4. How the *AB* were written

The only evidence of the working methods of successive annalists lies in the text itself. All the writers saw themselves as continuing a tradition established by the *RFA*, for instance, following the practice of using 25 December as the start of the new year, and maintaining an interest in 'the deeds of kings' throughout the Carolingian world. In the 830s, each annal seems to have been written up from material collected and noted in the course of each year. The chronological sequence within each annal seems accurate. After 843, Prudentius no doubt encountered more problems in obtaining, and arranging, his material. Some chronological errors within or across particular annals are best accounted for on the assumption that information reached him belatedly, and that he was unsure where to insert items as they came in. Nevertheless, errors are remarkably few.[50] The annals for 840 and 843 obviously caused difficulties. Otherwise, it seems reasonable to infer that Prudentius, like his predecessors, wrote up year by year.

Hincmar's working methods have recently been carefully reconsidered by Marlene Meyer-Gebel.[51] She has confirmed that most of his annals were written up year by year, and that Hincmar entered material several times a year. His chronology is thus accurate within the limits of the 4–8 weeks it normally took for data to reach him. But Meyer-Gebel has also been able to show that Hincmar, especially in the later annals of his section, sometimes attempted a more thematic treatment. Long paragraphs reveal the writing-up of a sequence of events after their outcome was known. Examples occur in the 869 annal, where the account of Lothar II's visit to Italy was obviously written up in the knowledge that he never returned, and in the 877 annal, where again

50 Below 851:73, n. 9. Other alleged (but not certain) errors: 857:85, n. 8; 859:91, n. 11.

51 Meyer-Gebel 1987.

52 Below: 203.

events are depicted in the light of hindsight.[52]. Hincmar had access to such 'official' documents as papal letters and records of royal inaugurations, and sometimes quoted them verbatim in the *AB*.[53] He made still more efforts than his predecessors to incorporate information from widely divergent geographical areas. In several of the annals for the 870s, especially, his shaping of material as narrative pushes the very limits of the annal form. He was capable of manipulating plural 'stories' to present meaningful juxtapositions and a carefully structured interweaving of plot and sub-plots. Although so far such an analysis has been attempted only for the 873 annal,[54] the approach could fruitfully be applied elsewhere in his section.

In Hincmar's case, the possibility of retrospective tampering with his predecessor's work needs to be considered. It seems to have been Hincmar's anxiety about an item in Prudentius's 859 annal which evoked the heartfelt denial expressed in the marginal note discussed above. It is well known that Hincmar tampered a little with canon law and patristic texts to suit his own book: in his famous dispute with his nephew the bishop of Laon, the arch-accuser of the other's forgeries was himself a forger.[55] In the case of the *AB*, the tampering may have taken the form of interpolation. Three possible instances can be noted here. First, the entry about the assembly held by Charles 'against custom' in June 846 at Épernay, a Rheims *villa*, has a ring of local indignation, while the additional bitter comment that 'reverence for bishops had almost never been so disregarded since Christian times began' has no parallel in Prudentius's section of the annals, but seems to echo the complaint in a Rheims manuscript recording the assembly of Épernay.[56] A second likely interpolation occurs in the 849 annal, where a fierce denunciation of the heretic Gottschalk and his 'pestiferous teachings on the subject of predestination' jars not only with Prudentius's otherwise phlegmatic style but with his sympathetic response to Gottschalk in the *AB* and in his theological work. Further, the passage continues with an approving mention of the synod convened to condemn Gottschalk by 'the venerable man Hincmar who was in charge of the metropolitan see of Rheims'.[57] A third possible

53 Below 863: 107; 867: 142; 869: 158; 870: 166 and 168; 877: 204; 878: 208 and 213.
54 Nelson 1988b.
55 Fuhrmann 1990.
56 *MGH Capit.* II, no. 257. p. 261; Hartmann 1989: 216-17.
57 Below: 67. Eighteenth-century scholars already identified this as a Hincmarian interpolation; Bouquet 1749-52, VII, 56-7.

instance of Hincmarian insertion (and trumpet-blowing) occurs in the annal for 856, where a brief narrative passage breaks the chronological sequence to record in a single long sentence the arrival of King Æthelwulf at Charles's court in July and his marriage to Charles's daughter in October, when 'after Bishop Hincmar of Rheims had consecrated her and placed a diadem on her head' she was given 'the title of queen'.[58] For this occasion, Hincmar composed the first of his four coronation rites: the other three are all carefully recorded in Hincmar's own section of the *AB* [59] and were no less carefully preserved as a group in a Rheims manuscript.[60] Perhaps it should be added, though, that Hincmar did no more than interpolate. He did not, after all, delete the passage that so worried him in Prudentius's 859 annal. On the whole, we can probably safely assume that, with a few exceptions, Hincmar left Prudentius's text as he found it.

5. The manuscripts

It is no coincidence that very few manuscripts of the *AB* exist: Prudentius's one manuscript was copied, as we have seen, by Hincmar, who then added his own annals to his manuscript. There is no evidence that any other manuscripts of the complete text existed in the ninth century. 'M', containing the annals from 830 to part-way through 837, is the only extant manuscript of any part of the *AB* which does not derive from Hincmar's own. 'M' is a twelfth-century compilation made at St-Arnulf, Metz.[61] Here, the first eight annals of the *AB* follow the *Prior Metz Annals*, whose last annal covers the year 830: the Metz compiler has tacked his two sources together, without troubling about the overlap for the year 830. This proves that his source for the *AB* annals was not a manuscript in which they appeared as a continuation of the *RFA*. Instead, that source, available at Metz in the twelfth century, can plausibly be identified as a copy of the annals for 830 to mid-837, made for Drogo, who in the late 830s was both archchaplain and archbishop of Metz. The 837 annal in 'M' lacks its final paragraph: further evidence that its ultimate source was a work in the very process of compilation, hot from a palace clerk's hand.

58 Below: 83.

59 Below 866: 133-4; 869: 158-62; 877: 204-6.

60 Nelson 1986a (1977a): 138, n. 1; 149, n. 3; 152-3.

61 MS Berlin. Deutsche Staatsbibliothek, Meerman lat. 141. See Ganshof 1949: 166-8; Levillain 1964: xxxix-xli, liii-iv. 'M' breaks off after the sentence ending: '... promised to stay loyal in future', below: 37.

'C' is a seventeenth-century copy of part of Hincmar's now lost manuscript.[62] Flodoard, when he copied an extract from the 867 annal into his *History of the Church of Rheims* around the year 960, probably also used Hincmar's manuscript.[63] A copy of the whole *AB* seems to have been taken in the tenth century, either by or for the community of St-Vaast, Arras. A large compilation was made, to span the whole history of Gaul, starting from antiquity, and ending with full coverage of the ninth century through the *RFA*, the *AB* and, finally, the *Annals of St-Vaast* (which cover the years 873-900).[64] The original manuscript of this large composite work is now lost, but from it was copied in the eleventh century MS 'D', now at Douai.[65] 'D' is unfortunately incomplete, lacking one or more quires containing the *AB* from 845 onwards.[66] Also in the eleventh century, either at St-Vaast or at St-Bertin, another copy of the St-Vaast compilation was made: this manuscript was dismembered in the later Middle Ages, but the parts remained in the library of the abbey of St-Bertin. 'O', the part containing the *AB*, is now in the municipal library of Saint-Omer.[67] This, the oldest complete text of the *AB*, formed the basis of the edition of Levillain/Grat. From 'O' was copied, also in the eleventh century, the *AB* manuscript now in Brussels ('B').[68] Another now-lost copy of Hincmar's manuscript was apparently taken in the late tenth or early eleventh century by or for Aimoin of Fleury. In the eleventh-century Continuation of Aimoin's *Historia Francorum* are incorporated the *AB* annals from the middle of 869 onwards. This work in turn was copied at St-Germain-des-Prés, in the eleventh-century manuscript 'A' and in the thirteenth-century manuscript 'P' (of which only a fragment survives).[69] Given this small manuscript-family, it is unsurprising that the influence of the *AB* on subsequent medieval historiography was slight.

---

62 MS Paris, BN, Mélanges Colbert, vol. XLVI. fols. 283-313. See Poupardin 1905; Ganshof 1949: 163; Levillain 1964: xviii-xxi.

63 Flodoard III, c. 17, pp. 507-8; and in III, c. 5, p. 479, and c. 12, pp. 488-9, briefer extracts from *AB* 862. See Levillain 1964: xxii, xxxviii-xxxix.

64 Ganshof 1949: 164-6; Levillain 1964: xxv-xvi.

65 MS Douai, Bibl. publique 795. Levillain 1964: xli-iii.

66 'D' breaks off at fol. 118v just after the start of the 844 annal.

67 MS Saint-Omer, Bibl. munic. 706. Levillain 1964: xxiii-xxxii

68 MS Brussels, Bibl. royale 6439-51. Levillain 1964: xxxi i i -xxxvii.

69 MSS Paris, BN lat. 12711 and 12710. Levillain 1964: xliii-xlvii.

6. The *AB* in print and in translation

The *AB* were first printed in Paris in 1641 by François Du Chesne, from a copy of manuscript 'O' made by a colleague of Bolland.[70] This edition was reproduced in the eighteenth century by L. A. Muratori in his *Rerum Italicarum Scriptores* (a tribute to the many notices of Italian affairs in the *AB*) and by M. Bouquet, *Receuil des historiens de la France* (a pioneering collection of national historiography).[71] In 1829, G. H. Pertz edited the *AB* from manuscripts 'O' and 'B' in the folio *Scriptores* series of the *Monumenta Germaniae Historica*.[72] In 1871, A. Deshaines published a new edition using 'D' as well as 'O' and 'B'.[73] G. Waitz published an edition in 1883 for the *MGH* series *in usum scholarum*.[74] René Poupardin's discovery of manuscript 'C' made a new edition desirable. Félix Grat worked on this intermittently until his death in 1940; Léon Levillain took up Grat's work and had completed the edition but not the notes when he died in 1952. The edition, with Levillain's introduction and (incomplete) notes, was finally published, thanks to additional work by Jeanne Vielliard and Suzanne Clémencet, in 1964.[75]

A German translation was published by J. von Jasmund in 1857. This was reprinted (with some modernisation) by R. Rau in volume II of his *Quellen zur karolingischen Reichsgeschichte*.[76] French translations were published by L. Cousin in 1683 (of the annals from 843 only) and by F. P.-G. Guizot in 1824 (of the annals from 840 only).[77] A translation was left incomplete by A. Giry (died 1897) and Levillain left a draft translation among his papers.[78]

For this English translation, I have used the edition prepared by Grat. The introduction to that edition by Levillain remains a first-rate guide to the text and the manuscript tradition, and I have drawn on it extensively in my own comments above. Nevertheless the usefulness

---

70 Du Chesne (Chesnius) 1641: III, 150-261.

71 Muratori 1723: II, i, 495-570; Bouquet 1749-52: VI, 192-204. VII, 57-124, VIII, 26-37.

72 Pertz 1826: 419-515.

73 Deshaines 1871.

74 Waitz 1883.

75 Levillain 1964; Grat 1964.

76 Rau 1957(?): II, II-287.The translation is basically von Jasmund's. the edition that of Waitz.

77 Cousin 1683, 406-694: Guizot 1824, 127-316.

78 See Lot-Halphen 1909: iii; Levillain, 1964: lxxvii-viii.

of Levillain/Grat even for students who read Latin is reduced by the absence or incompleteness of notes for much of the text, and by the fact that the most recent of the references are now forty years old. The extensive notes that accompany my translation are intended to supply enough background information and cross-references within the *AB* to enable non-specialist readers to identify people and places in the text, and to understand the events described. I have given references to modern secondary works in English where possible. Since most of the specialist literature is in French and German, I have often cited books and articles in those languages, but where interpretations are contentious, I have tried to indicate these. For the sake of brevity, author, date and page(s) are given in the notes, and full references in the Bibliography. I have also supplied cross-references to other ninth-century historical sources, especially annalistic ones of which translations are forthcoming in the Manchester University Press series. (References to the notes to the *Annals of Fulda* are to T. Reuter's translation.) I have given references to the standard (usually *MGH*) editions of primary materials in Latin (especially councils, capitularies and papal letters) as guides to further study, even though no translations yet exist.

I have left certain words untranslated: *villa* sometimes means 'estate', sometimes 'estate-centre' (hence, in some cases, 'palace', or 'aristocratic residence'), sometimes 'village'. *Civitas* means a place where there is a bishop's see, for which the translation 'city' or 'town' seems misleading. *Honor* denotes an office (usually that of count), but can also mean lands or estates not necessarily attached to an office. *Castellum* is a type of fortification for which 'castle' is clearly a mistranslation. Other untranslated terms (like *emporium, mansus* and *accola*) are explained in the notes.

I have translated *beneficium* as 'benefice' (avoiding the anachronistic 'fief'); *Dani* as 'Danes' and *Nor(t)manni* as 'Northmen' throughout, rather than translating both as 'Vikings' (the normal term in English-language historiography). Place-names are given in forms most familiar to English-speaking students (thus, 'Liège' rather than 'Lüttich', 'Cologne' rather than 'Köln', but 'Trier' rather than 'Trèves'). When the reference is to a particular church or monastery, a saint's name is hyphenated (e.g. 'St-Denis', 'St-Martin'); without hyphen, the reference is to the saint as a person. All places mentioned in the text will be found on one or both of the maps. Personal names are standardised, anglicised and modernised where possible, and otherwise given in their simplest form. (Thus 'Louis' for *Ludoicus* or *Hludouuicus*; 'Robert' for *Rotbertus*; 'Ermentrude' for *Ermendrud* or *Hyrmintrudis*; 'Hincmar' for *Ingmarus* or *Hincmarus*.) The one exception is *Karlomannus*: to avoid confusion, where the reference is to Charles the Bald's son, I have rendered this as 'Carloman'; where the reference is to Louis the German's son, I have rendered 'Karlmann'. For clarification, some brief additional information (such as a bishop's see, or a ruler's kingdom) has sometimes been supplied in square brackets.

I have put all dates in their modern forms, and supplied dates for liturgical feasts (Easter, The Purification, etc.) and periods of time (Lent). Note that the annal year starts on 25 December.

In February, an assembly was held there at which he decided[1] to undertake a campaign with all the Franks into the lands of Brittany.[2] It was Bernard the chamberlain[3] who was the strongest advocate of this course. Not long afterwards, on Ash Wednesday [2 March], the Emperor left Aachen, sorely troubled with pain in his feet, and he decided to make a rapid advance on Brittany by the coastal route. He left the Lady Empress behind at Aachen.[4] The whole people were much opposed to this campaign because of its difficulties, and they refused to follow the Emperor to Brittany. Some of the magnates,[5] knowing the people's critical attitude, summoned them to a meeting so as to wean them away from the loyalty they had sworn to the Lord Emperor. And so the whole people, who ought to have been marching to Brittany, met up at Paris, and went on to force Lothar to come from Italy and Pippin from Aquitaine[6] to attack their father: the plan was to depose him, to destroy their stepmother and to kill Bernard. Bernard got wind of this, and fled to Barcelona.[7] When the plot was denounced

---

1 'There', i.e. Aachen, and 'he', i.e. Louis the Pious, are references back to the entry for 829 in the *RFA*. For the *AB* as the continuation of the *RFA*, see above, Introduction: 5.

2 On relations between Brittany and the Carolingian Empire, see Davies 1990; Smith 1992.

3 Bernard was the son of William, a cousin of Charlemagne, who was appointed Count of Toulouse in 789, founded the monastery of Gellone, and died in 806. For Bernard's family and subsequent career, see below 834, n. 11 (Herbert); 844 and n.1 (Gauzhelm); cf. Wollasch 1957b; Riché 1975: 17-21. Bernard was appointed count of Barcelona in 827 at the latest and chamberlain in 829; *RFA* 827 (and compare 820), 829. See Ward 1990: 225-7. The importance of the post of chamberlain, or treasurer, is clear from Hincmar, *De Ordine Palatii*, cc. 22, 32, trans. Herlihy 1970: 208-27.

4 *RFA* s.a. 819 records the Emperor's marriage to Judith, a daughter of Count Welf whose lands lay in Alemannia. See Ward 1990.

5 Among these, Matfrid, formerly Count of Orléans, and Hugh, formerly Count of Tours, played the most conspicuous roles. See Astronomer c. 44; Thegan c. 55; and for their disgrace in 828, *RFA* s.a.

6 Lothar, Louis the Pious's eldest son by Ermengard, was born in 795, designated co-emperor in 817, and sent to rule Italy in 822 and again (after a return to Francia from 824) in 829: *RFA* s.a. Pippin, Louis's second son, born c. 797, was sent to rule Aquitaine in 814: *RFA* s.a.

7 His county since 827 at the latest: *RFA* s.a. and cf. *RFA* 820. For Bernard's position in 830, cf. *AF* s.a.

to the Lord Emperor, he immediately travelled to meet with them at Compiègne. There Pippin, who had with him a large proportion of the people, with Lothar's consent took away from the Emperor his royal power, and also his wife whom they veiled and sent to the convent of St-Radegund at Poitiers. They also tonsured her brothers, Conrad and Rudolf, and shut them up in monasteries.[8] After Easter Week [17–24 April], Lothar arrived from Italy: there and then he held an assembly and ordered Bernard's brother Herbert to be blinded[9] and he imprisoned various of the Lord Emperor's faithful men.

When all these events had taken place, the Lord Emperor together with his son Lothar gave notice of another assembly to meet around 1 October at Nijmegen, where the Saxons and East Franks could gather.[10] There an army flocked together, consisting of many from each side, that is from the Lord Emperor's side and from Lothar's. The Lord Emperor had regained control of the situation. He ordered those responsible for what had been done to him, whose double-dealing had been detected and their plot exposed, to be kept in custody until the meeting of another assembly to be held at Aachen. It was adjudged, further, by all the bishops, abbots, counts and other Franks, that his wife, who had been taken away from him unjustly and without due process of law and judgement, should be brought back before this assembly that had been arranged, and if any free man wanted to charge her with any crime, either she should defend herself according to the laws, or she should undergo the judgement of the Franks.[11] From Nijmegen the Lord Emperor hastened to winter at Aachen.

831

Around 1 February, he held a general assembly, as had been arranged. He ordered the attendance of those men who, the previous year, had offended against the Lord Emperor through their sedition, first at Compiègne and then at Nijmegen, so that their cases could be discussed and judgement passed. It was adjudged, first of all by his sons and then by all those present, that they should suffer the death

---

8 Nithard I, 3 adds that these were in Aquitaine, and that Conrad and Rudolf were in Pippin's custody.

9 Nithard I, 3 adds that he was sent as a prisoner to Italy.

10 Astronomer c. 45 has an interesting account suggesting that the Emperor showed much skill in handling this assembly and exploited the support of the non-Frankish peoples east of the Rhine.

11 For this procedure see Brunner 1928(ii): 505-6. On the judgement of the Franks, cf. Nelson 1986a (1983a): 102.

penalty. Then the Lord Emperor, with his usual magnanimity, granted them life and limb, and sent them to be held in custody in various places. Lothar too, because he had given his sympathies to those men more than he should have done, appealed to his father's merciful nature. To this assembly came the Lady Empress, as she had been ordered to do; standing there in the sight of the Lord Emperor and his sons, she declared her willingness to purge herself on all the charges levelled against her. Then the whole assembled people were solemnly asked if anyone wanted to charge her with any crime. When no one was found who wanted to bring any wrongdoing whatsoever against her, she purged herself according to the judgement of the Franks of all the things of which she had been accused. When the assembly was over, the Lord Emperor allowed Lothar to go to Italy, Pippin to Aquitaine and Louis to Bavaria.[1]

The Lord Emperor himself arrived at Ingelheim on about 1 May. There Lothar came to him, and he received him honourably. All those men, too, who had been sent into exile were brought before him and pardoned, and they gained the favour of the Lord Emperor.

Now he held a third general assembly at the *villa* of Thionville and there envoys came from the Amir al-Mamoun of Persia[2], seeking a treaty. They soon got what they sought, and went home again. There also came envoys of the Danes with the same request[3] and they too went home after having their treaty confirmed. Many embassies came to him from the Slavs[4] and were duly heard, dealt with and given leave to depart. Count Bernard presented himself and gave satisfaction on all

---

1 Louis the German, born c. 806, was sent to rule Bavaria in 825: *RFA* s.a. There is no mention in the *AB* of the division-project, almost certainly of early 831, whereby the arrangements of 817 were changed to exclude Lothar from Francia proper and divide it between Pippin, Louis and Charles: *MGH Capit* II, no. 194, pp. 20–4. Nithard I, 3 hints at this project.

2 Caliph of Baghdad 813–33, son of Harun al-Rashid. He was at war with the Byzantines. See Canard 1966: 709–10. Perhaps he hoped for Frankish help.

3 For the background to Frankish attempts to exploit dynastic conflict in Denmark in the preceding two decades, see *RFA* for 812, 814, 817, 819, 821–3, 825–8; Wood 1987.

4 The background to those contacts, which attained a new importance in Louis the Pious's reign, is sketched by Vlasto 1970: ch. 2.

5 But it seems unlikely that Bernard was reinstated in the office of chamberlain. In 832 he was in Aquitaine where he and Pippin were accused of disloyalty to the Emperor and Bernard was deprived of his lands and offices: Astronomer c. 47; *AX* for 831 (in error for 832). Already in 831 it looks as if Adalard the seneschal had become the most influential figure at the Emperor's court. See Lot 1970a (1908): 591–2.

the charges of which he had been accused, swearing an oath to the Lord Emperor and to his sons.[5] Those of the sons who had been present returned to their own lands, the Lord Emperor waited for some time for Pippin to arrive there, and then sent special envoys to order him to come. Pippin promised to do so, but put off coming.

After Martinmas [11 November] the Lord Emperor arrived at Aachen to winter there; and there, a few days before Christmas, Pippin came to him. The Lord Emperor received him less favourably than he had been used to doing before, because of Pippin's disobedience.

832

Pippin, resentful because he had not been honourably received by his father, made his own plans. On the Eve of Holy Innocents' Day [27 December] at the first hour of the night, he fled with a few of his own men and made for Aquitaine as fast as he could. At this, the Lord Emperor was deeply upset and angered: he had never thought that such things could happen where his son was concerned or that he could actually flee his father's presence. He therefore summoned together his advisers from every side and took counsel with them as to what should be done about Pippin's behaviour. It was decided that the Lord Emperor's general assembly should be announced as to be held in the *civitas* of Orléans, and that Lothar should go to the assembly direct from Italy, while Louis should come to Aachen and go on from there in company with his father.

Everything had been thus settled, and messengers sent out everywhere to make the necessary arrangements, when it suddenly came to the ears of the most righteous Emperor that Louis with all the Bavarians, free and unfree, together with as many Slavs as he could draw to his cause, was planning to attack Alemannia, which had already, some little while ago, been given to his brother Charles by his father,[1] to lay waste and plunder it, and annex it to his own kingdom and get all the people of that kingdom [of Alemannia] to promise loyalty to him, and when all those things had been perpetrated, he was going to attack Francia with that same army and invade and conquer as much of his father's kingdom as he possibly could. The Lord Emperor, as soon as he had found out all this, immediately changed his plans, and ordered all the West and East Franks and the Saxons too to assemble at Mainz to meet him on 18 April. On hearing this

1 In 829: Thegan c. 35; Nithard I, 3, and again in 831, cf. 831, n. 1. This is the first mention in the *AB* of the future Charles the Bald.

summons, everyone hastened to the Lord Emperor with all speed, wanting to offer him all the help they could. It was at this time that there was an eclipse of the moon after sunset on 19 April.

The Lord Emperor arrived at Mainz and there the whole people came to the assembly which he had fixed for them. The very next day, with a strong force of Franks and Saxons, he crossed the rivers Rhine and Main, and pitched camp in the vicinity of the *villa* of Tribur. His son Louis with his army was encamped near Worms at the *villa* called Langbardheim: his hopes were being buoyed up with empty promises, for both his own men and those of the counts and vassals of the Lord Emperor and of Charles who were with him were promising him that all the East Franks and Saxons would give their support to him. The man urging this most strongly with his treacherous plots and schemes was Matfrid[2], to whom the Lord Emperor the year before had granted life and limb and possession of his inheritance, after he had previously been condemned to death. When Louis learned that his father had crossed the Rhine with such a large force of faithful men, his boldness was undermined and he lost all hope of gaining the power he had so unjustly sought. He wasted no time but retreated hastily with his men to Bavaria along the same route by which they had come; and many of those with him went over again to the Lord Emperor. Hearing of Louis's sudden retreat, the Lord Emperor advanced to the place from which Louis had withdrawn, and found much devastation there.

He bore all these adversities patiently, as is his usual way.[3] He did not go in pursuit of his son but proceeded with his whole army at a slow pace into Alemannia, finally reaching Augsburg on the river Lech. There he got that son of his who had been led so much astray to come before him. But Louis promised, swearing an oath, that he would never again perpetrate such things in future nor connive with others for any such purpose.

When the assembly was over, he allowed his son peacefully to return to Bavaria, while he himself disbanded his army and came to Salz by way of Austrasia [i.e. Franconia]. There the Lady Empress came to meet him. The pair reached Mainz[4] by a river journey, and there Lothar met his father.

It was announced again that a general assembly would be held at Orléans on 1 September, and every free man was to come there ready

2 Cf. n. 5 to 830.

3 See above, Introduction: 6.

4 Thegan c. 40 says 'Frankfurt'.

to go on campaign. When he arrived there, he received the annual gifts in the customary way, and soon left to hasten to Limoges. Then he summoned his son Pippin to him and reproached him asking, among other things, why he had fled from his father's presence without permission. Wishing with fatherly affection to win him over again, he ordered Pippin to go to Francia, to stay for a while in a place to which his father would assign him, until such time as he should soothe his father's feelings by mending his own ways.[5] Pippin pretended to agree to this and set off, but he turned back from the journey, and scorned to carry out his father's orders. Meanwhile the Lord Emperor was returning through other parts of Aquitaine, to Francia. When Pippin's action was reported to him, he did not return to Francia as soon as he had planned but, on account of this news, delayed in those parts for some days longer, finally coming to Le Mans[6] at Christmas.

833

When the Holy Days had been celebrated there, he reached Aachen by a direct route. He had not been staying there for many days when news arrived that his sons had again got together in an alliance to revolt against him and were aiming to attack with a large force of his enemies. After taking counsel, he reached Worms before the beginning of Lent and there he spent that period and celebrated Easter [13 April] and Pentecost [1 June]. He summoned an army and made plans to advance against them, so that if he had been unable to divert them from their shameless course of action by peacemaking words, he could check them by force of arms, lest they do harm to the Christian people. At last, wanting to finish what they had begun, his sons joined forces in the region of Alsace at a place called Rotfeld.[1] Lothar came from Italy bringing Pope Gregory[2] with him, Pippin from Aquitaine, and Louis from Bavaria with a very large number of men. When the Lord

---

5 The *AB* account here obscures the fact that the Emperor had already decided to take Aquitaine from Pippin and give it to Charles instead: Nithard I, 4; *AF* for 832; Astronomer c. 47.

6 The Emperor's nominee Aldric was consecrated bishop on 22 December: Goffart 1966: 264; Le Maître 1980.

1 A marginal note in manuscript 'O' seems to have glossed Rotfeld as follows: 'near Colmar, and since then called "the Field of Lies"'. On this manuscript see Introduction: 16.

2 Gregory IV (827-44). For his role in legitimising Lothar's rebellion, see Paschasius Radbertus, *Epitaphium* II, pp. 86-9; Ganz 1990a: 546-7. Fried 1990: 267-73 rates Gregory's authority very significant in 833. Astronomer c. 48 suggests a more marginal role.

Emperor met with them, he was completely unable to prevent them from continuing on their wilful course: rather, it was they who deceived the people who had come with the Lord Emperor, by evil persuasions and false promises, with the result that everyone deserted him.[3] For some of his men – those against whom the rebels' anger raged most fiercely – slipped away and took themselves off to the lands of their friends and kinsmen and of their faithful men. The Lord Emperor's wife was taken away and sent into exile in Italy at the *civitas* of Tortona. Lothar seized royal power, and let the Pope return to Rome, Pippin to Aquitaine, and Louis to Bavaria. Lothar himself brought his father with him as a prisoner by way of Metz to Soissons, and there left him under the same strict custody in the monastery of St-Médard. He also took his father's son Charles away from him and sent him to the monastery of Prüm,[4] something that grieved his father very much indeed.

Then, on 1 October, Lothar held a long-planned assembly at Compiègne. The bishops, abbots, counts and all the people assembled there formally presented him with the annual gifts and promised their loyalty. Also to Compiègne came envoys from Constantinople: they had been sent to Lothar's father, but instead reached Lothar and handed over their letters and presents to him. In this assembly, they dreamed up many crimes to impute to the Lord Emperor, with Ebbo Bishop of Rheims[5] standing out among them all as a kindler of false charges. They harrassed him for so long that they forced him to lay aside his weapons and change his garb to that of a penitent,[6] driving

---

3 A note in manuscript 'O' adds at this point: 'But Bishops Drogo [of Metz] the Emperor's brother, Modoin [of Autun], Wiliric [of Bremen] and the above-mentioned Aldric [of Le Mans] stayed with him [i.e. the Emperor], together with some other bishops, abbots, counts and others of his faithful men.'

4 This monastery in the Eifel region (see map 1) had longstanding associations with the Carolingian dynasty. Note that Charles was not tonsured - perhaps because Lothar felt bound by his oath to protect his half-brother and godson (Nithard I, 3) or because he feared hostile Frankish aristocratic opinion.

5 An intimate of Louis the Pious while still king of Aquitaine, Ebbo was born of a slave-mother who was Louis's nurse. He was freed by Louis, and made archbishop of Rheims in 816: a unique case of such social advancement in the Carolingian period. Thegan c. 44 is a diatribe against him for his lowly origin, and for exploiting his post to advance his own kin (in fact, usual conduct on the part of holders of high office). By contrast, Flodoard II, c. 19, p. 467 preserves quite a favourable judgement on Ebbo's career. For a brief account, see McKeon 1974b.

6 Penance entailed disqualification from bearing arms, and hence in practice rendered Louis incapable of ruling, though the bishops involved claimed no authority to depose an emperor. See Halphen 1977: 204-6; Nelson 1986a (1977a): 135-6 and 146, n. 2.

him into the gates of Holy Church so that no one would dare to speak with him except those specially deputed for that purpose. But after a while they were afraid that he might be snatched away from that place by some of those who had remained loyal to him. So Lothar himself came to that monastery and took his father away with him against his will and kept him with him at Compiègne, still under sentence of excommunication. Then, when the assembly had been concluded, Lothar hastened to Aachen to winter there, and forced his father to accompany him, still under the same conditions. He reached Aachen on St Andrew's Eve [29 November]. But after a few days, it came about that Lothar and Louis had a meeting at Mainz to discuss various matters. There Louis begged his brother Lothar most earnestly to act more gently towards their father and not hold him in such strict confinement. When Lothar refused to listen, Louis left in sadness. From then on, he kept thinking over with his men how he might rescue his father from his imprisonment.[7] Lothar reached Aachen a few days before Christmas.

834

The Lord Emperor was being kept at Aachen. He was not being more humanely treated in any way at all: on the contrary, his enemies raged against him much more cruelly, trying day and night to weaken his spirit with such intense sufferings that he would voluntarily renounce the world and take himself off to a monastery. But he kept saying that he would never make any such commitment as long as he had no real power over his own actions. Louis, however, when he realised that his request to Lothar to treat their father more mildly would carry no weight at all with that brother of his, sent envoys to his brother Pippin and told him of all that had been done to their father: he begged him to remember his father's affection, and the duty he owed him, and to join him [Louis] in rescuing their father from his tribulation. Pippin at once summoned an army of men from Aquitaine and from beyond the Seine[1] while Louis summoned the Bavarians, Austrasians, Saxons, Alemans and the Franks on this side of the Ardennes;[2] with all these

7 Thegan cc. 45, 47 gives a similar account of the role of Louis the German in 833. Astronomer cc. 49-50 stresses the swing in aristocratic opinion in Francia and in other parts of the empire. Cf. also Nithard I, 4.

1 I.e. the region between Seine and Loire. The annalist writes from the perspective of Aachen.

2 Again note the Aachen perspective. Cf. the same phraseology in Nithard II, 3 describing Lothar's approach from the east. The Charbonnière forest, covering part of the Ardennes, was an historic frontier between Neustria and Austrasia. See Nelson 1986a (1985): 215-16.

troops they began to move rapidly on Aachen. When Lothar heard of
this, he left Aachen and brought his father all the way to Paris, still
under the same conditions. He found Pippin already arrived there with
his army but prevented from crossing the Seine by exceptionally high
floodwaters: much flooding of other rivers too and unheard-of burst-
ing of their banks created great difficulties for many people. But now
when Lothar learned for certain that Louis too was heading rapidly
towards the same area with such a great number of troops, he was
stricken with terror. Leaving his father in that same place, Lothar fled
with his men. This was on 28 February. When he had gone, the
bishops who had been present there came and reconciled the Lord
Emperor in the church of St-Denis, and clad him in his royal robes and
his weapons.[3] Then his sons Pippin and Louis along with other faithful
men came to him and were joyfully received by his fatherly heart. He
offered warmest thanks to them and to the whole people because they
had been so quick and keen to offer help.

After he had held an assembly with them, he let Pippin and the rest of
the people return home, but he had Louis come with him all the way
to Aachen and there they celebrated the feast of Easter together [5
April]. When the festival days were over, he summoned his close
advisers and those magnates who were in the vicinity, and eagerly set
about discussing with them how he might be able to summon his son
Lothar to him. He dispatched messengers to every part of his realm
with orders to bring the people the news of his own liberation and to
remind them to make every effort to fulfil the obligations of loyalty
which they had promised him; also to say that he had forgiven them,
for the love of God, whatever wrongs they had done against him.

Lothar, having set off from Paris, got to the town [urbs] of Vienne in
Provence. He stayed there for a while, imposing many burdens on the
men of those parts. The Lord Emperor, when he learned that Lothar
was there, sent envoys to tell him that his father had forgiven him all
that he had done against him, and to tell him to return in peace to his
father. But Lothar scorned these messages and refused to come,
remaining fixed in his obstinacy. There were other developments:

3 The date: Sunday 1 March. Perhaps some of the bishops mentioned above 833
   n. 3 were among those who reconciled Louis. Nithard I, 4 stresses the
   importance of aristocratic initiative. On the ritual, cf. 835 n. 2. The *AB* say
   nothing about Ebbo, who, according to Flodoard II, c. 20, p. 472, fled from
   Rheims 'with the help of certain Northmen who knew the route and the
   harbours of the sea and the rivers that flow into it', and sought the protection
   of the Northmen he had got to know during his mission-work in the 820s. He
   was later persuaded to return to Francia and stand trial; below 835: 33.

when those who were the Lord Emperor's faithful men in Italy – Bishop Ratold,[4] Count Boniface,[5] Pippin, the Emperor's kinsman[6] and a number of others – realised that some of his enemies wanted to bring about the death of his wife, they sent men as fast as they could who rescued her and brought her safe and sound to Aachen to the presence of the Lord Emperor.

At this time also, the following were killed on the expedition sent against Lambert[7] and Matfrid[8] and other accomplices of Lothar: Counts Odo, and William his brother, and Fulbert; Abbot Theoto of St-Martin[9] and a number of others. Meanwhile a fleet of Danes came to Frisia and laid waste a part of it. From there, they came by way of Utrecht to the *emporium* called Dorestad[10] and destroyed everything. They slaughtered some people, took others away captive, and burned the surrounding region.

Now Lothar came with his men to Chalon-sur-Saône, took it by storm

---

4 Bishop of Verona. Astronomer c. 29 notes his service to the Emperor during the revolt of King Bernard of Italy in 817. Cf. below n. 6.

5 Count of Lucca: *RFA* 828. On Boniface's family, see Wickham 1981: 58-60.

6 Great-nephew of Louis the Pious and son of King Bernard of Italy who had died in 818 from blinding as a result of his revolt: *RFA* 817; he was given a countship in Francia sometime between 834 and 840: Nithard II, 3.

7 Count of Nantes in the early 820s: Ermold III, l. 1552, p. 120; *RFA* 825. On his family, see Dhondt 1948: 318-22; Boussard 1968: 18.

8 Cf. 830, n. 5. Astronomer c. 52 places this battle after Whitsun (25 May). Its importance is suggested by a number of contemporary writers. The rich Loire valley region was a cockpit of aristocratic rivalries.

9 This casualty list may be compared with those given by Nithard I, 4 and Astronomer c. 52. Odo had been made count of Orléans in 828 in place of Matfrid. He was a kinsman of Bernard of Barcelona (Astronomer c. 45). He married, probably c. 828, a sister of Count Gerald of Paris and of Adalard (cf. above 832, n. 5): their daughter was to marry Charles the Bald in 842. According to Levillain 1938: 31-46, Odo was a first cousin of Louis the Pious. His inherited lands and first countship lay in the Worms area but he transferred his interests westwards in the mid-820s thanks to imperial patronage. Cf. Werner 1959b: 154-5, 163, though apparently with some reservations about Levillain's reconstruction. Odo's brother William was the Emperor's constable and count of Blois at the time of his death: Adrevald I, c. 21, col. 925. Note the military service owed by Theoto abbot of St-Martin, who was also the Emperor's archchancellor. Adrevald mentions that the bishop of Orléans and the abbot of Fleury were also summoned to serve in this campaign.

10 For the political situation in Frisia as the outcome of inter-Danish rivalries see Wood 1987: 43. For the meaning of *emporium* as a trading-place for prestige goods, and for archaeological evidence of the economic role of Dorestad, see Hodges 1990b: 74-7, 122-5; Hodges 1990a: 206-7, 209-15. For the very large output of the Dorestad mint in the late 830s, Coupland 1988.

and set it on fire, and took prisoner the counts who were in the city. Three of them he killed[11] and the rest he led away with him under strong guard. He had Bernard's sister, a nun, put in a barrel and drowned in the river Saône.[12] Then he came to Orléans.

The Lord Emperor, getting word of all these doings, summoned his army to Langres in mid-August. There he received the annual gifts, and immediately set off on a campaign through the regions of Troyes, Chartres and the Dunois to liberate the people from those who had wrongfully seized the realm. He arrived near the stronghold [castellum] of Blois at the same time as his son Louis, and to this place his son Pippin also came with his army to meet his father and bring him help. Lothar, staying in his camp not far away, threatened battle with his forces but was in fact quite incapable of carrying out such a threat. Then the Lord Emperor, moved by his usual desire to show mercy, sent to tell Lothar to come peacefully to him for he would forgive him and all his men all the things they had said against him. He granted Lothar Italy, just as Pippin, the Lord Emperor's brother, had held it in the time of the Lord Charles,[13] and to the others he granted life and limb and their hereditary possessions and to many of them their benefices too. When Lothar came to him with his men, his father bound him with the strong bonds of solemn oaths, that neither he nor his men should ever afterwards do such things again nor agree to others' doing them. When all these arrangements had been confirmed, he made Lothar go back to Italy with those men who preferred to follow him. He himself arrived in the neighbourhood of Orléans. He granted permission to return home to Pippin, to Louis and to the whole army. Then he came by way of Paris to Attigny, where about Martinmas [11 November] he held an assembly with his advisers. When the affairs of the realm had been settled, he went off to winter at Thionville.

---

11 Two of these are named by Nithard I, 5 and Astronomer c. 52. 'Senila' sounds like a Goth, and 'Gozhelm' can probably be identified as the count of Roussillon and brother of Bernard of Barcelona; Wollasch 1957b: 184.

12 Her name, Gerberga, and more details are given by Nithard I, 5 and Astronomer c. 52: she was condemned as a witch. Cf. Thegan c. 52: '(Lothar) tortured her for a long time and then he executed her by the judgement of the wives of his wicked counsellors.'

13 Charlemagne's son Pippin was king of Italy from 781 until his death in 810.

835

He celebrated the feast of Christmas joyfully at Metz, having been received there most handsomely by his brother Drogo, bishop of that *civitas*.[1] He spent the festal days there, and then returned to his own palace at the *villa* of Thionville. About the time of the Feast of the Purification of Holy Mary [2 February] he held there a general council of nearly all the bishops and abbots, both canonical and regular, of his whole empire. At this council, among other provisions for ecclesiastical discipline, the following events were particulary fully discussed: in the year immediately preceding, the most devout Emperor had been deposed undeservedly, through the treachery of evildoers and enemies of God, from the realm, honour and royal title which he had inherited from his father; then after some time it had been decided and confirmed by everyone in concord and unanimity that since the evildoers' factions had been destroyed by God's help, he, restored now to his ancestral honour and clothed again as he deserved in the royal splendour, should be acknowledged by all in the most loyal and unswerving obedience and subjection as emperor and lord. Each one present at the council drew up with his own hand a full account of thse findings and of his own confirmation thereof, and authenticated it with his own signature. The outcome of the whole affair, how it had been dealt with, discussed, settled and finally confirmed in suitable fashion by the signatures of everyone: all this was put together, set out in full detail in one collection, bound as a small volume, and agreed by all as an accurate account. They then wasted no time in making it as widely known as possible, bringing it to everyone's attention with most devoted and heartfelt and kind concern, and with an authority most worthy of so many reverend fathers. For they gathered at Metz in the church of the blessed protomartyr Stephen, completed the celebration of mass, and read out the account of the whole affair publicly to all who were present. Then the holy and venerable bishops lifted from the most holy altar the crown, symbol of rulership, and with their own hands restored it to his head, to the utmost joy of everyone.[2] Furthermore, Ebbo, former archbishop of Rheims, who had

---

1 Drogo (801-55) was Charlemagne's son by a concubine, Regina. Louis the Pious kept him and two other half-brothers at court during the first years of his reign, but in 818, anxious that they might become foci for rebellion, he had them tonsured; Nithard I, 2. Abbot of Luxeuil in 820, Drogo was made bishop of Metz in 823. He became Louis's archchaplain in 834.

2 The date was 28 February. Astronomer c. 54 gives more details. Brühl 1962: 278-9 discusses the significance of this ritual as a 'confirmatory coronation'.

once been a kind of standard-bearer of that whole conspiracy, ascended a high place in that same church and voluntarily confessed before everyone that the Emperor had been unjustly deposed; that everything done against him had been evilly done and wickedly plotted, against all the rules of equity; and that afterwards the Emperor had been deservedly, justly and worthily established again on his own throne of empire.

When all these things had been solemnly completed, they returned to the palace of Thionville. There Ebbo confessed to a capital crime at a plenary session of the synod,[3] proclaimed his unworthiness of so great an office as that of bishop, and confirmed this in his own writing: then he resigned from that office by the consent and the judgement of everyone.[4]

When these and other affairs of state had been justly dealt with, all were dismissed to their homes, while the Emperor himself celebrated the holy time of Lent also at Thionville, and the most holy feast of Easter [18 April] at Metz where he again stayed with Archbishop Drogo. Then he set out for the general assembly which he had given notice would be held at Tramoyes near the *civitas* of Lyons.[5] When this had been held in June, and the annual gifts had been received and the Marches of Spain, Septimania and Provence had been set in order,[6] he returned to Aachen. But while he was still at that assembly, the Northmen fell on Dorestad in a second assault, laid it waste and looted it savagely. The Emperor, very angry, reached Aachen and made arrangements for effective defence of the coasts. He spent the autumn hunting-season in the Ardennes[7] and returned from there to winter at Aachen.

3 Apparently Ebbo confessed to some sexual misdemeanour. It was later alleged by his partisans that he was deposed on Louis's orders. This was essentially true, but it looks as if canonical procedures were carefully observed: Louis now had his episcopate well in hand. See Devisse 1975: 74–86; Nelson 1990d: 155–6.

4 At this point, L/G: 17 identified the break between Fulco's section of the *AB* and that of Prudentius. None of the manuscripts shows any sign of this change in authorship. See Introduction: 6–7.

5 The Emperor's sons Pippin and Louis were also present; Thegan c. 57.

6 Astronomer c. 57 could suggest that the troubled state of these regions resulted from the revived ambitions of Bernard of Barcelona. Unfortunately this source's chronology seems disordered at this point.

7 For the social and political significance of the royal hunt, see Nelson 1987: 166–72. The *AB*'s silence on such hunts in 830–34 probably reflects more than a lack of interest on the annalist's part, for hunts are mentioned in *RFA* 817, 829, and again in *AB* 835–6, 838–9.

836

After spending the feast of Christmas there, he again sent envoys to Lothar, warning him about the obedience and deep respect he owed his father, and impressing upon him by a great number of arguments the value of peace and concord. So that he should recognise this more explicitly, he was ordered to send to his father those envoys of his in whom he had greatest confidence, through whom he could negotiate about his own honour and security, and who could hear what his father's wishes were in regard to him and would be able to report this back to him faithfully. Lothar did not go so far as to question his father's orders, and in May he sent to the Emperor's presence at Thionville Abbot Wala,[1] Richard the Usher[2] and Count Eberhard.[3] Discussions were held with these envoys about the coming of Lothar in person. It was settled on our side that he and his men should have a safe conduct to come to his father's presence and then to return home, and it was promised on oath by his envoys for their part that he would come without delay to his father's presence at the assembly appointed.

When all these things had been dealt with, the Emperor spent some days hunting around Remiremont. After that, in September, he came to the assembly that had been announced at Worms. There he had

1 A cousin of Charlemagne, Wala lost favour in 814 and became a monk at Corbie. He regained favour in 822, when he was sent with Lothar to Italy as a leading counsellor (*RFA* 822). Thereafter he consistently supported Lothar and withdrew with him to Italy in 834. He received the abbacy of Bobbio, but was deprived of Corbie which he had held since 826; Weinrich 1963: 70-89; Ganz 1990b.

2 Richard, former chief of ushers to the Emperor, sided with Lothar in 833: Thegan c. 47, and postscript, labels him *perfidus*. He too went with Lothar to Italy in 834, and the Emperor confiscated lands previously granted him in the Ardennes. His family lands were in the Metz area. The chief of ushers (door-keepers: *ostiarii*) seems to have become a major court post in Louis the Pious's reign: he may have functioned as a master of ceremonies.

3 Son of Count Unroch (*RFA* 811), Eberhard was a Frankish magnate who became duke of Friuli probably in 828 (cf. *RFA* 828), but also held lands in northern Francia (the lower Meuse region) and in Alemannia. He does not seem to have been as closely identified with Lothar's cause as Richard was (above n. 2): in 836 he was considered *fidelis* at the Emperor's court (Thegan postscript) and it may have been then that he married Gisèle, daughter of Louis the Pious and Judith; Nelson 1990c: 152. For further details on what modern historians have labelled the 'Unruoching' family, Werner 1965: 133-7. Note that the names of Richard and Eberhard are missing from all *AB* manuscripts due to scribal error in the archetype, but Thegan postscript warrants their restitution. See L/G: 18, note 'n'.

received the annual gifts in the usual way and was awaiting Lothar's arrival when news came that he had been stricken with fever and could not possibly come. Abbot Hugh[4] and Count Adalgar[5] were immediately dispatched to ask Lothar about his illness, his recovery, and his intentions of coming later; also about the restitutions of property which though it belonged to churches in Francia was situated in Italy and had thus been subjected to unchecked spoliations by Lothar's supporters; and finally about those bishops and counts who had lately with loyal devotion accompanied the Empress from Italy,[6] for the Emperor wanted their sees, counties, benefices and their own property to be restored to them. To all this Lothar replied through orders given to his envoys that he could not agree on every point, and he suggested some alternative terms.

At that same time, the Northmen again devastated Dorestad and Frisia.[7] But Horic, king of the Danes,[8] through his envoys sent to that assembly offered terms of friendship and obedience and declared that he had in no way given his agreement to their urgent requests [to support the attacks]. He also complained about the killing of the envoys he had sent to the Emperor. They had been massacred a short while before near Cologne through the unauthorised action of certain men. The Emperor very rightly avenged the slaughter of these envoys, sending *missi* specifically to see to this.

The autumn hunting-season was spent at the palace of Frankfurt, and then he returned to Aachen. Envoys from Horic arrived there seeking an amount equivalent to the blood-money for those Northmen who had recently been perpetrating such attacks on our own borders and whom he, Horic, had captured and had killed.[9] Aznar, count of Hither

---

4 Hugh, a son of Charlemagne and his concubine Regina, was a full brother of Drogo; see 835, n. 1. Tonsured in 818 and sent to the monastery of Charroux in Poitou, he was given the rich abbacy of St-Quentin probably in 822 or 823 and became archchancellor in 834, presumably as a reward for loyalty to Louis the Pious.

5 Werner 1965: 133-7 links the name with the family of Count Unroch, a Frankish magnate prominent in the early ninth century. He can perhaps be identified with the Adalgar below, 838.

6 See 834, nn. 4-6.

7 Cf. 834, n. 10.

8 Horic son of Godofrid had emerged as winner in a fierce power-struggle in Denmark; *RFA* 827. The *Life* of Anskar cc. 25, 26 gives an impression of Horic's authority in the 840s. Cf. below 845, n. 3; 847, n. 5. See Wood 1987: 42-3, 45.

9 My reading follows that of Vogel 1906: 71 and n. 2.

Gascony, who some years previously had defected with Pippin,[10] died a horrible death. His brother Sancho Sanchez took control of that region despite Pippin's denial of permission.

Then also Abbot Wala died in Italy.[11] Lothar had relied heavily on his advice.

837

After the Christmas celebrations were over, the Emperor held an assembly of bishops at Aachen on the feast of the Purification of the ever-virgin Mary [2 February].[1] At this assembly there took place many and varied discussions on the state of the Holy Church of God: it was made plain and set out clearly what was the proper function of each social order [ordo]. Furthermore, a letter was sent to Pippin from this assembly of venerable bishops. In it, they warned him at some length about his own salvation, and also urged him to remember the practice of his forefathers, especially his most righteous father, and restore to God's churches the property which had previously been battened on and ruined by his own supporters:[2] otherwise he would arouse God's anger against himself on this account. Pippin gave his assent to the advice of so many fathers, restored everything and assigned to each church precisely what was its due, confirming the documents with his own seal-ring. Thus the Emperor, when he had put the coastal defences of Frisia in order, came to Thionville in May and received the annual gifts. Then he set out for Rome to arrange for the defence of the holy Roman Church and to pray there. He had

10 Aznar Galindez, a Basque, had been appointed a count in the Aragon valley early in the ninth century. He was involved in a struggle against the ruler of Pamplona in the 820s; *RFA* 824. Collins 1983: 250-1 outlines his subsequent career on the basis of a tenth-century Spanish source. See also Collins 1990b: 373, and for Gascony in this period, Collins 1986, chs. 4, 5. Prudentius, involved in the production of the *AB* at this point, was himself probably a kinsman of Aznar; Nelson 1990b: 26.

11 Either on 31 August or 12 September; Weinrich 1963: 88, n. 139.

1 This may be an error, through confusion with the Aachen assembly on 6 February 836; L/G: 20 n. 2. But it is possible that there were February assemblies in consecutive years.

2 Restitutions of secularised church property were often demanded by ecclesiastics in this and succeeding reigns. Such demands, and the extent of their implementation, depended on political circumstances. Though it is not clear that the problem was worse in Aquitaine than elsewhere, Louis the Pious may have tried to use this pretext to interfere in Pippin's kingdom, perhaps especially in Anjou which Pippin had acquired from his father in 834/5; Oexle 1969: 153-4, 156 and n. 88. See also Collins 1990b: 371-2.

meanwhile sent envoys to Lothar warning him to receive his father with due filial respect and to see that supplies were available in suitable quantities along the Emperor's route.

The Northmen at this time fell on Frisia with their usual surprise attack. Coming upon our people unprepared on an island called Walcheren, they slaughtered many of them and plundered even more. They stayed on the island for a while, levying as much tribute as they wanted. Then they fell on Dorestad with the same fury and exacted tribute in the same way. When the Emperor heard about these attacks, he postponed his planned journey to Rome and wasted no time in hurrying to the fort of Nijmegen close by Dorestad. When the Northmen heard of his arrival there, they withdrew immediately.

Now the Emperor summoned a general assembly and held an inquiry in public with those magnates to whom he had delegated the task of guarding that coast. It became clear from the discussion that partly through the sheer impossibility of the task, partly through the disobedience of certain men, it had not been possible for them to offer any resistance to the attackers. Energetic abbots and counts were therefore dispatched to suppress the insubordinate Frisians. Now too, so that from then on he would be better able to resist their incursions, he gave orders that a fleet should be made ready to go more speedily in pursuit in whatever direction might be required.

But Lothar meanwhile ordered the Alpine passes to be guarded by very strong barriers.[3] Lambert, Lothar's greatest supporter,[4] died, and so did Lothar's father-in-law Hugh.[5]

Meanwhile the Bretons, impelled by a kind of impudence, made an attempt at revolt. The Emperor sent an expedition and crushed their rebellion. They returned the land they had taken from our people, gave hostages and promised to stay loyal in future.

---

3 These passes, in the Carolingian period chiefly the Mont Cenis and the *Mons Iovis* (later known as the Great St Bernard), were crucially important to any transalpine political action; Duparc 1951. See map 1.

4 See 834, n. 7.

5 According to Thegan c. 28, Hugh was descended from Duke Eticho, whom modern scholars have identified as holding power in Alsace in the mid-seventh century. Lothar married Hugh's daughter Ermengard in October 822; *RFA*. Bertha, another daughter of Hugh, had married Gerald count of Paris c. 819; Louis 1946: 30-3. Astronomer c. 56 says that Lambert and Hugh died at the same time as Wala, lists others in Lothar's following who died in Italy in this epidemic, and adds that such mortality among noble Franks distressed Louis the Pious.

After all this, in the presence and with the agreement of Louis [the German] and of Pippin's envoys and of the whole people whose presence had been commanded in the palace at Aachen, he gave to his son Charles the greater part of the Belgic provinces, that is: the whole of Frisia from the North Sea and the boundaries of Saxony as far as the boundaries of the Ripuarian Franks; within the boundaries of the Ripuarians the counties of Mulekewe, Ettra, Hamaland and Maasgau; also all the territory between the Meuse and the Seine right as far as Burgundy including the Verdun area; moving from Burgundy, the districts of the Toulois, Ornois, Blois, Blaisois, Perthois, the two Barrois [Bar-sur-Aube and Bar-le-Duc], the Brénois, Troiesin, Auxerrois, Sénonais, Gâtinais, Melunois, Etampois, the pays de Châtres and the Parisis; then along the Seine to the Channel and up the coast as far as Frisia: in other words, all the bishoprics, abbacies, counties, royal estates [*fisci*] and everything situated within these boundaries with all pertaining thereto in whatever region they might be situated.[6] Thus at the Emperor's command and in his presence the bishops, abbots, counts and royal vassals who held benefices in the above-listed places commended themselves to Charles and confirmed their fidelity with an oath.[7]

838

After all this, when the feasts of Christmas, Epiphany [6 January] and the Presentation [2 February] were over and just as the Lenten fast was beginning [Ash Wednesday, 6 March], word came to the Emperor that Louis [the German] had sought a private meeting with his brother Lothar in the remote valleys of the Alps.[1] Because his son had presumed to do this without his knowledge or agreement, the Emperor was very angry and sent out official messengers [*cursores*] to go as fast as possible in every direction to summon up his faithful men from all sides. When they had all come hastening from everywhere, he revealed to them the suspicious meeting held by his sons and warned them to hold themselves fully prepared for resistance should necessity require that. When Louis learned of this, he came to his father on the latter's orders in the week of the Octave of Easter [21-27 April]. After

6 These details, which Nithard I, 6 reproduces word for word, presumably come from an official document. Astronomer c. 59 says the grant was made at Judith's instigation.

7 Nithard I, 6 mentions by name Hilduin abbot of St-Denis and Gerald count of Paris. Cf. below 856, n. 13.

1 Cf. *AF*.

discussing everything in great detail, he swore on oath, along with
those in whom he had most confidence, that he had not contemplated
anything at all at that meeting with Lothar against his father's honour
or the loyalty he owed him. So Louis was dismissed to his own lands
with orders to come to meet the Emperor at Nijmegen in May. For the
Emperor was planning to proceed there as arranged so that through
his presence, the sort of damage that occurred in previous years becase
of the pirates' savagery and our men's fecklessness might now be
avoided. An assembly of faithful men was held and quantities of
equipment and supplies were distributed around the coastal areas.
While this was happening Danish pirates sailed out from their
homeland but a sudden severe storm arose at sea and they were
drowned with scarcely any survivors.

Louis [the German] made no delay in appearing before his father's
presence as he had been ordered to do. There was a great argument,
quite different from what ought to have happened. Louis lost whatever
territory beyond and on this side of the Rhine[2] he had wrongfully
withdrawn from his father's authority. The Emperor resumed these
lands, namely Alsace, Saxony, Thuringia, Austrasia and Alemannia.

Meanwhile fleets of Saracen pirates attacked Marseilles in Provence,
carried off all the nuns, of whom there was a large number living there,
as well as all the males, both clergy and laymen, laid waste the town
[urbs] and took away with them en masse the treasures of Christ's
churches.

The Emperor reached his general assembly at Quierzy in mid-August
as he had planned.[3] There, in his presence and with the approval of
Pippin, now complying with his father's wishes, a grant was made, to
take immediate effect, to his brother Charles of part of Neustria,
namely the duchy of Le Mans and all the western shores of Gaul
between the Loire and the Seine.[4] At the same time Charles was
invested with his sword-belt.[5]

2 Note again the viewpoint of Aachen; cf. 834 n. 2. Louis the German was
   confined to Bavaria: *AF*.

3 Nithard I, 6 and Astronomer c. 59 date this assembly to September. Nithard
   alone mentions a plot (*seditio*) at this point, adding that it was easily suppressed. It is linked by Oexle 1969: 164, n. 129 with opposition to the grant of
   Neustria to Charles.

4 This region was an ancient Merovingian duchy which became a Carolingian
   sub-kingdom in the eighth century: Boussard 1968: 7-18; Classen 1972: 110-11.
   Cf. below, 856.

5 I.e. the weapons of manhood: Charles was now fifteen, the Frankish age of
   majority. Cf. Nelson 1989a. Nithard I, 6 adds that Charles was given a crown.

When the assembly had been dissolved, the Emperor made a point of visiting Paris and the churches of the holy martyrs in order to pray there. While Charles was despatched to the Le Mans region, the Emperor himself made a series of short stays at Ver, Compiègne and other places in the vicinity suitable for hunting. At the invitation of his brother Hugh, abbot of the monastery of the blessed martyr Quentin, he celebrated that martyr's feast there [31 October] with due honour and much enthusiasm. He then went to Attigny where he received Charles on his return from the west. Here too came envoys from Horic to report that because of his loyalty to the Emperor he had captured and ordered to be killed the majority of those pirates who had lately attacked our territory. Horic also requested that the Frisians and Obodrites[6] be given over to him. The request seemed to the Emperor so thoroughly inappropriate that he utterly scorned and ignored it. In fact some time before, while the Emperor was applying himself to his hunting at Ver, Counts Adalgar and Egilo,[7] who had previously been sent against the Obodrites and the Wilzes[8] after they had renounced their allegiance, returned bringing hostages with them and reporting that those people would from now on be submissive to the Emperor. He now resumed the journey previously begun and set out to winter at Frankfurt. On 5 December in the middle of the night the full moon suffered an eclipse. Pippin, the Emperor's son and king of Aquitaine, died on 13 December leaving two sons, Pippin and Charles.

News came to the Emperor while he was making his way towards Frankfurt that his son Louis had surrounded that place with lines of hostile troops and entrenched himself there.[9] Not only was he thus blocking his father's coming to stay the winter at the palace there but he was trying to stop him crossing the Rhine. On receipt of this news the Emperor was greatly angered and ordered his faithful men to be called up from every region. He himself continued on his route and reached Mainz.

6 The Obodrites (or Abodrites) were a northern Slav people settled on the lower Elbe; Vlasto 1970: 142-3.

7 Adalgar; see above 836 n. 5; Egilo can perhaps be identified with the man mentioned by Nithard II, 3 as an important supporter of Charles the Bald in summer 840.

8 The Wilzes were a Slav people settled on the east bank of the Elbe, neighbours, and often enemies, of the Obodrites (above n. 6).

9 On 29 November, according to *AF*.

839

When the feasts of Christmas and Epiphany were ended, he sent out faithful men over and over again to urge Louis to come to a peaceful settlement. But he was completely unable to sway him. On the contrary, from his position in forts [*castella*] built on the other side of the Rhine, Louis obdurately maintained his hostile stand and continued to bar the river-crossing to the Emperor, stuck at Mainz. But the Emperor was deeply worried about spilling the blood of a people who felt themselves one. He was not too proud to switch his men to another site suitable for making the crossing. But all along the opposite bank he could see his son's men entrenched and ready to oppose anyone who might try to get across. It was a wretched sight: on this side the righteous father, on the other the undutiful son, so far apart from each other. This situation forced the Emperor to return to Mainz. His faithful men flocked to him from every direction. He could not tolerate for much longer the sufferings imposed on them by the harsh winter. He got nearly 3,000 men across the Rhine just downstream from Mainz, and he received the Saxons who came to meet him. Louis, who until then had felt sure his father could not make the crossing, learned that he had done so. The Austrasians, Thuringians and Alemans whom Louis had involved in his rebellion were now deserting him. He fled in panic and retreated to Noricum, now called Bavaria, the realm given to him by his father some time before.[1] The Emperor, mindful of how a father should behave, forbore to pursue his son. He welcomed and bound with oaths those who had fled from Louis and thrown themselves on the Emperor's mercy, while those who had fomented or favoured conflict were justly punished for their crimes, some by loss of property, others by exile. The Emperor then reached Frankfurt where he stayed for a few days and lost no time in setting in order the German frontier regions and their inhabitants and subjecting them more firmly to his control. Then during Lent he moved quickly into the regions of Alemannia to the royal *villa* called Bodman.[2]

Meanwhile something very distressing happened, something to be bewailed by all the children of the Catholic Church. Rumour spread the news and the Emperor found out that the deacon Bodo, an Aleman by birth and deeply imbued from his earliest childhood in the Christian religion with the scholarship of the court clergy and with sacred and

1 *RFA* 817.

2 On the northern shore of Lake Constance.

secular learning, a man who only the previous year had requested permission from the Emperor and the Empress to go on pilgrimage to Rome and had been granted this permission and been loaded with many gifts: this man seduced by the enemy of the human race had abandoned Christianity and converted to Judaism. First he entered into discussion about apostasy and his own perdition with some Jews whom he had brought with him to sell to the pagans. He was not afraid to make his cunning plans and having let these Jews be taken away and kept only one companion with him, a man rumoured to be his nephew, he renounced the Christian faith – we weep to say it – and professed himself a Jew. Thus he was circumcised, let his hair and beard grow and adopted – or rather usurped – the name of Eleazar. He assumed a warrior's gear, married a Jew's daugher and forced his nephew mentioned earlier also to convert to Judaism. Finally, overcome by the most despicable avarice, he entered the Spanish town of Zaragoza in mid-August along with some Jews.[3] It was only with difficulty that the Emperor could be persuaded to believe this news at all, which clearly showed to everyone what a very distressing episode this was for the Emperor and Empress and indeed for all those redeemed through the grace of the Christian faith.

Furthermore, on 26 December, that is St Stephen's Day, a great flood far beyond the usual coastal tides covered nearly the whole of Frisia. So great was the inundation that the region became almost like the mounds of sand common in those parts which they call the dunes. Every single thing the sea rolled over, men as well as all other living creatures and houses too, it destroyed. The number of people drowned was very carefully counted: 2,437 deaths were reported. Then in February an army of fiery red and other colours could often be seen in the sky, as well as shooting stars trailing fiery tails.

Now after Easter [6 April] when the Emperor was heading back into Francia, the king of the English sent envoys to him to ask the Emperor to grant him permission to travel through Francia on his way to Rome on pilgrimage.[4] He also warned the Emperor to devote even more careful attention and concern to the salvation of the souls of those subject to him. For the minds of the English had been quite terrified

3 Cf. below 847. Bodo's career is discussed by Cabaniss 1952-53; Blumenkranz 1960. The political background is sketched by Collins 1983: 191-2; cf. Löwe 1988.

4 Æthelwulf of Wessex (839-58) did not in fact travel to Rome until 855: see below. For contacts between West Francia and Wessex at this period, see Stafford 1990.

by a vision that one of them had seen. The king took pains to send the Emperor a detailed account of this vision which went as follows:

The vision of a certain pious priest of the land of the English, revealed to him after Christmas while he was transported out of his body.

One night when that pious priest was asleep, a certain man came to him and told him to follow him. So he got up and did so. This guide then led him to a land he did not know at all and there he saw many wonderful buildings standing. One was a church into which he and his guide went and there he saw a lot of boys reading. He asked his guide if he might be so bold as to inquire who these boys were. The guide replied: 'Ask what you like and I will gladly show you.' When he got so close to them that he could see what they were reading, he saw that their books were written not only in black letters but also in letters of blood; it had been done so that one line was written out in black letters, the next in bloody ones. He asked why the books were written out like that with lines of blood and his guide answered: 'The lines of blood you can see in those books are all the various sins of Christian people, because they are so utterly unwilling to obey the orders and fulfil the precepts in those divine books. These boys now, moving about here and looking as if they are reading, are the souls of the saints who grieve every day over the sins and crimes of Christians and intercede for them so that they may finally be turned to repentance some day. And if those souls of the saints did not cry out to God with incessant weeping, there would already have been an end to so many evil men in the Christian people some time ago. You'll recall that this very year, fruit came forth in abundance on the land and on the trees and vines too, but becase of the sins of men most of this fruit perished and never came to be consumed or used by anyone. If Christian people don't quickly do penance for their various vices and crimes and don't observe the Lord's Day in a stricter and worthier way, then a great and crushing disaster will swiftly come upon them: for three days and nights a very dense fog will spread over their land, and then all of a sudden pagan men will lay waste with fire and sword most of the people and land of the Christians along with all they possess. But if instead they are willing to do true penance immediately and carefully atone for their sins according to the Lord's command with fasting, prayer and alms-giving, then they may still escape those punishments and disasters through the intercession of the saints.'

There also came envoys from the Greeks sent by the Emperor Theophilus. They were Theodosius, metropolitan bishop of Chalcedon, and Theophanus the Spatharius and they brought gifts worthy for an emperor, and a letter.[5] The Emperor received them with due ceremony on 18 May at Ingelheim. The purpose of their mission was to confirm the treaty of peace and perpetual friendship and love between the two emperors and their subjects. They also brought congratulations and exultation in the Lord on the victories that our Emperor had gained with Heaven's help in his wars against foreign peoples. Theophilus in friendly fashion urged the Emperor and his subjects to offer up thanks to God for all these victories. He also sent with the envoys some men who said they – meaning their whole people [*gens*] – were called Russians[6] and had been sent to him by their king whose name was the Khagan for the sake of friendship, so they claimed. Theophilus requested in his letter that the Emperor in his goodness might grant them safe conducts to travel through his empire and any help or practical assistance they needed to return home, for the route by which they had reached Constantinople had taken them through primitive tribes that were very fierce and savage and Theophilus did not wish them to return that way in case some disaster befell them. When the Emperor investigated more closely the reason for their coming here, he discoverd that they belonged to the people of the Swedes.[7] He suspected that they had really been sent as spies to this kingdom of ours rather than as seekers of our friendship, so he decided to keep them with him until he could find out for certain whether or not they had come in good faith. He lost no time in sending a letter to Theophilus through the same envoys to tell him all this, and to add that he had received them willingly for the sake of his friendship for Theophilus and that if they were found to be genuine, he would supply them with means to return to their own fatherland without any risk of danger and send them home with every assistance, but if not, he would send them with envoys of ours back to Theophilus for him to deal with as he might think fit.

When all these matters had been settled the Emperor came to the

---

5 Theophilus (829-42) sent this embassy to confirm his predecessor's treaty with Charlemagne of 812; Grierson 1981: 912.

6 This is the earliest evidence for the name *Rus*, identifying Scandinavians in lands east of the Baltic. The term *khan* had been used for chiefs of Slavs and Huns in *RFA* 782, 805.

7 The Swedes were well enough known to the Frankish court since the mission of St Anskar from 829 onwards; Sawyer 1982: 54-5, 134-5; Wood 1987.

town [urbs] of Worms on 30 May as previously arranged. There he received some of his faithful men to whom he had given special orders to hasten there for this purpose. His son Lothar arrived from Italy and the Emperor showed not the slightest reluctance to receive him with fatherly affection.[8] Lothar fell at his father's feet like a suppliant in the presence of everyone and humbly begged forgiveness for his earlier wrongdoings. The Emperor was moved by that merciful nature which was always so exceptionally strong in him: he forgave Lothar with fatherly love and kindness whatever he and his supporters had done against him in former years, but on condition that they should never again attempt any action against the Emperor with their evil machinations. To some of Lothar's supporters he gave not only outright grants of land but also *honores* consisting of benefices.[9] In addition he ordered that a detailed survey of the realm be made and two more or less equal shares defined, and he actually offered Lothar the choice of whichever share he preferred. The details of the division were as follows. One share consisted of: the kingdom of Italy and part of Burgundy, namely the Val d'Aosta, the county of Valais and the county of Vaud as far as Lake Geneva; then the eastern and northern part of the Rhône valley as far as the county of Lyons; the counties of Escoens, Varais, Portois, Saintois and Chaumont; the duchy of the Moselle region; the counties of the Ardennes and of Condroz and from there along the course of the Meuse as far as the sea; the duchy of the Ripuarian Franks, Wormsfeld and the Speyer district; the duchies of Alsace and Alemannia, Chur, the duchy of Austrasia including Schwalefeld and Nordgau and Hesse; the duchy of Thuringia with its marches; the *regnum* of Saxony with its marches; the duchy of Frisia as far as the Meuse; the counties of Hamaland, Betuwe and Teisterbant; and Dorestad. The other share consisted of: Burgundy, that is the counties of Geneva, Lyons, Chalon, Amous, Oscheret, Langres and Toul, and from there along the course of the Meuse to the sea; the territory between the Meuse and the Seine, and that between the Seine and the Loire including the Breton March; Aquitaine and Gascony with the marches pertaining to them; Septimania with its marches; and Provence.[10] When Lothar chose the eastern share, the Emperor assigned the western one to his son Charles on condition that they

---

8 Nithard I, 7 gives the background to Louis the Pious's rapprochement with Lothar and, again, mentions Judith's influence.

9 The phrase *beneficiarii honores* suggests a significant extension of the meaning of *honor* to cover benefices.

10 The *AB* is the only source to give details of this division.

should remain in loyal obedience to him as long as he lived and actually get possession of their shares after he was dead. He received many kinds of oaths from Lothar and then allowed him to return to Italy.

Then the Emperor gave notice of a general assembly to be held near Chalon on 1 September. After this he sent envoys to Louis ordering him never to dare to leave the frontiers of Bavaria without his father's express command, and to confirm his agreement to this by oath: otherwise he should be in no doubt at all that his father would advance to Augsburg at the beginning of September to attack him. The Emperor's troops were therefore arranged as follows: some were assigned to his son Charles at Chalon to attack and crush the Aquitanian rebels, for some of the Aquitanians had recently joined the Younger Pippin [II] in defecting from the Emperor;[11] and some were sent to advance along with the Saxons against the incursions of the Danes and Slavs who were getting restive again. The Emperor himself stayed in the fortress [castrum] of Kreuznach and exerted himself vigorously in hunting. He decided to await there the arrival of the envoys he had sent to Bavaria. They came back and, accompanied by envoys from Louis, came into the Emperor's presence. They reported that Louis had not yet complied with his father's orders but had promised that he would do so on condition that his own request be met, namely that the Emperor's faithful men should swear an oath to him [Louis]. Now it happened that the magnates from whom he was demanding this oath were absent at that point, so the Emperor decided to trust to his good faith and compliant promises until he himself should return from Aquitaine with a divinely granted victory: then if Louis had stuck to his orders he would receive him graciously, but if he had made any moves to the contrary his father would lose no time in attacking him with all the force at his disposal. Some of Louis's supporters had recently been punished by loss of their property for their complicity in the revolts he had organised against his father. But now at Louis's request the Emperor granted that each of these men should have his property restored – on condition, however, that they make every effort to keep their faith to the Emperor without any violation, and plot no secret incitement of the faithful men of the realm by any kind of deceit or treachery. Envoys were duly despatched on

11 Astronomer c. 61 gives more details of the situation in Aquitaine. Ademar of Chabannes makes further inferences from the Astronomer; Gillingham 1990: 46-7. See below n. 15.

special missions to receive confirmations by oath to this effect.

Two expeditions were mounted: a Saxon one against the attacks of the Sorbs[12] and Wilzes who had recently left several *villae* of the Saxon March in flames; and a combined Austrasian–Thuringian one against the rebellious Obodrites and the people called the Linones.[13] Meanwhile the Emperor himself took a pleasant form of exercise hunting in the Ardennes. He gave orders that the rest of the faithful men of his whole realm should come to meet him at Chalon at the beginning of September, as he had previously announced.

Some pirates attacked part of Frisia and imposed great sufferings on our frontier territories. Also, Horic sent envoys to the Emperor. One of them was a man whose advice he seemed to trust more than anyone else's and always to act on, and with him he sent his own nephew. They brought gifts of precious things native to their country with the object of consolidating the peace and the alliance still more firmly. They were joyfully received and gifts were bestowed on them. They had lodged complaints about the Frisians and their troublesome behaviour, so the Emperor despatched able leaders [*duces*], who at an appointed date were to settle these grievances fairly and justly on every point.

The Emperor received his faithful men at Chalon and redirected his whole army to Aquitaine. Pitching camp straight away almost three miles from Clermont, he held a meeting with those Aquitanians who publicly commended themselves to his son Charles in their traditional way, their loyalty to the Emperor and his son being strengthened by the pledging of an oath. Then he gave orders that the Empress and their son should go on ahead of him to Poitiers, while he hastened by forced marches to the stronghold [*castrum*] called in the vernacular Carlat, because some of Pippin's supporters were reported to be there. This stronghold had had nothing added to it by any engineer's design: it stood on a natural rock protected by precipices all round, except on the eastern side where it was separated from the surrounding land only by a very small gap. In this stronghold they had taken their stand, but the Emperor besieged them and forced them to yield, though with his typical generosity he granted them life and limb and their inherited property. Then he directed his campaign to the region of Turenne where the rebels were trying in vain to conceal themselves and

12 The Sorbs were a Slav people settled southwards of the Wilzes on the east bank of the Elbe.

13 The Linones were part of the larger grouping formed by the Wilzes.

continue their resistance. They now roamed about in different directions, scattered and seeking flight wherever they could.[14] But the Emperor's army suffered much distress from the prolonged hot weather that autumn and the fierceness of the sun. Most men went down with fever, some died and some got home after a dreadful journey. The seriousness of this situation imposed itself on the Emperor: hampered by the harshness of the winter that was now coming on, he released the rest of his army and withdrew to winter quarters at Poitiers.[15]

Meanwhile the Saxons fought a battle at Kesigesburg against those Sorbs who are called the Colodici and thanks to heavenly help won the victory. The Sorbian king Czimislav was killed and Kesigesburg and eleven forts [castella] were captured. Another king was hurriedly made amidst all these upheavals, and oaths were taken from him and hostages too, and much of their land was confiscated.

Also the Emperor's envoys, sent to Horic to make a treaty, received oaths from him and concluded a permanent peace.

840

The Emperor celebrated the feasts of Christmas and Epiphany and also the Purification of the blessed ever-virgin Mary [2 February] at Poitiers, and was applying himself to crushing the Aquitanian rebels, when as Lent approached he received some bad news. His son Louis, with his long-accustomed insolence, was taking over control of the realm as far as the Rhine.[1] Furious at this news the Emperor left the Empress and their son Charles with a sizeable part of the army at Poitiers while he himself came to the palace at Aachen, and after celebrating Easter there [28 March], crossed the Rhine and went into Germany.[2] His son was driven to flight and sought in person the

---

14 The details here suggest that Prudentius either himself accompanied the emperor on the Aquitanian campaign or had information from someone else who did so. Charter evidence confirms that Pippin II did have support in the Carlat–Turenne area; Levillain 1926: 185-200. Astronomer c. 61 gives further information on Louis's campaign, and Lupus Ep. 17 suggests that it was on the whole successful.

15 Astronomer c. 61 makes clear the role of Ebroin of Poitiers as a supporter of Louis the Pious in Aquitaine. Perhaps Louis appointed Ebroin in 839 as archchaplain to his son Charles the Bald; Grierson 1934: 241-2. Ebroin occupied that post from 840 until his death, perhaps in 853: Oexle 1969: 189-91.

1 Cf. *AF* for an account less sympathetic to Louis the Pious.

2 Carolingian writers used *Germania* in the classical sense to mean territory east of the Rhine.

support of the pagans and of peoples beyond the frontiers, giving them large bribes. The emperor abandoned any further pursuit of him. On 13 May, before the ninth hour of the day, an eclipse of the sun was seen by a lot of people in many different places. The Emperor, on his way back from pursuing his son, was stricken by illness. On 26 June, on an island in the Rhine downstream from Mainz, within sight of the palace of Ingelheim, he died.[3]

Lothar, when he heard the news of his father's death, left Italy and thrust into Gaul – thereby breaching the laws of nature. Puffed up by the imperial title, he took up arms against both his brothers, Louis and Charles, and attacked first one, then the other, engaging them in battle, but with very little success in either case. The business was settled to the satisfaction at any rate of his own vanity, and on terms of some kind he left his brothers alone for the time being. But he did not stop plotting against them, secretly and openly, with all the evilness of his greed and cruelty.[4]

841

Louis on the other side of the Rhine, Charles on this side, subdued or won over everyone in their respective areas, some by force, some by threats, some by granting them *honores*, some on other special terms. Lothar, during Lent, led a force to Mainz against Louis. Louis was prepared for him, and while he maintained his resistance, Lothar held off for a long time from crossing the river. Then, when by some breach of faith on the part of the people on Louis's side[1] Lothar did cross, Louis made for Bavaria. A large force of Lothar's men also tried to stop Charles from crossing the Seine. But Charles got across the river by a combination of forceful shrewdness and shrewd force, put them all to flight and did so a second and a third time too.[2]

---

3 Astronomer c. 63 gives further details: Bishop Drogo was at Louis's deathbed, and Louis was buried at St-Arnulf, Metz.

4 For Lothar's political successes in August 840 and the ensuing months, see Nelson 1985: 260-1. Nithard II, 1 and 4, gives details of the truces arranged by Lothar with first Louis the German, then Charles the Bald.

1 *AF* also mention treachery by some of Louis's supporters.

2 Nithard II, 5 and 6 details Charles's moves in the early months of 841, from northern Aquitaine (Bourges) to Neustria (Le Mans). He crossed the Seine by boat north of Rouen, having had to make a long detour because Lothar's supporters had destroyed the bridges further upstream. *AFont* 841 dates Charles's crossing to 31 March. As Charles moved south-east via Paris to Troyes, arriving on 15 April, Lothar's partisans fled; Nithard II, 6.

Lothar, when he got news that his men had fled and that Charles was advancing, came back across the Rhine and after leaving garrisons in position against Louis, set off against Charles. Louis then hurled his men on the troops which Lothar had stationed to resist him, slew many of them and put the rest to flight.[3] Then he moved quickly to bring reinforcements to his brother Charles.

Meanwhile Danish pirates sailed down the Channel and attacked Rouen, plundered the town with pillage, fire and sword, slaughtered or took captive the monks and the rest of the population, and laid waste all the monasteries and other places along the banks of the Seine, or else took large payments and left them thoroughly terrified.[4]

Charles, full of joy and affection, came to meet Louis as he approached. There was a complete union between them: they were bound by brotherly love, and they even pitched camp together, sharing each other's company and counsels. They made every effort, by sending very frequent missions, to come to an agreement with Lothar for peace and harmony and the government of the whole people and realm. Lothar played with them by equally frequent sending of envoys and with oaths, until at last he received from Aquitaine the younger Pippin, son of his brother Pippin who had died a while before. It was in the region of Auxerre, at a place called Fontenoy, that Lothar made his attempt to deprive both his brothers of their shares of the realm by a military victory. Since it had proved quite impossible to draw him back to peace and brotherly concord, his brothers attacked on the morning of 25 June, a Saturday. Many were slain on both sides; still more were wounded. Lothar suffered a shameful defeat and fled.[5] The slaughter of the fugitives continued on all sides, until Louis and Charles, afire with generous feelings, ordered an end to the carnage. To uphold the standards of Christianity, they refrained from pursuing the fugitives any further from their camp, and for the same reason gave orders to the bishops to remain on the spot next day to bury the corpses of the dead, so far as time might allow. In this battle George bishop of Ravenna was taken prisoner. He had been sent by Pope Gregory to Lothar and his brothers to arrange a peace, but he had been detained by Lothar and not allowed to go on to his brother. He

3 More details in *AF* and Nithard II, 9.

4 *AFont* gives details of the ransoms paid by St-Wandrille: 26 lb. (of silver) for sixty-eight prisoners and 6 lb. (!) for the monastery.

5 Nithard II, 9 and 10 gives a detailed account of the preliminaries and a brief account of the battle itself, stressing like the *AB* the significance of Pippin's arrival. See Nelson 1986a (1985): 204–5.

was now sent home with due honour.[6] Lothar, having turned tail, reached Aachen. To renew the struggle, he applied himself to winning over the Saxons and other frontier peoples. He went so far as to offer those Saxons called *Stellinga*[7] – there is a very large number of them among that people – the choice between some kind of written law and the customary law of the ancient Saxons, whichever they preferred. Always prone to evil, they chose to imitate pagan usage[8] rather than keep their oaths to the Christian faith.

Lothar, to secure the services of Harald, who along with other Danish pirates had for some years been imposing many sufferings on Frisia and the other coastal regions of the Christians, to the damage of Lothar's father's interests and the furtherance of his own, now granted him Walcheren and the neighbouring regions as a benefice. This was surely an utterly detestable crime, that those who had brought evil on Christians should be given power over the lands and people of Christians, and over the very churches of Christ; that the persecutors of the Christian faith should be sent up as lords over Christians, and Christian folk have to serve men who worshipped demons.[9]

Partly by terror-tactics, partly by conciliation, Lothar got large numbers of Saxons, Austrasians, Thuringians and Alemans under his control. Charles settled affairs in Aquitaine, so far as his resources would let him, travelled through Francia by way of Le Mans, Paris and Beauvais, and won over the men of the Haspengau more by love than by fear.[10] Lothar crossed the Rhine, aiming to attack Louis, but having failed to achieve any of his plans, he suddenly turned against Charles. He reckoned Charles could be easily beaten now that he had moved a fair distance away from his brother Louis. Charles fell back on Paris, crossed the Seine, and for a while blocked all Lothar's moves. Lothar, prevented from crossing the river, made for its upper reaches, and went by way of the Morvois district to Sens. From there he reached Le

6 For a highly critical view of Archbishop George's activities and an account of Fontenoy showing the crucial importance of Pippin's role in the battle, see Agnellus of Ravenna cc. 173, 175, pp. 389-91.

7 The *Stellingas* were Saxon peasant rebels. Nithard IV, 2 also denounces Lothar for abetting them. See also *AF* 842 n. 5.

8 The Latin is *ritus paganorum.*

9 Prudentius is very critical of Lothar, but Louis the Pious had granted Harald the county of Rüstringen in 826; *RFA*. Wood 1987: 43. The implication here is that Lothar had induced Harald to defect from Louis sometime in the 830s, presumably 833-34, but perhaps later too.

10 Nithard III, 3 gives fuller details of Charles's moves. For the significance of the Haspengau (Hesbaye) see Nelson 1986a (1985): 220-11.

Mans without further obstacle, ravaging everything with such acts of devastation, burning, rape, sacrilege and blasphemy that he could not even restrain his men from damaging those whom he was planning to visit. He lost no time in carrying off whatever treasures he could find deposited in churches or their strong rooms for safe-keeping – and this, even though the priests and clergy of other ranks were bound by oath to preserve those things. Even nuns and women dedicated to God's service he forced to take oaths to himself. Charles was kept busy for some time in the Paris region; then he reached Châlons to celebrate Christmas there.

842

From Châlons, he went to Troyes, then going by way of the Azois district and the city of Toul, he crossed the wild country of the Vosges and joined up with his brother Louis near the town of Strasbourg. Lothar, after so savagely devastating the western regions of Gaul – without any benefit whatsoever to himself or to his supporters – now crossed the Seine near Paris and returned to Aachen. When he got news that his brothers had joined up, he was very angry.

Louis and Charles, to bind more securely to themselves the loyalty of the people subordinate to each, bound themselves by a most solemn oath to each other. The faithful men on each side likewise bound themselves by oath, swearing that if ever one of those two brothers should try to do any harm to the other, everyone would utterly abandon that stirrer-up of discord, and would turn instead to the brother who stood by the fraternal alliance.[1] When all this had been done, messages were sent to Lothar urging peace. But Lothar banned their envoys from seeing or holding talks with him, and he and his supporters made the necessary military preparations to fight it out with his brothers. While he took up residence in the palace at Sinzig almost eight miles from the Moselle, and stationed guards to deny any crossing of that river, Louis reached the fort [castrum] of Koblenz with a naval force and Charles came up with cavalry. There they boldly started to cross the Moselle, whereupon Lothar's guards took to their heels. Lothar, terrified by his brothers' unexpected arrival, retreated. He took all he could from the palace at Aachen and from the palatine chapel of St-Mary and from the royal treasury, including a silver plate

---

1 Nithard III, 5 gives the texts of these oaths in Romance and Old High German. See Nelson 1986a (1985): 210-11.

of wonderful size and beauty. On it there shone a map of the whole world and it also showed the stars and the various movements of the planets at proportionate distances from each other, with the more important signs of the Zodiac.[2] Lothar had this great plate cut up into pieces and distributed amongst his men – who despite being induced by such a large bribe, still continued to desert in droves from every section of his army. He fled by way of Châlons, spent Easter [2 April] at Troyes and made for Lyons. Louis celebrated that feast at Cologne, Charles at the palace of Herstal.[3] Abandoning any pursuit of their brother, they welcomed the men of those regions who came to them to take refuge. Only when they had received large numbers of these men did they follow their brother's route, but still at a rather slow pace. Lothar, albeit reluctantly, began negotiations with his brothers about peace terms, sending his most trusted envoys.[4] The neighbourhood of the town of Mâcon was chosen for this purpose, and to it men came from both sides. The river Saône separated the two camps, and they met on an island in this river to hold plenary discussions face-to-face.[5] There mutual forgiveness was sought and given for all the wrongs they had done to each other in the past, and each swore to his brothers an oath of peace and fraternity. They decided that a meeting should be held at Metz at the beginning of October to make detailed arrangements for the division of the whole realm into equal parts.

At that time, a fleet of Northmen made a surprise attack at dawn on the *emporium* called Quentovic,[6] plundered it and laid it waste, capturing or massacring the inhabitants of both sexes. They left nothing in it except for those buildings which they were paid to spare. Moorish pirates sailed up the Rhône to near Arles, ravaging everything on their route, and got away again completely unscathed, their ships loaded with booty.

From Mâcon Charles now entered Aquitaine and moved about the

2 This plate was mentioned, along with two others, in Charlemagne's will; Einhard, *Life of Charlemagne*, c. 33.

3 Prudentius omits the division-project agreed between Louis and Charles at Aachen in March, described by Nithard IV, 1. See Nelson 1986a (1985): 218–20. By its terms Lothar would have been excluded from Francia altogether.

4 Nithard IV, 3 says talks began at Mellecey near Chalon (Saône-et-Loire) and names Lothar's envoys as Joseph (bishop of Ivrea), Eberhard (marquis of Friuli) and Egbert.

5 Nithard IV, 4 dates the meeting to 15 June and names the island as *Ansilla*.

6 Nithard IV, 4 seems to date this attack to April or May. It was also noted in *ASC* 842. For the importance of Quentovic up to this time, see Lebecq 1989; Hodges 1990a: 212–13.

region.[7] But he made no delay in going to the assembly at the time and place agreed. Lothar received Greek envoys at Trier,[8] let them depart again, and at the time of the assembly was staying at the *villa* of Thionville.

Louis marched throughout Saxony and by force and terror he completely crushed all who still resisted him: having captured all the ringleaders of that dreadful example of insubordination – men who had all but abandoned the Christian faith and had resisted Louis and his faithful men so fiercely – he punished 140 of them by beheading, hanged fourteen, maimed countless numbers by chopping off their limbs, and left no one able to carry on any further opposition to him.

Meanwhile, the Beneventans were quarrelling among themselves, and some Saracens were invited over from Africa. Originally intended to be helpers, they now turned into fierce enemies and took by force a number of the Beneventans' *civitates*.[9]

In October, Charles went from Metz to Worms and joined up with his brother Louis. They stayed there for some time; envoys were sent to Lothar from each of them alternately and detailed and lengthy discussions took place concerning the shares into which the realm was to be divided.[10] It was finally decided that *missi* of outstanding ability should be selected from throughout the realms under their control, and thanks to their efforts a more detailed survey could be made, on the basis of which a really fair division of the realm between the three brothers would be completed in the time appointed[11] and in a definitive way, beyond all subsequent questioning. When these *missi* had been sent out, Louis made his way back to Germany, while Lothar stayed in the middle region of the Frankish realm. Charles came to the palace of Quierzy, and there married Ermentrude, niece of Count Adalard.[12]

---

7 Nithard IV, 4 says that Egfrid count of Toulouse put some of Pippin's supporters to flight, and that Duke Warin and others were left in charge of Aquitaine by Charles. Pippin remained at large, however.

8 Grierson 1981: 903 and n. 31 suggests that the Byzantines were seeking Frankish co-operation against increasingly serious Saracen attacks on Italy. A marriage alliance was proposed between a Byzantine princess and Lothar's eldest son Louis. But see below 853.

9 This and subsequent (844, 845) references to events in the Lombard principality of Benevento imply that Prudentius had access via Charles's court to an Italian source. Cf. below 846: 63.

10 These negotiations took place at Koblenz; Nithard IV, 5.

11 The truce was extended to 14 July 843; Nithard IV, 6.

12 Nithard IV, 6 says the nuptials were 'completed' on 14 December. The

Then he set off for St-Quentin to honour the memory of the martyr–
saint, and to celebrate Christmas. Meanwhile there was an earthquake
in western Gaul.

843

Lothar and Louis behaved peacefully, keeping themselves within the
boundaries of their own realms; Charles travelled about in Aquitaine.
While he was still based there, the Breton Nominoë and Lambert, who
had recently defected from their allegiance to Charles, slew Rainald
duke of Nantes, and took large numbers of prisoners.[1] So many and
such great disasters followed, while brigands ravaged everything
everywhere, that people in many areas throughout Gaul were reduced
to eating earth mixed with a little bit of flour and made into a sort of
bread. It was a crying shame – no, worse, a most execrable crime – that
there was plenty of fodder for the horses of those brigands while human
beings were short of even tiny crusts of earth-and-flour mixture.

Northmen pirates attacked Nantes, slew the bishop and many clergy
and lay people of both sexes, and sacked the *civitas*.[2] Then they at-

wedding-day, i.e. presumably the day the ecclesiastical blessing was given, was
commemorated on 13 December according to the specifications of two charters
issued by Charles to St-Denis in 862; T. 246 and 247. Ermentrude was the
daughter of the Count Odo killed in 834; above 834, n. 9. Her mother's brother
Adalard (above 831, n. 5) was an important supporter of Charles the Bald in
840-41 and count of Tours. For further details on Ermentrude's life see Hyam
1990. On Adalard's career see Werner 1958: 274-5 and 1959b: 155-6.

1 *AAng* date this battle to 24 May. For the reliability of this source see Gillingham 1990: 49-51. A tenth-century Angers chronicle fragment says the battle
was fought at Messac (dep. Île-et-Vilaine), 40 km north-east of Redon;
Coupland 1987: 13-17. Adrevald c. 33 depicts the conflict as a feud (*perduellio*)
between the *marchiones* Rainald and Lambert. Rainald fought against Vikings
on the island of Noirmoutier in 835; *AAng*. He can probably be identified with
the Rainald who was an important supporter of Charles against Pippin II in
839-40; Astronomer c. 61; Lupus Ep. 17. See also Oexle 1969: 176-7. Rainald
received the countship of Nantes probably in 841. The chronicle fragment says
Lambert, after defeating Rainald, briefly took control of Nantes but was
thrown out a fortnight or so later, before the Vikings arrived. The *Chronicle of
Nantes*, c.6, pp.14-18, invents an alliance between Lambert and the Vikings. This
Lambert was probably a kinsman (?son) of his namesake, above: 30 and n.7; 37.

2 *AAng* 843 says these Northmen were *Westfaldingi*, i.e. Norse originally from
Westfold; Smyth 1977: 18-19, 30-1. They may have come to Francia from
Ireland; Vogel 1906: 64-5. Ermentarius (writing c. 860), trans. Herlihy 1970:
8-13, says they had sixty-seven ships, and that they gave into captivity those
whom they did not slay. The *Chronicle of Nantes*, c. 6, partly dependent on a
contemporary account (Charles the Bald is referred to as the reigning king),

tacked the western parts of Aquitaine to devastate them too. Finally they landed on a certain island,[3] brought their households over from the mainland and decided to winter there in something like a permanent settlement.

Charles went as arranged to meet his brothers, and joined up with them at Verdun.[4] There the shares were allocated: Louis got everything east of the Rhine and on this side of it he got the *civitates* and districts of Speyer, Worms and Mainz; Lothar got the lands between the Rhine and the Scheldt where it runs into the sea, and inland by way of Cambrai, Hainaut, the regions of Lomme and of Mézières and the counties which lie next to each other on the western side of the Meuse down as far as where the Saône runs into the Rhône, and down the Rhône to where it flows into the sea, likewise with the counties situated on both sides of it. Beyond these limits, though, all he got was Arras,[5] and that was through the generosity of his brother Charles. Charles himself was given everything else as far as Spain. Solemn oaths were sworn, and finally everyone departed to their various destinations.[6]

At that time, the Beneventans restored peace amongst themselves, and with God's help the Saracens were driven out of those parts.

and the Angers chronicle fragment (see previous note), date the capture of Nantes to 24 June, St John's Day. Later accounts add details, such as that the bishop was slain during Mass. Some of the details in the *Chronicle of Nantes* also look like later embellishments.

3 Probably Noirmoutier. Cf. above n. 1.

4 The detailed description of this division has not been preserved, but it can be reconstructed by reference to the 870 division of the Middle Kingdom, below 168-9, and see map II. The *AF* note the role of the leading men in the definition of the three shares; see also Ganshof 1956 (1971); Classen 1963: 6-20.

5 I.e. the monastery of St-Vaast just outside the city of Arras, which thus constituted an enclave held within Charles's territory by Lothar, then by Lothar II until 866, below 132. Lothar bestowed the valuable lay-abbacy first on Matfrid, son of the late Matfrid count of Orleans (above 830, n. 5), and then on Adalard (above 831, n. 5; below 849, n. 1).

6 Prudentius is silent on the events of the latter part of 843 in Charles's kingdom; Nelson 1990b: 28. For Charles's first Breton campaign (October), Guillotel 1975-76: 10-14; and for his attempt at Coulaines (November) to establish a consensual base for his regime, Magnou-Nortier 1976: 98-108; Nelson 1986a (1977a): 147-8.

844

The winter was a very mild one, made more so by the mild weather's lasting right up to the beginning of February.

Bernard, count of the Spanish March, had for a long time now had great plans and thirsted for the heights of power. He was found guilty of treason by judgement of the Franks, and was executed in Aquitaine on Charles's orders.[1] Pope Gregory died and Sergius succeeded him and occupied the see of Rome in his place, and was ordained in that apostolic see.[2] Lothar sent his son Louis to Rome with Drogo bishop of Metz: they were to take measures to prevent any future pope being consecrated there, on his predecessor's death, except on Lothar's orders and in the presence of this representatives.[3] They reached Rome and were received with due honour by the pope, who, when the negotiations had been concluded, consecrated Louis king by anointing him, and invested him with a sword.[4] Bishop Drogo was designated papal vicar in the regions of the Gauls and Germanies.[5] Siginulf, Duke of the Beneventans, made his submission to Lothar along with all his men, and as a self-imposed penalty gave him 100,000 gold pieces.[6] The Beneventans, who had previously bestowed their loyalties elsewhere, when they found out about this accepted Siginulf and applied them-

1 Cf. above 830, n. 3. Levillain 1937a: 363 and Auzias 1937: 187 assumed that Bernard was holding Toulouse against Charles. But Bernard's trial and execution could have happened elsewhere in Aquitaine before Charles reached Toulouse; Malbos 1970: 8. Charles was at Limoges in February, and Castel-Ferrus (Tarn-et-Garonne), 60 km. north-west of Toulouse at the end of April; T. 32, 34, 35. *AF* imply that Bernard had come voluntarily to Charles, perhaps offering support. Cf. the situation in January 841 when Charles, after attacking Bernard, made terms with him; Nithard IV, 5. But by 844 Charles evidently no longer trusted Bernard's promises to bring over Pippin II. Hincmar, below 864: 119, again specifies that Bernard was condemned 'by the judgement of the Franks'.

2 Gregory IV died on 25 January 844. Sergius II was consecrated very quickly without awaiting confirmation from Lothar.

3 Influence over papal elections was always important to the Carolingian rulers of Italy; the contemporary biographer, *Liber Pontificalis, Vita Sergii II*, cc. viii-xv, pp. 87-90, describes the ravaging of papal territories by Louis II, Drogo and the Franks to punish the Roman aristocracy for their faithlessness: see previous note. Sergius and the Romans had to swear an oath of fidelity to Lothar as emperor: Delogu 1968b: 142-3.

4 15 June; Brühl 1962: 323.

5 Drogo's powers as papal vicar north of the Alps reflect Lothar's ambitions to interfere in ecclesiastical affairs in his brothers' realms. Little came of this; Devisse 1975: 35-52.

6 Also recorded in *Liber Pontificalis, Vita Sergii II*, c. xvii, p. 90.

selves to driving the remnants of the Saracens out of their territory. Lambert, with his Breton allies, ambushed certain *markiones* of Charles's on a bridge over the River Maine and slaughtered them.[7]

Charles was besieging the city of Toulouse and an army was hastening from Francia to join him. Pippin, son of the late Pippin,[8] met this army in the county of Angoulême: in a short time and without casualties amongst his own men, he scattered it so completely that once the leaders had been killed, the rest who had started to flee even before battle was joined, with the exception of a very few who got away, were either taken prisoner or allowed to return home only after being stripped of all they had and bound by solemn oaths.[9] In this unexpected battle, the following were slain: Hugh, priest and abbot,[10] son of the late Emperor Charlemagne, brother of his successor Louis, and uncle of the three kings Lothar, Louis and Charles; Abbot Richbod, another close kinsman of those kings,[11] being through his mother a grandson of Charlemagne; Counts Eckhard,[12] and Hrabanus;[13] and a

7 The date of this attack is unknown: the later evidence cited by Lot and Halphen 1909: 117-19, n. 5, should be treated sceptically. *AAng* gives the names of two of the victims as Bernard and Harvey son of Rainald. Adrevald c. 33, col. 937 names only Harvey. Bernard was identified by Ademar as count of Poitou; Oexle 1969: 172-3; but see Gillingham 1990: 45, n. 33. For Rainald see above 843, n. 1. The river Maine in north-western Aquitaine flows into the Sèvre Nantaise some 12 km. south-east of the Loire at Nantes. In earlier Carolingian usage, *marchiones* (*markiones*) constituted a group of counts with collective responsibility for a march; Werner 1980: 210-11 and n. 93.

8 Prudentius does not give Pippin I the title king, presumably to invalidate Pippin II's assumption of the royal title. There is no MS warrant for the 'restitution' of the word *rex* here by Waitz 1883: 30.

9 *AX* add that the son of Bernard fought on the side of 'King Pippin'. The date was 14 June. Nelson 1986a (1985): 235-7, argues that Nithard was killed fighting for Charles's side in this battle. Its location in the Angoumois cannot be precisely identified. Lupus Ep. 35 implies that also among Pippin's supporters was Turpio, an Aquitanian noble probably to be identified as the count killed in a Viking attack on Angoulême in 863, *AAng*, s.a. In the agreement of 845, below 61, the Angoumois went to Pippin.

10 Cf. above 836, n. 4. His death is also mentioned by *AF* and by several monastic annals. His corpse was taken for burial to the monastery of Charroux (dep. Vienne). His epitaph describes Pippin II weeping to find his naked corpse on the battlefield; *MGH Poet. Lat.* II: 139.

11 Abbot of St-Riquier, probably an appointee of Lothar's in 840; Nelson 1986a (1985): 224-5. It is not known which of Charlemagne's daughters was Richbod's mother.

12 Possibly count of Amiens; Grierson 1939: 84-6.

13 *AF* adds that he was the standard-bearer. He can perhaps be identified with the Rabano sent as Charles's envoy to Louis the German in 841; Nithard III, 3. Werner 1959b: 160-1 suggests that he was a close relative of Hrabanus Maurus.

great many others. The following were taken prisoner: Ebroin, bishop of Poitiers,[14] Ragenar, bishop of Amiens;[15] Abbot Lupus,[16] the two sons of Count Eckhard;[17] another Eckhard;[18] Counts Gunthard and Richwin;[19] Engilwin[20] and a fair number of other nobles.

The Breton Nominoë, at that same time, insolently crossed over the boundaries assigned to him and his predecessors. Laying waste the whole countryside far and wide and setting fire to most of it, he got to Le Mans where he received news that Northmen had suddenly attacked his own territory. So he was forced to go back there.

Louis king of the Germans attacked the people and lands of the Slavs. Taking some prisoner and slaying others, he subdued, by force or favour, nearly all the petty kings of those regions.[21]

The Northmen launched a major attack on the island of Britain, in that part which is largely inhabited by Anglo-Saxons. After a battle lasting three days, the Northmen emerged the winners: plundering, looting, slaughtering everywhere, they wielded power over the land at will.[22]

Meanwhile the brothers, Lothar, Louis and Charles, after many mutual exchanges of envoys with brotherly affection, met together in October at Thionville.[23] They had amicable discussions for some days on

14 Cf. above 839, n. 15.

15 830/34–49.

16 Lupus abbot of Ferrières mentions his own capture and release ('thanks to the help of a man named Turpio') in Ep. 35 written only six weeks later.

17 Cf. above n. 12. One of these sons, also called Eckhard, may have been count of Amiens.

18 This second Eckhard has been identified as a later count of Autun and member of the family of the 'historic Nibelungen' by Levillain 1937b: 351-7, 381, 394-6. On this family, Martindale 1977: 18-20.

19 Count Gunthard cannot be identified. Richwin was probably a recipient from Charles early in 843 of lands belonging to the church of Rheims, and also the envoy sent by Charles to Louis the German in November 843; Werner 1959b: 159-60. His countship lay in the Rheims area. He was a leading supporter of Charles down to 860, his last appearance in the records.

20 Probably identifiable as a magnate with lands around Amiens; Grierson 1939: 82-4.

21 Cf. AF.

22 Cf. ASC 840 (for 843) on the defeat of Æthelwulf at Carhampton (Somerset).

23 For the decrees of this council presided over by Drogo, see MGH Conc. III, 27-35. They included a veiled request for an ending of the vacancy in the see of Rheims (c. 2) and a strong protest against the granting of abbeys to laymen (c. 3; see below n. 24). Otherwise the bishops showed a sympathetic and realistic attitude towards royal demands on ecclesiastical resources; Nelson 1986a (1983b): 122.

matters of vital concern, and confirmed that their obligations of mutual fraternity and love would not be violated in future. They promised that sowers of discord would be vigilantly guarded against and condemned; they also promised to restore church property which had been most shamefully dismembered, through the pressures of these hard times, and openly handed over to persons totally unfit, in other words, to laymen.[24] From Thionville the three brothers also sent envoys to Pippin, Lambert and Nominoë to discuss peace terms and to urge them to waste no time in coming to their brother Charles as obedient men and to remain faithful in future. If they refused, the brothers gave notice that they would join together boldly in warlike fashion, at an appropriate time, and advance against them forthwith to take revenge on such traitors.

The Northmen sailed up the Garonne as far as Toulouse, wreaking destruction everywhere, without meeting any opposition. Then some of them withdrew from there and attacked Galicia, but they perished, partly because they met resistance from missile-throwers, partly because they were caught in a storm at sea. Some of them, though, got to the south-western part of Spain, where they fought long and bitterly with the Saracens, but were finally beaten and withdrew to their ships.[25]

845

A very hard winter. In March, 120 ships of the Northmen sailed up the Seine to Paris, laying waste everything on either side and meeting not the least bit of opposition. Charles made efforts to offer some resistance, but realised that his men could not possibly win. So he made a deal with them: by handing over to them 7,000 lb [of silver] as a bribe, he restrained them from advancing further and persuaded them to go away.[1]

24 Felten 1980 shows that the granting of abbeys, i.e. control of their material resources, to laymen was a recent practice, resulting from previous generations' lavish monastic endowments and royal needs for the wherewithal to reward service. Lay-abbacies aroused noisy but selective protests from churchmen adversely affected.

25 The rather later Spanish sources for these events are summarised by Collins 1983: 195. They bear out the *AB* account.

1 The chief of this group of Northmen was called Ragnar; *TransSG, AX, AFont. AF* mentions the payment by Charles. The silver pound was now an abstract currency unit: the '7,000' was made up of gold and silver bullion as well as coin. *AX* blames Charles's feebleness (*desidia*) but says that over 600 Northmen died in Gaul. See below: 62.

Count Folcrad and the rest of the Provençals defected from Lothar and usurped for themselves power over the whole of Provence.[2]

Horic, king of the Northmen, sent 600 ships up the Elbe in Germany against Louis. The Saxons opposed them, and when battle was joined, by the help of our Lord Jesus Christ, emerged victorious. The Northmen went away from there, and attacked and captured a certain *civitas* of the Slavs.[3]

A terrible famine consumed the western regions of Gaul, and as it got worse many thousands of people died. Charles came to Fleury where stands the monastery of St-Benedict, twelve leagues from Orléans, and there he received Pippin, son of Pippin,[4] who gave him oaths of fidelity to the effect that henceforth he would be faithful to him as a nephew ought to be to his uncle and would give him aid to the best of his ability whatever needs might arise. Then Charles allowed him lordship of the whole of Aquitaine, except for Poitou, Saintonge and Aunis.[5] So all the Aquitanians who until then had been with Charles hastened forthwith to attach themselves instead to Pippin.

The Beneventans finally went to war again with the Saracens, as their old disputes flared up once more.

The Northmen went back down the Seine to the open sea. Then they devastated all the coastal regions, plundering and burning. God in his goodness and justice, so much offended by our sins, had thus worn down the lands and kingdoms of the Christians. Nevertheless, so that the pagans should no longer go unpunished in falsely accusing the most all-powerful and most provident Lord of improvidence and even powerlessness, when they were going away in ships loaded with booty from a certain monastery which they had sacked and burned, they

2 The revolt was brief. Folcrad still held his countship in 860; Poly 1976: 41.

3 The *AF* say this place was Hamburg. The *AB* figure of 600 ships is implausible; Wallace-Hadrill 1975: 219. Cf. Horic's concern later in 845 to avoid conflict with the Carolingians; below 62, and *TransSG*. See Wood 1987: 47-8.

4 See above 844, n. 8. Fleury (St-Benoît-sur-Loire) is some 32 km. upstream from Orléans.

5 This meeting took place in June; T. 71. Charles presumably saw the concession forced on him by the defeat in the Angoumois as a temporary expedient. 'Lordship' (*dominatus*) fell short of kingship, and Charles intended to reserve his own rights as overlord; cf. a charter of December 845 (L. LI) in which Pippin II refers to Charles as his *patronus*. The regions retained by Charles in north-western Aquitaine where he had always had support were economically as well as strategically important; below 848, n. 5.

were struck down by divine judgement either with blindness or
insanity, so severely that only a very few escaped to tell the rest about
the might of God. It is said that their king Horic was so disturbed
when he heard about this that he sent envoys to King Louis for peace
talks, and was ready to release all the captives and make every effort
to restore all the stolen treasures.[6]

Lothar attacked Provence and soon recovered all his power there.[7]

The Danes, who had ravaged Aquitaine the year before, returned and
attacked Saintonge. They won the fight, and settled down there to stay
quietly for a while.

Charles made a rash attack on Brittany with a small force. His men
deserted, and things went badly with luck against him.[8] He made a
hasty retreat to Le Mans where he got his army into order again and
prepared for another attack on Brittany.

846

Danish pirates went to Frisia, extracted as large a tribute as they
wanted and then fought a battle which they won. As a result they
gained control of nearly the whole province. A terribly fierce north
wind lashed the crops and vines during the whole winter almost up to
the beginning of May. Wolves attacked and devoured with complete
audacity the inhabitants of the western parts of Gaul. Indeed in some
parts of Aquitaine they are said to have gathered together in groups
of up to 300, just like army detachments, formed a sort of battle-line
and marched along the road, boldly charging *en masse* all who tried to
resist them.

Charles held a general assembly of his people in June. He convened it,
breaching custom, at a *villa* belonging to the church of Rheims, called
Épernay. At this assembly the most necessary admonition of the
bishops of the realm about the affairs of the church was treated as if it
did not matter a straw: practically never, since Christian times began,

---

6 This whole passage seems to depend on information from St-Germain (the
'certain monastery'); cf. *TransSG*.

7 Cf. *AF*.

8 Cf. *AF*. The timing of this attack, far out of the campaigning season, was
determined, according to Lupus Ep. 44, by news of dissension 'beyond the
usual' among the Bretons. The date of the ensuing battle was 22 November;
AFont. It took place at Ballon a few kilometres north of Redon; Guillotel 1975-
76: 16-17.

can reverence for bishops be found to have been so totally disregarded.[1] A man had been found one day in Lent having intercourse with a mare: by the judgement of the Franks he was burned alive.[2] From Épernay, Charles with his army went into Brittany, and made a peace-treaty with Nominoë, duke of the Bretons. Solemn oaths were exchanged between them.[3]

In May of this year, so much rain fell on the *civitas* of Autun that the flood waters burst through walls and even bore off barrels full of wine into the River Yonne. And what is even more amazing, the flood took a whole vineyard, with its earth, vines and all its trees completely intact, just as if it was a solid thing, and transported it from one side of the River Yonne and set it down on the other, as if it had grown there in that field quite naturally.

In August, the Saracens and Moors got to Rome up the Tiber, laid waste the basilica of St Peter Prince of the Apostles, and along with the very altar which had been placed over his tomb, they carried off all the ornaments and treasures.[4] Then they took up a position on a mountain 100 miles from the city, an extremely well-defended site. But they were mercilessly attacked and killed by some of Lothar's commanders. Another enemy force reached the tomb of the blessed Apostle Peter, but they were crushed by the people of the Campagna and all of them were slain.

Louis king of the Germans set out against the Slavs, but went back again seriously worried as much by the disputes among his own men as by any enemy victory.[5]

Louis, Lothar's son, king of Italy, joined battle with the Saracens but was defeated and only got back to Rome with difficulty.

---

1 This passage looks like an interpolation by Hincmar into Prudentius's text. See Introduction: 14. Note that Prudentius makes no mention of the Synod of Meaux–Paris, June 845/February 846 (*MGH Conc.* III, 61-127), though he perhaps attended it.

2 The mention of 'the judgement of the Franks' seems to imply a customary penalty; Brunner 1928: 781. But cf. Exod. 22: 19.

3 Lupus Ep. 81 reveals that among the agreed terms was Charles's removal of Lambert from Neustria. Lambert was given the lay-abbacy of St-Colombe, Sens.

4 The date was 27 August; *Liber Pontificalis, Vita Sergii II*, c. civ, pp. 99-100, with comments of Duchesne 1955: 104. *AX* and *AF* also show the shock created by this event.

5 Cf. *AF* and n.2.

847

Envoys of 'Abd al-Rahman [II] king of the Saracens came from
Cordoba in Spain to Charles to seek a peace and draw up a formal
treaty. Charles received them with fitting ceremony at Rheims, and
later let them leave.[1]

Bodo, who some years earlier had abandoned the truth of a Christian
and gone over to the perfidy of the Jews, made such further progress
in evil that he devoted himself to urging all the Christians living in
Spain under the king and people of the Saracens that they should
abandon Christianity and convert to the insanity of the Jews or the
madness of the Saracens, or, said Bodo, they would all certainly be
killed.[2] A tearful petition was sent about him by all the Christians of
that realm, to King Charles, and the bishops and other clergy in his
kingdom, requesting them to demand the apostate Bodo to stop
presenting the Christians who lived down there with such a choice
between persecution or death.

The Danes came to the western region of Gaul where the Bretons live,
defeated them in three battles, and completely overpowered them.
Nominoë, beaten, fled with his men; later he softened up the Danes
with bribes and got them out of his territories.

Pope Sergius died on 27 January, and Leo was elected in his place.[3]

The Saracens, their ships loaded down with the vast quantity of
treasures they had taken from St-Peter's basilica, were on their way
home, when during the sea-voyage they blasphemed with their foul
mouths against God and our Lord Jesus Christ and his apostles.
Suddenly there arose a terrible storm from which they could not
escape, their ships were dashed against each other, and all were lost.
The sea tossed up some of the corpses of the drowned Saracens on the

---

1 The probable reason for this embassy from 'Abd al-Rahman II (822-52) was to
stop Charles intriguing with Musa, governor of Tudela, a persistent rebel
against the amir; Sanchez-Albornoz 1969: 28-9; cf. below 848, n. 7, and also
with Spanish Christians who sought Charles's protection, after the activities of
Christian zealots at Cordoba had provoked the amir's wrath, leading to
martyrdoms; Collins 1983: 212-18.

2 Cf. above 839, n. 3. Presumably this further information about Bodo reached
Francia via the Cordoban envoys.

3 Leo IV (847-55) was apparently elected on 27 January (the day of Sergius's
death) and consecrated without Lothar's prior approval, on 10 April; *Liber
Pontificalis, Vita Leonis IV*, pp. 106-7. Neither *AF* nor *AX* mention his accession.
Leo's fortifying of St-Peter's was in fact done on Lothar's orders; Duchesne
1955(ii): 137.

shore, still clutching treasures to their breasts. When these treasures were found, they were taken back to the tomb of the Blessed Apostle Peter.

The Irish, who had been attacked by the Northmen for a number of years, were made into regular tribute-payers. The Northmen also got control of the islands all around Ireland, and stayed there without encountering any resistance from anyone.[4]

Lothar, Louis and Charles sent envoys to Horic, king of the Danes, ordering him to restrain his own people from their attacks on Christians: otherwise, they said, he should be in no doubt at all that they would make war on him.[5]

At that time, the Moors and Saracens attacked Benevento and laid waste Beneventan territory right up to where it bordered Rome's.

Danes attacked and plundered the coastal regions of Aquitaine. They laid siege to the town of Bordeaux for a long time. Another group of Danes occupied and took possession of the *emporium* called Dorestad and the island of Betuwe.[6]

The army of Louis, king of the Germans, fought the Slavs with such success that Louis recovered what he had lost to them the previous year.

848

The Slavs launched a violent attack on Louis's realm, but he overcame them, in Christ's name.[1] Charles attacked the contingent of Northmen who were besieging Bordeaux and manfully defeated them.[2] Lothar's army fought the Saracens who had taken Benevento, and Lothar was victorious. In Aquitaine some Jews betrayed Bordeaux to the Danes:

4 Cf. *Annals of Ulster* 847: 306-7.
5 Prudentius omits the meeting of Charles and his brothers at Meersen, late February–early March, *MGH Cap.* II, no. 204, pp. 68-71, as a result of which the envoys were sent to Horic.
6 Cf. *AF* 850. Betuwe is the area just south of Dorestad between the Rivers Lech and Waal; map 1.
1 Cf. *AF*.
2 *AFont* says that Charles attacked during Lent (12 February – 25 March) and captured nine Danish ships on the river Dordogne. The assembly over which Charles presided at Limoges on 25 March (Lot and Halphen 1909: 190-1) is a reconstruction of Ademar's which should be treated sceptically.

having taken the town, they ravaged and burned it.[3]

The Aquitanians were driven by Pippin's idleness and incompetence to turn to Charles instead. At Orléans nearly all the high nobility, along with the bishops and abbots, elected Charles as their king and then solemnly consecrated him with an anointing of holy chrism and episcopal benediction.[4]

Greek pirates ravaged Marseilles in Provence. No one offered any resistance and the pirates left unscathed. The Northmen laid waste the township [vicus] of Melle and set it on fire.[5] The Irish attacked the Northmen, won a victory with the aid of our Lord Jesus Christ, and drove them out of their land. Consequently the king of the Irish sent envoys bearing gifts to Charles to make a friendship-treaty and alliance with him; the Irish king also sought permission to travel through Charles's kingdom on a pilgrimage to Rome.[6] The Moors attacked Benevento again.

William, son of Bernard, captured Ampurias and Barcelona by guile rather than force.[7]

849

Lothar and Charles let wiser counsels prevail and returned to peace

3 *AFont* mention a night attack and the capture of Bordeaux's commander William. Lot and Halphen 1909: 190, n. 2 observe that the 'Jews' betrayal' is 'une plaisante invention' of Prudentius.

4 The date was 6 June; T. 246, 247, 363. The impression given in the *AB* that this was a consecration to the kingship of Aquitaine is misleading; Levillain 1903. See also Nelson 1977a: 245-6, and 1977b: 60-2. The *AB* say nothing about Charles's summer campaign in Aquitaine against Pippin; *AFont.* The collapse of Pippin's position is indicated by the absence of any further charters after 848.

5 Site of the largest silver-mine in the Carolingian Empire and of a major mint; Richard 1893; Grierson 1965: 521.

6 Cf. *Annals of Ulster* 848: 306-7, listing four victories 'against the heathen'.

7 Born in 826, William was the elder son of Bernard of Septimania (above 830, n. 3) and Dhuoda whose *Manual* was addressed to him; Riché 1975; Claussen 1990. Nithard III, 2 and *AX* (above 844, n. 9), throw light on William's earlier career. Levillain 1939: 136 identifies him with the commander of Bordeaux, above n. 3. William's appearance in Barcelona may be linked with the collapse of Pippin's cause in Aquitaine and perhaps with the death of the previous count, Sunifred; d'Abadal 1980. William received help from 'Abd al-Rahman (Eulogius of Toledo Ep. 3, *PL* 115, col. 845), perhaps in revenge for Charles's aid to Musa, above 847, n. 1. *AFont* says that William drove the governor of Barcelona and the Spanish March, Aledramn, from the city. Cf. below 849, n. 9. Presumably Aledramn was a recent appointee of Charles's.

and brotherly concord.[1]

In Gaul, during the night of 17 February, while the clergy were performing the nocturnal liturgy, there was a violent earthquake, but there was no destruction of any buildings.

A man called Gottschalk, a 'Gaul' [in that he was] a monk and priest of the monastery of Orbais in the diocese of Soissons, puffed up by his learning, had given himself over to certain false teachings. He had got to Italy, under the guise of pious motives, and been thrown out from there in disgrace. Then he had assailed Dalmatia, Pannonia and Noricum, constructing by the pestiferous things he said and wrote teachings quite contrary to our salvation, especially on the subject of predestination. At a council of bishops in the presence of Louis king of the Germans, he was exposed and convicted. After that he was compelled to return to the metropolitan *civitas* of his diocese, namely Rheims, where that venerable man Hincmar was in charge. There he was to receive the sentence his perfidy deserved. That most energetic practitioner of the Christain faith, King Charles, summoned a synod of the holy bishops of the Rheims archdiocese and ordered Gottschalk to be brought before them. He was duly led forward there, publicly flogged, and compelled to burn the books containing his teachings.[2]

Louis and Charles met together in brotherly love. They were clearly held by such strong bonds of fraternal affection that each handed over to the other in public a staff and each commended his realm, wife and children to the other, should he outlive him.[3]

1 *AFont* say this meeting happened in January at Péronne. *AF* 846 and 848, give a reason unmentioned by *AB* for the previous bad relations between Lothar and Charles: Giselbert, a vassal of Charles, had abducted Lothar's daughter, and only made his peace with Lothar in 848. Lothar had also tried to embarrass Charles by reopening the question of the validity of the deposition of Ebbo of Rheims (above 835, n. 3) and by maintaining some support for Pippin II; *MGH Cap.* II, no. 204, p. 70. Werner 1959b: 156 suggests that Adalard left Charles's kingdom for Lothar's as part of a general entente at Péronne, but Lupus Ep. 36 implies Adalard moved east in 844. He was given a countship in the Moselle region.

2 This passage looks like another Hincmarian interpolation: see Introduction: 14. Gottschalk was a Saxon by birth. His political friendship with Ebbo in the 830s may help to explain Hincmar's hostility. Prudentius's own views on predestination were close to Gottschalk's. For the East Frankish synod of Mainz, 848, see *AF*. Charles then summoned a synod at Quierzy in late March; Hartmann 1989: 227-8. After his condemnation here, Gottschalk was imprisoned in the monastery of Hautvillers near Rheims. For his career and theology, see Nineham 1989; Ganz 1990a; Marenbon 1990.

3 The meeting probably took place in May. It implies that Charles was hedging his bets where Lothar was concerned.

Charles marched into Aquitaine. Nominoë the Breton, with his usual treachery, attacked Anjou and the surrounding district. The Northmen sacked and burned the city of Périgueux in Aquitaine, and returned unscathed to their ships. The Moors and Saracens sacked the Italian city of Luni, and without meeting the least resistance ravaged the whole coast along to Provence.

Charles, son of Pippin, left Lothar and wanted to join his brother Pippin who was moving about in Aquitaine. He was captured by faithful men of King Charles and led into his presence.[4] He had certainly deserved a death-sentence for his treachery against his own uncle and godfather,[5] but mercy prevailed and he was spared.

In June at Chartres where King Charles was holding an assembly, Charles son of Pippin, mounting the ambo of the charch when Mass was over, addressed them all in person and announced that for love of God's service and under no compulsion from anyone, he wished to become a cleric. Then and there he received the benediction from the bishops present, and was tonsured as a cleric.[6]

Louis king of the Germans was ill, but sent his army against the Slavs. This army was defeated in a disgraceful fashion:[7] they found out as they fell or fled what a grave disadvantage their commander's absence had meant for them.

Charles went into Aquitaine, and managed to subdue nearly everyone by peaceful means, by Christ's favour.[8] Then he made arrangements, at his own discretion, for the government of the Spanish March.[9] The Breton Nominoë ran amok with his usual insolence.[10]

4 *AF* 851 also says Charles of Aquitaine had previously been in Lothar's kingdom. *AFont* says he and several of his associates were captured in March by Count Vivian (of Tours).

5 Charles of Aquitaine was born probably in the late 820s, and baptised at some date in the early 830s (?early 831) when his father Pippin I had effected a *rapprochement* with Louis the Pious; Schieffer 1960: 44-5. The young Charles the Bald had stood as godfather to his nephew and namesake.

6 *AF* and *AFont* add that Charles of Aquitaine was sent to Corbie. Cf. below 854.

7 Cf. *AF*.

8 *AFont* gives details of this campaign; the abbot of Fontenelle (St-Wandrille) played a conspicuous part in bringing about the capitulation of Toulouse.

9 In October Charles met Aledramn, above 848, n. 7, at Narbonne or Albi; T. 118, 119, 120. Presumably Aledramn was sent back to Barcelona with reinforcements.

10 *AFont* says Nominoë got as far as Angers. The ecclesiastical aspect of Nominoë's hostility to Frankish overlordship is discussed by Smith 1982, and his record of raiding in Anjou by Smith 1985: 98-105.

850

In the Spanish March, William, son of Bernard, captured counts Aledramn and Isembard by a trick.[1] But he himself was captured by a still craftier trick and was killed at Barcelona.[2] The Moors ravaged everything as far as Arles without meeting resistance from anyone. But on their way home, they were forced back by a contrary wind, and slain. Lothar sent his son Louis to Rome, where he was received with due honour and anointed emperor by Pope Leo.[3]

Horic, king of the Northmen, was attacked by two of his nephews and war ensued. The nephews were induced to make peace by a partition of the realm.[4] Roric, the nephew of Harald, who had recently defected from Lothar, raised whole armies of Northmen with a vast number of ships and laid waste Frisia and the island of Betuwe and other places in that neighbourhood by sailing up the Rhine and the Waal. Lothar, since he could not crush Roric, received him into his allegiance and granted him Dorestad and other counties.[5] Another band of Northmen plundered the inhabitants of Mempisc, Thérouanne and other coastal districts, while yet others attacked the island of Britain and the English but they were beaten by the English with the aid of our Lord Jesus Christ.[6]

851

The Breton Nominoë died.[1]

---

1 Cf above 848: 66, n. 7; 849: 68, n. 9. Count Isembard was the son of Warin; *AFont*; cf. above 842: 54, n. 7. His county lay in Burgundy.

2 *AFont* links William's downfall with loss of Muslim support, and makes his death sound like a formal execution instigated by 'Aledramn and certain Goths'. William apparently still had the *Manual* written for him by his mother; Riché 1975: 49.

3 Schlesinger 1965: 799 argues that the imperial title was now linked with rulership of Italy and lacked any connotation of Frankish overlordship. But it also carried the right to intervene in papal elections and protect the papacy; see below 858, n. 10.

4 Apparently to the exclusion of another nephew, Gudurm; *AF* 854.

5 Cf. *AF* 850 and above 841, n. 8.

6 This was the West Saxon victory at Aclea; *ASC* 851.

1 On 7 March; *AAng*. The 850 annal has omitted Charles's campaign into Brittany that summer, and Nominoë's capture of Rennes and Nantes following the Franks' withdrawal; *AFont*. Charles seems to have been on the point of a counter-offensive from Tours; T. 136, when Nominoë died.

Lothar, Louis and Charles held a meeting at the palace of Meersen.[2] They stayed there in brotherly fashion for a few days, and then on the collective advice and with the consent of their leading men they issued the following decrees[3] which they confirmed by their own monograms:

c. 1. That between us we blot out the evildoing that existed before, and all perpetrators of discords and of rebellions and evil plottings and injurious acts against each other; and may all this, along with all malice and rancour, be so utterly rooted out from our hearts that henceforth none of it should ever return to our memories to cause any retribution for evildoing or any discord or improper action.

c. 2. That with God's help such great good feeling of true charity should ever henceforth remain between us, from pure heart and good conscience and faith unfeigned, without deceit or dissimulation, so that no one of us should covet his brother's realm or his faithful men or wish ill to anything pertaining to royal security and prosperity and honour; nor should he willingly accept falsehoods and criticisms compounded of secret whisperings.

c. 3. That each one of us, wherever he can, should help his equal wherever his need may be, with counsel and aid, whether he give these in person or through a son or through his faithful men, so that he may be worthy, as he should, to hold his realm, his faithful men, his prosperity and his royal *honor*; and each one of us should truly compete with the others to show that in his brother's adversity (should that come about) he grieves in a brotherly way, and rejoices in his brother's prosperity. And that same good faith, which we have confirmed between us previously as to be kept henceforth, each of us will likewise keep to the children of his brother should that brother die and he himself survive him.[4]

c. 4. And because the peace and tranquillity of the realm keeps being disturbed by unstable and disrespectful men, it is our will that to whichever of us such a man may come wishing to evade reason and justice for the things he has done, none of us should receive or

2 Probably in May; Lot and Halphen 1909: 227-8, n. 3.

3 *MGH Cap.* II, no. 205, pp. 72-4, followed by the *adnuntiationes* of the three rulers not given by Prudentius. For his motives in including the text verbatim, see Nelson 1990b: 29, and for the manuscript transmission of this and other capitularies, Nelson 1986a (1983a): 93-6, 112.

4 Cf. the agreement of Louis and Charles in 849, above: 67; and Charlemagne's similar provisions in the 806 *Divisio, MGH Cap.* I, no. 45, c. 5, p. 128 (trans. Loyn and Percival 1975: 93).

retain that man for any purpose whatsoever, unless to bring him to right reason and due emendation. And if he evades right reason, all should join together to pursue him, into the realm of whomsoever he may come, until either he be brought to reason or wiped out from the realm.

c. 5. Likewise it should be done concerning him who is corrected or excommunicated by any bishop whatsoever for any capital and public crime or who before being excommunicated commits a crime, and then moves to another realm and the rule of another king so as not to receive due penance, or, if he has received it already, so as not to carry it out according to the law, and meanwhile during his flight marries a close kinswoman incestuously or a nun or some woman he has carried off or a woman already married whom it was not permitted for him to have back there in the realm he came from: let this sort of man,[5] when the bishop to whose charge he belongs shall have made him known to us, be keenly and diligently sought out, lest he find a place to stay and hide in the realm of another of us and infect with his sickness the faithful people of God and of us; but let him be constrained by us, that is through the officers of the state, and let him be compelled to return to his bishop, together with the diabolical loot which he brought with him, and receive due penance for whatever public crime he may have committed, or, if he has already received it, then let him carry it out according to the law.

c. 6. That our faithful men, each one in his rank and status, may be truly secure in respect of us, because henceforth we shall neither condemn anyone, nor deprive anyone of his *honores* nor oppress him nor afflict him with undeserved machinations contrary to law and justice and authority and just reason; and by the common counsel of those men, that is to say of those truly faithful to us, according to the will of God and the best interests of all, we shall offer our assent for the restitution of the holy Church of God and for the welfare of the realm and for the royal *honor* and the peace of the people committed to us, to this end that they may not only not contradict us nor resist the carrying-out of these measures, but may indeed be faithful to us and obedient and true helpers and fellow-workers with true counsel and sincere aid for the carrying-through of those things which we have commanded, just as every man in his

5 A case in point was Giselbert, who carried off Lothar's daughter; above 849, n. 1. Cf. the vulnerability of noble women in tenth-century Saxony; Leyser 1979: 64.

rank and status ought in rightness to be to his prince and lord.[6]

c. 7. That just as we have once joined together, both we brothers with each other, and we three together with our faithful men and our faithful men with us, and all of us together with God, so we should reunite ourselves and, so that God may be propitious unto us, let us offer to him as a devoted gift that each one of us all, without any attempt to excuse or justify himself, should acknowledge in what things, whether individually or collectively, we have acted or consented to others' acts against his commands and the decrees of his saints, in the affairs of the church and in those of the realm, and we should bring these all out into the open, one by one, in public, and no one of us should spare himself or his friend or his kinsman or his ally and especially not himself, in any worldly way, so that he may be able to spare in the spiritual way that leads to salvation; rather, as we already provided in the preceding chapter, let us strive with all our might, with true counsel and sincere aid, to vie with one another in amending those things in common, as speedily as we reasonably can.

c. 8. And if anyone of those who are bound by it, of whatever rank and status, shall depart from this agreement, or withdraw himself from it or speak against this common decree, let the lords[7] with their truly faithful men carry out these things according to the will of God and to law and just reason whether that man wills or not who resists and speaks against divine counsel and command and against this agreement. And if any one of the lords shall depart from this common decree, or withdraw himself from it, or – may this not happen! – act against it, when a large number of the faithful men of our lords, and the leading men of the realms, shall have met together in unity, we shall decree, with God's favour, by the counsel of those lords who have observed these commands and by the judgement of the bishops and by the common consent of all, what action should be taken about the man who after being duly admonished has remained obstinately incorrigible.[8]

And in order that the above-spoken *capitula* may be the more steadfastly observed inviolably by us with the Lord's help, and also in order

6 This chapter recalls the provisions of Coulaines (843); Nelson 1986a (1977a): 147-8

7 As in c. 6, 'lords' (*seniores*) refers to the rulers Lothar, Louis and Charles.

8 This provision is reminiscent of the oaths of the faithful men at Strasbourg, above 842 and n. 1.

that you may more surely believe that we shall observe them, we have confirmed them by putting our own signatures beneath them.

After this, Danish pirates ravaged Frisia and the inhabitants of Betuwe. Running amok right up to the monastery of St-Bavo which they call Ghent, they burned the monastery and then after reaching Rouen they proceeded on foot as far as Beauvais which they burned. On their way back, they were intercepted by our forces and some of them were killed.[9]

Erispoë, son of Nominoë, came to Charles, and giving him his hands, was received in the town of Angers. Then he was endowed with royal vestments as well as with the authority of the command his father had held. In addition Rennes, Nantes and the Pays de Retz were given to him.[10]

The Saracens held Benevento and other *civitates*, and occupied them undisturbed.

King Louis ravaged nearly all the Slavs and subjected them to his control.[11]

Pope Leo, fearing the attacks of the Saracens, fortified the church of St-Peter all round with a wall and continued this wall right up to the city, thus linking the church to the city of Rome.[12]

9 Against the implication here that these Vikings came from the North Sea, *AFont* says that they had previously been active in Aquitaine (Bordeaux). Vogel 1906: 130 and n. 4, inferred that there were two fleets, one on the Seine, the other on the Scheldt. Lot 1970b: 684-5 and n. 24 preferred the *AB* to *AFont*, while accepting the latter's placing of the Franks' successful counter-attack at Vardes (dep. Seine-Inf.). But the Vikings on the Seine in 851 as later (below 852, 858, 861) no doubt comprised several different groups. Cf. Sawyer 1982: 91-2. *AFont*'s dating of the burning of St-Wandrille to 9 January 852, and of the Vikings' burning of Beauvais, defeat by the Franks, and departure from the Seine to early summer 852, is accepted against the *AB*'s mention of all these under 851 by Coupland 1987: 35-6.

10 'Giving hands' implies an oath. 'Royal vestments' may imply the donor's claims to superior, imperial status; Smith 1992, ch. 4. Still, the Franks did not acknowledge Erispoë as king any more than they had his father. The substantial territorial grants to Erispoë (which remained permanently part of Brittany; Smith 1985: 106) are left unexplained in the *AB*, where there is no mention of the serious defeat of Charles's forces, and the death of the Franks' commander Count Vivian, at the Bretons' hands on 22 August; *AFont*; *AAng*; Regino s.a.860. Guillotel 1975-76: 25-6 locates the battle at Jengland, a few kilometres from Redon on the left bank of the river Vilaine.

11 Cf. *AF*.

12 Leo acted on the orders of the Emperor Lothar; Duchesne 1955 (ii): 137. Hitherto St-Peter's, across the Tiber from Rome itself, had lacked defences.

852

The Northmen went to Frisia with 252 ships, but after receiving payment as large as they asked for, they headed off elsewhere.[1] The Moors took Barcelona because the Jews betrayed it to them.[2] They slew nearly all the Christians, laid waste the town, and went away unscathed.

Charles invited his brother Lothar to come and have talks with him at Augusta of the Vermandi, a place made distinguished by the body of the blessed martyr Quentin.[3] He received him in brotherly fashion, treated him with due honour, negotiated with him fraternally, loaded him royally with gifts and kindly escorted him on his way back.

The brothers Lambert and Warner, those major causes of discord, were both killed, one by a trick, the other after being sentenced to death.[4] The Breton Salomon became Charles's faithful man and a third of Brittany was bestowed on him.[5] Sancho count of Gascony captured Pippin son of Pippin, and kept him under close guard until he got him into Charles's presence.[6] Charles brought him, still a prisoner, to Francia and after meeting with Lothar gave orders for Pippin to be

1 This raid occurred in 851. See below n. 8.

2 Cf. the similar allegation above 848 and n. 3.

3 The reference to St-Quentin as *Augusta Viromandorum* reflects the characteristic classicising style of Prudentius; Introduction: 6. This meeting did effectively seal an alliance between Lothar and Charles.

4 *AFont* 850 say that Warner was captured by Count Gauzbert and brought before Charles, *AFont* 851 that Lambert was killed by 'the youngest Gauzbert', and Warner executed on the king's orders. *AFont* distinguish three Gauzberts without suggesting that they were related (though the editor assumes they were father, son and grandson). Lambert, probably a kinsman of the Count Lambert who supported Lothar, above 834, n. 7 and 836, n. 5, had defected from Charles and allied with the Bretons in 843 above and n. 1 and 844 with n. 7. He had been reconciled with Charles and given the countship of Angers in 845/6, then transferred to Francia, above 846, n. 3, then given the countship of Nantes with the Breton March in 849, but again defected, along with his brother, and allied with the Bretons in 850; *AFont*. See Dhondt 1948: 89-92; Oexle 1969: 187-8.

5 Salomon was Erispoë's cousin, and Charles was evidently exploiting rivalry between the two. The territorial definition of the grant is nowhere stated, but Smith 1985: 108 points to evidence that it may have consisted of the counties ceded to Erispoë in 851.

6 Auzias 1937: 264 identifies Sancho with the brother of Aznar mentioned above, 836. Eulogius of Toledo, *PL* 115, col. 845, shows Sancho in revolt against Charles in 849 or 850. Auzias 1937: 265-7, in a plausible reconstruction, suggests that Sancho was then supporting Pippin II, that he was captured by the rebel Musa (above 847, n. 1), released as a result of pressure exercised by Charles, and subsequently therefore handed over Pippin to Charles. T. 149 (6 September) shows Charles at Angoulême (though the charter may not be genuine).

tonsured in the monastery of St-Médard at Soissons.

Louis, son of Lothar, reached Benevento and laid siege to the city of Bari, but when he had breached the walls, he listened to very bad advice and drew back from from he had begun. His counsellors told him that he would be completely defrauded of most of the treasures within the city, if access were left open to all and sundry. So he withdrew to his camp, and forebade anyone to get into the city. After they had gone away, the Moors that night repaired the breached section of the wall with balks of timber, so effectively that they had nothing to fear from their enemies when they came up next morning. Thus after expending so much labour in vain, Louis with his army simply went home.

'Abd al-Rahman, king of the Saracens in Spain, died at Cordoba, and his son succeeded to his realm.[7]

Godefrid, son of Harald the Dane, who had once been baptised at Mainz in the Emperor Louis's time,[8] now defected from Lothar and took himself off to his own people. He collected a strong force from among them, and attacked Frisia with a large number of ships, then went to the area around the River Scheldt, and finally to the Seine.[9] Lothar and Charles came up to meet him with their whole army, and blockaded him from either bank of the Seine.

853

During this blockade, they celebrated Christmas. But the men in Charles's contingent did not want to fight, so he had to withdraw having achieved no advantage at all. Charles got Godefrid to make peace with him on certain agreed conditions.[1] But the rest of the Danes settled down there right through to March without needing to feel the

7 Mohammed I (852-86).

8 Cf. *RFA* 826; *AF* 850, n. 1.

9 *AFont* dates their appearance to 9 October and names their leaders as Godefrid and Sidroc. For Godefrid's father, Harald, see above 841, n. 9. Sidroc is not previously documented. *AF* misdates this attack to 850. Vogel 1906: 128-9 inferred that the *AB* here give a resumé of Godefrid's career since the 840s, and that the unattributed raid on Frisia mentioned at the beginning of this annal occurred in 851. This interpretation seems preferable to the suggestion of Lot 1970c: 686-7 that the first entry under 852 was a misplaced interpolation which really belonged with the last section of this annal.

1 *AFont* say the Northmen successfully demanded permission to winter at Jeufosse (dep. Seine-et-Oise); Lair 1897: 14-17. *AF* 850 say that Charles granted Godefrid 'land to live on', a statement rejected by Lot 1970: 688, n. 11, suggesting that a cash payment was made instead. But cf. *AF* 850, n. 2.

least anxiety: they ravaged, burned and took captives all the more savagely for being completely unrestrained.[2]

Lothar and Charles celebrated Epiphany [6 January] with great joy at the palace of Quierzy. Lothar became godfather to Charles's daughter;[3] and a few days later set out for home.

In July the Danes left the Seine and went to the Loire where they sacked the town of Nantes and the monastery of St-Florent[4] and its neighbourhood.

In April Charles summoned a synod of bishops to meet in the monastery of St-Médard at Soissons. He himself, presiding over the synod, had two priests and monks of St-Médard defrocked for having made plans to get Pippin away by stealth and then flee with him to Aquitaine. Hincmar, bishop of Rheims, on the judgement of the synod, deposed all those priests, deacons and sub-deacons of his church whom Ebbo had ordained after he was deposed.[5] Pippin swore an oath of fidelity to King Charles and moreover donned a monk's habit and promised to observe the monastic rule in the usual way.[6]

From Soissons, Charles came to Quierzy where along with certain of his bishops and professed abbots[7] he issued four statements and confirmed them with his own hand. The first of these ran as follows: no one is predestined by God to punishment, and there is only one predestination by God pertaining either to the gift of grace or to the retribution of justice. The second was this: that free will towards the good which we lost in the first man has been returned to us by grace, through the care and aid of Christ. The third was: that God wills in a general sense that all men may be saved, although not all are saved. The fourth was: Christ's blood was shed for all, although not all are

2 Lot 1970: 688 and n. 13 suggests that this 'more savage' behaviour was perpetrated by Sidroc's pagan followers and distinguishes them from the 'Christian, half-civilised' Godefrid.

3 This daughter's name is unknown. For godparenthood and *compaternitas* as forms of alliance between spiritual and biological fathers, see Angenendt 1984: 102–5, 121–6.

4 St-Florent-le-Vieil (dep. Maine-et-Loire), on the south bank of the Loire some 50 km. upstream from Nantes.

5 Prudentius himself was chosen as a judge–assessor for this hearing; Devisse 1975: 92. For doubts on the validity of Ebbo's deposition, hence on the status of the clerks he ordained in 840, see above 849, n. 1, and below 866, n. 13.

6 In 852, Pippin had simply received a clerical tonsure: now he was further bound by the stricter obligations of a monastic profession. Cf. Nelson 1988b: 110.

7 I.e. not lay-abbots. Prudentius means to suggest that not very many bishops and abbots were present. See next note. The synod met in May.

redeemed by the mystery of the passion.[8]

Almost all the Aquitanians abandoned Charles, and sent envoys to Louis king of Germany with hostages to convey their submission to him.[9] Louis for his part moved sharply against Charles: for some time past, a number of grounds for conflict between them had existed. The Wends plotted against Louis with their usual perfidy.

The most Christian Queen Ermengard had died two years previously.[10] The Emperor Lothar now took as mistresses two serving-women from a royal *villa*: one of them, named Doda, bore him a son whom he ordered to be called Karlmann. His other sons, like their father, gave themselves up to adulterous affairs.[11]

On 8 November, Danish pirates from Nantes heading further inland brazenly attacked the town of Tours and burned it, along with the church of St-Martin, and other neighbouring places. But because the attack had been known about beforehand with complete certainty, the body of St Martin had already been taken away to the monastery of Cormery and the treasures of his church to the *civitas* of Orléans.[12]

The Bulgars allied themselves with the Slavs, and lured, so it is said, by our bribes, they moved sharply against King Louis of Germany. But God took a hand in the fight and they were defeated.[13]

8 Though Prudentius was present at Quierzy, he did not share the views contained in the four *capitula* which were essentially Hincmar's formulation; *MGH Conc* III, no. 28, pp. 294–7. See Ganz 1990a: 297, and cf. above 849, n. 2. Hincmar was looking for a compromise under pressure from Charles who feared political problems arising from doctrinal dispute; Devisse 1975: 199–205.

9 This assertion must be qualified in the light of *AF* 854; see also below 854, n. 2. Louis seems to have been alienated by Charles's increasingly close relations with Lothar, and perhaps also by Charles's poaching of Louis's faithful men, the sons of Conrad; below 858, n. 15.

10 Ermengard, daughter of Hugh (above 837, n. 5) had died on 20 March 851.

11 Apparently a reference to Lothar II's relationship with Waldrada; below 857. This has often been classed as a *Friedelehe* (concubinage with a noblewoman) by modern historians; Wemple 1981: 90; Bishop 1985: 57, though the term is not contemporary. Lothar later attempted to argue that he had been married to Waldrada before 855; Konecny 1976: 104. She belonged to a noble family (but not to the imperial aristocracy), probably one with lands in the Remiremont area in the Middle Kingdom: Schmid 1968: 128–34. Hugh, the son she had by Lothar II, may have been born as early as 855; Werner 1967: family-tree, though Konecny 1976: 108 and n. 51 dates his birth 'c. 860'.

12 This attack and the burning of St-Martin are also mentioned by *AF* and *AX*. The monks and their relics were back at Tours by August 854; T. 167.

13 Prudentius, suggesting that Charles encouraged Louis's Slav enemies, clearly sympathised with Louis. See Introduction: 9.

The Greeks were equally aroused against King Louis of Italy, Lothar's son, because he had betrothed himself to the daughter of the Emperor of Constantinople but kept putting off the actual marriage.[14] Also the Romans, in dire straits as a result of Saracen and Moorish attacks, lodged complaints with the Emperor Lothar because of the total neglect of their defence.[15]

854

Charles, suspecting the good faith of his brother Louis, came to meet Lothar in the township [*vicus*] of Liège. There they held lengthy discussions concerning their sincere and unbreakable alliance, and finally before all who were present they swore mutual solemn oaths on holy relics to this same effect. Each commended to the other his sons, magnates and realm.[1]

Meanwhile Louis the Younger, son of Louis king of the Germans, was dispatched by his father to the Aquitanians at their request.[2] He crossed the Loire and was welcomed by those of them who had asked him to come.[3] Charles swiftly launched a campaign into Aquitaine during Lent,[4] and stayed there until after Easter. [22 April] His people devoted all their efforts to looting, burning and taking people captive: they did not even restrain their greed and insolence in the case of the churches and altars of God.[5]

14 Cf. above 842, n. 8. Grierson 1981: 903, n. 31.

15 Prudentius omits the meeting between Charles and Lothar at Valenciennes in November, and the important West Frankish assembly at Servais that followed; *MGH Cap.* II, nos. 206, 260; Nelson 1986a (1983a): 98.

1 The meeting took place in February; *MGH Cap.* II, no. 207, pp. 74-6. Cf. the meeting between Charles and Louis above, 849 and n. 3.

2 *AF* imply that Louis the Younger was sent right at the beginning of 854.

3 *AF* identify these as the *cognatio Gauzberti*. Gauzbert's death is recorded for March 853 by *AAng*; cf. Regino, wrongly under 860: 'Gauzbert was beheaded on Charles' orders.' Werner 1965: 138-9 and, less confidently, Oexle 1969: 145-6 identify Gauzbert as a member of the so-called 'Rorgonides-clan'. But this is uncertain. The sole source to identify Gauzbert as count of Maine is Ademar, on whose unreliability see Gillingham 1990. If Gauzbert's kinsmen may be located in Poitou and included Bishop Ebroin (above 839, n. 15) then it is possible that the latter was involved in the appeal to Young Louis; Oexle 1969: 191, and hence his disappearance from the records from this time on. Oexle thinks it likelier that Ebroin predeceased Gauzbert.

4 Lent began on 7 March.

5 Note again Prudentius's implied criticism of Charles and hence sympathy for Louis.

Lothar held discussions with his brother Louis on the Rhine, about fraternal behaviour in regard to Charles. But though at first they were snapping fiercely at each other, in the end they came back into agreement and made a peace-compact. Charles was greatly disturbed when he learned this. He returned from Aquitaine having achieved nothing and invited his brother Lothar to come to meet him at his palace of Attigny. They met together there and confirmed the agreement they had previously concluded.[6]

The Danes stayed on the Loire. They sailed up as far as the stronghold of Blois which they burned. Their aim was to reach Orléans and wreak the same havoc there. But Bishop Agius of Orléans and Bishop Burchard of Chartres got ready ships and warriors to resist them; so the Danes gave up their plan and headed back to the lower waters of the Loire. Other Danish pirates also laid waste the part of Frisia next door to Saxony.

Lothar and Charles sent envoys to their brother Louis to maintain the terms of their agreement and to ask him to recall his son from Aquitaine. Charles then went back into Aquitaine himself.[7] Pippin, son of Pippin, who had been tonsured and had received the monastic habit in the monastery of St-Médard and who had taken a vow to stay there, now entered Aquitaine,[8] and most of the people of that land quickly went over to him. King Charles put off dealing with the Pippin affair for the meantime. Instead he drove his nephew Louis out of Aquitaine, forcing him to flee back to Germany to his father.[9] Pippin's brother Charles, now ordained as a deacon, got away from the monastery of Corbie.[10] King Charles had his son Carloman tonsured and dedicated him to the church.[11]

---

6 This meeting took place in June; *MGH Cap.* II, no. 26, p. 277. For the 'previous agreement', above 854: 78.

7 T. 164 could suggest July as the date, and Cosne as the crossing-point of the Loire.

8 The suggestion that Charles deliberately connived at Pippin's escape is rejected by Auzias 1937: 278-9. Cf. the previous attempt, above 853, engineered by two monks at St-Médard.

9 *AF* date Louis's departure to the autumn.

10 *AF* 856 suggest that Louis the German may have been behind his escape. Contacts between Corbie and its daughter-house of Korvey in Saxony were close.

11 Carloman was probably born in 848 or 849. His father was evidently intending to exclude him from the royal succession; Nelson 1986a (1979): 81-2; Nelson 1988b: 109.

The Danes fought amongst themselves in a civil war. They battled like madmen in a terribly stubborn conflict lasting three days. When King Horic and other kings with him had been slain, almost the entire nobility perished too.[12] Pirates of the Northmen came up the Loire again and burned the *civitas* of Angers.

855

Lothar gave the whole of Frisia to his son Lothar, whereupon Roric and Godefrid headed back to their native Denmark in the hope of gaining royal power.

Lothar was ill. This inspired his brothers Louis and Charles to re-establish good relations.

The Northmen attacked Bordeaux, a *civitas* in Aquitaine, and moved about all over the countryside at will.

At the request of the Aquitanians, Charles designated his son Charles[1] their king and sent him there to them. Charles also gave an honourable reception to King Æthelwulf of the Anglo-Saxons who was hastening on his way to Rome.[2] Charles gave him all the supplies a king might need and had him escorted right to the boundary of his realm with all the courtesies due to a king. Lothar lodged a complaint against Charles on the grounds that his good faith was suspect. Many things contrary to the Catholic faith were stirred up in Charles's realm, and he himself was not unaware of them.[3]

In August Pope Leo died and Benedict succeeded him.[4] That same month, two shooting stars, one larger, one smaller, were seen travelling from the western part of the sky to the eastern. This

---

12 Cf. *AF* and n.2.

1 Born 847 or 848. Charles the Bald however continued to exercise royal power in Aquitaine; Martindale 1990a: 126-9.

2 *ASC*; Asser in Keynes and Lapidge 1983: 234.

3 Probably an allusion to the four *capitula* of Quierzy, above 853: 76, which had been severely criticised by a Lotharingian synod at Valence in January 855; Hartmann 1989: 267-9, and which Prudentius himself did not really accept; Ganz 1990a: 293-4, 298. See also Devisse 1975: 220-2.

4 Leo IV died on 17 July. Benedict III was consecrated on 29 September after the failure of an imperially-backed attempt to install the priest Anastasius, whom Leo IV had excommunicated for political offences. Benedict nevertheless had to accept the presence at Rome of the Emperor Louis's representative, Bishop Arsenius of Orte, a close relative of Anastasius; Duchesne 1955 (ii): 103, 149; Kelly 1986: 105-6; and below 865, n. 4, and 868, n. 9.

happened ten times with them appearing alternately: while the larger star stayed, the smaller was sometimes quite invisible.

The Emperor Lothar, worn down by illness and despairing of life, entered the monastery of Prüm in the Ardennes. Totally renouncing the world and his realm, he was tonsured and humbly assumed the life and habit of a monk. He disposed of his realm between those of his sons who were there with him: his namesake Lothar got Francia, while Charles got Provence.[5] Six days later on 29 September he died, and found a burial place, as he had wished, at Prüm.

In mid-October, the Aquitanians assembled at Limoges. There all together, they set up Charles the Younger, son of King Charles, as their king, and when he had been anointed by the bishops they put the crown of the realm on his head and handed over the sceptre.

The Northmen sailed up the Loire. They left their ships and tried to reach Poitiers on foot. But the Aquitanians came up to meet them and beat them so soundly that hardly more than 300 of them escaped. Roric and Godefrid, on whom success had not smiled,[6] remained based at Dorestad and held sway over most of Frisia.

Louis king of the Germans was troubled by frequent Slav revolts.[7]

856

An extremely cold and dry winter. A serious pestilence carried off a sizeable part of the population. Louis king of Italy, son of Lothar, complained to his uncles Louis and Charles: he claimed a share in his father's realm in Francia for, he maintained, he had got Italy through the generosity of his grandfather the Emperor Louis.[1] The Aquitanians[2] spurned the young Charles whom they had so recently set up as their king. Pippin, who had been brought out of his imprisonment, escaping from the monastery of St-Médard, they turned from a monk into someone that looked like a king. King Charles made peace terms with the Breton Erispoë, to whose daughter

5 Cf. *AF*. Lothar II was aged about twenty, the Young Charles of Provence about ten.

6 Cf. above, beginning of this annal. Presumably they had failed to gain power in Denmark.

7 Cf. *AF*.

1 Louis had been recognised as king of Italy in 840; Eiten 1907: 140.

2 Prudentius's failure to distinguish between different factions in Aquitaine is particularly evident in this annal.

D

he betrothed his own son Louis.[3] He also gave Louis the duchy of Le
Mans as far as the road that leads from Paris to Tours.[4] The leading
men of the late Emperor Lothar made his son Lothar king of Francia
and anointed him too.[5]

On 18 April, Danish pirates came to Orléans, sacked it and went away
again without meeting any opposition.

Nearly all the counts of King Charles's kingdom[6] formed a conspiracy
against him with the Aquitanians. They invited Louis king of the
Germans to bring their plans to fruition.[7] But he was detained for a
long time on an expedition against the Slavs during which he lost a
large part of his army.[8] The plotters could not put up with this delay
and so were reconciled again to King Charles.[9] And the Aquitanians
now spurned Pippin, and renewing instead their acceptance of the
Young Charles, the son of King Charles, whom they had previously
driven out, they brought him back into Aquitaine.

In mid-August, other Danish pirates again sailed up the Seine. They
ravaged and plundered the *civitates*, monasteries and *villae* on both
banks of the river, and even some *civitates* further away. Then they
chose a place on the bank of the Seine called Jeufosse, an excellent

---

3 The meeting took place at Louviers (dep. Eure), near Pîtres, in February; T.
  180, 181, 182. Erispoë was granted the Breton March and the county of
  Nantes. Charles was enlisting him as the key supporter of the subkingdom of
  the nine–year–old Louis the Stammerer. See Smith 1985: 110-13.

4 Cf. above 838, n. 5.

5 Cf. *AF* 855 and n. 3.

6 Again Prudentius's words cannot be taken literally. The opposition to Charles
  seems to have followed from his grant to his son, above. Hence the conspirators
  were holders of countships and lands in Neustria, who feared displacement.
  Werner 1959a: 166, n. 83 and 1959b: 113-15 argues, from a misdated passage
  in Regino, that Robert had been granted a 'duchy' comprising Neustria and the
  Breton March in 852 and therefore was the leader of the 855 conspiracy.
  Robert had certainly been given important honours in the Loire valley,
  including the countship of Angers, in 852. There is no evidence as to whether
  Charles tried to compensate Robert before installing Louis at Le Mans; but
  Robert evidently resented the favour shown to Erispoë, above n. 3. Robert is
  undocumented between November 853 and 858: below and n. 8.

7 Louis the German had had Charles, brother of Pippin II of Aquitaine, made
  archbishop of Mainz the previous February; *AF*. The conspirators' aim was
  probably the reinstatement of Pippin II.

8 Cf. *AF*.

9 Charles offered an amnesty in return for assurances of future fidelity; *MGH
  Cap*. II, nos. 262, 264, 265, the last two manifestos addressed 'to the Franks and
  Aquitainians'.

defensive site for a base camp, and there they quietly passed the winter.[10]

In July Æthelwulf king of the western English, on his way back from Rome, was betrothed to King Charles's daughter Judith. On 1 October, in the palace of Verberie, he received her in marriage. After Hincmar, bishop of Rheims, had consecrated her and placed a diadem on her head, Æthelwulf formally conferred on her the title of queen, which was something not customary before then to him or to his people.[11] When the marriage had been sealed by mutual exchange of royal gear and gifts, Æthelwulf sailed with Judith to Britain where his kingdom lay.

Louis emperor of Italy and his brother Lothar king of Francia met together with their brother, the boy Charles, at Orbe.[12] Louis and Lothar quarrelled so fiercely about the shares of their father's realm that they almost decided to settle the issue by judgement of battle. But finally they assigned Provence and the duchy of Lyons to their brother Charles, according to what their father had planned: this was after the magnates of those parts had got the boy out of the clutches of his brother Lothar who was trying to have him tonsured as a cleric.[13]

Saracens from Benevento made a surprise attack on Naples which they ravaged and plundered and completely destroyed.

857

On 28 December [856] Danish pirates attacked Paris and burned it. Those pirates who were based in the region of the lower Loire sacked

10 Cf. above 853, n. 1.

11 Stafford 1981 argues convincingly that the West Saxons' downgrading of the status of the king's wife was a means of reducing tensions arising from a determinate system of royal succession. Stafford 1990 argues that Charles sought this alliance with a powerful warrior-dynasty to concert resistance to the Vikings and to counter opponents at home. Judith's consecration was intended to secure her position in Wessex. Æthelwulf's motives are examined by Enright 1979.

12 In modern Switzerland (canton Vaud), on the route from Francia via the Jura Mountains to Lake Geneva.

13 One of the leading magnates was Gerald, former count of Paris (above 837, n. 7), who had gone over to Lothar in the autumn of 840, become count of the palace in the Middle Kingdom, and received the duchy of Lyons comprising the counties of Lyons and Vienne c. 844. His wife Bertha was a sister of the Empress Ermengard, so he was uncle of the young Charles of Provence. Lothar in 855 had probably also appointed him regent for the boy-king who referred to him in a charter of 10 October 856 as *parens et nutritor*, Louis 1946: 51-4.

Tours and all the surrounding districts as far as the stronghold of Blois.

Some of the Aquitanians were persuaded by certain of the Franks[1] who were secretly plotting against Charles to desert the Younger Charles and ally again with Pippin. King Charles and his nephew Lothar exchanged solemn oaths and made a treaty.[2] Louis king of Germany and Louis emperor of Italy did likewise.[3] Pippin allied himself with Danish pirates, sacked Poitiers[4] and ravaged many other places in Aquitaine. Lothar wickedly kept concubines, and put aside his wife the queen.[5]

At Cologne, while Bishop Gunther was standing there, a very thick cloud with frequent thunderbolts came down over the church of St-Peter. A flash of lightning suddenly burst through the crypt of the church like a sheet of flame, killing a priest, a deacon and a layman, and then being lost in the bowels of the earth. Again at Trier in August, while Bishop Theutgaud was celebrating mass with the clergy and people, a black, black cloud came down over the church, terrifying everyone with thunderclaps and lightning flashes, threatening the bell-tower and filling the church with such gloom that people could hardly see each other. A dog of huge size was seen to run right round the altar: then it suddenly disappeared in a gaping hole in the ground.[6]

1 Cf. above 856, n. 6. Prudentius omits both the assembly at Quierzy in February, *MGH Cap.* II, nos. 266, 267, where Charles and his *fideles* attempted to deal with the lawlessness resulting from political disturbances (*mobilitas, perturbationes*), and the meeting of Louis the German with Lothar II at Koblenz, also in February; *AF* and n. 1.

2 This meeting took place at St-Quentin in March. The treaty was recorded in a capitulary, *MGH Cap.* II, no. 268, in which Charles attributed his recent problems to his own illness and to Viking attacks as well as to revolt. After conventional expressions of familial solidarity, Charles and Lothar promised co-operation in punishing malefactors who fled from one kingdom to the other.

3 They met at Trento in north-east Italy, perhaps in July; Dümmler 1887-88 (i): 418-19. Note the designation of Louis as 'emperor of Italy'; cf. above, 850, n. 3.

4 Poitiers was evidently being held against Pippin II, but neither the bishop nor the count of Poitiers at this time can be identified. Conjectures about the countship based on Ademar should be resisted.

5 Lothar had married Theutberga in 855. Her kinsmen held lands in western and southern Lotharingia; see below, 860, n. 7; Hyam 1990: 156, 167. The only 'concubine' Lothar II is known to have kept is Waldrada; above 853, n. 10.

6 Cf. *AF* and n. 6. Note that Prudentius puts his report of these events at Cologne and Trier immediately after his mention of Lothar's repudiation of Theutberga, presumably seeing portents of the Lotharingian archbishops' later connivance with Lothar's plans for a divorce; below 860 and n. 1.

The Danes who were coming up the Seine ravaged everything
unchecked. They attacked Paris where they burned the church of SS-
Peter and Genevieve and all the other churches except for the
cathedral of St-Stephen, the Church of SS-Vincent and Germain and
also the church of St-Denis: a great ransom was paid in cash to save
these churches from being burned. Other Danes stormed the *emporium*
called Durestad and ravaged the whole island of Betuwe and other
neighbouring districts.

Erispoë, duke of the Bretons, was slain by two Bretons, Salomon and
Almar, who had been opposing him for a long time.[7] Certain of King
Charles's magnates allied themselves with the Aquitanians and com-
mitted many acts of plunder and other kinds of violence.

As the Danes attacked his *civitas*, Frotbald bishop of Chartres fled on
foot and tried to swim across the river Eure but he was overwhelmed
by the waters and drowned.[8]

858[1]

On the very night of Christmas and on the following day, there was a
violent and recurring earth-tremor at Mainz, and a great pestilence
followed.[2] In the district of ... [3] the sea threw up a certain tree, torn
out by the roots, which had previously been unknown in the provinces
of Gaul: it had no leaves, but instead of boughs it had little tiny
branches like blades of grass, thick-spread in places but longer, and
instead of leaves it had things shaped like triangles and in colour like
human nails or like fishbones, quite tiny and attached to the very tips
of the grasslike branches as if they had been stuck on from outside, just
like those little things made of various kinds of metals which are fixed

7 Cf. above 852, n. 3, and below 874.
8 This record of Frotbald's death may be a misplaced marginal note to the 858
  annal; L/G: 75, n. 2. A Chartres necrology dates the deaths of Frotbald and
  twelve companions to 12 June 858; Coupland 1987: 45, 48.
1 In MS 'O' (see Introduction: 16) this annal begins: 'This was the year when
  Charles attacked that island in the Seine called Oissel where he endured grave
  danger as many people realised at the time, and when his brother Louis
  attacked him with all his army, but, by the granting of God's mercy, withdrew
  without honour.' This later note was perhaps added to correct the bias of
  Prudentius's silences; Nelson 1990b: 31, and Introduction: 9.
2 *AF* date this earth-tremor to 1 January. Prudentius seems to treat it as a
  portent of plague.
3 There is no blank here in the manuscripts but a place-name seems to have been
  lost.

on to sword-belts or on to the body-armour of men or horses by way of ornament.

In the Sens district one Sunday in the church of St-Porcaria, while the priest was celebrating mass, a wolf suddenly came in and disturbed all the menfolk present by rushing about; then after doing the same thing among the womenfolk, it disappeared.

Æthelwulf, king of the West Saxons, died. His son Æthelbald married his widow, Queen Judith.[4]

Bjørn, chief of one group of the pirates on the Seine, came to King Charles at the palace of Verberie, gave himself into his hands and swore fidelity after his own fashion. Another group of those pirates captured Abbot Louis of St-Denis[5] along with his brother Gauzlin,[6] and demanded a very heavy fine for their ransom. In order to pay this, many church treasuries in Charles's realm were drained dry, at the king's command. But even all this was far from being enough: to bring it up to the required amount, large sums were eagerly contributed also by the king, and by all the bishops, abbots, counts and other powerful men.[7]

King Charles's counts now defected from him[8] and allied with the

4 Asser c. 17 says this marriage was 'contrary to the practice of all pagans' as well as 'against God's prohibition', but Stevenson 1904: 214–15 cites other examples, pagan and Christian. See also Stafford 1990: 151 and n. 74.

5 Charles's archchancellor from the beginning of his reign, Louis was made abbot of St-Denis later in 840. He was a grandson of Charlemagne through his mother Rotrud, and his father was Rorgo count of Maine. Lot 1970a (1908a): 729–31 dated the capture of Louis and his half-brother (see following note) to Easter Day, 3 April 858; but Coupland 1987: 47–8 argues convincingly that the pair had been captured in 857 and released probably in February or March 858.

6 Gauzlin (Fr. Josselin) was a son of Rorgo and hence a (much younger) half-brother of Abbot Louis. Born c. 830 and offered as an oblate to the monastery founded by his father at Glanfeuil, he was educated among the clergy of Rheims. He joined Charles's chancery as a notary in 860 and succeeded Louis as archchancellor in 867; Tessier 1955: 39–45. For his later career, see below, 871.

7 For the total of Louis's ransom, 686 lb. gold and 3,250 lb. silver, see Lot 1970 (1908a): 728, n. 2; Coupland 1987: 163. Gauzlin was ransomed by his *alma mater*, the church of Rheims.

8 A synodal letter of June 859, below s.a. and n. 8, lists nine of the rebels by name, including two, perhaps three, counts: Robert of Angers (above 856, n. 6), Odo of Troyes (below, n. 17), and Harvey, identified as a count in 866 and perhaps already count in 858 (his county cannot be identified, but for a probable kinsman, see above 844, n. 7). Levillain 1937a: 240, n. 2 argued that Prudentius misplaced events in this annal, that the counts' defection occurred well before Easter and that it was occasioned by Charles's taking of oaths of

Bretons, and compelled his son Louis with his followers to leave the Le Mans region in terror, to cross the Seine and flee to his father.

King Lothar strengthened his alliance with his brother Charles, king of Provence, by giving him two bishoprics out of his own share of the realm, and also two counties, Belley and Tarentaise.[9] For his part Charles virtually handed over his kingdom to that same brother of his, Lothar; the arrangement was that, if Charles were to die before taking a wife and begetting sons, Lothar would succeed him by hereditary right.

In May, in the township of Liège where the body of St Lambert the bishop lies at rest, so great a flood of rain suddenly fell that the water burst forth violently, hurling into the river Meuse houses, stone walls and buildings of all kinds along with people and whatever else it met with in its path right up to the church of St-Lambert itself.

The Danes attacked Saxony but they were repulsed.

Pope Benedict died. Nicholas took his place,[10] more through the presence and favour of King Louis [i.e. Emperor Louis II] and his magnates than through election by clergy.

King Lothar was forced by his own people to take back the wife he had put aside:[11] but instead of readmitting her to his bed, he had her locked up.

In July, King Charles came to the island of Oissel in the Seine to besiege the Danes ensconced there.[12] There the Young Charles, his son, arrived from Aquitaine and along with him came Pippin, now a

fidelity at Quierzy on 21 March; *MGH Cap.* II, no. 269. The list of lay magnates who took the oath includes an 'Odo', but no Robert or Harvey. (Note that Archbishop Wenilo of Sens, absent from the list of ecclesiastical magnates, did take the oath soon afterwards.) There seems, anyway, no good reason to reject Prudentius's ordering of events.

9 These belonged geographically with Provence; Louis 1946: 59; L/G: lxiii.

10 Benedict III died on 17 April. Nicholas I was consecrated on 24 April in the presence of the Emperor Louis II. Trusted imperial agents like Arsenius of Orte were to play major parts during Nicholas's pontificate. Members of the papal entourage also attempted to bolster imperial ideology; Delogu 1968b: 161.

11 Theutberga purged herself by ordeal of charges of incest before an assembly of Lotharingian bishops; her champion emerged from the boiling water, as Hincmar put it, 'uncooked': *PL* 125, col. 659. The probable reason for the rapprochement was that a faction supporting the queen and her brother Hubert (below 860, n. 9) had temporarily got the upper hand at Lothar's court.

12 Cf. above 85, n. 1. Oissel is just south of Rouen; Coupland 1987: 46.

layman. King Charles received Pippin and handed over to him some counties and monasteries in Aquitaine. In August too, King Lothar hastened to that same island of Oissel, to bring help to his uncle. They stayed there till 23 September, without making any progress in the siege. Then they went home. Meanwhile those counts of King Charles's realm who for five years now had been inviting Louis king of the Germans actually induced him to come.[13] He reached the royal *villa* of Ponthion on 1 September and then got to Sens[14] by way of Châlons and the Queudes area. From there he pushed on into the Orléans district where he received those Aquitanians and Neustrians and also Bretons, who had pledged themselves to come over to him. Then he returned to the Queudes area by almost the same route. When King Charles heard news of all this, he marched rapidly to the *villa* of Brienne by way of Châlons, and from there, when the leading men of Burgundy[15] rallied to him, he sent a message to Louis who was in hot pursuit. But though messengers hurried between them, no peace terms could be arranged. Finally, on the third day, that is 12 November, when the lines of battle had already been drawn up on both sides, Charles, realising that his men were deserting him, retreated[16] and made for the remoter parts of Burgundy. Louis received those who had defected from Charles, and reached Troyes,[17] where he distributed to

13 Cf. above 853, n. 8; 856, n. 6. Again Prudentius misleads. *AF* names the envoys from the West as Abbot Adalard (of St-Bertin) and Count Odo (of Troyes). Adalard was used by Charles as an envoy in October 856. Odo may have sworn fidelity in March 858 (above n. 8). They, at least, do not seem to have opposed Charles consistently since 853.

14 Archbishop Wenilo of Sens was the only prelate to defect to Louis; below 859, n. 6.

15 They probably included Count Isembard of Autun, above 850, n. 1, who was among those swearing fidelity at Quierzy, above n. 8, and whom (or possibly his son) T. 208 shows as the recipient of a *villa* from Charles on 20 June 859; the bishop of Autun, whose church's privileges were confirmed by Charles in T. 205, 206; and the bishop of Auxerre, where Charles assisted at the translation of the relics of St Germain on 9 January 859: T. 200. *AF* 858 says that 'the sons of Conrad', who had been sent westwards as spies by Louis the German, had gone over to Charles. These were Abbot Hugh of St-Germain, Auxerre, and Conrad, subsequently count of Auxerre. Their move west may date to 853, however, when Hugh first appears as abbot of St-Germain (T. 156, 30 June). See Nelson 1992: ch. 7.

16 The *AF* account shows that Charles still had an army but was outnumbered. This source may well exaggerate the extent of defections to Louis. Cf. below 859, n. 2.

17 Count Odo of Troyes was now a leading supporter of Louis in West Francia; above, n. 13. Prudentius's position as bishop of Troyes affected his recording of events at this time; Nelson 1990b: 30-1.

those who had invited him counties, monasteries, royal *villae* and grants of land outright. Then he turned back to the palace of Attigny. King Lothar went to meet him there and an agreement was made between them, after which Lothar went home. Louis went, by way of Rheims and the Laon district to St-Quentin, that is, to the monastery of the martyr–saint, to celebrate Christmas there.[18]

Meanwhile a certain monk of the monastery of SS-Vincent and Germain returned from Cordoba in Spain bearing with him the bodies of the blessed martyrs George the Deacon and Aurelius, and the head of Nathalie, and he placed them at the *villa* of Esmans where they were to be preserved in reliquaries.[19]

859

The Danes ravaged the places beyond the Scheldt. Some of the common people living between the Seine and the Loire formed a sworn association amongst themselves, and fought bravely against the Danes on the Seine. But because their association had been made without due consideration, they were easily slain by our more powerful people.[1]

King Charles recovered his strength, attacked his brother Louis when he least expected it and drove him from the bounds of his realm.[2] King Lothar hastened to his uncle Charles, and on the Sunday at the beginning of Lent [5 February] they publicly exchanged solemn oaths in person in the palace of Arcis and reaffirmed their common front

18 Louis may have been hoping for a consecration at Rheims when he summoned the West Frankish bishops to meet him there on 25 November. They refused, and instead those of the Rheims and Rouen provinces held a synod at Quierzy, whence under Hincmar's leadership they directed a famous letter to Louis, playing for time but not encouraging his hopes; *MGH Conc.* III, no. 41, pp. 403-27.

19 The monk was Usuard, whose *Martyrology* was dedicated to Charles; Dubois 1965. Riché 1981 (1977): 41-2 shows Charles's interest in hagiography. Usuard's visit to Cordoba was well-timed: the martyr movement there had recently produced a new stock of relics; Collins 1983: 212-18. Usuard and his colleagues had originally been looking in Barcelona for relics of their patron St Vincent of Zaragoza when they heard of the Cordoban martyrs; Wattenbach, Levison and Löwe 1957: 363 and n. 221. For the *villa* of Esmans (dep. Seine-et-Marne) in the Senonais, see T. 363.

1 Lot 1970a (1908a): 740, n. 2, and L/G: 80, n. 1 understand the sentence to mean that 'our people' were killed by the 'more powerful Vikings'. But *incaute* ('without due consideration') has overtones of subversion (cf. *AF* 842, n. 5) and this passage constitutes important evidence for social conflict *between* Franks.

2 Charles the Bald later celebrated 15 January as the date of this recovery: T. 246, 247.

against all their enemies. Charles distributed to laymen some monasteries which previously used to be held by clerics.

Danish pirates made a long sea-voyage, sailed through the straits between Spain and Africa and then up the Rhône.[3] They ravaged some *civitates* and monasteries, and made their base on an island called the Camargue.

King Charles caused meetings of bishops to be held in various places,[4] but he was there in person, along with his nephews Kings Lothar and Charles, at the synod held four miles from Toul at the *villa* of Savonnières.[5] There he presented his list of charges against Wenilo archbishop of Sens.[6] But the case was deferred because of Wenilo's absence. From Savonnières, Charles hastened to discussions with his brother King Louis on an island in the Rhine between Andernach and Koblenz. The conclusion of the talks was postponed until 25 October at the *civitas* of Basel. Louis appeared, but Charles, after setting out, turned back, because Lothar was not going to be there.[7]

The Aquitanians nearly all transferred their loyalties to the Young Charles. Pippin allied himself with Count Robert and the Bretons.[8]

In August, September and October, armies were seen in the sky at night: a brightness like that of daylight shone out unbroken from the east right to the north and bloody columns came streaming out from it.

Danes launched new attacks, and laid waste, by firing and plundering, the monastery of St-Valery [sur-Somme], the *civitas* of Amiens and

3 Smyth 1977: 62-6 suggests that the leaders of these Vikings were the sons of Ragnar Lothbrok.

4 One of these met at Langres in April, another at Metz in May–June: *MGH Conc.* III, nos. 44, 45, pp. 432-44. See further *AF* 859, n. 1.

5 The decrees of this assembly dealt with the restoration of ecclesiastical order in Charles's kingdom; *MGH Conc.* III, no. 47, pp. 447-63. See also McKeon 1974a/6; and below n. 8.

6 The most serious charge was that Wenilo failed to provide his church's military service, offering it instead to Louis the German; Nelson 1986a (1983b): 122-3. Wenilo's defection had also put supporters of Louis in control of the Sens area: *MGH Conc.* III, no. 47, pp. 464-7.

7 See *AF* 859, n. 4

8 A letter sent from the bishops at Savonnières names Robert, Odo, Harvey and a number of other rebels in the Loire valley area; *MGH Conc.* III, pp. 482-5, and see Werner 1959b: 151. For Salomon, see above 857: 85. The bishops at Savonnières also wrote to the Breton bishops urging them to remind Salomon of the fidelity he owed Charles; *MGH Conc.* III, pp. 480-1, and see Smith 1992: ch. 6.

other places round about.[9] Others of them also attacked with the same fury the island in the Rhine called Betuwe.

These who were still on the Seine made a night attack on the *civitas* of Noyon. They took captive Bishop Immo along with other nobles, both clerics and laymen, and after laying waste the *civitas* carried the prisoners off with them and slew them on their march.[10] Two months earlier, they had also killed Ermenfrid bishop of Beauvais at a certain *villa*,[11] and the previous year they had slain Baltfrid bishop of Bayeux.

For fear of those same Danes, the bones of the blessed martyrs Denis, Rusticus and Eleutherius were removed to Nogent [sur-Seine], one of the *villae* belonging to St-Denis in the Morvois district. There on 21 September the bones were reverently placed in reliquaries.

Lothar handed over to his brother Louis king of Italy a part of his realm, namely what he held beyond the Jura Mountains: that is to say, the *civitates* of Geneva, Lausanne and Sion, along with the bishoprics, monasteries and counties except for the hospice on the *Mons Iovis* [Great St Bernard] pass, and the county of Pümplitz.[12]

Wenilo bishop of Sens was reconciled to King Charles without any episcopal hearing.

Pope Nicholas faithfully confirmed and catholicly decreed concerning the grace of God and free will, the truth of double predestination, and the blood of Christ and how it was shed for all believers.[13]

9 This attack was probably led by Weland; below 861, 95. Lupus Ep. 106, ii, p. 138 shows successful resistance at Corbie led by Abbot Odo.

10 Since the Vikings usually held noble prisoners to ransom, some resistance on Immo's part may be surmised. His death can be dated to late 859 (he attended Savonnières, but his successor attended the Synod of Tusey in October–November 860); see next note.

11 If this was a fortified residence (cf. below 868: 143), Bishop Ermenfrid too may have been attempting resistance. Grierson 1935: 166-7, n. 6 argues that the news of his death was false as his name was on the attendance-list of the synod of Tusey. But McKeon 1974a: 80-1 notes problems with this list. Prudentius correctly dated the death of Baltfrid of Bayeux to 858.

12 The power-base of Theutberga's brother Hubert lay in this area; below 864: 121, and n. 28. Since Louis II proved unable to establish effective control there, Lothar's grant may hardly have been a real concession. See below 860, n. 9.

13 Prudentius may have been justified in attributing his own views to Nicholas I; Nelson 1990b: 31. Cf. above 10-11.

860

A long winter with continuous snowfalls and hard frost from November to April.

Lothar hated his queen, Theutberga, with irreconcilable loathing, and after wearing her down with many acts of hostility, he finally forced her to confess before bishops that she had had sodomite intercourse with her brother Hubert. For this crime, she was immediately condemned to penance and shut away in a convent.[1]

King Charles, deceived by the empty promises of the Danes on the Somme, ordered a tax to be levied on the treasures of the churches and on all *mansi* and on traders – even very small-scale ones: even their houses and all their equipment were assessed so that the tribute could be levied on them.[2] For the Danes had promised that if 3,000 lb of silver, weighed out under careful inspection, were handed over to them, they would turn and attack those Danes who were busy on the Seine and would either drive them away or kill them.

On the night following 4 April, when the ninth moon had begun, a sort of horned darkness – the very same shape as the shining moon is said to have – appeared across the middle of the moon causing it to shine on at either end but be obscured in the middle. It is also said that on 7 April the sun, having risen, suffered a sort of shadiness in the middle of its orb, and as this slid away to the sun's lower part, another dark spot came quickly in from the upper part and likewise ran down the sun's orb to the bottom. This happened in the tenth moon.

The Danes on the Somme, since the above-mentioned tribute was not paid to them, received hostages, and then sailed over to attack the Anglo-Saxons by whom, however, they were defeated and driven off.[3] They then made for other parts. The Danes who were still on the

1 Theutberga's confession and condemnation took place at two synods at Aachen in January and February; *MGH Capit.* II, pp. 463-6, 466-8. See Hartmann 1989: 275-8. Hincmar summarised these decisions, and gave his own views, in his *de Divortio*, *PL* 125, cols. 629-32, 637-9. Theutberga was accused of both anal ('sodomite') intercourse and of having had an abortion. Her conception of a child by Hubert was attributed to witchcraft. Hincmar's interest in these details is commented on by Devisse 1975: 377. For Hubert, see below, n. 9. For further literature on the Lotharingian divorce, see Bishop 1985; Kottje 1988.

2 This is an important indication of the scale of commerce in northern Francia at this date. For *mansi*, see below 130, n. 4.

3 *ASC* 860 records a victory of the men of Hampshire and Berkshire over 'a great ship-army' that had attacked Winchester.

Rhône got as far as the city of Valence, ravaging as they went. There they destroyed everything around, and then returned to the island on which they had made their base.[4]

Kings Louis, Charles [the Bald] and Lothar met on 1 June at the fortress called Koblenz. There they held lengthy peace negotiations, and finally confirmed their harmony and friendship by swearing an oath in person.[5]

Louis emperor of Italy was attacked by a faction amongst his own people. He raged against them, and against the Beneventans, with fire and sword.

The Danes who had been on the Rhône made for Italy, where they took Pisa and other *civitates*, sacked them and laid them waste.

King Lothar, fearing his uncle Charles, allied himself with Louis king of Germany, and to obtain this alliance handed over part of his kingdom, namely Alsace, to Louis.[6] Lothar's wife, fearing the hatred and dark schemes of her husband, fled to her brother Hubert in the realm of Charles.[7]

4 Above 859: 90.

5 The decisions reached, *MGH Capit.* II, no. 242, pp. 152-8, consisted of (a) general provisions about peace and justice within the Frankish *regnum*; (b) a reaffirmation of concord between Louis, Charles and their three nephews; (c) a promise by Charles to restore the family-lands of those who had defected to Louis the German in 858, provided that they were loyal in future; (d) a promise by Louis to do the same for Charles's supporters with lands in East Francia; and (e) an undertaking by Charles to consider restoring the grants (*alodes*) and *honores* received from him by those defectors. The last clause shows that Charles had much more control over the disposition of new *alodes* and *honores* than over inherited lands; Nelson 1986b: 54.

6 This transaction shows the weakness of Lothar II, and implies that Louis the German had won over some magnates in Alsace; but for evidence that Lothar II retained, or recovered, control of this region, see below 867, n. 7

7 Hubert had been endowed by Lothar II with the abbacy of St-Maurice, Agaune (modern Switzerland, canton Valais), on the main route leading to the Mons Iovis Pass (modern Great St Bernard). In 857, Pope Benedict III complained that Hubert enjoyed the company of actresses (*scenicae mulieres!*) and kept hawks and hunting-dogs; *MGH Epp.* V, p. 613. Hubert's arrival in West Francia had probably followed Lothar's grant to his brother Louis II of the area around St-Maurice; above 859: 91. But Hubert retained his interests there; below 864: 121. Hincmar, *de Divortio*, *PL* 125, cols. 698-9, criticised Hubert's welcome in Charles's kingdom. Prudentius omits (and was himself absent from) the Council of Tusey (October–November 860) where bishops from fourteen provinces in the kingdoms of Charles the Bald, Lothar II and Charles of Provence discussed predestination and problems over church property as well as the Lotharingian divorce; McKeon 1974a; Ganz 1990a: 300-1. Hartmann 1989: 265-6, 270-2 notes that royal pressure for unity determined the treatment of theological issues.

King Charles bestowed the monastery of St-Martin [Tours] on his son Louis. [8]

861

In January, the Danes burned Paris and with it the church of SS-Vincent the martyr and Germain the confessor. Also, traders who were fleeing back up the Seine by ship were chased and captured. Other Danish pirates also came to the district of Thérouanne and ravaged it.[1] On 30 March, in the fourteenth moon, after the eighth hour of the night, the whole moon turned completely black.

King Charles ordered that his son Lothar, who was lame, should be made a cleric in the monastery of St-John.[2]

Prudentius bishop of Troyes, originally named Galindo, a Spaniard by birth, was at first a most learned man: it was he who some years ago had resisted the predestinationist Gottschalk. But later, excited by bitter feelings, he became a very keen defender of that heresy against certain bishops who had previously been allied with him in resisting the heretic. Then he died, still scribbling away at many things that were mutually contradictory and contrary to Faith: thus, though racked by a long illness, he put an end at the same time both to living and to writing.[3]

Karlmann, son of Louis king of Germany, made an alliance with Rastiz, petty king of the Wends, and defected from his father. With Rastiz's help he usurped a considerable part of his father's realm, as far as the River Inn. Louis deprived Karlmann's father-in-law Ernest of his *honores* and expelled Ernest's nephews from his realm.[4] They went

---

8 This grant could imply that Charles had regained control in the Touraine, and may also show an attempt to re-establish Louis the Stammerer in a Neustrian sub-kingdom; cf. above 856: 82 and n. 3.

1 The Vikings who attacked Paris were probably those who had been based at Oissel since 858, above 87. The 'other pirates' were the Vikings who had been on the Somme in 859 and attacked England in 860, above 90 and 92. See also below 95.

2 Réôme (dep. Côte-d'Or). Prudentius's section of the *AB* appears to end with this entry, though there is no break in the manuscripts. See Introduction: 9-11.

3 This passage is surely by Hincmar. His hostility to Prudentius arose in part from their differences over predestination; above 849, n. 2; 860, n. 7, but probably still more from Hincmar's attempts to defend his control of Rheims's proprietary shurches (and tithe-revenues) in the diocese of Troyes; Hincmar, *De Ecclesiis et Capellis* p. 76, and Stratmann 1990: 8-14.

4 The nephews were Uto and Berengar, below 129; their father was Count Gebhard of Lahngau, and Ernest was duke of Bavaria; cf. AF 861, n. 6.

to Charles, along with Adalard, uncle of Queen Ermentrude and also their kinsman, whom Lothar was attacking at the instigation of his uncle Louis.[5] Charles received them warmly and comforted them with *honores*. Moreover nearly all those who had recently defected from Charles to Louis now returned to Charles: they were rewarded by him with high favour and *honores*.[6]

The Danes had lately come back from the English and burned Thérouanne. Under Weland's command, they now sailed up the Seine with over 200 ships, and besieged the fort built by the Northmen on the island of Oissel with those Northmen inside it too.[7] To support the besiegers, Charles ordered a levy to be raised from his realm to bring in 5,000 lb of silver and a large amount of livestock and corn, so that the realm should not be looted. Crossing the Seine, he came to Meung on the Loire where he received Robert with *honores* agreeable to him.[8] Just at this time, Guntfrid and Gauzfrid,[9] on whose advice Charles had received Robert, defected from Charles to Salomon duke of the Bretons along with their associates, in an unheard-of way, and with a treacherousness like that of barbarians.

Meanwhile the other group of Danes with sixty ships sailed up the Seine and into the *Tellas* and from there they reached those who were besieging the fort, and joined up with them.[10] The besieged were forced by starvation, filth and general misery to pay the besiegers 6,000 lb made up of gold and silver and to make an alliance with them. So they sailed away down the Seine as far as the sea. But they were

5 For Adalard's earlier career, see above 842: 55, n. 12; 67, n. 1. The nature of the kin-tie between him and Gebhard is uncertain: their mothers may have been first cousins. Adalard's expulsion from Lothar's kingdom confirms the influence of Louis the German over Lothar at this time. See below, n. 17.

6 Cf. above 858, n. 8.

7 For their previous agreement with Charles to attack the Vikings at Oissel, see above 860: 92. The *AB* omit the assembly of Quierzy in June 861, where measures promulgated against the refusal of good coin, *MGH Capit.* II, no. 271, pp. 301-2, were provoked by the circulation of debased and counterfeit coin; Metcalf and Northover, 1989; Coupland 1991c.

8 Robert kept the countship of Angers.

9 Guntfrid and Gauzfrid are linked again in 862, below: 00. Gauzfrid was a son of Count Rorgo of Le Mans (died c. 842) and may himself have been count of Le Mans in the 850s; Oexle 1969: 147. Guntfrid's kinship with him is likely but cannot be proved.

10 The ingenious interpretation of this combined attack offered by Lair 1897: 24-6 has been challenged by Coupland 1987: 56-7, identifying the location as Oissel (not Oscelle) and rejecting Lair's identification of the River 'Tellas' as the Epte.

prevented from putting out to sea by the winter now coming on. So they split up according to their brotherhoods[11] into groups allocated to various ports, from the sea-coast right up to Paris. Weland with his company came up the Seine to the fort of Melun. Former occupants of the besieged fort, with Weland's son, now occupied the monastery of St- Maur-des-Fossés.

Hincmar archbishop of Rheims, at a synod of his province held at the church of the martyr-saints Crispin and Crispian outside the city of Soissons, deprived Bishop Rothad of Soissons of episcopal communion, according to the decrees of the canons, until he should become obedient, because he had refused to obey the rulings of the church.[12]

Charles sent his son Louis, under the guardianship of Adalard, Queen Ermentrude's uncle, to protect the realm against the Northmen.[13] Charles himself was invited by certain people there[14] to take over the realm of Provence, because Charles son of the late Emperor Lothar was thought to be incompetent and unsuited to hold the office and title of a king. Charles, taking his wife with him, travelled through Burgundy as far as the *civitas* of Mâcon.[15] There things began to turn out badly, and many acts of pillage were perpetrated on the people of that region.[16] Charles therefore returned to the palace of Ponthion. There he gave audience to a mission brought on behalf of his brother Louis and his nephew Lothar by Adventius bishop of Metz and Count Liutard.[17] He dismissed them, and then celebrated Christmas Day joyfully as is customary.

11 *Sodalitates.* These bands, perhaps fictive kin-groups, were apparently basic to the Vikings' military organisation; Sawyer 1982: 54–5; Gillmor 1988: 83. Cf. Musset 1965: 214–15.

12 The *acta* of this synod are lost. On the case of Rothad, see Nelson 1991. Hincmar's letters show that as metropolitan he had been complaining of Rothad's conduct since the mid-850s.

13 Louis's command was evidently based around the lower Seine; see below 862: 100. The appointment of a guardian (*baiulus*) implied that Louis's father was still treating him as a minor. Louis's fifteenth birthday, the age of majority in Frankish law, would fall on 1 November 861.

14 Evidently a faction opposed to Charles of Provence's leading supporter in the region, Gerald count of Vienne; see above 856, n. 13.

15 Ermentrude's presence could suggest hopes for a joint consecration as king and queen of Provence; Schlesinger 1970: 457.

16 Hincmar's disapproval of Charles's attempted takeover is evident in the mention of pillage. See also Staubach 1982: 179, n. 335. For Hincmar's anxieties over lands of the church of Rheims situated in the kingdom of Provence, and hitherto protected by Count Gerald, see Hincmar's letter to Gerald, *MGH Epp.* VIII, no. 142.

17 Adventius bishop of Metz (855–75) was often used by Lothar II as an envoy to

862

Charles came by way of Rheims to Soissons where he got news from a reliable source concerning his daughter Judith, widow of Æthelbald king of the English.[1] Before this she had sold up the possessions which she had acquired in the kingdom of the English, returned to her father and was being kept at Senlis under his protection and royal and episcopal guardianship, with all the honour due to a queen, until such time as, if she could not remain chaste, she might marry in the way the apostle said, that is suitably and legally. Charles now learned that she had changed her widow's clothing and gone off with Count Baldwin,[2] at his instigation and with her brother Louis's consent. Charles also learned that his son Louis, incited by Guntfrid and Gauzfrid, had abandoned his father's faithful men, fled by night with only a few men and, a deserter now, made his way to those who were inciting him to action.[3] When he heard all this, Charles took counsel with his bishops and other magnates of his realm. After the judgement of secular law had been pronounced, Charles asked the bishops to make known the canonical sentence on Baldwin, and on Judith, who had run away with a thief and made herself fall to an adulterer's share, according to the edicts of the blessed Gregory to the effect that 'if anyone shall have stolen away a widow to become his wife, let him and all who consent

Charles the Bald; Staubach 1982: 167 and nn. 283-7. He had good contacts with Hincmar and with Charles, who wrote to Nicholas I on Adventius's behalf in 864; *MGH Epp.* VI, pp. 222-3. Count Liutard (? of Metz) may have been a kinsman of Gerald; above n. 14; Levillain 1941: 189-97. Hincmar omits any mention of a meeting between Lothar II and Louis the German and his sons in December 861. But Schmid 1968: 115-23 has shown the likelihood that such a meeting occurred: Lothar's response to Charles's designs on Provence was a request to Louis the German to meet him at Remiremont. Thence Lothar and Louis sent a letter to Nicholas I protesting against Charles's 'solliciting of their faithful men'; *MGH Epp.* VI, p. 213. See also Staubach 1982: 178-80.

1 Above 858, n. 4. Æthelbald had died in 860.

2 Baldwin's counties, unspecified in any ninth-century source, were probably Flanders (an area much smaller than the later medieval county) and Ghent. Hincmar, *MGH Epp.* VIII, nos. 155, 156, feared that Baldwin might seek help from Roric, the Viking lord of neighbouring Frisia (above, 850: 69). Baldwin and Judith certainly sought help from Lothar II (below 862: 103) and from Pope Nicholas I; *MGH Epp.* VI, nos. 7, 8, pp. 272-5. Note the suggestion here in the *AB* that Baldwin's abduction of Judith was linked with Louis the Stammerer's rebellion against his father. See next note.

3 Cf. above 856: 82 and n. 3; 861: 95 and nn. 9, 13.

to his deed be anathema'.[4]

The abbacy of St-Martin, which Charles had ill-advisedly granted to his son Louis, he now granted, still not very advisedly, to Hubert, a married cleric.[5] Then Charles arrived at Senlis, where he waited, expecting the people to assemble there to him so that troops could be positioned along both banks of certain rivers, namely the Oise, Marne, and Seine, and defensive measures taken to stop the Northmen from coming up to plunder.[6] But Charles now received news that a select force of Danes, picked from amongst those encamped at Fossés, was making for Meaux with a few ships. Charles made all speed in that direction with those men whom he had with him. But he could not catch up with them, because the bridges had been destroyed and the ships taken over by the Northmen. He therefore followed some indispensable advice and rebuilt the bridge across to the island by Trilbardou, thereby cutting the Northmen's access to the way down the river.[7] He also assigned squadrons to guard both banks of the Marne. The Northmen, now tightly hemmed in by these moves, gave hostages chosen by Charles, and on his orders: the conditions were that they should return without any delay all the captives they had taken since sailing up the Marne, and either, on some prearranged assembly-date, should withdraw from the Seine with the other Northmen, and seek the open sea, or, if the others would not withdraw with them, should unite with Charles's army to attack those who refused to go. Thus, when ten hostages had been given, they were allowed to return to their own people. About twenty days later, Weland himself came to Charles and commended himself to him, while he and the men he had with him swore solemn oaths in their own way. Then he returned to the ships and with the whole Danish fleet sailed down the Seine to Jumièges, where they decided to repair their ships and await the Spring equinox. When the ships had been repaired, the Danes made for the open sea, and split up into several flotillas which sailed off in different directions according to their various choices.

4 The citation is from Gregory II's Roman Synod of 721, also cited in the *acta* (composed by Hincmar) of the assembly of Savonnières in 862; *MGH Capit.* II, no. 243, c. 5, pp. 160-1.

5 Cf. above 860: 93-4, and nn. 7, 8.

6 See Coupland 1987: 57-8 and 130-4 for Charles's strategy of containment up to 862. Hildegar, *Vita Faronis* cc. 129-31, p. 202, describes a Viking attack on Meaux early in 862, which caused Charles to move swiftly south from Senlis.

7 Coupland 1987: 173 emends Hincmar's *ad insulam* to *ad Insulas*, and identifies the location as Isles-les-Villenoy, near Trilbardou. For the political context of the Viking attack on Meaux, see below n. 20.

Most of them made for the Bretons, who live in Neustria with Salomon as chief; and these Danes were joined by the ones who had been in Spain.[8] Salomon hired twelve Danish ships for an agreed fee, to use against Robert. These Robert captured on the river Loire and slew every man in the fleet, except for a few who fled into hiding. Robert, unable now to put up with Salomon any longer, made an alliance against Salomon with the Northmen who had just left the Seine, before Salomon could ally with them against him. Hostages were exchanged, and Robert paid them 6,000 lb of silver.[9]

Weland with his wife and sons came to Charles, and he and his family became Christians.[10]

Karlmann, son of King Louis of Germany, made peace with his father, after his father had granted him that part of the realm which he had previously invaded, and after he had given a solemn oath never to invade any territory beyond that without his father's voluntary agreement.[11]

Then Louis, son of King Charles, took the advice of Guntfrid and Gauzfrid, and approached Salomon. He was given a strong contingent of Bretons, and with these he attacked Robert, his father's faithful man, and laid waste the Anjou region and wherever else he could reach, with sword, fire and general devastation.

Robert then attacked the Bretons as they were returning with enormous quantities of plunder, slew more than 200 of the Bretons' leading men and prised their booty from them. Louis made another attempt to fight back, but Robert drove him into flight and all his companions were scattered while he himself only just managed to get away.

Charles, king of the Aquitanians, son of King Charles, had still not yet reached the age of fifteen. Stephen prevailed on him to marry the

---

8 These Vikings were probably not the same as those mentioned above, 844: 60. There had been other attacks on Spain in the 850s.

9 Though all manuscripts have simply '6,000', L/G: 89, note 'r' supply 'libris'. (If 6,000 d. were meant, this would have amounted to 25 lb, which seems implausibly low. Cf. the ransom of Abbot Louis, above 858, n. 7.) This was apparently a hire-fee made by Robert as a 'private' payment, rather than a royally-organised tribute.

10 Information earlier in this annal suggests that Weland was no longer in overall control of this confederation, hence perhaps his quest for Frankish support. See further below 863: 110-11.

11 Cf. above 861: 94; *AF* 862: 55.

widow of Count Humbert without his father's will or consent.[12] His brother Louis, moreover, following in his footsteps, right at the beginning of Lent married the daughter of the late Count Harduin and sister of his great favourite Odo.[13]

Their father Charles caused all the leading men of his realm to assemble about 1 June, with many workmen and carts, at the place called Pîtres, where the Andelle from one side and the Eure from the other flow into the Seine.[14] By constructing fortifications on the Seine, he closed it off to ships sailing up or down the river. This was done because of the Northmen. He himself went with his wife to have talks with his son Charles on the Loire at a place called Meung, having first given oaths of safe-conduct through messengers. Charles went back to Aquitaine like a man subdued, but despite his humble words, his spirit was still unbowed.

His father returned to Pîtres, whither he had previously summoned an assembly and a synod to meet at the same time.[15] While he went on with the work of constructing the fortifications, he discussed with his faithful men the affairs of the holy church and of the realm. Rothad bishop of Soissons was a singularly stupid man, who had been deprived by a provincial synod of episcopal communion, according to the rules of the church. He now presented himself, with characteristic contumacy, before a council of four provinces.[16] This assembly of brother-bishops decided to refrain from deposing him completely pending his appeal to the apostolic see. But Rothad, after the judgement of that provincial council from which he had appealed, asked for twelve judges

---

12 For the Young Charles, see above 855: 80. His exact date of birth is unrecorded. Stephen can probably be identified as the son of Count Hugh, and Hugh's county may have been Bourges (Auzias 1937: 305-12) or possibly Nevers. According to L/G: 90, n. 3, Humbert was count of Bourges. There is no direct evidence; but another Humbert is mentioned by John VIII as a magnate in Berry in 878: *MGH Epp.* VII, no. 135, p. 119.

13 The bride was Ansgard. Harduin's county seems to have lain in northern Neustria; *MGH Capit.* II, no. 260, c. 7, p. 275. Harduin's wife was named Guerimbourg. Their son Odo was identified with Odo of Troyes by Levillain 1937a and L/G: 91, n. 3; but Werner 1959b: 154 and n. 35 convincingly distinguishes the two. The marriages of Charles the Bald's two elder sons without his permission represented a serious threat to his authority.

14 This site has been identified at Pont-de-l'Arche (dep. Eure), about 2 km. downstream from the palace of Pîtres; Hassall and Hill 1970; Dearden 1989; Dearden 1990.

15 The decisions of this assembly show the bishops collaborating with Charles to deal with the punishment of criminals; *MGH Capit.* II, no. 272, pp. 302-10.

16 Sens, Rheims, Rouen and Tours.

to be appointed by this council of four provinces to carry out its judgement.[17] Like another Pharoah in the hardness of his heart, and replicating ancient times in being a man turned into a monster, Rothad was deposed just outside Soissons because of the excesses described in the list of his bad deeds, since he refused to be corrected.

Meanwhile a miracle occurred at Thérouanne. On the morning of the day of Mary's Assumption [15 August], the slave-woman of a certain citizen of that town began to iron a linen garment, the sort called in the vulgar tongue a shirt [camisium], so that it would be all ready for her master to wear when he went to mass. The first time she put the iron down on it and pushed it across it, the shirt became stained with blood. And so it went on: whenever the slave put the iron across, blood followed it, until the whole garment was quite dyed in the blood pressed on to it. Hunfrid, the venerable bishop of that civitas,[18] had the shirt brought to him and kept in the church as a witness to the miracle. Because the feast of Mary's Assumption had not previously been celebrated by the inhabitants of his diocese, he gave orders that this solemn occasion should be celebrated by all and kept as a feast with due reverence.[19]

Louis, who had recently defected from his father, returned to him and asked forgiveness from him and from the bishops too for his excesses. He bound himself by most strict and solemn oaths to be loyal to his father in future. His father granted him the county of Meaux and the abbacy of St-Crispin, and ordered him to come to him in person from Neustria along with his wife.[20] Hunfrid marchio of Gothia[21] had been

17 Cf. above 861: 96. Rothad had previously appealed to Pope Nicholas over the head of his metropolitan, Hincmar of Rheims. The procedure of appointing twelve judges was laid down in canon law; Devisse 1976: 592-4.

18 Hunfrid's family connections in the Moselle region have been explored by Hennebicque 1981: 294-7. My translation here assumes the bishop's slave was a woman. (The Latin mancipium is neuter.)

19 Hincmar was interested in promoting devotion to the Virgin; Devisse 1976: 916. See also below: 102.

20 Bishop Hildegar of Meaux may have been a supporter of Louis's rebellion; and Charles the Bald may therefore have colluded in the Viking attack on Meaux, above: 98 and n. 6. This would explain the strong criticism of Charles in Hildegar's Vita Faronis, cc. 123-5, pp. 200-1. Louis's wife, unnamed here, was Ansgard.

21 Against the view of Dhondt 1948: 210 that Hunfrid was a Goth and represented 'national' separatism, it now seems clear that he was a Frankish appointee of Charles: Collins 1990a: 178-9. The title marchio here signifies command of the frontier region of the Spanish March, with the additional connotation of headship over a number of counts; Werner 1980: 211-21, esp. 216-17, n. 96. Gothia is an alternative name for Septimania.

accused of breach of faith by Waringaud, but at the request of his faithful men King Charles did not allow the affair to become an occasion for war: he restored peace between Hunfrid and Waringaud.

Louis king of Germany summoned his nephew Lothar to Mainz and asked him to join with him in a campaign against the Wends called ....[22] and their chief. Lothar at first promised to come but later failed to make good his promise. But Louis, leaving his son Charles at home because he had lately got married to the daughter of Count Erchangar,[23] took with him his son Louis and attacked the Wends. Having lost some of his leading men, he had no success at all, so he took hostages and returned to his palace at Frankfurt on the Main. The Danes plundered and laid waste a great part of his kingdom with fire and sword. Also enemies called Hungarians, hitherto unknown to those peoples, ravaged his realm.[24]

Lothar had been demented, so it was said, by witchcraft and ensnared in a blind passion by the wiles of his concubine Waldrada for whom he had cast aside his wife Theutberga. Now with the backing of his uncle Liutfrid[25] and of Walter, who because of this were his special favourites, and with the consent – an abominable thing this is to say – even of certain bishops of his realm, Lothar crowned Waldrada and coupled with her as if she were his lawful wife and queen, while his friends grieved and spoke out against this action.[26] Hincmar bishop of Rheims, when King Charles came to the city, summoned his suffragan bishops and on 17 September with due solemnity dedicated the new mother church of that province to the honour of St Mary, to whom the ancient church had been consecrated.

Louis king of Germany sent smooth-talking envoys to his brother Charles and asked him to come to a meeting in the neighbourhood of

---

22 Though a word is missing from the manuscripts (L/G: 93, note 'd'), *AF* 862, with n. 2, allow the name 'Obodrites' to be supplied.

23 This is the future Charles the Fat, then aged twenty-three. His father- in-law was a count in Alsace. The marriage may have been arranged by Louis the German to fit with his plans for the future partition of his realm; see below 866, n. 1. Cf. Nelson 1988b: 116-17.

24 This is the earliest mention in any source of a Hungarian attack.

25 Liutfrid was the brother of Lothar II's mother Ermengard, and son of Count Hugh of Tours, above 837, n. 5. Walter was at the centre of Lothar's diplomacy; *MGH Epp.* VI, pp. 209, 215, 327. See also Schmid 1968: 109.

26 The two Lotharingian archbishops, Gunther of Cologne and Theutgaud of Trier, and their suffragans, supported Lothar's plans. Cf. above 857, n. 6. Waldrada's coronation proclaimed her status as queen.

Toul.[27] Because Charles refused to hold talks with Lothar until he had told his brother the reasons why he was displeased with Lothar, quite a battle of words ensued. Finally Charles and the bishops who were with him sent to Louis and the bishops who were with him a written text drawn up in *capitula*,[28] showing the grounds on which Charles refused to communicate with Lothar unless he would undertake either to give a reasonable explanation on these points or would show some improvement, according to rightful authority. When Lothar gave an undertaking on these terms, Charles and the bishops with him received Lothar into communion. As for the texts of the *adnuntiationes*[29] from their meeting, which had been written down and read out to the counsellors, and which they ought to have issued to the people, Louis and Lothar totally rejected them. In this they were following the advice especially of their counsellor Conrad, Charles's uncle, who was trying hard in his usual fashion with an arrogant yet superficial knowledge of the world which brought little benefit to himself, still less to others, to prevent the people from finding out what accusation Charles was making against Lothar.[30] But Charles, against their wishes, made it fully known to everyone that he had refused to communicate with Lothar before he gave the undertaking mentioned above, for two reasons: first, because Lothar had abandoned his wife and taken another woman, contrary to the authority of the Gospel and of the apostles, and second, because Lothar and his mistress had had communication with excommunicated persons, namely the wife of Boso,[31] and Baldwin who had stolen away Charles's daughter and

27 The envoys, including Bishop Altfrid of Hildesheim, were sent during the summer. Hincmar misleads in suggesting that the initiative in seeking a meeting came from Louis rather than Charles; Prinz 1965: 258-60. The meeting took place at Savonnières in November. In the official communiqué, *MGH Capit.* II, no. 243, pp. 159-65, Louis, Charles and Lothar II reaffirmed the commitments made at Koblenz, above 860, n. 5.

28 Literally, 'under separate headings': the normal form of Carolingian public documents and a subject on which Hincmar was expert; Nelson 1986a (1983a): 106, n. 71.

29 Oral statements ('announcements') made by Carolingian kings to their faithful men at assemblies; Nelson 1986a (1983a): 109, and cf. Nelson 1986a (1977a): 150-1.

30 For Conrad, see above 830: 22; *AF* 858, n. 13. His career from c. 840 was spent in the East Frankish kingdom; Borgolte 1987: 165-70. Though Hincmar's dislike of him is clear, Conrad could be seen as a peacemaker in a family quarrel.

31 This Boso was the brother of Theutberga and Hubert, and held a countship in the kingdom of the Emperor Louis II. His wife Engeltrude was the daughter of Matfrid; above 830, n. 5. On Engeltrude's case, see further below 863: 109 and n. 16.

married her.[32] Thus the brothers left each other, after agreeing on the venue of a further meeting in the following October, on the border between the counties of Mouzon and Voncq.

Louis made for Bavaria, either to reconcile, or to resist his son Karlmann who had rebelled against his father with the aid of Rastiz petty king of the Wends.[33] Charles returned from the Toul district by way of Ponthion, and from there went along the bank of the Marne to Senlis, where he most reverently celebrated Christmas.

863

In January Danes sailed up the Rhine towards Cologne, after sacking the *emporium* called Dorestad and also a fairly large *villa* at which the Frisians had taken refuge, and after slaying many Frisian traders and taking captive large numbers of people. Then they reached a certain island near the fort of Neuss.[1] Lothar came up and attacked them with his men along one bank of the Rhine and the Saxons along the other and they encamped there until about the beginning of April. The Danes therefore followed Roric's advice and withdrew by the same way they had come.

Charles, son of the Emperor Lothar and king of Provence, who had long suffered from epilepsy, died.[2] His brother Louis, so-called emperor of Italy, came to Provence and won over as many of the leading men of that realm as he could. On hearing news of this, Lothar made straight for Provence, and through the mediation of members of their households and of their close associates, he and Louis agreed on an assembly to which they would both return at the same time to negotiate with each other about the kingdom of Provence. Louis then returned to Italy, Lothar to his own kingdom.

King Charles went to Le Mans and proceeded from there to the

32 Above 862: 97, n. 2.

33 *AF* 863, n. 1.

1 This is the last mention of Dorestad in the *AB*. Coupland 1988 shows that its decline postdates the 840s, and was not caused solely by Viking activity. See also Verhulst 1989. According to *AX* 864: 20-1, the island was near Xanten, some 60 km. downstream from Neuss: having burned the church of St-Victor at Xanten, 'the plunderers made for a nearby small island, built a fort, and stayed there for a while'.

2 25 January. Ado of Vienne, pp. 322-3, describes the outcome of the ensuing contest over the succession to this kingdom: Louis II got Provence and Transjurane Burgundy, Lothar II the rest.

monastery called Entrammes.[3] There Salomon duke of the Bretons came with the leading men of his people to meet Charles, and commended himself to him, swearing an oath of fidelity which he also made all the leading men of Brittany swear. He paid Charles, moreover, the tribute owed by his land according to ancient custom.[4] In consideration of his oath of fidelity, Charles granted him part of the region called Between-the-two-waters, and also the abbey of St-Aubin at Angers as a benefice. He received, and graciously granted *honores* to, Gauzfrid and Rorgo and Harvey[5] and the others who had recently, as often before, defected from him. From Entrammes he returned to Le Mans and celebrated Easter there.

Hunfrid *marchio* of Gothia grabbed Toulouse from Raymund and usurped it for himself.[6] He did so without King Charles's knowledge, by a conspiracy, in the usual way of the Toulousans, who are always withdrawing that city's allegiance from their counts.

King Charles, returning from the regions beyond the Seine, received Liutard bishop of Pavia representing Louis emperor of Italy, Gebhard bishop of Speyer representing his brother Louis king of Germany, and Count Nanthar representing Lothar, Charles's nephew, all of whom came seeking peace[7] which it was always Charles's aim, likewise, to preserve, so far as the hostility of his opponents allowed. He also received from his brother Louis another envoy called Blitgar, who requested that if Louis's son Karlmann, now abandoned by the Wend Rastiz and a fugitive from his father, should come to Charles, he should not receive him. Not long afterwards, Karlmann, deceived and deserted by his own men,[8] was received back by his father Louis on

3 Dep. Mayenne, equidistant between Le Mans and Rennes.

4 Salomon's position had been weakened by the events of 862, above: 99. For Breton tribute, see Davies 1990: 106.

5 Gauzfrid and Rorico were brothers; below 866: 129. They were sons of Rorgo count of Le Mans; above 861, n. 9. Harvey was probably a kinsman (?son) of the Harvey killed in 844; above 844, n. 7. He may also be identified with one of the two Harveys listed among the rebels of 858; above 859, n. 8. Gauzfrid, Rorico and Harvey appear as counts in 866, below: 129, presumably thanks to their reception of *honores* in 863.

6 Raymund seems to have succeeded his brother Fredelo as count in the early 850s; Levillain 1938: 20-1. The Young Charles, king of Aquitaine, may well have been involved in Hunfrid's revolt; Calmette 1917.

7 This embassy came to discuss the succession to Provence; Calmette 1901: 87-8.

8 *AF* 863: n. 4.

condition that he gave a solemn oath. Louis kept him with him in free custody.

Charles received the envoys of Pope Nicholas with due ceremony at Soissons in the monastery of St-Médard. They were Radoald bishop of Porto and John bishop of Cervia. Charles kept them with him for a while, and granted forgiveness to Baldwin who had sought refuge at the threshold of the apostles. It was to obtain this that the legates had come.[9] So Charles then dismissed them, generously endowed with gifts, to return with letters to the apostolic see.

Legates also came from the pope to Metz to hold by apostolic delegation a synod in mid-June, to consider the divorce which had occurred between Lothar and his wife Theutberga, and the substitution for her of his concubine Waldrada whom he had joined to himself in marriage, contrary to both ecclesiastical and secular laws. At this synod, the two legates, corrupted by bribes, concealed the pope's letters and carried out none of the things that had been entrusted to them by sacred authority. But in order to give the impression that they had achieved something, with the connivance of Hagano, a crafty and very greedy Italian bishop,[10] they ordered Gunther archbishop of Cologne and Theutgaud his fellow-archbishop of Trier to go to Rome with the childish nonsense which the bishops of Lothar's realm had had written out and had subscribed in that synod,[11] so that the case might be settled by the judgement of the pope. But the pope was fully aware of all that had gone on. He wished to condemn Radoald on another similar charge, for he had lately been corrupted by greed in Constantinople along with his fellow bishop Zacharias.[12] The pope himself therefore now summoned a synod. Radoald, when he got wind of this, fled by night and disappeared. Gunther and Theutgaud, when they came to Rome, were condemned by the pope first in the synod and afterwards in the church of St-Peter, in the following terms:[13]

9 For Nicholas's intervention on behalf of Baldwin and Judith, above 862, n. 2.

10 Bishop of Bergamo. His role suggests the influence of Louis II.

11 For the letter of the Lotharingian archbishops, see below 864: 113-16. The Synod of Metz condemned Theutberga, as Lothar wished; Devisse 1976: 441-2; Hartmann 1989: 280-2.

12 For the mission of Radoald and Zacharias to Constantinople in 861, see Dvornik 1948: 74-91; Dvornik 1966: 450-4; Grégoire 1966: 109. The Patriarch Ignatius had resigned in 858 under pressure from the regime of the young Emperor Michael III (855-67), and been replaced by Photius. Pope Nicholas had at first approved, but in 862 decided to support Ignatius. See below 864: 120 and n. 30. For Nicholas's stance, see Ullmann 1972: 105-6.

13 Copies of Nicholas's letter circulated widely; cf. *AF* 863: 58-60. See *MGH Epp.* VI, nos. 18-21, pp. 284-7.

Nicholas, bishop, servant of the servants of God, to our most reverent and most holy confrères Hincmar of Rheims and Wenilo of Rouen and all our confrères, the archbishops and bishops established in the realm of the glorious King Charles. That crime which Lothar the king – if that man can truly be called a king who reins in his appetites by no healthy control of his body but rather with weakness yields to its unlawful motions – committed against two women, namely Theutberga and Waldrada, is manifest to all. But almost the whole world was reporting to us, as it flowed to the threshold or seat of the apostles, even though those who wrote this to our apostolate were absent in person, that in such a deed Lothar formerly had as authors and supporters Bishops Theutgaud and Gunther. This we were all the more reluctant to believe, in so far as we used to hope never to hear any such thing about bishops, until those very men, coming to Rome at the time of the council, were found before us and the holy synod to be exactly as they had so very often beforehand been said to be by many people: that is, they were caught by that very document which they had set out with their own hands and which they wished us to confirm with our own hand, and while they were trying to set a trap for the innocent, they were ensnared in their own toils. Thus has been fulfilled, at God's instance, what is read in the Book of Proverbs [1: 77]: 'The net is thrown in vain before the eyes of the birds.' Thus they were bound and fell. But we who were falsely being said to have fallen into that crime, by God's favour have risen up again with the defenders of justice, and we are upright. Therefore with the holy synod decreeing along with us, they stand in our presence indubitably deposed and excommunicated from episcopal office and removed from the government of episcopacy. Wherefore let your fraternity, guarding as it does the norm of the canons and observing the sanctions of the decrees, take care not to presume to receive in the catalogue of high priests those whom we have flung aside. The sentence of deposition which we have delivered against the above-mentioned Theutgaud and Gunther, together with other decrees which we have promulgated, the holy synod sanctioning them with us, is shown attached below.

c.1. *That the synod assembled at Metz by archbishops Theutgaud and Gunther is utterly annulled.*
The synod which recently, that is under the most pious Emperor Louis in the eleventh Indiction, in the month of June, was summoned together in Metz by bishops who had acted in advance

of our judgement and who rashly violated what was instituted by the apostolic see, we judge to be now and henceforth and for all eternity void; and we ordain that it be reputed along with the robber-synod of Ephesus[14] to be damned by apostolic authority in perpetuity; and we decree that it should not be termed a synod, but because it favoured adulterers, it should be called a brothel.

c.2. *The depositions of Archbishops Theutgaud and Gunther.*

Theutgaud bishop of Trier, primate of the Belgic province and Gunther bishop of Cologne, now before us and the holy synod by reason of their deeds, in as much as they acknowledged and judged the case of King Lothar and his two women, namely Theutberga and Waldrada, offering a document on this matter confirmed by their own hands, and affirming with their own mouths to the many before whom they spoke that they had done nothing more nor less nor otherwise, and confessing themselves publicly and orally to have violated the sentence which our most holy brother Archbishop Tado of Milan and others of our fellow-bishops requested should be sent out from the apostolic see against Engeltrude, the wife of Boso,[15] and which we, afire with divine zeal, canonically delivered under assurance of anathema, in all of which matters we have found them to have exceeded in many respects the apostolic and canonical sanctions and wickedly to have defiled the rule of equity: them we judge to remain utterly removed from all office of high priesthood, declaring them, by the judgement of the Holy Spirit and the authority of St Peter, to be deprived of all governmental powers pertaining to the episcopate. If they should in future presume to act as bishops according to their previous custom and to do anything which pertains to that sacred office, then they shall lose all hope of restitution in any other synod or any opportunity of satisfaction, and all who communicate with them shall be thrown out of the Church, and especially if they are already aware that this sentence has been delivered against those men.

c. 3. *Other bishops.*

Other bishops who are said to have been accomplices of these men, namely Theutgaud and Gunther, or adherents thereof, if in association with them they commit seditions, conjurations or conspiracies, or if in adhering to them they dissent from their head, that is, from

14 The proceedings of the Council of Ephesus (449) had been denounced by Pope Leo I as a 'robbery'; Chadwick 1967: 201-3.

15 See following note.

the see of Peter, they shall be held bound by the same condemnation with those. But if they come to their senses and become wise henceforth of their own accord in harmony with the apostolic see, whence it is manifest that they took the source of their episcopal office, or if they confess by sending messengers to us with their written admissions, may they know that pardon shall not be denied them by us, nor need loss of their offices through us in any way be feared, on account of presumptuous acts or subscriptions made to profane deeds which they have since retracted.

c. 4. *The case of Engeltrude.*[16]

Engeltrude, daughter of the late Count Matfrid, who abandoned her own husband Boso and, look, has now for about seven years been running about here and there, a vagabond, we recently lawfully anathematised, along with her supporters, but on account of her contumacies we have thought it fit that she should again be knotted in the bonds of anathema. Therefore by the Father and the Son and the Holy Spirit, the one and true God, and by all the holy fathers and by the universal holy catholic and apostolic Church of God and by us, let her be utterly anathema, with all her accomplices, and those who communicate with her and those who aid her, in such a way that, as we have already decreed, if anyone presumes in any way to communicate with her or to favour her, let him, if he is a cleric, be bound by the same bond and let him lose the office of the clericate; and monks and laymen, if they are disobedient to this present decree, let them likewise be anathematised. But of course, if that woman returns to her husband, or comes hastening to Rome, to the apostolic see of the blessed Peter, there is no doubt that we shall not deny her forgiveness after due satisfaction. Yet let her remain in the meantime bound under the previous bond of anathema by which we formerly bound her and now bind her. If anyone in ignorance communicates with that Engeltrude while she is hastening or running to Rome for this purpose, to the apostolic see of blessed Peter, or if anyone knowingly offers her the means to come, let him be held bound by no bond on account of this.

c. 5. *The sentences and interdicts of the apostolic see.*

If anyone willfully ignores the dogmas, mandates, interdicts, sanctions or decrees healthfully promulgated by the bishop of the

---

16 Cf. above 862, n. 31. Engeltrude had gone off with one of her husband's vassals and found protection with Lothar II; Wemple 1981: 87 and n. 64. She later threatened to seek refuge with the Northmen; Hincmar, *de Divortio*, PL 125, cols. 754–5.

apostolic see, for the catholic faith, for ecclesiastical discipline, for the correction of the faithful, for the emendation of the wicked or for the interdiction of imminent or of future evildoers, let him be anathema.

May your holinesses fare well in Christ.

Charles held a synod in the palace of Verberie on 25 October. There he lawfully vindicated the abbey of St-Calais against Bishop Robert of Le Mans, who wished to hold the abbey through the commendation of the apostolic see as a lawful possession of his bishopric.[17] Charles sent the recently-deposed Rothad[18] to Rome, as the lord pope had commanded him to do, with letters and representatives from himself and from the bishops. In response to an appeal from the pope, he received his daughter Judith back into his good graces.[19] He also received with customary ceremony the envoy of Mohammed king of the Saracens who came with many large gifts and with letters speaking of peace and a treaty of friendship. He decided to wait at Senlis for a suitable time to send this envoy in dignified fashion back to his king with honour and due protection and all the help he needed.[20]

Then from Senlis, he made his way towards Aquitaine, with a strong force, to receive his son Charles in strength, or, if he refused to come, to attack him instead. He reached Auxerre: there, on the advice of his faithful men, and in accordance with the pope's request, he permitted his daughter Judith to be joined in lawful matrimony to Baldwin with whom she had eloped. From Auxerre he went on to Nevers, where his son Charles came to him and was duly received. His father ordered him to swear fidelity and due subordination with a solemn oath, and he had all the leading men of Aquitaine again swear loyalty to him.[21]

Two Northmen who had recently left their ships with Weland and come asking to be baptised as Christians now revealed – and it

17 T. 258 is the record of this judgement. The claims of Le Mans to jurisdiction over St-Calais had been supported in a series of forgeries; Goffart 1966.

18 Above 862: 101.

19 Above 863: 106.

20 For Mohammed amir of Cordoba, above 852, n. 6. He was probably anxious about a possible alliance between Hunfrid and rebels at Zaragoza in his own territory; cf. *Trans. SS Aurelii et Georgii* cc. 2, 5, *PL* 115, cols. 941, 943. Charles's dealings with Cordoba may also have been linked with the suppression of his son's revolt in Aquitaine; above 863, n. 5, and below 864: 111.

21 Nevers was a characteristic choice of meeting-point on 'Charles's' bank of the Loire: his son therefore had to make the crossing.

afterwards turned out to be true – that this had been a trick, and they accused Weland of bad faith. Weland denied this. So, according to the custom of their people, one of the Northmen challenged him to single combat in King Charles's presence, and killed him in the fight.[22]

Meanwhile he received the sad news that the Northmen had come to Poitiers, and though the city was ransomed, they had burned the church of the great confessor St Hilary.[23] He celebrated Christmas in the same place near Nevers where he had received his son.

864

Charles arranged his troops and ordered the Aquitainians to advance against the Northmen who had burned the church of St-Hilary. He himself returned to Compiègne taking with him his son and namesake Charles, and he sent his *missi* to Gothia to receive the submission of the *civitates* and fortresses there.[1]

The Northmen got to Clermont where they slew Stephen, son of Hugh, and a few of his men, and then returned unpunished to their ships.[2] Pippin, son of Pippin, who had changed back from being a monk to become a layman and an apostate, joined company with the Northmen and lived like one of them.[3]

The Young Charles, whom his father had recently received from Aquitaine and taken with him to Compiègne, was returning one night from hunting in the forest of Cuise. While he meant only to enjoy

22 Above 862: 99 and n. 10.

23 Like other major cult-sites, St-Hilary was outside the city-walls; Claude 1960: 99 and plan of Poitiers. Brühl 1975: 175-6 suggests that the monastery contained a royal palace, which was destroyed in 863. This might explain the shift of Charles's interest to Bourges.

1 This mission was clearly linked with the suppression of Hunfrid's revolt.

2 I identify this Stephen with the man mentioned above 862: 99-100 and n. 12. Cf. Wollasch 1959: 23, n. 25. The man killed in 864 was a count, probably of the Auvergne: Nicholas I, *MGH Epp.* VI, p. 623. The killers may have been Vikings who came from the River Charente where they had attacked the Angoumois in 863, *AAng*; Vogel 1906: 199. Coupland 1987: 62-3 thinks it more likely that they were Loire Vikings who had attacked Poitiers in 863. They may already have been allied with Pippin II; see next note, and cf. above 857: 84.

3 'Apostate' here has the technical sense of a monk who has abandoned his profession. *Ritum eorum servat* has been taken to mean 'followed their religion'; Wallace-Hadrill 1975: 226. But *ritus* can mean 'habits' or 'way of life': e.g. above 841: 51, n. 8; and *RFA* 823. See further Coupland 1992; and below n. 19. Clerical anxieties generated a myth of proselytising Viking paganism; but in fact Viking religion was eclectic; Wood 1987: 49-58.

some horseplay with some other young men of his own age, by the devil's action he was struck in the head with a sword by a youth called Albuin. The blow penetrated almost as far as the brain, reaching from his left temple to his right cheekbone and jaw.[4]

Lothar, son of Lothar, raised 4 *denarii* from every manse in his whole kingdom, and handed over the sum in cash, plus a large quantity of flour and livestock and also wine and cider, to the Northman Rodulf, son of Harald, and his men, all this being termed a payment for service.[5]

Louis, so-called emperor of Italy, goaded on by Gunther to his own harm, regarded those legates of his brother Lothar whom the pope had degraded, as described above, as having been directed to Rome by means of his (Louis's) guarantees and intervention. In fury, showing no self-restraint, he travelled with his wife[6] to Rome taking those legates Theutgaud and Gunther along with him, with the intention of having the two bishops reinstated by the pope or, if the pope refused to act, laying hands on him to do him some injury. When the pope heard about all this, he proclaimed for himself and for the Romans a general fast with litanies, so that through the intercessions of the apostles, God might make the emperor well-disposed and respectful towards divine worship and the authority of the apostolic see. When the emperor had reached Rome, and was staying near the church of St-Peter, the clergy and people of Rome, celebrating their fast with crosses and litanies, approached the tomb of St Peter. As they began to climb the steps in front of St-Peter's basilica, they were thrown to the ground by the emperor's men, and beaten with all kinds of blows. Their crosses and banners were smashed, and those who could escape simply fled.

There was a wonderful cross, most worthy of honour, which had been very beautifully worked by Helena of holy memory: she had placed in it the wood of the life-giving cross, and handed it over to St Peter as the greatest of gifts. This cross was smashed in all the uproar, and thrown into a pool of mud. From there, so they say, the pieces were

---

4 Regino, 870: 101, gives more details of the accident, and identifies Albuin as brother of Bivin and Betto. Ado, p. 323, says the Young Charles was 'dishonoured by his injury' (*dehonestatus iniuria*). He never recovered; below 866: 134.

5 These were probably the Northmen who had sailed up the Rhine in 863, above: 104. For Rodulf, see Wood 1987: 44. For *denarii* and manses, below 130, n. 4.

6 The Empress Engelberga played a conspicuous role in Carolingian politics during the next decade; Odegaard 1951, and below: 113; 866: 130; 872: 177.

retrieved by some Englishmen and returned to the cross's custodians. When the pope, who was staying in the Lateran palace, heard about these crimes, and learned soon after from a reliable source that he himself was to be taken prisoner, he secretly boarded a boat and got himself across the Tiber to the church of St-Peter, where he stayed for two days and nights without food or drink.

Meanwhile the man by whose presumption the venerable cross had been broken died, and the emperor went down with fever. He therefore sent his wife to the pope. With her safe-conduct the pope came to the emperor and after long conversations had been held, as is fitting should take place between them, the pope returned to Rome, to the Lateran palace. Then the emperor ordered the degraded Gunther and Theutgaud, who had come with him, to return to Francia. Then Gunther sent to the pope by his brother the cleric Hilduin,[7] accompanied by Gunther's men, the list of points devilishly inspired and hitherto unheard-of, which Gunther had sent with the following preface to the bishops of Lothar's realm when he returned to Rome in the entourage of the Emperor Louis, as already mentioned. Gunther gave Hilduin further instructions that if the pope refused to receive this list, he should lay it on the body [i.e. tomb] of St Peter:[8]

To their holy and venerable brothers and fellow-bishops, Gunther and Theutgaud send greetings in the Lord. We implore your fraternity to afford us who so earnestly pray for you the immediate solace of your holy prayers, and we ask you not to be disturbed nor frightened on account of the things that rumour has perhaps adversely reported to you about us. We have trust in the most merciful goodness of our Lord, that the snares of our enemies will not prevail either against our king or against us, God helping us.

The lord Nicholas, who is called pope and who numbers himself as an apostle amongst the apostles, and who is making himself emperor of the whole world, had wished to condemn us, at the instigation and prayer of those with whom he has conspired and whom he is known to favour. Nevertheless he has found people

---

7 According to *AX* 871: 29, Hilduin was Gunther's nephew. This is likely to be correct if *AX* was written by a Cologne cleric, as argued by Löwe 1951: 78-9. In 862, Hincmar had successfully resisted Lothar II's efforts to have Hilduin installed as bishop of Cambrai; *MGH Epp*. VIII, nos. 152-4. Brown 1989: 38-45 shows that Hilduin's family connections extended very widely in all three Carolingian successor-kingdoms.

8 This manifesto was widely circulated; cf. below n. 10. Gunther attempted to circulate his own propaganda; Fuhrmann 1958: 8-9, 17-19; Nelson 1991.

E

resisting his madness, with Christ's help, in every way possible, and whatever he has done thereafter he has later had great cause to regret.

We have sent you this list of points written out below so that you can learn from them the grounds of our complaint against the said pope. We had left Rome and gone far away. Now we have been summoned back to Rome again. As we begin our return journey there, we have written you this brief letter, so that you may not be surprised that we are making still longer delays. Visit our lord king [Lothar II] often, both in person and through your messengers and letters; comfort him; win over to him as many friends and faithful supporters as you can; especially keep inviting King Louis with frequent admonition, and inquire diligently with him concerning the common good, for our peace will lie in peace between those kings.[9] Be calm in spirit and tranquil in heart, lords and brothers, because we hope to announce to you, God willing, such things in which, without error, you will be able to observe, with the spirit of the Lord instructing you, what you ought to do and how to do it. Only take care to advise the said king in every way you can to remain unmoved amongst all the various insinuations made to him, until he himself can also know the true explanation of these things. Besides, most beloved brothers, it is necessary for us, and worthy of praise, that we should keep inviolably before God and men that faith we promised to our king. May Almighty God deign to keep you in his holy service.[10]

'c. 1. Hear, Lord Pope Nicholas. Those fellow-bishops, our fathers and brothers, directed us to you, and thus we came voluntarily to consult your magisterial authority on those matters about all of which we, as seemed good to us and as we could make known to our associates and supporters by setting out in writing the authorities and reasons for our view, likewise judged that your wisdom, having investigated everything thoroughly, should show to us your feel-

---

9 The archbishops clearly regarded Louis the German as potentially sympathetic to Lothar's divorce.

10 *AF* omit the archbishops' prefatory letter, but give the following *capitula* (except the last) though in a text slightly different from that in *AB*. For the variants, see L/G: 108-10. The *AB* text has been doctored: L/G: 108, n. 1, suggest that Hincmar tried to make it look more critical of Nicholas and so weaken the archbishops' position. Alternatively, Hincmar slightly softened the tone of the original to make the criticisms stick better; Nelson 1990b: 35. See also next note.

ings and your wishes. And if your holiness should better investigate all this, we humbly beg that you will instruct and teach us accordingly, for we are prepared, together with our confrères, to acquiesce with sound proofs in whatever you may more rightly and convincingly recommend.

c. 2. But we have awaited your reply for three weeks, and you gave us no expression of certainty, no sound teaching, but only admitted publicly one day that we seemed to be excusable and innocent according to the assertion of our own published statement.

c. 3. Finally, having been summoned, we were led into your presence. We suspected no act of hostility. But you had bolted all the gates of the place and laid a plot against us in the way a gang of criminals might do. You had collected a mob, a mixed bunch of clergy and laymen, and you made an attempt to crush us by violence amidst so many of them. You wanted to condemn us, by your own will and tyrannical fury alone,[11] without any synod or canonical trial, without any prosecutor, or any witness, or any discriminating direction of the case or any convincing proof from authorities, without receiving any oral confession from us, and in the absence of any other metropolitans and diocesan bishops, our fellows and confrères, and utterly without any collective expression of opinion.

c. 4. But we have in no way at all accepted your abusive sentence, so alien to fatherly kindness, so removed from brotherly love, which you delivered against us without justice or reason and against the canonical laws. Nay, rather, together with the whole assembly of our brothers we have despised and rejected it as abusive and groundlessly given. And you also, you who favour and communicate with condemned and anathematised persons and those who reject and despise sacred religion: we have no wish to receive you into our communion or our fellowship. We are satisfied that, arrogantly exalting yourself above it, you despise the communion and fraternal society of the whole Church, and that by rendering yourself unworthy through the swelling of your pride, you have cut yourself off from that society.

c. 5. Therefore in the temerity of your foolishness you have inflicted ruin on yourself by your own sentence of anathema, shouting out: "He who does not keep the apostolic precepts, let him be anathema."

11 Here the original attributed the pope's fury to the 'criminal teaching' of Anastasius, the papal librarian and counsellor; see below 868: 145 and n. 9.

These you know *you* are violating and have violated many many times, rendering void, as far as you could, the divine laws and the sacred canons, and refusing to follow in the footsteps of your predecessors the Roman pontiffs.

c. 6. Now therefore, because we have proof by our own experience of your fraudulence and cunning, we have not been provoked as it were by reaction against the abuse you have heaped on us, but we have been fired by zeal against your wickedness: without regard for our own insignificance, we have before our eyes the whole body of our order which you are trying to bludgeon by force.

c. 7. We shall sum up the essence of our argument on the specific case. Divine and canon law most clearly proves, and the secular laws, likewise worthy of respect, lay down that it is not lawful for anyone to hand over a free-born virgin in concubinage to any man, especially if the girl was never willing to give her consent illicitly to such a union: because she was linked with her husband by the consent of the parents, in conjugal faith, affection and love, let her forthwith be deemed, not his concubine, but his wife.'[12]

Pope Nicholas refused to receive this document. Hilduin, mentioned above, fully armed and with a troop of Gunther's men, entered the church of St-Peter without showing any respect, wanting to throw that diabolical text on the body of St Peter, as his brother Gunther had ordered him to do, should the pope refuse to receive it. When the guards refused them admission, Hilduin and his accomplices started hitting them with clubs, so fiercely that one of them was killed on the spot. Then Hilduin threw that document on St Peter's body, and he and those who had come with him, protecting themselves with unsheathed swords, made their way out of the church, and having completed the whole sorry business, returned to Gunther.

A few days later, the emperor left Rome. His following had committed many acts of devastation there, destroying houses, raping nuns and other women, killing men and breaching the privileges of churches. He reached Ravenna, where he celebrated Easter [2 April] in an acceptable manner with the respect due to God and the apostles. That very

12 The archbishops stated uncompromisingly that Waldrada had been married to Lothar in the sight of canon and secular law: there is no question of a *Friedelehe*. (This 'customary union', or 'quasi–marriage', is a modern historians' invention, unfortunately accepted by Wemple 1981: 34–5, 90.) Nicholas scotched a rumour that he had restored the archbishops; *MGH Epp.* VI, p. 313, and was unimpressed by their legal arguments; Kottje 1988.

Good Friday [30 March], Gunther had reached Cologne, and presumed, godless man, to celebrate mass and consecrate the sacred
chrism. Theutgaud, however, showed proper respect and abstained
from his official functions, as he had been commanded to do. With the
co-operation of the other bishops at his court, Lothar deprived
Gunther of his archbishopric. Entirely on his own initiative, he
granted it to Hugh, son of King Charles's uncle Conrad and of Lothar's
own aunt, a tonsured cleric but one who had only been ordained a
subdeacon and who in his own morals and way of life fell far short of
the standards even of a good layman.[13] Gunther, furious at this, went
back again to Rome, carrying off with him what was left of the
Cologne cathedral treasure: he wanted, according to the pope's
command, to set out all Lothar's and his own false arguments about
Theutberga and Waldrada.

The bishops of Lothar's realm also sent their own envoys to the pope
with statements of penitence and canonical professions to the effect
that in the case of Theutberga and Waldrada they had greatly deviated
from the truth of the Gospels and from apostolic authority and from
the sacred rules.[14] Lothar too in his false fashion had already sent
Bishop Ratold of Strasbourg to the pope with documents, expressing
excuses for his conduct and his voluntary correction of it.[15] Lothar
himself went by way of Gondreville and Remiremont to meet his
brother at the place called Orbe.[16]

Charles, as the pope had ordered, sent Rothad to Rome accompanied
by Bishop Robert of Le Mans bearing letters, and the bishops of his
realm also sent their representatives to the apostolic see with
synodical letters about Rothad's case.[17] But Louis [II] refused all these

13 For Hugh's earlier career and the fact that he was also a nephew of Louis the
German, see above 858: 88 n. 15. Hugh's mother, and Lothar's mother
Ermengard, were sisters. Hugh had moved to the Middle Kingdom in 861 but
may not have lost the abbacy of St-Germain, Auxerre, until 863, when Charles
the Bald gave it to his lame son Lothar; T. 261. Hugh's appointment to the see
of Cologne reflected the influence of Louis the German. At the same time,
Lothar's abandonment of Gunther was a conciliatory move towards the pope
and an attempt to dissociate himself from the excesses of Gunther's nephew
Hilduin in Rome, above, n. 7.

14 Adventius of Metz's statement in his own defence survives; *MGH Epp.* VI, pp.
219-22, and he evidently had a hand in those of the other Lotharingian bishops:
Staubach 1982: 196-7.

15 *MGH Epp.* VI, pp. 217-19. Staubach 1982: 197-9 argues persuasively for
Adventius's authorship.

16 Cf. above 856, n. 12.

17 Above 863: 110.

envoys permission to travel through his lands.[18] The envoys of both
the king and the bishops secretly made known to the pope the reasons
why it was impossible for them to come to Rome. Then the rest of them
journeyed back to their own fatherland. But Rothad feigned illness and
stayed at Besançon, and when the others had gone he made his way via
Chur, with the help of his backers Lothar and King Louis of Germany,
to Emperor Louis of Italy, intending to reach Rome with his aid.

The *missi* sent by King Charles [to Gothia] returned from their task,
having accomplished little of what they set out to do. Hunfrid left
Toulouse and Gothia behind, and travelled through Provence to
somewhere in Italy; whereupon Charles again sent other *missi* to
Toulouse and into Gothia to receive the *civitates* and fortresses.[19]

Louis king of Germany marched with an army to meet the Khan of the
Bulgars named ... ,[20] who had promised that he was willing to become
a Christian. Louis planned, if things seemed to go well, to go on
afterwards to the Wendish march to settle matters there.

Northmen sailed to Flanders with a large fleet, but when they met
with resistance from the local people, they sailed up the Rhine and laid
waste the neighbouring regions of the kingdoms of Lothar and Louis
on both banks of the river.

On 1 June at a place called Pîtres, Charles held a general assembly, at
which he received not only the annual gifts but also the tribute from
Brittany. This was sent to him by Duke Salomon of the Bretons,
following the customs of his ancestors, and it amounted to 50 lb of
silver.[21] Then Charles ordered fortifications to be constructed there on
the Seine to prevent the Northmen from coming up the river. With the
advice of his faithful men and following the custom of his predecessors
and forefathers he drew up *capitula* to the number of thirty-seven, and
he gave orders for them to be observed as laws throughout his whole
realm.[22]

18 Louis II was worried about a possible deal between Charles the Bald and Pope
Nicholas over the Lotharingian succession; below: 121.

19 For the earlier sending of *missi* to Gothia, above 864: 111. Calmette 1917: 161
points out that Hincmar conflates the chronology here. There must have been
a time-lag between the return of the first group of *missi* and the sending of the
second.

20 The manuscripts omit the khan's name: Boris. See *AF* 863, n. 3; and below 866:
137-8. Boris had allied with Louis the German in 863 against their common
enemy, the Moravians; Sullivan 1955: 91.

21 Cf. above 863, n. 4.

22 Hincmar had a hand in drafting these. See Nelson 1986a (1983a): 97-100;
Nelson 1990a: 15-16.

The Aquitanians by a trick captured the apostate Pippin, and removed him from his association with the Northmen. He was presented before the assembly at Pîtres, and having been condemned by the leading men of the realm as a traitor to his fatherland and to Christianity, and then sentenced to death by the general assembly, he was held in strictest custody at Senlis.[23]

Bernard, a son of the late tyrant Bernard according to both the flesh and his behaviour, received the king's permission and left the assembly one night with his military retinue, on the grounds that he wanted to return to his own *honores*.[24] But hiding himself in a wood, he waited for a time and place to commit a malicious act of slaughter: some people said his intended victim was the king who had ordered his father's execution by the judgement of the Franks, while others said his plan was to kill Robert and Ranulf, the king's faithful men.[25] This was reported to the king, who sent men to take Bernard prisoner and bring him into the royal presence. Thereupon Bernard fled, and the king, by judgement of his faithful men, confiscated the *honores* he had given him, and granted them instead to his faithful man Robert. Egfrid, who some while before had allied with Stephen to draw away the young Charles from obedience to his father, was now taken prisoner by Robert and presented to the king at the assembly at Pitres. At the earnest request of Robert himself and of others of his faithful men, the king forgave Egfrid all the crimes he had committed against him and, when he had confirmed his loyalty by oath, bestowed royal favour on him and allowed him to depart unharmed.[26]

Returning from Pîtres, Charles reached Compiègne around 1 July. The envoy of Mohammed king of the Saracens, who had come to him the

---

23 Pippin was captured by Count Ranulf of Poitou, according to the tenth-century Continuator of Ado of Vienne, p. 324. The indictment of Pippin was drawn up by Hincmar, *MGH Epp.* VIII, no. 170, pp. 163–5. Pippin seems to have died soon after the assembly of Pîtres. There is no further information on his fate.

24 This Bernard was the son of Bernard of Septimania executed in 844, above: 57 and n. 1. He was born on 22 March 841; Dhuoda, pref., pp. 84–5. The *honores* given him by Charles included (or perhaps consisted of?) the county of Autun; below 866: 131. Bouchard 1986: 65–8 does not deal with this phase of Bernard's career.

25 For Robert, see above 858, n. 8; 859, n. 8; 861: 95. Ranulf, above n. 23; Oexle 1969: 147, 182–7.

26 Egfrid (Acfred) was a noble whose interests extended from Poitou to the Angoumois; Nelson 1992: chs. 5, 6. He was probably a kinsman (?son) of the man appointed count of Toulouse by Charles in 842; Nithard IV, 4. For Stephen and the revolt of the Young Charles, above 862: 99.

previous winter, he now endowed with many large gifts and sent him back to his own king accompanied by *missi* in honourable fashion.[27]

Karlmann, son of Louis king of Germany, who was staying with his father in free custody, pretended to be going hunting, gave his father the slip and fled. With the consent of the *marchiones* who had betrayed him before, he reoccupied the same marches of which his father had deprived him.[28] His father pursued his trail, and made him come to him on condition that the status quo would be restored, and granted him *honores*. Returning from there to the palace of Frankfurt, while hunting a deer in a thicket, Louis fell from his horse and was hurt in the ribs. He stayed in bed in a neighbouring monastery, sending his son Louis on ahead to the palace at Frankfurt, where his wife was. He himself followed, having made a speedy recovery.

Pope Nicholas again sent letters to all the archbishops and bishops throughout the Gauls, the Germanies and the Belgic province, to confirm the deposition of Theutgaud archbishop of Trier and Gunther archbishop of Cologne. To the other bishops of Lothar's realm, who had consented to the divorce of Theutberga and the bringing-in of the concubine Waldrada in her place, but who had sent to the pope to make their professions, Nicholas gave letters granting indulgence, as he had promised to do in the document reproduced above.[29] He convoked a synod at Rome for the beginning of November, announcing that here he would finally confirm the deposition of the two former archbishops, and deal with the cases of Lothar and of Ignatius patriarch of Constantinople, who had been deposed the year before, and a certain layman tonsured and hurriedly ordained bishop in his place.[30] Theutgaud and Gunther came to this synod of their own accord, thinking that through the Emperor Louis's intervention they would be able to obtain their reinstatement by the pope.

Louis, so-called emperor of Italy, was gravely wounded by a stag which he was trying to shoot with an arrow while it stood on a rocky place. Pope Nicholas requested Louis, through Arsenius the *apocrisi-*

27 Above 863: 110.

28 The *AF* omit this further revolt of Karlmann. But for the identity of one of these *marchiones*, see AF 863, n. 4.

29 Above 863: 109. Nicholas's letters: *MGH Epp.* VI, nos. 29, pp. 295-7, confirming the deposition of the archbishops, and 30, 31, pp. 297-9, forgiving the other Lotharingian bishops.

30 Above 863, n. 12. Pope Nicholas after 862 refused to acknowledge Photius. Grégoire 1966: 112-13 links the pope's refusal with his interest in converting the Bulgars, below: 137.

arius,[31] for permission to send legates to Charles on certain ecclesiastical matters. But Louis refused: he believed that the pope wished to send those envoys to Francia with hidden designs against himself.

Hubert, a married cleric and abbot of the monastery of St-Martin, who was holding on to the abbacy of St-Maurice and other *honores* belonging to Emperor Louis of Italy against his will, was killed by his own men.[32] Theutberga, Hubert's sister, cast aside by Lothar, came over into Charles's protection. Charles granted her the convent of Avenay,[33] and committed the abbacy of St-Martin to Engilwin, a deacon of his palace.[34]

Robert count of Anjou fought against two companies of Northmen who were based on the Loire. Of one, he slew every man, except for a few who got away; the other larger group attacked from behind, and Robert was wounded, and having lost a few of his men, he decided to withdraw. But after a few days he recovered.

865

King Charles celebrated Christmas in the palace of Quierzy. Then he moved to the *villa* of Ver, and about the middle of February at the *villa* of Douzy he received with due ceremony his brother Louis who came bringing his sons.[1] There when they had considered matters with the faithful subjects of both together, they sent Bishops Altfrid [of Hildesheim] and Erchanraus [of Châlons] on a mission to their

31 Originally denoting the resident papal ambassador at Constantinople, this title was given in the ninth century to a senior papal envoy. In 881, in the *De Ordine Palatii*, cc. 19, 20, Hincmar alleged that the title was also used for the senior cleric at the Carolingian court; Löwe 1972 shows this claim was wishful thinking.

32 For Hubert's earlier career, above 860: 92-3; 862: 98; and for his brief tenure of the abbacy of Lobbes, Dierkens 1987: 109. According to *AX* 864: 23, he was killed 'by the sons of Conrad', meaning Conrad the Younger and Hugh, above 858, n. 15, and above n. 13. See also Borgolte 1987: 258-9, 290-1.

33 Above 860: 93. Theutberga's whereabouts between 860 and 864 are uncertain. Avenay (dep. Marne) near Rheims was a convent used to endow Carolingian princesses; Hyam 1990: 163 and n. 67.

34 St-Martin, Tours, had been vacated by Hubert's death. The appointment of the palatine clerk Engilwin (perhaps son of the Engilwin above 59, n. 20) showed Charles's determination to keep control of this important house. Engilwin became bishop of Paris in 871.

1 See the capitulary-record in *MGH Capit.* II, no. 244, p. 165. A future partition of the Middle Kingdom was probably discussed. *AF* 864: 62 reveal that a formal pact was agreed, and that its guarantors on Charles's behalf were Engelram and Hincmar himself. Hincmar says nothing about this in the *AB*.

nephew Lothar, who kept saying often that he was going to go to Rome. Charles and Louis ordered him first to follow their and the pope's urgent pleas and to make good the wrongs he had committed against divine and human laws in the Church he had scandalised by his reckless behaviour: then, they said, when he had set his kingdom in order, he might if he wished hasten to the threshold of the apostles to seek and obtain forgiveness. But Lothar suspected them of wanting to take away his kingdom from him and divide it between themselves. So he sent his uncle Liutfrid[2] to his brother the emperor of Italy, asking him to get the pope to send letters to his uncles on his behalf so that they would keep the peace so far as his kingdom was concerned and not harm his interests in any way. The Emperor Louis got the pope to do this.

Meanwhile, Northmen based on the Loire made their way up the river with a favourable wind, divine judgement thus making it easy for them, to launch a full-scale attack. They reached the monastery of St-Benedict known as Fleury and burned it. On their way back they burned Orléans and the monasteries both in the *civitas* and round it, except for the church of the Holy Cross which, despite great efforts on the part of the Northmen, the flames proved unable to consume. So they sailed back down the river and after ravaging all the neighbouring districts they returned to their base.

From Douzy, Louis made his way to Bavaria, brought his son Karlmann back on to completely friendly terms with him and returned the marches he had taken away from him. Then he returned to the palace at Frankfurt.

Charles came by way of Attigny to Senlis where he celebrated Lent and Easter [22 April]. Bernard, son of a certain Bernard and of Count Rorgo's daughter,[3] was sent into Gothia where Charles entrusted part of that march to him. Thus Charles came at length to the *villa* of Ver and received the bishops and other leading men of Aquitaine who had come to meet him there. At their insistent request Charles allowed his son Charles, though still not properly recovered,[4] to return to Aquitaine with the title and power of a king.

2 Above 862, n. 25.

3 Rorgo's daughter Blichild had probably married the *marchio* Bernard killed in Poitou in 844, above: 58 with n. 7. Hincmar here clearly distinguishes between their son Bernard *marchio* of Gothia, and Bernard 'son of the tyrant Bernard', above 864, n. 24.

4 For the Young Charles's injury, above 864: 112.

Pope Nicholas sent Arsenius bishop of Orte, his close adviser, with letters to the brothers Louis and Charles and also to the bishops and magnates of their kingdoms.[5] The letters contained the things that Lothar had requested, using his brother's influence. Nicholas sent these letters, not as popes had been accustomed to write to kings, to honour them, that is, with apostolic mildness and the usual signs of respect: rather, he sent them with malicious and interfering threats. Arsenius came, by way of Chur and Alemannia, to present the pope's letters to Louis king of Germany in the palace of Frankfurt, and from there he went to Lothar at Gondreville. To Lothar, and to the bishops and leading men of his realm, Arsenius handed over the pope's letters. These said that unless Lothar took back his wife Theutberga and put aside Waldrada, as soon as Arsenius had reported back, Nicholas would have to cast Lothar out from all Christian society, as a man whom the pope had often before, in many letters preceding these ones, warned would be excommunicated and ejected from the fellowship of Christians.[6]

Thus about the middle of July Arsenius came from Lothar to Charles at the palace of Attigny, and handed over with due formality letters exactly like the ones to Louis and Lothar. He also brought Rothad back with him and presented him to Charles. Rothad had been canonically deposed by the bishops of five provinces[7] and reinstated by Pope Nicholas, not according to the rules, but according to an arbitrary and overbearing decision. For the sacred canons say that, if a bishop, thrown out of his office by the bishops of his province, has recourse to Rome, the Roman bishop should write to the bishops of the surrounding and nearby province so that they themselves may look into the case with the utmost care and make their decision according to the faith of truth; and if he who has again been deposed by them sets the Roman bishop in action, let the Roman bishop either send from his side men who, having the authority of him who sent them, may judge along with the bishops, or let him trust the bishops to be adequate to

---

5 On Arsenius bishop of Orte (855-68), Schieffer 1980, and above 855, n. 4. For these papal letters, *MGH Epp.* VI, nos. 33, 38, pp. 301-3, 309-12, to Charles and Louis the German, no. 34, pp. 303-5, to the bishops asking them to warn Charles 'to keep out of the kingdom of the emperor's brother'. The *AB* say nothing of the Synod of Pavia (February 865) summoned by Emperor Louis II, which requested Nicholas to forgive the Lotharingian archbishops; Fuhrmann 1958: 4-6; Hartmann 1989: 284-5.

6 *MGH Epp.* IV, no. 35, p. 305.

7 Above 863: 100, n. 16. The fifth province was Bourges.

impose an end to the business.[8] The pope chose to adopt neither of these courses: instead, setting aside the judgement of the bishops who, following the sacred rules, after passing sentence reported the whole case to the apostolic see in chronological sequence, he himself restored Rothad by his own power alone. He therefore sent the restored Rothad to Charles with letters in which it was stated that, if anyone, without exception, refused Rothad anything pertaining either to the status or the property of his bishopric, he was to be anathema.[9] Thus without any seeking of information from the bishops who had deposed him or any consent on their part, Rothad was restored to his see through the legate Arsenius.

After all this, Arsenius made his way to Douzy to meet Lothar, bringing with him Theutberga who had for some time now been living with due honour in Charles's realm. After receiving an oath from twelve men swearing on Lothar's behalf,[10] Arsenius restored Theutberga to him in matrimony, although no ecclesiastical satisfaction was performed by Lothar, following the sacred canons, to atone for his public adultery. The oath taken before Theutberga on Lothar's behalf, as dictated and brought from Rome by Arsenius himself, went as follows:

'I, so-and-so, promise with an oath, by these four holy Gospels of Christ which I touch with my own hands, and by these relics of the saints, that my lord King Lothar, son of the late most serene Emperor Lothar of pious memory, now and henceforth will receive Theutberga his wife as his lawfully married lady, and shall hold her thus in every way, as it behoves a king to hold the queen his wife. And she shall have on account of the dissensions already mentioned, no harm either in life or in limb, either from my said lord Lothar, or from any man acting at his instigation or with his help or even

8 Hincmar here referred to canon 7 of the Council of Sardica (343), transmitted in the Dionysio–Hadriana Collection of canon law, *PL* 67, col. 178: this decreed that if a bishop thought himself unfairly treated in a provincial synod, he must complain direct to the pope, and his judges themselves must refer the case to Rome. Rothad had appealed to the archbishop of Trier. For Hincmar, it was vital to refute Trier's claims to superiority over Rheims: Fuhrmann 1972: 197-8; Devisse 1976: 588-9.

9 *MGH Epp.* IV, nos. 69, pp. 384-8 (to Charles); 70, pp. 389-91 (an extremely cold letter to Hincmar); no. 71, pp. 392-400 (to the bishops of Gaul). The partial translation of no. 71 in Baldwin 1970: 158-61 illustrates Nicholas's tone when dressing down Frankish bishops.

10 This legal procedure is widely attested in the early medieval West; Brunner 1928: 520-1. Hincmar had probably obtained a copy of this document from Bishops Isaac of Langres and Erchanraus of Châlons, below: 125.

with his consent. But he will treat her in such a way as it behoves a king to treat his lawful wife, on condition, however, that she from now on may so keep herself, as it behoves a wife to do, having regard to her lord's honour in all things.'

These are the names of those who took this oath: of the counts – Milo, Rathar, Erland, Theutmar, Werembald, Roculf; of the vassals Erlebald, Wulfrid, Eidulf, Bertmund, Nithard, Arnost.

This was sworn on the four Gospels of God, and on the most precious wood of the holy cross of our Lord, and on other relics of the saints, in the place called Vendresse, on the third day of August in the thirteenth indiction. This was done in the time of the triply blessed, coangelic and apostolic Nicholas, through the mediation and arrangements of the venerable Bishop Arsenius, envoy and *apocrisiarius* of the highest holy catholic and apostolic see, having apostolic authority and being the legate of that same Lord Nicholas the apostolic one.

The names of the bishops in whose presence the oaths were given are as follows: Arduic archbishop of Besançon, Remedius archbishop of Lyons, Ado archbishop of Vienne, Roland archbishop of Arles, Adventius bishop of Metz, Atto bishop of Verdun, Franco bishop of St-Lambert [Liège], Ratald [sic] bishop of Strasbourg, Fulcric the chaplain and imperial envoy. From the kingdom of Charles: Isaac bishop of Langres, and Erchanraus bishop of Châlons.[11] From the hands of these two bishops, acting on behalf of King Charles, Queen Theutberga was received by the venerable Bishop Arsenius, legate of the apostolic see, together with the above-named archbishops and bishops, and in the presence in that place of noble men from various kingdoms and with a multitude of the people, who saw and heard these oaths in public, but a complete list of whose names we have been unable to put down on this page.'

That same day, Bishop Arsenius, legate of the apostolic see, together with all the above-named archbishops and bishops, restored and gave

11 The presence of Archbishop Ado of Vienne (860-75) indicates papal and imperial pressure on Lothar II: Ado had close ties with Rome, and wide-ranging contacts throughout the Carolingian world; see Lupus Ep. 110, translated with comments by Dubois and Renaud 1984: xiii-xiv, n. 1. Of Charles's envoys, Bishop Isaac of Langres (859-80) was a protégé of Hincmar whose installation in this frontier see in 859 had signified Charles's political recovery; Bishop Erchanraus of Châlons (858-68) was a key figure at Charles's court and in the diplomacy of the 860s.

Queen Theutberga into the hands of King Lothar, not only on the oath
cited above, but also on pain of adjuration and excommunication in the
following terms: that if Lothar should not observe and fulfil in every
respect the conditions set out above, he would have to render account
not only in this present life but also at the eternal and terrible
Judgement of God to the Blessed Peter prince of the apostles, and
would be damned by him eternally in that Judgement and and
condemned to burn in perpetual fire.

Meanwhile Lothar sent his envoys to Charles, with the wish and
request that a friendship treaty be made between them and confirmed
on each side. This he obtained on the intervention of Queen
Ermentrude. Coming to Attigny, Lothar was received by Charles in
friendly fashion and with due honour, and welcomed into the alliance
he had sought. Arsenius also came back there, bringing a letter from
Pope Nicholas full of the most terrible curses, hitherto unheard-of in
the moderately-expressed statements of the holy see, on those who
some years before had looted and stolen a large quantity of treasure
from Arsenius, unless they found the means to restore what they had
taken from him, to make satisfaction. This letter was read out, and also
another about the excommunication of Engeltrude, who had abandoned her husband Boso and fled with an adulterer into Lothar's
realm.[12] Bishop Arsenius received back, under Charles's protection, the
villa called Vendeuvre which the Emperor Louis [the Pious] of pious
memory had handed over to St Peter but which a certain Count Guy
had held for some years.[13]

Then, having accomplished at Charles's court everything he had come
to him to do, Arsenius went on with Lothar to Gondreville. Theutberga had preceded him there. He stayed there too for a few days on
account of Waldrada, who was to be brought to him there and then
taken by him to Italy. He celebrated mass on the day of St Mary's
Assumption [15 August], with Lothar and Theutberga both attired in
royal splendour and wearing their crowns.[14] Then he left Gondreville

12 Above 863, n. 16.

13 Perhaps identifiable with one of Charles's closest counsellors of the 860s,
   though he was dead before 869, when Charles made arrangements for his
   liturgical commemoration (T. 325, and cf. T. 379, 441). Guy's *honores* had been
   in Burgundy; *MGH Capit.* II, no. 281, c. 31.

14 This ritual was a demonstration of Theutberga's recovered queenly dignity;
   Brühl 1962: 288-9. This may have been the occasion for the production, at the
   behest of 'Lothar king of the Franks', of the carved rock-crystal (now in the
   British Museum) depicting the biblical story of Susannah who was wrongly
   accused of adultery and subsequently vindicated.

with Waldrada and made for Orbe where, it was said, Louis emperor of Italy was to come to hold a meeting with Lothar. From there travelling through Alemannia and Bavaria to receive the patrimonies of the church of St-Peter in the surrounding regions, he returned to Rome.

From Attigny Charles marched to resist the Northmen who had sailed up the Seine with fifty ships. On this march, through the negligence of the guards, he lost three splendid crowns and some exceptionally fine armills and some other precious things. He found them all again after a few days, except for a few gems which had been lost in the turmoil and disruption.

The Northmen on the Loire made their way on foot to Poitiers without meeting any resistance, burned the *civitas* and returned to their ships unscathed. But Robert slew more than 500 of these Northmen based on the Loire, without losing any of his own men, and sent to Charles the standards and weapons captured from the Northmen.

Charles, for his part, came up to the place called Pîtres where Northmen still were. Now there were bridges over the Oise and the Marne at two places called Auvers and Charenton, but the local people who had built them long ago could not repair them because of the attacks of the Northmen. On the advice of his faithful men, Charles therefore ordered these bridges to be repaired by men drafted from more distant regions to perform labour services in order to complete the fortifications on the Seine, but on condition that this was treated as a special case of urgent need and that the men who would now repair these bridges should never at any future time suffer any disadvantage through performing labour services on this particular job.[15] Guards were assigned to keep watch on both banks of the Seine. Then in mid-September, Charles moved to the *villa* of Orville to do some hunting. But the guards still had not taken up their positions on this [i.e. the east] bank of the Seine, so those Northmen dispatched about 200 of their number to Paris to get wine. Failing to find what they sought there, they came back to their people who had sent them, without suffering any losses. More than 500 of them planned to advance from there beyond the Seine to sack Chartres, but they were attacked by the troops guarding the west bank of the Seine and after losing some men killed and some wounded, they retreated to their ships.

15 Cf. legislation at Pîtres in 864 (*MGH Capit.* II, no. 273, c. 27) imposing generalised obligations of fortress- and bridge-building; Nelson 1989b: 196-9. See also Gillmor 1989: 99-100.

Charles sent his son Louis into Neustria. He neither restored nor withheld his royal title, but he endowed him with only the county of Anjou, the abbacy of Marmoutier and some *villae*. To Robert, however, who had been *marchio* in Anjou, he gave the counties of Auxerre and Nevers, in addition to the other *honores* he held already.[16]

Louis king of the Germans welcomed home the army he had sent against the Wends and which had had a successful campaign. His son and namesake had betrothed himself to Adalard's daughter against his father's will, thereby greatly displeasing him.[17] Charles went to Cologne to meet his brother Louis and to talk with him. Amongst the other things they discussed, Charles managed to reconcile the father and son following the latter's presumptuous action, but on condition that he should no longer marry Adalard's daughter. Then Louis went back to Worms, and Charles to Quierzy. He received the news *en route* that on the 18 October, Northmen had got into the monastery of St-Denis, where they stayed for about twenty days, carrying off booty from the monastery to their ships each day, and after much plundering without encountering resistance from anyone at all, they returned to their camp not far from the monastery.[18]

Meanwhile Northmen on the Loire joined forces with Bretons and attacked Le Mans. They sacked it without opposition, and sent back to their ships. The Aquitanians fought with Northmen based on the Charente under their chief Sigfrid,[19] and slew about 400 of them: the rest fled back to their ships.

16 Angers had become the base of the Breton march since the grant of Nantes to Erispoë (above 851: 73); Werner 1980: 207, n. 95. For Robert's countship of Autun, see above 864: 119 and n. 24. His transfer from Neustria to Burgundy belies the view of Dhondt 1948, followed by James 1982: 175, that Charles the Bald pursued a deliberate strategy of creating territorial principalities. Conrad (II), previously count of Auxerre (above 858, n. 15), had transferred his interests to the Middle Kingdom in 864; Wollasch 1957a: 211-12.

17 Cf. *AF* 866, n. 1, though *AF* make no mention of this attempted marriage-alliance. Louis the Younger, like others, was exploiting the uncertain situation in the Middle Kingdom. Fried 1984: 10 points out that Charles the Bald was also threatened by his nephew's move. Adalard's lands lay near Trier. If, as is possible, he had no son (below 872, n. 3), then his daughter would have been a valuable heiress.

18 Vogel 1906: 214 and n. 2; Coupland 1987: 67. The Oissel Vikings were taking advantage of Charles's absence from his kingdom. Adalard and the others charged with the defence of this area in 861 (above: 96) had clearly failed: perhaps Adalard in angling for a marriage-alliance with Louis the Younger (see preceding note) already planned to return to the Middle Kingdom.

19 *AAng.* 486. Vogel 1906: 211.

Charles received at Compiègne the envoys he had sent to Mohammed at Cordoba the previous year. They came back with many gifts: camels carrying couches and canopies, fine cloth of various kinds and many perfumes. From Compiègne he went to the *villa* of Rouy. There he summoned Adalard, to whom he had entrusted the organisation of defence against the Northmen, and also his own close relatives Uto and Berengar.[20] Because these men had achieved nothing of any use at all against the Northmen, Charles deprived them of the *honores* he had bestowed on them and regranted those *honores* to various other people.

The Northmen who had sacked St-Denis became ill with various ailments. Some went mad, some were covered in sores, some discharged their guts with a watery flow through their arses: and so they died. After dispatching troops to keep guard against those Northmen, Charles returned to Senlis to celebrate Christmas. There he got the news that his son Abbot Lothar of St-Germain was dead.[21]

866

On 29 December a contingent of those Northmen who were based on the Loire broke out into Neustria to plunder. They attacked Counts Gauzfrid, Harvey and Rorgo who were coming up together against them.[1] In the fight Gauzfrid's brother Rorgo was killed, and the Northmen fled back to their ships having lost a great many of their men.

King Charles's uncle Rudolf died of a bile complaint.[2]

Northmen sailed up the Seine to the fort at Melun. Charles's squadrons advanced on both banks of the Seine, and the Northmen disembarked to attack what looked like the larger and stronger squadron, commanded by Robert and Odo.[3] The Northmen put them

20 Cf. *AF* 866, n. 3.

21 On 14 December. Lothar had become abbot of St-Germain, Auxerre in 863; above, 864, n. 13. In 866, Charles gave this abbacy to his son Carloman; Wollasch 1957a: 215, n. 148; 216.

1 Above 861, n. 8, and 863, n. 4.

2 On 6 January. He was the brother of Conrad, Judith and Emma. His career since 845 seems to have been spent in Charles the Bald's kingdom, where, according to his epitaph, he held the lay-abbacy of St-Riquier for thirty years, and was 'second to none among Charles's courtiers'; *MGH Poet. Lat.* III, nos. 91, 92, pp. 352-3.

3 Werner 1959b: 154 identifies Odo as the former count of Troyes, and Robert's long-time ally; above 858, n. 8, and 859, n. 8, who, though he never recovered

to flight even without a battle, and returned to their own people, their ships loaded with booty.

Charles made peace with those Northmen at the price of 4,000 lbs of silver, according to their scales. A levy was imposed throughout the realm to pay this tribute: 6 *denarii* were required from each free manse, 3 *denarii* from each servile one,[4] 1 *denarius* for each *accola*, and 1 *denarius* also for every two *hospitia*;[5] a tenth of the value of all the goods owned by traders; and a payment was also required from priests, according to what resources each had. The army tax[6] was also levied from all free Franks. Then 1 *denarius* was exacted from every manse, free and servile alike; and finally, in two stages, the taxes being raised by each of the magnates of the realm from his own *honores*, Charles collected the amount he had agreed to pay those Northmen, both in silver and in wine.[7] Furthermore, any slaves who had been carried off by the Northmen and escaped from them after the agreement was made were either handed back or ransomed at a price set by the Northmen; and if any one of the Northmen was killed, whatever price the Northmen demanded for him was paid.

Emperor Louis of Italy, together with his wife Engelberga, advanced to Benevento against the Saracens.[8] Lothar, acting, so some allege, at

the countship of Troyes, had become count of Mâcon, perhaps by 866. Alternatively, the Odo of the 866 annal is the brother-in-law of Louis the Stammerer: above 862, n. 13.

4 A *denarius* was worth one-twelfth of a *solidus*, and weighed approximately 1,3/ 4 g. of silver. As for its purchasing power: in the famine-year 794, Charlemagne decreed that 1*d* should buy twelve 2-lb wheaten loaves, *MGH Capit.* I, no. 28, c. 4, p. 74; in 864, the Edict of Pîtres mentioned sellers of bread and meat 'by pennyworths', *MGH Capit.* II, no. 273, c. 20, p. 319. In ninth-century West Francia, many peasants paid out between 8*d* and 18*d* in annual rent to their lords; Devroey 1985: 485; Spufford 1988: 47. A manse (*mansus*) was a fiscal unit, nominally a holding sufficient to support one peasant household, perhaps 20– 50 ha. in extent.

5 An *accola* was a smaller holding than a manse, a *hospitium* smaller still; Doehaerd 1971: 107.

6 The *heribann*, originally a fine of 60 *solidi* imposed on Franks who failed to obey a summons to the host, seems to have functioned in the ninth century as a regular payment in lieu of personal service from better-off free peasants.

7 Grierson 1990: 63, following Joranson 1923: 62-92 and Lot 1924: 76-8 takes this passage to mean that after a first set of taxes had failed to raise the amount required, a second levy was imposed, and then two further payments were required from the magnates. On my reading, only two levies were made, the magnates being responsible for collection in both cases, and the total value being reached by payments in cash or in wine.

8 The Benevento campaign was an important move of Louis II into southern Italy; Wickham 1981: 62.

the instance of his brother the Emperor Louis, took back the see of Cologne from Hugh, and handed it over, on receipt of a bribe, to Gunther's brother Hilduin.[9] But in reality the see's adminstration remained in Gunther's hands with the exception of the bishop's sacramental functions, and both the metropolis of Cologne and the church of Trier for a long time lacked pastors, which was against the sacred rules and involved great danger for many people.

Charles endowed Count Robert with the abbacy of St-Martin, which he had taken away from Engilwin; and on Robert's advice divided the *honores* beyond the Seine amongst Robert's accomplices. Bernard, son of Bernard, had hung on to the county of Autun to the exclusion of Robert. Now, on Robert's advice, Charles entrusted it to his own son Louis so that he could take charge of it.[10]

In June the Northmen moved from the island near the monastery of St-Denis and sailed down the Seine until they reached a place suitable for making repairs to their ships and for building new ones, and there they awaited the payment of the sum due to them. Charles marched to the place called Pîtres with workmen and carts to complete the fortifications, so that the Northmen might never again be able to get up the Seine beyond that point.

Louis king of Germany moved his army against some of his people in the Wendish march who were plotting rebellion.[11] He forestalled this quickly, suppressed those responsible without fighting a battle, and told the army, which had not yet been fully mobilised, to stay at home.

In July the Northmen reached the sea. One group of them returned for a while to the Ijssel district and enjoyed everything they wanted, except that they did not manage to make an open alliance with

9 For Hugh, see above 864, n. 13; for Hilduin, above 864, n. 7.

10 Werner 1959b points out that this distribution of *honores* beyond the Seine to Robert's clients turned out to have long-term importance for 'Robertine' control of Neustria. Hincmar seems to be referring to the lands of St-Martin, Tours: hence the pejorative term 'accomplices'. The reference here to the county of Autun illuminates the statement above 864: 119 about the transfer of 'Bernard's *honores*' to Robert. Having gauged the strength of Bernard's hold on Autun, Robert preferred to concentrate on Neustria. Though *AB* do not say so, it seems likely that the county of Angers was now returned to Robert and relinquished by Louis the Stammerer, above 865, n. 16. Robert's recommendation that Autun be assigned to Louis thus seems entirely self-interested. I can see no justification for the claim of L/G: 126-7, n. 3, that the assigning of Autun to Louis made it 'a consecrated territory' and thus 'obliged Bernard to renounce it'.

11 *AF* 866, and n. 2.

Lothar.[12]

Charles went with his wife to a *villa* of the abbey of St-Quentin called
La Vignole, to meet Lothar. In return for certain mutually convenient
arrangements agreed between them, so it was said, Charles received
from Lothar the grant of the abbacy of St- Vaast.[13]

In August Charles went to Soissons, and participated in the synod
summoned on Pope Nicholas's orders. At this synod, following the
pope's recommendation, it was decided to defer the question of Wulfad
and his colleagues who had been ordained by Ebbo, the former
archbishop of Rheims, after his deposition.[14] For out of reverence for
the pope and respect for the sacred rules, those rules could not be
openly overturned; and if the king and others made too great efforts
to favour Wulfad's cause, schism and scandal could not otherwise be
avoided. The decision given according to the rules by a synod of the
bishops of five provinces concerning the removal of Wulfad and the
others had been confirmed by the subscriptions of Pope Benedict and
Pope Nicholas. It was therefore decided that Wulfad and the rest
might be received as validly ordained, following the precedents of the
indulgence of the Nicene Council concerning those ordained by the
condemned Meletius, and also the tradition of the African Council
concerning the Donatists,[15] only on condition that Pope Nicholas
should be willing to alter his sentence which he himself had confirmed.

12 The Ijssel district is in Frisia. Apparently these Northmen wanted to be
   granted land in Frisia, as previous groups had been; above 841, n. 8; 850, n. 5. ﹅
13 Cf. above 843, n. 5. Lothar II's grant reveals the difficulties of his position.
   Nicholas I complained, *MGH Epp.* VI, no. 48, pp. 329-32, about this 'nefarious
   pact to ruin Theutberga'.
14 See above 853, n. 5. Hincmar's personal interest is clear: if Ebbo's consecrations performed after his deposition were valid, this called in question
   Hincmar's own position at Rheims; Devisse 1976: 603-8. Wulfad can perhaps
   be identified with the former chancellor of Pippin II of Aquitaine; if so, Wulfad
   presumably abandoned Pippin in 848 or 849. He was a favoured palace clerk of
   Charles the Bald from the early 850s, and served as tutor to Charles's third son
   Carloman. For Wulfad's intellectual milieu, see Marenbon 1981. The Synod of
   Soissons was attended by seven archbishops and twenty-eight bishops:
   Charles, determined to resolve the problem of Ebbo's clerks, concerted plans
   with the pope behind Hincmar's back; Mansi XV, cols. 707-9; Devisse 1976:
   602-15.
15 Bishop Meletius was condemned by the Council of Nicaea (324), but the
   consecrations he had performed were accepted; Chadwick 1967: 124, 131. 'The
   African Council' was Hincmar's usual way of referring to the Council of
   Carthage in 418; for the relevant decree, see Dionysio-Hadriana, *PL* 67, cols.
   200-1, asserting that those baptised as infants by Donatist heretics could
   validly be ordained as clerics.

Thus the synod assembled by Archbishop Eogil of Sens sent letters to Pope Nicholas setting out the terms just outlined as well as other matters it had met to consider; and it then broke up without any conflict arising among the bishops.[16] Now according to the decrees of Pope Innocent, what the urgent need of some particular time has once discovered should, when that need has ceased, 'itself cease, and this just as plainly as it was urgently needed before; because the lawful ordering of the world is one thing, quite another the usurpation which a particular time impels to come into existence for the present only'.[17] Thus what was now being sought most urgently was nothing other than some way by which Wulfad could be made a bishop; and it seemed to some people more tolerable, for the sake of avoiding dissension, to put this urgent matter again on the agenda, since it was as pressing now as it had been before, than to arouse uproar in the church and in the sphere of royal power. The situation was like that of Paul carrying out the ritual practices of the Law, following the opinion of James and the elders of Jerusalem in having Timothy circumcised, even after the Law had been abolished.[18] When things had been arranged in this way, Charles, acting entirely on his own decision before the case had been settled, now entrusted the archdiocese of Bourges to Wulfad, since the former archbishop, Rodulf, had recently died.[19]

Before the bishops left Soissons, Charles asked them to give his wife Ermentrude consecration as queen. Charles himself witnessed their performance of the rite in the church of St-Médard, and joined with

16 Eigil, a former abbot of Prüm with many contacts in the Middle Kingdom, came west in 861. Charles first gave him the abbacy of Flavigny (dep. Côte-d'Or), then appointed him Wenilo's successor at Sens in 865. Hincmar briefed him carefully to speak on his behalf to Pope Nicholas during this mission to Rome, and also entrusted him with a letter of his own to the pope. For the letter of the Synod of Soissons, see Mansi XV, col. 728; Hincmar's letters to Eigil and to Nicholas, *MGH Epp.* VIII, nos. 185-8 (cf. Introduction: 10.) Nicholas replied with sharp rebukes to the bishops, and to Hincmar; *MGH Epp.* VI, nos. 79, 80, pp. 414-22, 422-31. Cf. below 867, n. 3. Nicholas ordered that Ebbo's clerks be reinstated in a year's time if no real charge could be brought against them.

17 Innocent I, Ep. 17, *PL* 20, col. 532. Hincmar cites from Dionysio–Hadriana, *PL* 67, col. 260.

18 The reference is to Acts 15-16. Controversy arose in the early Christian community at Jerusalem over whether gentile converts had to be circumcised. Paul decided to circumcise Timothy in order to accommodate the views of the Jewish brethren: a good precedent for political compromise.

19 On 16 or 17 July. For Rodulf's career in Aquitaine, see Martindale 1990b: 30-42. Bourges was increasingly important to Charles's control of Aquitaine in the late 860s.

them to put the crown on her head.[20]

From Soissons, Charles went with the queen to the palace of Attigny to meet Lothar. To Attigny also they summoned back Theutberga, Lothar's queen but in name only, who had had permission to go to Rome. They decided on a joint embassy to entrust to Pope Nicholas things which they believed needed to be treated in strictest confidence: Charles's envoy was Archbishop Eigil of Sens, while Lothar sent Archbishop Ado of Vienne and Walter,[21] his closest adviser. After this, Charles dispatched his son Carloman, abbot of St-Médard,[22] to arrange the handing over of the archbishopric of Bourges to Wulfad. The synod had been dissolved, as stated above, and letters had been sent from it to Pope Nicholas, with Archbishop Eigil as carrier, when Carloman and Wulfad reached Bourges in September. Some bishops, less well versed than they should have been in ecclesiastical law, were immediately won over by Wulfad's faction and swayed by the threats of Carloman, acting on his father's authority: by these bishops Wulfad, contrary to all the laws of the church, was clothed as it were with a vestment of malediction instead of with the ordination of a bishop. Aldo bishop of Limoges, acting as one who 'dis-ordered' Wulfad rather than conferred orders on him, was stricken with illness during the very consecration-rite itself and died soon afterwards.[23]

Charles's son the Young Charles, king of the Aquitanians, had had his brain disturbed by the blow on the head he had received a few years before.[24] He suffered from epileptic fits for a long time, and then on 29 September he died at a *villa* near Buzençais. He was buried by his brother Carloman and by Wulfad in the church of St-Sulpice at Bourges. William, Charles's cousin, and son of the late Count Odo of Orléans, was taken prisoner in Burgundy by some of Charles's men. Charles had him beheaded as a traitor near Senlis.[25]

20 This consecration took place on 25 August. The *Ordo* composed by Hincmar shows that the recent death or disability of four of Charles's sons had made the queen's fertility again a matter of concern; Hyam 1990: 159.

21 Ado of Vienne, above 865, n. 11; Walter, above 862, n. 25.

22 For Carloman, above 854, n. 1 and for Wulfad as his tutor, above 866, n. 14. Wulfad had been abbot of St-Médard in the 850s. Carloman received the abbacy in 863.

23 Werner 1966: 435-6 suggests that Aldo was a kinsman of Wulfad. For Hincmar's attitude, see above 866, n. 14.

24 Above 864: 112.

25 William may have supported the rebellion of Bernard son of Bernard in Autun, above 866, n. 10, but 'treason' implies that he sollicited intervention from the Middle Kingdom. There is no other information on William's career. Though

Northmen, about 400 of them, allied with the Bretons, came up from the Loire with their horses, attacked Le Mans and sacked it. On their way back they got as far as Brissarthe where they came on Robert and Ranulf, and also Counts Gauzfrid and Harvey, with a strong force of warriors – had God been with them. Battle was joined, Robert was killed and Ranulf fled, stricken by a wound from which he later died. When Harvey too had been wounded and some others killed, the rest retreated to wherever their own lands were.[26] Ranulf and Robert had refused to accept punishment for their previous misdeeds in assuming, one the abbacy of St-Hilary, the other that of St-Martin, contrary to the rules, for they were laymen: so they deserved to suffer the retribution that befell them.[27]

Louis, son of King Louis of Germany, started a rebellion against his father. He was egged on by Werinhar and others, whom his father had deprived of their *honores* because of their disloyalty.[28] Young Louis also roused Rastiz the Wend to come plundering right up to Bavaria, so that while his father and his faithful men were fully engaged in that region, he himself might be freer to continue with what he had begun. But Karlmann, to whom his father had granted that march, took energetic measures to push Rastiz back within his own borders. The elder Louis, with the wisdom born of long experience in such situations, marched rapidly to the palace at Frankfurt where after an exchange of oaths he summoned Young Louis to come to him and they exchanged promises on oath to wait till 28 October. The elder Louis therefore went back with all the speed he could muster to strengthen his march against Rastiz, intending to return to meet his brother Charles and his nephew Lothar near Metz on the eighth day before Martinmas [3 November]. Charles let his men know that he was

Odo of Orléans had been Queen Ermentrude's father, above 834, n. 9 and 842, n. 12, Hincmar here identifies William not as Charles the Bald's brother-in-law but as his cousin. Levillain 1938: 31-44 worked out the genealogical link, without drawing attention to the fact that Charles and Ermentrude must have been related in the fourth degree. No contemporary mentions this.

26 The fight at Brissarthe happened on 15 September. Robert's death is mentioned by *AX* and *AF* (both s.a. 867), presumably because of his origin and connections in Franconia. Regino 867 gives further details of the fight. For Ranulf, see above 864, n. 23; for Gauzfrid, above 861, n. 9; Harvey, above 863, n. 5. Lot 1970a (1902): 427-33 treats Brissarthe as a mere skirmish; but it is symptomatic of the scale of much ninth-century warfare. Cf. France 1985: 92-4; Gillmor 1988: 91-2, 106-9.

27 Ranulf had held St-Hilary, Poitiers; Robert held St-Martin, Tours. Hincmar strongly disapproved of lay-abbacies.

28 *AF* 866, nn. 1-3.

going to Metz prepared for war, with as large an army as he could raise just then; it was composed mostly of the bishops' contingents.[29]

At the same time Charles granted the counties of Tours and Anjou, along with the abbacy of St-Martin and other abbacies to the cleric Hugh, son of his uncle Conrad, and dispatched him to Neustria in Robert's place.[30] Charles kept for himself the chief *villa*, and the other most choice ones, belonging to the abbey of St-Vaast, as he had done before in the case of St- Quentin, and divided all the rest among some of his men, with more detriment to his own soul than any benefit to them.[31]

Thus continuing on the campaigning-route he had announced, taking his wife along with him, he advanced by way of Rheims to the Metz district and reached Verdun. There he met envoys from his brother Louis, who brought the message that he had no need for any reason whatsoever to bring an army with him when he came to meet his brother, since Louis had received his own son's submission on terms which he, the father, had laid down, and the rebellion that had been stirred up against him had now been completely suppressed. Louis added that it was not feasible for him to come all the way to Metz at that time to meet Charles, because he was hastening away to Bavaria on urgent matters affecting the realm. Charles then stayed at Verdun for about twenty days, and ravaged the city and its neighbourhood in the way an enemy force would do. At this point he got word that Lothar was coming. Lothar had been at Trier along with the bishops of his realm trying hard to get Theutberga to incriminate herself again on a false charge and to take the veil; but he could not make her do so. In the end Charles made his way back to Rheims by the same route he had gone on, while his men ravaged everywhere they passed through.[32] From Rheims he went to Compiègne, where he celebrated Christmas.

The previous year, inspired by God and taking as a warning the portents and afflictions that befell the people of his realm, the king of the Bulgars had thought carefully about becoming a Christian, and had

29 This was a winter expedition: Charles relied on the church's military service, especially for such campaigns; Nelson 1986a (1983b). Louis the Younger's revolt gave Charles a pretext to move eastwards into the Middle Kingdom.

30 For Hugh, see above 864, n. 13, and 866: 131.

31 Above 866, n. 13. Charles may have been lay abbot of St-Vaast (see below 867: 140) and St-Quentin for the rest of his reign.

32 Throughout this passage, Hincmar's tone is implicitly very critical of Charles. The reasons for this attitude in 866 are hinted at above 866: 132 and n. 14; Nelson 1990b: 37.

been baptised.[33] But his leading men were very angry and stirred up his people against him, aiming to kill him. All the warriors there were in all the ten counties of that realm came and surrounded the king's palace. But he invoked Christ's name and came forth against that whole multitude with only forty-eight men who, burning with zeal for the Christian faith, stayed loyal to him. As soon as the king came out from the city gates, there appeared to him and his companions seven clerics, each holding a burning candle in his hand, who thus advanced ahead of the king and his men. Now to the rebels it seemed that a great flaming mansion was falling on them, and the horses of the king's men, so it seemed to their opponents, advanced walking on their hind legs and struck them down with their front hooves. Such great terror gripped the rebels that they could not get themselves ready either to flee or to fight, but flung themselves on the ground unable to move. The king killed fifty-two of the leading men who had been most active in stirring the people up against him, but he let the rest of the people go away unharmed. Sending messengers to Louis king of Germany who was bound to him by a peace treaty, he requested a bishop and priests, and he received with due reverence those whom Louis dispatched.[34] Louis also sent to ask his brother Charles for sacred vessels, and sacred vestments and books to help those priests in their ministry. On receipt of this request, Charles received from the bishops of his realm a large sum, and dispatched it to Louis to be sent on to the king.

The king of the Bulgars dispatched his son and many of the leading men of his realm to Rome, and he sent to St Peter, along with other gifts, the armour he had been wearing when in Christ's name he triumphed over his enemies. He also sent a number of questions concerning the sacraments of the faith to Pope Nicholas to get his ruling on them, and he asked for bishops and priests to be sent him from the pope.[35] All these requests were met. But Louis emperor of

33 For Boris's earlier dealings with Louis the German, above 864: 118, and n. 20. Now accepting Christianity from Byzantium, he took the baptismal name Michael; Vlasto 1970: 159. This whole passage seems to have been added to the 866 annal as an afterthought.

34 *AF* 867 and n. 1.

35 Boris's request to Nicholas I was a move to maintain his freedom of manoeuvre *vis-à-vis* the Byzantine emperor and also Louis the German: both were interested in converting the Bulgars; Obolensky 1966: 498-9; Vlasto 1970: 159-61. For Nicholas's *responsa* to the Bulgars, *MGH Epp.* VI, no. 99, pp. 568-600, see Sullivan 1955: 92-5. Boris eventually accepted Greek missionaries and the authority of the patriarch of Constantinople, however.

Italy, on hearing of all this, sent to Pope Nicholas with orders that the weapons and other things which the king of the Bulgars had sent to St Peter should be redirected to him. Some of these things Pope Nicholas did send on to him, using Arsenius as his envoy, while Louis was still in the Benevento area; but the pope sent excuses about the others.

867

Louis abbot of St-Denis, grandson of the Emperor Charles through his eldest daughter Rotrude, died on 9 January.[1] King Charles retained the abbacy of that monastery for himself, making arrangements for the monastery's administration and working of its lands to be handled on his behalf by a provost, a dean and a treasurer, while a mayor of the household took responsibility for its military contingent.

About the middle of Lent [c. 6 March], he went to the *villa* of Pouilly on the Loire; there he summoned the leading men of Aquitaine to meet him, and he set his son Louis over those Aquitanians as king, assigning him household officers from his own palace.[2] He returned from Pouilly to spend Easter [30 March] at St-Denis. Then he proceeded to Metz to hold discussions with his brother Louis king of Germany.

On 20 May, at the palace of Samoussy, he received Archbishop Eigil of Sens with letters from Pope Nicholas concerning the reinstatements of the clerics of the church of Rheims, that is, Wulfad and his colleagues. Nicholas was making such strenuous efforts for them to be treated as reinstated in their clerical grades that he attributed in those letters many things to Archbishop Hincmar of Rheims which by obvious common sense were known to be untrue.[3] Archbishop Eigil also brought to the lord Charles letters from Pope Nicholas to Lothar and the bishops of his realm concerning the case of his wives, namely Theutberga and Waldrada; Eigil transmitted the pope's command that

1 Above 858, n. 5.

2 Louis's Aquitanian sub-kingdom was evidently to be under Charles's control. Letters of Nicholas I to Aquitanian nobles (*MGH Epp.* VI, nos. 40 (865), 43 (866), pp. 314, 317-18) threatening excommunication for expropriators of church lands reveal Charles's influence. Martindale 1990a: 126-32 argues that royal power in Aquitaine grew weaker as Charles's reign went on. For a different view, see Nelson 1992 ch. 8.

3 Nicholas's rebuke to Hincmar, above 866, n. 16, accusing him of mishandling evidence and misinterpreting canon law, reached Rheims in May 867. Hincmar rebutted the charges in *MGH Epp.* VIII, nos. 198, 199. In 867, Hincmar came to terms with the *fait accompli* of Wulfad's installation at Bourges; Devisse 1976: 625, n. 389.

Waldrada be sent to Rome.[4] On the pope's behalf, Charles gave these letters to Lothar when he came to meet him at the palace of Attigny; from there Charles went on to a meeting with his brother,[5] and having left him, returned home, on the way visiting Lothar again in the forest of the Ardennes.

He announced a general summoning of the host throughout his whole realm, and gave notice that his assembly would be on 1 August at Chartres, from where he would advance into Brittany to subdue the Breton chief Salomon.[6] Meanwhile envoys went to and fro between them until they managed to make peace terms on condition that, after Charles had given hostages, Salomon's son-in-law Pascwethen, on whose advice he relied heavily, should come to Charles at Compiègne around 1 August, and both parties thereafter should stick to whatever was then settled and confirmed there, but that the people who had been summoned to the host should meanwhile stay at home in a state of readiness and, if it proved necessary and the king required it, they should come to Chartres on 25 August prepared to go on campaign.

Louis king of Germany sent his son Louis to campaign with the Saxons and Thuringians against the Obodrites. He ordered the rest of the people in his realm to stand in readiness so that, as soon as he might give the command, being already prepared, they would be able to attack rapidly.

Lothar was suspicious of Charles, so he went to Frankfurt to see Louis on his return from Metz, and reconciled himself with the man who had previously been quite hostile to him. To Hugh, his son by Waldrada, he gave the duchy of Alsace and commended him to Louis.[7] He also committed the rest of his realm to Louis, on the grounds that he was about to go to Rome and would send Waldrada on there ahead of him. Returning from Frankfurt, he summoned up the host throughout his realm to the defence of the fatherland, as he explained, against the Northmen, for he expected that Roric, whom the local people (the new name for them is Cokings) had driven out of Frisia, would return

4 *MGH Epp.* VI, nos. 46, pp. 322-5 (to Lothar), 47, pp. 325-8 (to the bishops).
5 At Metz, below: 139.
6 The Bretons had allied with Northmen to attack Le Mans in 866, above: 135. Note that in 867, Charles's giving of hostages guaranteed Pascwethen's safe conduct to Compiègne. Hincmar took part in the military preparations on Charles's side; *MGH Epp.* VIII, no. 198, p. 206. Devisse 1976: 619, n. 342 suggests that the shortness of the 867 annal betrays Hincmar's lack of time.
7 Hugh's date of birth is unknown, but may have been in 855. Lothar had granted Alsace to Louis the German in 860, above: 93 and n. 6.

bringing some Danes to help him.[8]

Charles, having given hostages, received Salomon's envoy Pascwethen at Compiègne on 1 August. He granted to Pascwethen, in his capacity as Salomon's representative, the county of Coutances with all the fiscal lands, royal *villae* and abbeys therein and properties wheresoever pertaining to it, except for the bishopric; and Charles confirmed this with a solemn oath sworn by all his leading men. In return, he received from Salomon's representative acting on his behalf a solemn oath of fidelity and peace and guaranteed help against his enemies, on the condition that Salomon and his son should hold this grant along with those he held previously and should show themselves faithful men to Charles and his son.[9] When this arrangement had been settled, Charles, acting on Pope Nicholas's authority, gave notice of a synod to be held at Troyes on 25 October. He made arrangements to do some hunting and spend autumn at St-Vaast and then stay at the *villa* of Orville and its neighbourhood.[10]

A synod of the provinces of Rheims, Rouen, Tours, Sens, Bordeaux and Bourges assembled at Troyes on 25 October. There certain bishops, as usual supporting Wulfad to curry favour with King Charles, started working against Hincmar, thereby acting against the truth and the sacred authority of the canons. But Hincmar opposed their efforts with reason and authority, the majority decision prevailed, and those bishops who had assembled there sent to Pope Nicholas by common consent a letter in which were listed all the events around which the case turned. Bishop Actard of Nantes was to take the letter to Rome.[11]

The gist of the letter was the same as that of the letter of Bishop Hincmar of Rheims which he had sent to Rome the previous July, using as carriers clerics of his disguised as pilgrims to avoid the snares set by his enemies. Actard received the letter drawn up in the Synod

8 For Roric's previous career, above 850, n. 5 and 863, n. 1. See also Wood 1987: 44. The Cokings have been taken to be inhabitants of Tokingen (Oostergoos) in the Netherlands, or alternatively the followers of a chieftain named Kok.

9 For these negotiations see Smith 1992. Charles's concessions were partly offset by his retention of control of the see of Coutances. Salomon remained loyal to Charles thereafter.

10 This *villa* was probably Orville on the Oise, near Quierzy; see below 877, n. 18.

11 The synodal letter of Troyes, Mansi XV: 791-6. The synod marked a compromise, accepting Wulfad's consecration but still (thanks to Hincmar's influence) registering problems over Ebbo's clerks. Actard, bishop of Nantes since 843, was to be high in royal favour for the rest of Charles's reign.

at Troyes and signed with the seals of the archbishops present there,
and which he was now to carry. Then along with certain bishops, he
went back to Charles, as Charles himself had ordered. Charles forgot
the fidelity and all the labours which, for his honour and for the secure
holding of his realm, the oft-mentioned Hincmar had undertaken for so
many years: he ordered Actard to hand over the letter, broke the
archbishops' seals, and read all that had been done at the synod.
Because Hincmar had not ended up by being silenced at that synod, as
Charles had wished, the king had a letter written to Pope Nicholas at
his dictation and in his name in opposition to Hincmar and he sealed
this letter with the *bulla* bearing his own name and sent it to Rome
along with the synodal letter by the same carrier, Actard.[12]

Now Hincmar's clerics mentioned above had arrived in Rome in
August, and found Pope Nicholas very ill, and greatly harrassed and
preoccupied by the dispute he was carrying on against Michael and
Basil, the Emperors of the Greeks, and against the eastern bishops.[13]
The clerics therefore stayed at Rome until October, when Pope
Nicholas received agreeably what Hincmar had written and wrote
back to say that he would be given satisfaction on every point.[14] He
also sent another letter to Hincmar and to the other archbishops and
bishops holding office in Charles's realm, informing then that the
Emperors of the Greeks and also the eastern bishops were laying false
charges against the holy Roman Church, indeed against the whole
Church that uses the Latin language. These were their accusations:
that we fast on Saturdays; that we say the Holy Spirit proceeds 'from
the father and from the son' [*filioque*]; that we forbid priests to have
wives; that we forbid priests to anoint with chrism the foreheads of the
baptised. Those Greeks also say that we Latins make chrism from
river-water; and they blame us Latins for not abstaining, as is their
custom, from eating meat during the eight weeks before Easter and
from eating cheese and eggs for seven of those eight weeks. They
allege further that at Easter, in Jewish fashion, we bless and offer a
sheep on the altar, along with the Lord's body. They are also enraged

12 Hincmar's allegation that Charles broke the seals of the archbishop's letters is
   almost certainly false; Devisse 1976: 627. For Charles's own use of sealed
   letters, Tessier 1955: 35-7.

13 Above 864, n. 30. In the summer of 867, the Greek clergy responded to
   Nicholas's deposition of Photius by declaring Nicholas deposed; Dvornik 1966:
   453. Basil had become co-emperor in 866.

14 Nicholas's final *rapprochement* with Hincmar was prompted by the need to rally
   the western Church. See next note.

against us because with us, clerics shave their beards; and they claim
that with us, a deacon can be ordained a bishop without having
received the office of priesthood.[15] On all these matters, the pope
ordered written replies to be sent to him from the metropolitans and
their fellow-bishops throughout every province in turn, and at the end
of his letter he addressed Hincmar as follows:

> Let Your Charity, brother Hincmar, once you have read this letter,
> make the utmost efforts to ensure that it is also taken to the other
> archbishops who hold office in the realm of our son the glorious
> King Charles; and fail not to urge them, each in his own diocese
> along with his suffragans in whoever's realm they are situated, to
> deal with these matters in a suitable manner; and take care to
> inform us of what they have discovered so that you may stand out
> as a strenuous doer of all the things contained in the frame of this
> present letter of ours, and also that you may be found in our sight
> a truthful and wise informant in all you write to us. Given on 25
> October in the first Indiction.

Hincmar received this letter on 13 December in the first Indiction. He
read it out to King Charles and many bishops in the palace of Corbeny,
and he made efforts to ensure that it was sent around to the other
archbishops, as he had been instructed to do in the papal mandate.

Pope Nicholas had died on 13 November. Pope Hadrian succeeded him
in his pontificate, by the election of the clergy and by the consent of
the Emperor Louis.[16] When Actard reached Rome with the letters
mentioned above, he found Hadrian already ordained in the apostolic
see. Now Arsenius, a man of great cunning and excessive greed, caused
Theutgaud and Gunther to come to Rome, deceiving them with false
hopes of their restitution, in order to extract money from them. They
stayed in Rome for a long time, and lost nearly all their supporters. In
the end Theutgaud died there, and Gunther nearly died too.

Lothar sent his wife Theutberga to Rome, so that she would

---

15 *MGH Epp.* VI, no. 100, pp. 600-9. Nicholas's letter marked an important stage
   in the alienation of the western from the eastern Church. Note that linguistic
   difference is taken to identify distinct churches. The addition of the phrase 'and
   from the Son' (*Filioque*) to the Latin Creed in Charlemagne's Francia (though
   not in Rome) had already aroused theological objections from the Greeks. For
   this and other charges against the Latins, Nicol 1967; Vlasto 1970: 161-2.

16 Hadrian II, consecrated on 14 December 867, was to prove more susceptible
   than Nicholas to the influence of the imperial court. For the role of Arsenius
   and Anastasius in this pontificate, see Devos 1967.

incriminate herself and he would then be able to be released from his marriage with her. But Pope Hadrian and the Romans did not believe such ludicrous tales, and she was ordered to return to her husband. Charles, with the consent of his brother Louis, ordered certain bishops to assemble at Auxerre at the beginning of February following, to deal with certain aspects of the Lothar case.

Then Charles, after receiving, so some people said, large bribes from Egfrid, who already held the abbacy of St-Hilary and many other rich benefices,[17] took away the county of Bourges from Count Gerald, in his absence and without making any allegation against him, and granted it to Egfrid instead.[18] But Egfrid was unable to make good his claim to the county at Gerald's expense. Charles therefore moved to Troyes, by way of Rheims, and from there reached Auxerre where he spent Christmas.

868

From Auxerre Charles went to the *villa* of Pouilly on the Loire. Meanwhile Count Gerald's men attacked Egfrid at a certain *villa*. Egfrid refused to emerge from the strongly-fortified house in which he had shut himself up; so they set fire to it and drove Egfrid out, chopped off his head and threw his body into the flames. Then Charles moved into Berry declaring that he would avenge this outrage. There so many evil deeds were done – churches broken into, poor folk oppressed, crimes of all kinds committed, and the land laid waste – that there are too many to list here: as is proved by the fact that many thousands of people died of hunger because of that devastation. But not only was no vengeance taken on Gerald and his companions, but no one even drove them out of Berry.

Those of Robert's *honores* which Charles had granted to his son after his father's death were now taken away and distributed among other

17 For Egfrid, see above 864, n. 26. He may have been a kinsman and/or client of Count Ranulf of Poitiers, above 866: 135, whom he succeeded in the lay abbacy of St-Hilary, Poitiers. Egfrid may have been the guardian of Ranulf's young sons; Werner 1959b: 167, n. 86.

18 L/G: 140, n. 5 cite no evidence for the suggestion that Gerald was the brother of Stephen son of Hugh (above 862, n. 12). Count Gerald of Bourges can be traced in a number of charters from that region, from 855 into the 860s; Wollasch 1959: 24, n. 27. He is certainly to be distinguished from Count Gerald of Vienne, below 870: 172. The history of Berry in this period is obscure; but note a serious Viking attack on Bourges in 867; Annals of Massay, *MGH SS* III, p. 169. Hincmar does not mention this in the *AB*.

men.[1] The sons of Ranulf also had their father's *honores* taken away from them;[2] and the abbacy of St-Hilary, which Ranulf had held, was granted to Archbishop Frotar of Bordeaux.[3] Charles then went back to St-Denis on Ash Wednesday [3 March], and from there proceeded to Senlis. Northmen sailed up the Loire, reached Orléans and having accepted a ransom, returned to their base unscathed.[4]

On the Saturday before Palm Sunday [10 April] Charles returned to St-Denis and celebrated Easter [18 April] there. Before returning from there to Senlis, on the second day of the Rogations [4 June], he received letters from Pope Hadrian brought by Adventius bishop of Metz and Grimland, Lothar's chancellor.[5] One of the letters was addressed to Charles: in it the pope commanded him to do no harm to the kingdom of the Emperor Louis nor to the kingdom of Lothar. The other letter, about Waldrada's absolution, was addressed to the bishops of Charles's realm, and other letters saying the same things were sent to the bishops of the realms of Louis and Lothar: absolution had been granted to Waldrada on condition that she did not stay with Lothar under any arrangements whatever.

Charles now reached Senlis, where he received Bishop Actard of Nantes back from Rome bringing him letters. One of these gave a reply on those matters which he had confided to Nicholas in opposition to Hincmar: among other things Hadrian insisted that from now on and forever this unprofitable issue should be allowed to drop.[6] Actard

1 This son was Odo, future king of West Francia (888-98). Robert's second son (also called Robert) was probably still very young. The *honores* were probably the counties of Auxerre and Nevers, above 865: 128, since Robert's Neustrian *honores* had already been granted to Hugh, above 866: 136. The suggestion that Robert's sons were Hugh's half-brothers, hence that their mother was Adelaide, widow of Conrad (died 863), and that she contracted a short-lived second marriage to Robert, has been shown to rest on a misunderstanding in the Chronicle of St-Bénigne, Dijon; Bouchard 1981: 512, n. 30.

2 Ranulf left three sons, the eldest of whom (another Ranulf) did later become count of Poitou; Dhondt 1948: 203. It is unclear who held the county of Poitou after Ranulf's death; Martindale 1990a: 130, nn. 77, 78.

3 Frotar, appointed archbishop of Bordeaux in 858, was given other ecclesiastical *honores* in Aquitaine during the 860s; Nelson 1990a: 15.

4 For Viking activity on the Loire, above 867, n. 18, and Vogel 1906: 226-7.

5 For Adventius, above 861, n. 17; for Grimland, Schieffer 1966: 376. Hadrian II's letters to Charles and to his bishops have not survived. His letter to Louis the German's bishops is extant: *MGH Epp.* VI, no. 5, p. 702.

6 Hadrian II's letter to Charles the Bald ordered the Ebbo affair to be 'consigned to silence', and thanked Charles for seeing to the restitution of Ebbo's clerks, above 866, n. 14. Hadrian also established rapport with Hincmar, *MGH Epp.* VI, nos. 7 and 10, pp. 704-7, 710-12.

brought a second letter, addressed to Hincmar, full of praises and warm appreciation of his faithfulness, and instructing him to act as his deputy in those parts in matters concerning Lothar. A third letter was addressed to the archbishops and other bishops on that side of the Alps: Hadrian ordered that Actard, since he had been unable to remain in his *civitas* because of the attacks of the pagans and the constant pressure of the Bretons, was to be installed by the bishops of the province, on apostolic authority, in the next see that fell vacant, preferably a metropolitan one.[7]

On the Wednesday following the first Sunday in Lent [10 March], thanks to Arsenius's plotting, his son Eleutherius cunningly deceived Pope Hadrian's daughter who was engaged to someone else, carried her off and married her himself. The pope was extremely upset. Arsenius made his way to the Emperor Louis at Benevento and, his health ruined by illness, he committed his treasure into the hands of the Empress Engelberga. Then, talking with demons, so it was said, without having received communion, he departed to Hell – his real home.[8] Once he was dead, Pope Hadrian got the emperor to send *missi* to judge Eleutherius according to Roman law. But Eleutherius, on the advice, so it was said, of his brother Anastasius, whom Hadrian at the very outset of his pontificate had appointed librarian of the Roman church, killed the pope's wife Stephanie, and his daughter, whom he himself had carried off. Then Eleutherius was slain by the emperor's *missi*. Pope Hadrian summoned a synod, and following the condemnation already long ago made against Anastasius, he condemned him again in the following terms:

This was written on the right hand side of the picture.[9]

In the reigns of our lords the Emperors and Augusti Lothar and Louis, on 16 December in the thirteenth Indiction (851). The ex-

---

7 For Actard, above 867, n. 11. The pope's letter, *MGH Epp.* VI, no. 8, pp. 707-9, repeated arguments advanced by Charles. Hincmar countered these by pointing out that many lay Christians still lived in Nantes side by side with pagan Northmen, and arguing that the bishop ought to tighten his belt; *PL* 126, cols. 218-21.

8 On Arsenius, above 865, n. 4. Hadrian was trying to assert his independence of this powerful Roman family, using imperial help to defeat Eleutherius. Anastasius returned to papal favour however, below: 178.

9 A reference to the commemorative wall-painting put up at Rome by Leo IV (847-55) to record a council on 16 December 850 at which Anastasius was excommunicated; *MGH Conc.* III, no. 24, pp. 230-1. For Anastasius, see Devos 1967, and above 855, n. 4. Against Hincmar's statement that he was Arsenius's son, Anastasius himself said he was Arsenius's nephew, *MGH Epp.* VII, p. 401.

F

communication which Bishop Leo made of the priest Anastasius, later repeated by Hadrian.

'Leo bishop, servant of the servants of God.

Anastasius, priest of our cardinal-church, whom we ordained in the *titulus* of St-Marcellus, and who departing from it went off without our pontifical knowledge to alien dioceses; whom we called to through messengers and through our letters, and for whom we begged our lords the emperors through our envoys that they might order him to return to his own diocese; who, hiding in this place and that, remained absent for two years, and though summoned to two of our councils refused to come, but was never found, because, as we have said, like the wandering sheep he was dwelling in secret in foreign regions, at the devil's instigation: let this man be deprived of communion from this day forth according to the canonical statutes and by the authority of Almighty God and of the blessed apostle Peter and also our apostolic authority, until he is presented to me in person for canonical judgement; and if he does not come, let him be forever excommunicate.'

Following the Roman pontiff, the archbishops of Ravenna and Milan and other bishops to the number of seventy-five gave their consent to this excommunication.

This was written on the left-hand side of the picture.

'Leo bishop, servant of the servants of God, to all bishops, priests, deacons, subdeacons and clerics of all grades, and to the whole Christian people.

You know, dearest brothers, that we are well and fully with you. For the advice and recollection of future time we now wish it to be made known again to Your Diligence that, at the devil's instigation and persuasion, Anastasius, priest of our cardinal-Church, whom we ordained in the *titulus* of St-Marcellus, has abandoned his province and his Church, contrary to the statutes of the fathers and see now! has been running about for the space of five years in alien dioceses, like a lost sheep. We, relying on our canonical authority, have called him back by apostolic letters for a third and a fourth time. But because he has put off returning, we have assembled two councils of bishops on his account, in whose assembled company, since we could not see him or have him present in person, we have by our common decree deprived him of holy communion, wishing indeed to lead him back, through the censure of this excommunication, to the bosom of his Holy Mother Church, from which he had departed. But setting at nought the apostolic warnings and those of the holy council, trapped by a mist of error, he utterly refused to come. We, then, just as, when we were staying in Ravenna, we promulgated with our own mouth concerning him in the church of St-Vitalis the martyr in the month of May on the twenty-ninth day thereof, in the first Indiction (854), so now again we have promulgated likewise in the church of St-Peter the apostle in the month of June, on the nineteenth day thereof, in the same Indiction (854): let him be declared anathema by the holy fathers and by us, and all who may wish to offer him help either in an election – which Heaven forfend! – to the pontificate, or in pontifical office, or any comfort whatsoever, let them be under the same anathema.'

After the Roman pontiff, the following consented in this anathema: John archbishop of Ravenna, Noting and Sigilfred, bishops of the lord emperor, and six bishops pertaining to the above archbishop, whose names we do not recall, and other bishops both from the city of Rome and from other cities to the number of fifty-six, not counting the priests and deacons of the holy Roman Church.

This was written on silver doors:

'In the name of the Father, and of the Son, and of the Holy Spirit. Here begins the holy and venerable synod which through the grace of God and has divine counsel was assembled in the church of St-Peter the apostle, in the seventh year of the pontificate of the most holy and coangelic and universal Pope Leo IV, and in the forty-second year of the imperial rule of the most unconquered Emperors Lothar and Louis,[10] in the month of December, on the eighth day thereof, in the second Indiction. In this holy and venerable synod so nobly celebrated, with the grace of God consoling it, after various pious and salvation-bringing admonitions and exhortations of bishops and priests and clerics and all Christians, Anastasius titular priest of the *titulus* of St-Marcellus was justly and canonically deposed, because he had deserted his own diocese, contrary to canonical authority, for five whole years, and to this very day remains in alien dioceses, and neither when summoned, nor excommunicated, nor even in the end anathematised, as the truthful picture of him in this synod shows he has been, has he been willing to come to the two councils of bishops assembled on his account.

10 'Forty-second' is an error, for which possible explanations are offered by L/G: 147, n. 1.

Therefore both by the supreme pontiff and by all the bishops then sitting in the synod to the number of sixty-seven, because of his foolish presumptuousness he has been deservedly, as we have said, deposed and deprived of sacerdotal honour, in the year, in the month, on the day and in the Indiction specified above.'

Pope Leo ordered it to be written up to this point.

Now after the death of Pope Leo of worthy memory, Anastasius, anathematised and deposed, returned with the backing of worldly power[11] from the secret places in which like a thief he had been skulking. Seduced by diabolical trickery and caught in a fog, in the manner of a brigand he invaded this church which he ought not to have entered at all, and like a savage and a barbarian, to the perdition of his own soul and the danger of this venerable synod, along with his most villainous accomplices and followers he destroyed and threw down that picture in the dust. The most blessed and distinguished Pope Benedict[12] restored and decorated it with colours flowing with light.

'Hadrian bishop, servant of the servants of God.

It is known to all the church of God what Anastasius did in the time of the popes our predecessors; and it is also clear to all what measures Leo and Benedict of holy memory, outstanding bishops amongst those pontiffs, took concerning him. One of them deposed, excommunicated and anathematised him, while the other defrocked him of his priestly vestments and received him into communion amongst the laity.

After that, our immediate predecessor, the most holy Pope Nicholas, would later have received him back, in like fashion, into the bosom of the Church, on condition that he then acted in a loyal manner with respect to the holy Roman Church. But his faithlessness has now become manifest to such an extent that, after plundering our patriarchate and stealing our synodal documents which he had found had been decreed by most holy bishops at various times concerning both him and others like him, he also

---

11 A reference to the influence of Louis II. Cf. above n. 9. Anastasius had made a bid for the papal throne immediately after Leo IV's death on 17 July 855.

12 Benedict III (855-58). He was consecrated on 29 September, perhaps the date of a council at Rome at which Anastasius was readmitted to lay communion. The sole evidence for this council is Hadrian II's statement deposing Anastasius, recorded in the AB's next paragraph, below; *MGH Conc.* III, no. 35, p. 372.

caused to be violated, by snatching it from us by stealth, that decree of the venerable synod which was made by those same holy pontiffs and reissued with the addition of the anathema. He compelled men to go out beyond the walls of this city, in the way thieves do, to sow discords between the most pious princes and the Church of God. He also caused a certain Adalgrim, who had sought asylum in the church, to be deprived of his eyes and tongue.

Now, as many of you, along with me, have heard from a certain priest named Ado, a kinsman of his, and as has been revealed to us in other ways also, he forgot our benefits and sent a man to Eleutherius urging him to commit murders, which as you know, alas! were committed.[13] Therefore on account of all these deeds, and many others whereby he smote and pierced the Church of the Lord, which indeed he has not ceased to strike at up to now with his secret machinations, we have decreed, by the authority of God omnipotent and of all the holy fathers, and of the venerable councils of the said fathers and also by the sentence of our judgement, that that same Anastasius is to be treated in exactly the same way as the pontiffs Lords Leo and Benedict solemnly and synodically decreed concerning him; neither adding nor subtracting anything whatsoever in his anathema or his case, except that he is to remain deprived of all ecclesiastical communion until he gives an account before the synod concerning all the charges on which he is accused to us; and whoever communicates with him in speech or with food or drink shall be held and bound by a like excommunication with him, because, in as much as he sought for himself higher things, which had so many times been forbidden him, and rashly usurped and ascended a forbidden place, our Church has complained enough and still does complain. But if he goes away, whatever the distance, from the city of Rome, or presumes to seek again, or to receive, either the priesthood or any clerical order or office whatsoever, because he will then be seen to be acting against the statutes of the said bishops and against the oath which he swore, never to depart more than forty miles from the city, nor to seek the priesthood nor the rank of clerical office, let him be under perpetual anathema, along with all his supporters, sympathisers and followers. Delivered in the sight of the whole holy Roman Church before this same Anastasius who has been placed at St-Praxedis, in the first year of the pontificate of Lord Hadrian supreme pontiff and universal pope, on 12 October in

13 Above: 145 and n. 8.

the second Indiction.'[14]

Lothar had his suspicions of Charles, and so he went off again to Louis and got him to agree that he would have an oath sworn to Lothar on his behalf that he would take no counter-action if Lothar should accept Waldrada as his wife. Then Lothar came to have talks with Charles in the palace of Attigny, and there he got Charles to agree that they should meet and talk again at the beginning of October following.[15]

Charles travelled on by way of the royal *villae* situated in the county of Laon. Without the prior knowledge of any bishop of his province, he ordered Hincmar bishop of Laon to come to answer a case in his own courts, in other words summoned him to secular judgement, because he had taken away benefices from certain of Charles's men.[16] But Bishop Hincmar protested that he did not dare to come, as he had been ordered, to a secular judgement, leaving aside that of the ecclesiastical courts. He did not appear at the place appointed for the secular judgement, instead informing the king of the reasons why he could not do so.[17] At this, King Charles ordered certain persons of low repute to go ahead and pronounce judgement, because the said bishop had not sent someone who could swear that he had been unable to appear; and since he offered no advocate to speak for him in the secular court, by the judgement of the said persons, whatever ecclesiastical property or moveable wealth the bishop had been holding for the use

14 Hincmar breaks the chronological order of events in this annal at the point where papal letters are received at Charles's court in June. He then inserts the whole story of Eleutherius and of Anastasius's second condemnation, a sequence spanning March to October. The final document can hardly have reached Hincmar before late November. In the remainder of the 868 annal are signs that Hincmar has tried, unusually, to write up events as a connected narrative; Meyer-Gebel 1987: 95-6.

15 These two meetings took place in July/August. Note that Hincmar omits the preceding meeting between Charles and Louis the German at Metz in June (at which Hincmar himself was present), when Lothar's two uncles agreed to partition his kingdom between them; *MGH Capit.* II, no. 245, pp. 167-8. For the date, Calmette 1901: 195-200; Schlesinger 1970: 458, n. 32.

16 The younger Hincmar, nephew of the archbishop of Rheims, had been consecrated to Laon in 858, and thereafter been one of Charles's most trusted servants. Charles increased the lands of the see of Laon to enable the bishop to grant more benefices thereon to the king's men. When some of these were dispossessed of their benefices by the bishop, they appealed to the king; McKeon 1978: 22-3; Nelson 1991.

17 At this stage of the dispute, Hincmar of Rheims supported his nephew's appeal to ecclesiastical privilege; McKeon 1978: 24-6. Hincmar addressed a lengthy treatise to Charles on this subject: part I of his *Pro Ecclesiae Libertatum Defensione, PL* 125, cols. 1035-60.

of the see was confiscated.

Thus the king came in mid-August to Pîtres, and received the annual gifts there. He measured out the fort into sections of a certain number of feet, and assigned responsibility for them to various men of his realm.[18]

Archbishop Hincmar of Rheims took Hincmar of Laon with him and went with other bishops to the king at Pîtres. Using written texts and oral arguments, he showed what great prejudice both episcopal authority and the universal church were suffering through such a judgement. He secured the king's agreement that after the bishop's reinvestiture with the property of which he had been stripped, as the sacred laws command, the case should be concluded in the province where it had to be judged by the judgement of specially-chosen judges, and then, if this should be necessary, by the decision of a synod.

At this same assembly the king received the *markiones*, Bernard of Toulouse,[19] and Bernard of Gothia,[20] and also another Bernard.[21] Furthermore, he met there an envoy of the Breton chief Salomon, through whom Salomon told Charles that he ought not to launch an assault himself against the Northmen based on the Loire, because he, Salomon, was all ready to attack them with a strong force of Bretons and only needed some help on Charles's part. In response the king sent

18 This passage supplies important evidence on the organisation of fortress-building. For parallels from ninth-century England, Hassall and Hill 1970; Gillmor 1989: 101 and n. 67.

19 Bernard count and marquis of Toulouse had been appointed to succeed Hunfrid, above 864: 118. Bernard was the son of Count Raymund, above 863: 105 and n. 6.

20 Above 865: 122 and n. 3.

21 The identity of this 'other Bernard' has caused much debate; Calmette 1951. Bouchard 1986 argues that he was Bernard son of the tyrant Bernard. Against this, Bernard son of Bernard is clearly identified as such when last mentioned in the *AB*, 866: 131 and when next mentioned, 869: 165. Further, there is no record of this Bernard's coming to terms with Charles before late 869: since 866, he had clearly been driven from Autun and attached himself to Lothar II and perhaps to Lothar's son Hugh. The three *markiones* of 868 should probably be linked with the setting-up of Louis the Stammerer's sub-kingdom, above 867: 138. All three *markiones* were clearly based in Aquitaine; see below 869: 153. The term *markio* had lost any necessary association with a particular march, and simply denoted a great magnate in one of the *regna*; Werner 1980: 216-17, and n. 97. Bouchard 1986 has not disproved the existence of a Count Bernard of the Auvergne, documented in charters of the monastery of Brioude. I therefore accept the identification of the 868 annal's third marquis Bernard as the count of the Auvergne; see Levillain 1948: 34-5, rebutting the objection of Dhondt 1948: 310-13 that this Bernard had died before April 868.

ahead Engelram, his chamberlain and master of the door-keepers and his closest counsellor,[22] with a crown made of gold and adorned with precious stones and all kinds of gear designed for regal display. He also sent his son Carloman, deacon and abbot, with a squadron of household troops,[23] as Salomon had asked him. Then from Pîtres he went on to his *villa* of Orville to do some hunting. The squadron which King Charles sent with Carloman across the Seine laid waste some territory, it is true, but did nothing of any use as far as resisting the Northmen was concerned – and that after all was the purpose for which they had been sent. On King Charles's orders they came back and each returned to his own home.

The men of Poitiers offered prayers to God and St Hilary and boldly attacked those Northmen for a third time.[24] They killed some of them and drove the rest to take flight. They gave a tenth part of all their booty to St-Hilary, and that was not counting voluntary offerings.

King Charles came to Quierzy on 1 December and summoned certain leading men of his realm, both some of the bishops and others, to meet him there. He was angry with Hincmar bishop of Laon because he had sent to Rome without the king's permission and obtained letters on which Charles had not agreed. He was in fact absolutely furious with the bishop for resisting him so contumaciously. For this reason the bishop went to his own see without leave from the king by whom he had often been summoned, yet to whom he still delayed coming. He roused the king against him more than befits the episcopal dignity.[25]

Charles went to Compiègne and celebrated Christmas there.

869

Now the bishop, though summoned through the other bishops to come to the king, still declined to obey the royal command. Charles there-

22 Engelram's importance in the 860s is confirmed by his acting as a negotiator on Charles's behalf, above 865, n. 1, and heading the list of counts in a royal judgement of 868 (T. 314).

23 Carloman was a secular clerk with a military household of his own; Nelson 1988b: 109-10.

24 Cf. above 863: 111 and 865: 127.

25 Note the shift in the attitude of Hincmar of Rheims to his nephew, whose appeal to Rome threatened the authority of his uncle as metropolitan. The pseudo-Isidorean decretals, forged by some of Ebbo's clerks c. 850, were used by Hincmar of Laon to invoke papal authority; Fuhrmann 1972: 219-24, and 1974: 651-72; McKeon 1978: 93-6.

fore dispatched to Laon a squadron of men mustered from as many counties of his realm as possible to bring the bishop to him by force. But the bishop sat himself on his throne with his clergy about him beside the altar. Thanks to the efforts of certain bishops, the troops did not drag him out of the church, but went back to Charles without him. The king then had all the free men of the see of Laon swear him solemn oaths. Still furious, he summoned a synod of all the bishops of his realm to assemble at Verberie on 24 April in the second Indiction, and he commanded that Hincmar of Laon be called before it.

Charles then went to the township of Cosne,[1] at an inconvenient time to travel since the weather was bad and there was a very serious famine, and met some of the Aquitanians there. But contrary to his expectations, he did not meet the *markiones*, namely the three Bernards.[2] He went back to Senlis, anxious and having achieved nothing.

From Senlis he moved on Ash Wednesday [16 February] to St-Denis where he passed Lent and celebrated Easter [3 April]. He began the construction of fortifications, made of wood and stone, going all around the monastery. Before leaving for Cosne, he had despatched letters throughout his realm, requiring the bishops, abbots and abbesses to see to the drawing up of *breves* of their *honores*, showing how many manses each held.[3] These were to be brought to the king at the beginning of May following. The royal vassals were to draw up similar surveys of the benefices held by counts, and the counts were to do likewise for the benefices held by their own vassals; and they were also to bring to the said assembly surveys of the buildings on their holdings. Charles gave orders that there should be sent to Pîtres one young warrior[4] for every 100 manses, and a cart with two oxen for he

1 Cosne-sur-Loire: a characteristic frontier-spot for Aquitaine, and equidistant between Auxerre and Bourges.

2 Above 868, nn. 19-21. The non-appearance of these men is sometimes taken to imply their opposition to Charles; Martindale 1990a: 131. But this is not clear from Hincmar's wording; and other evidence shows Bernard of Toulouse and Bernard of Gothia as reliable supporters of Charles. Cf. below 872: 177-8.

3 These *breves* were apparently not detailed surveys of tenants and their renders, but ennumerations of manses (above 866, n. 4) for each estate. Cf. Davis 1987. It seems unlikely that the 'realm' here meant more than Francia proper.

4 *Haistaldus*: compare Lombard *gastaldus*; Bullough 1985: 87, n. 47. L/G: 153, n. 1 prefer to translate 'young serf', but it seems more likely that these were men picked from the military followings of ecclesiastical and lay magnates, and thus with experience of building and guarding fortifications. The fort 'at Pîtres' was strictly speaking at Pont-de-l'Arche (dep. Eure), and may have consisted of a double bridge-head and a bridge which could be adapted to block the river; above 862, n. 14.

every 1,000 manses, along with the other dues which still greatly burden his realm.[5] These young men were to complete and then guard the fort which the king had ordered to be built at Pîtres out of wood and stone.

Lothar sent to both Charles and Louis asking them to make no trouble for him in his own kingdom until he returned from Rome. He received no such guarantee from Charles, but he did get one from Louis, so it is said. He therefore set off to Rome, to speak first of all with his brother the Emperor Louis, so that then, if he possibly could, through Louis's influence he might get Pope Hadrian's authorisation to put aside Theutberga and take Waldrada back. He ordered Theutberga to follow him to Rome. But, so it was said, the Emperor Louis replied that he could not abandon his siege of the Saracens for the sake of his brother's request: the king of the Greeks was speedily sending him more than 200 ships to help him against the Saracens.[6]

Lothar had begun his journey to Rome to settle the case of his wives at an unsuitable time, namely the month of June. Struggling to reach his destination, he got as far as Ravenna, where envoys from his brother met him bringing word that Louis ordered him not to go on any further, nor to stay any longer in his realm: they would meet together, Louis said, at a suitable time and convenient place, and he would do his best to satisfy Lothar's wishes. Lothar nevertheless did go down to Rome, and moreover continued all the way to his brother in Benevento. Using Engelberga as an intermediary, Lothar after petitions and gifts and a great deal of trouble got Louis to agree that Engelberga should accompany him as far as the monastery of St-Benedict on Monte Cassino. There, at the emperor's behest, he caused Pope Hadrian to come to Engelberga and himself, and after giving him many gifts, and again through Engelberga's intercession, he got the pope to say mass for him and to grant him holy communion on the understanding that since Pope Nicholas's excommunication of Waldrada he had not lived with her, had had no sexual intercourse with her, and had not even spoken with her at all. The wretched man,

5 This last phrase may have been added later in Charles's reign. It is clear, in any case, that Charles intended the new fortification to be permanently garrisoned. Gillmor 1989: 102-5 argues that these arrangements were new, shifting the burden on to the Church; but Hincmar had his own reasons for dwelling here on the Church's burdens. For the importance of fortifications, France 1979: 179-83.

6 Louis II was besieging Bari, held by Arabs from north Africa since 847 and used as a base for raiding southern Italy; Wickham 1981: 62, 154. The 'king of the Greeks' was the Emperor Basil I, below: 162.

like Judas, made a pretence of having a good conscience, and neither feared nor shrank from receiving holy communion with bare-faced effrontery on this understanding. His supporters along with him also took communion from Pope Hadrian: among them was Gunther, the originator and inciter of that public adultery, who received communion from the pope amongst the laity, after first giving him in front of everyone the following profession:

> I, Gunther, before God and his saints, profess to you my Lord Hadrian, highest pontiff and universal pope, and to the venerable bishops subject to you, and to the rest of this assembly, that I do not object to, but humbly accept, the sentence of deposition canonically given against me by the Lord Nicholas. Therefore I will no longer presume to touch the sacred ministry, unless in your mercy you wish to come to my relief. Nor do I wish ever to set in motion any scandal or any other opposition against the holy Roman Church or its pontiff, but I call you to witness that I shall show myself devoted to that holy mother Church and its bishop and remain obedient to them. I, Gunther, have subscribed with my own hand this profession made by me. Given on 1 June, in the second Indiction, in the church of St-Salvator which is in the monastery of St-Benedict at Cassino.

The pope received this profession from Gunther as he stood among the laity: it had been read out by him publicly among the laity in the presence of all. The pope then said to him:

> And I concede to you the communion of a layman on condition that as long as you live you observe what you have just now professed.

Engelberga then went back to her emperor, and Pope Hadrian returned to Rome with Lothar following in his footsteps. While the pope entered Rome itself, Lothar went to the church of St- Peter. No cleric came to meet him, but Lothar went up on his own, with only his personal retinue, to the tomb of St Peter. From there he went to the upper floor of a house near the church of St-Peter to find lodgings, but he found that the place had not even been cleaned out with a brush. He thought that mass would be bound to be sung for him next day, that is, on the Sunday (he had come to St-Peter's on a Saturday), but he could not get the pope to do this. On the Tuesday he entered Rome and had lunch with the pope in the Lateran palace: after giving him gifts in vessels of gold and silver, he got the pope to agree to bestow on him a cloak, a palm and a rod, which he duly did. Lothar and his followers interpreted these gifts as follows: with the cloak, Lothar was being reinvested with Waldrada; with the palm, Lothar showed himself the victor in what he had begun; and with the rod, he would beat down the bishops who resisted his will.[7]

Matters were arranged otherwise by the pope and the Romans, however. For the pope decided that Bishop Formosus[8] and another bishop also would have to be sent into the regions of the Gauls, to deliberate together with the majority of bishops on Lothar's requests. They were to report back their findings to the pope at the synod which he had already announced for the beginning of the following March at Rome. The pope ordered in his letters that four bishops from the realm of King Louis of Germany along with his envoys, and four bishops from Charles's realm along with his envoys, and certain bishops from Lothar's realm, should all come to this synod, on the understanding that they would confirm the deliberations and acts of the synod as representatives of the other bishops, both those of the West and also those of the East, whence the pope was hoping that by then his envoys would have returned: he had recently sent them to Constantinople to deal with the quarrel the Easterners had had with Pope Nicholas.[9]

Lothar left Rome in high spirits and got far as Lucca. There he was stricken by fever, and this disastrous sickness spread amongst his men. He watched them dying in heaps before his eyes. But he refused to recognise that this was a judgement of God. On 7 August he reached Piacenza. He survived through the Sunday, but about the ninth hour unexpectedly became almost unconscious and lost the power of speech. Next day [8 August], at the second hour, he died. Those few of his men who had survived the disaster committed him to earth in a little monastery near Piacenza.

Charles was staying at Senlis, and he and his wife too, having returned

---

7 For other ninth-century papal gifts of palms, Schramm 1955 (ii): 410-12; McCormick 1986: 370-1. The interpretation given to the rod implies that some of Lothar's bishops, perhaps indignant at his treatment of Gunther and Theutgaud, now opposed him; Staubach 1982: 252. Hincmar here seems to play down the real possibility that Lothar might have secured Hadrian's agreement to his divorce; cf. *AF* 869, n. 6.

8 Bishop of Porto and future pope (891-96).

9 Above 864: 120 and 867: 141. The papal envoys fell into the hands of pirates and did not return to Rome until December 870.

from Pîtres,[10] were dispensing in alms to holy places the treasures they owned in riches of various kinds, thus returning to the Lord what they had received from his hand. It was just then that Charles learned from a reliable messenger the news of Lothar's death.[11] He moved from Senlis to Attigny and there received envoys sent by certain bishops and also certain leading men of the kingdom of the late King Lothar. They asked Charles to stay where he was and not to enter the kingdom that had been Lothar's until his brother King Louis of Germany had returned from his campaign against the Wends. He had been threatened by them often during this year and the previous year, and though his men had fought against them, they had achieved virtually no success, but had in fact suffered very heavy losses.[12] The envoys therefore requested that Charles should stay at Attigny but send messengers to Louis at Ingelheim to let him know when and where he and Charles might meet and discuss the division of Lothar's realm.[13]

But the majority of the bishops and leading men of that realm urged him with wiser counsels[14] to try to reach Metz as fast as he conveniently could, promising that they would hasten to meet him either along his route there or at Metz itself. Charles realised that this latter advice was much more acceptable, being more in line with his own interests, so he acted swiftly in accordance with their plan. He reached Verdun and there he received many men from that realm who commended themselves to him, including Hatto bishop of Verdun and also Arnulf bishop of Toul. From Verdun he arrived at Metz on 5 September, and received into his commendation Adventius bishop of Metz, Franco bishop of Tongres (Liège), and many others.[15]

10 The capitulary issued at Pîtres in July 869, *MGH Capit.* II, no. 275, p. 337, was partly concerned with the fortifications, above, n. 5, and also with collaboration between ecclesiastical and secular personnel. Ermentrude's presence with Charles at Senlis refutes the idea that she had been repudiated; Hyam 1990: 156 and n. 21.

11 The news of Lothar's death arrived on 23 August (thus taking two weeks to come to Senlis from Piacenza), and Charles immediately moved east; Hincmar of Rheims to Hincmar of Laon, *PL* 126, cols. 533–4.

12 According to *AF* 869: 68–9, Louis the German had planned this campaign but fallen ill, so Karlmann led it, successfully.

13 As envisaged in the agreement of Metz, above 868, n. 15.

14 Hincmar's own bias is apparent; cf. the *AF*'s reference to 'the advice of evil men'.

15 The adherence of all these Lotharingian bishops was important, especially that of Adventius of Metz; above 861, n. 17. See Staubach 1982: 167. According to *AF*: 869, those Lotharingians who refused to come over to Charles were

And so on 9 September, on the insistence of everyone, the following statements were made and actions performed by the bishops present in the basilica of St-Stephen:[16]

In the year of the Lord's incarnation 869, in the second Indiction on 9 September, in the *civitas* of Metz, in the basilica of St-Stephen the martyr, Adventius bishop of that see in the presence of the king and the bishops made the following announcement to the people in speech and in written form:

'You know, and it is well known to many in several kingdoms, how many and great upheavals we endured in the time of our late Lord Lothar, for reasons very familiar to everyone here; and by what great grief and agony our hearts have recently been smitten by his unhappy death. Deprived, therefore, of our king and prince and desolated thereby, we have considered the sole recourse and especially beneficial advice for all of us to be that we turn ourselves, with fastings and prayers, to Him who is our helper in our troubles and in our tribulation and to whom belong counsel and the kingdom, and who, as it is written, shall give the kingdom to whomsoever He wills, and in whose hand are the hearts of kings and who maketh all to dwell united in one house and breaketh down the dividing-wall between them and maketh both into one [Eph. 2:14]; beseeching Him in His mercy to give into us a king and prince according to His heart, who may rule, preserve and defend us in judgement and justice in every rank and calling according to His will, and incline and unite all our hearts together to him whom He shall have foreknown and chosen and predestined for our salvation and benefit according to His mercy. Because, then, we in our unanimous agreement see it to be the will of God, who maketh the will of those who fear Him and heareth their prayer, that this man to whom we have freely committed ourselves is the legitimate heir of this kingdom, namely our present lord king and prince Charles, so that he may have charge over us and be of benefit to us, it seems good to us, if it pleases you, that as we shall demonstrate to you after hearing his words, we should prove by a most certain sign that

deprived of their benefices and hereditary lands. One lay magnate who supported Charles was Boso, below: 164.

16 Hincmar quotes the following documents from his own archive. He stage-managed the occasion and produced the liturgical *Ordo*; Nelson 1987: 163-4. The throne now known as the *Cathedra Petri*, Nees 1990, may well have been used by Charles in 869; Mütherich 1971: 271-3.

we believe him to be the prince chosen by God and given unto us. And let us not be ungrateful to God our benefector for His gifts, but let us offer thanks unto Him and pray that he who has been given to us may keep us for a long time in health and peace and tranquillity to the well-being and defence of His holy Church and the help and benefit of us all, and may govern us who obey him with faithful devotion and enjoy our hoped-for salvation under his administration in His service. And if it pleases him, it seems worthy for him and needful for us that we should hear from his mouth what it is suitable for his people loyal and united in his service, each man in his lay or ecclesiastical order, to hear from their most Christian king and to receive with devoted hearts.'

After this, King Charles himself pronounced the following statement to all present in that church:

'Because, as these venerable bishops have said, through the voice of one of them, they have given proof of your unanimity with unmistakable signs, and also you have acclaimed me as one who has come hither by the election of God for your salvation and benefit and rule and government, know that I with the Lord's help shall preserve the honour and worship of God and His holy churches and shall honour and make safe, and shall wish to keep honoured and safe, each one of you according to the dignity of his order and according to his person, so far as I know and can, and shall preserve law and justice for each man in his order according to the laws that apply to him, both ecclesiastical and secular, to this end that by each one of you, according to his order and rank and means, there may be shown to me royal honour and power and due obedience and aid for the holding and defending of the realm given to me by God, just as your ancestors showed unto my ancestors faithfully, justly and in accordance with reason.'[17]

After this, at the order and request of Adventius bishop of Metz and of the other bishops of the province of Trier, namely Hatto bishop of Verdun and Arnulf bishop of Toul, and also at the insistence of all the bishops of the province of Rheims, Hincmar bishop of Rheims publicly stated the following points in that church before the rest of the bishops and before the king and all who were present:

'Lest it might perhaps seem to anyone that I and the venerable

17 This statement, based on previous undertakings given by Charles and by his brothers, had the function of a coronation oath; Nelson 1986a (1977a): 149-51.

bishops of our province are acting incongruously or presumptu-
ously in involving ourselves in an ordination in another province
and in the affairs of that province, let such a one know that we are
not acting contrary to the sacred canons, for the churches of Rheims
and Trier, along with the churches committed to them, are deemed
sisters and fellow-members of one province in this Belgic region, as
ecclesiastical authority and most ancient custom demonstrate.
Therefore, they ought with unanimous consent both to make
synodal judgements, and to guard in harmony what has been laid
down by the holy fathers, on condition of keeping this privilege,
that whichever of them has been ordained the earlier, the bishop of
Rheims or the bishop of Trier, he shall take precedence. Divinely-
inspired law gives this command: "if thou shalt pass through thy
friend's harvest to collect ears of corn, thou shalt rub them in thy
hand to eat. Put not thy sickle to them", and "Reap them not with
thy sickle" [Deut. 23:25]. The harvest is the people, as the Lord
shows in the Gospel, saying, "the harvest is great, but the workmen
are few. Ask the lord of the harvest, therefore, to put workmen to
work in his harvest"[Matt. 9:37], meaning that you ought to pray
for us bishops, that we may speak worthy things unto you. The
friend's harvest is the people in the province committed to another
metropolitan. Hence, by exhorting you, as it were rubbing you by
the hand of our labours, we can and should draw you towards the
will of God and your salvation in the body of the unity of the
Church. To the parishioners of the provinces committed to other
metropolitans we do not put the sickle of judgement, however,
because it does not belong there nor do we consider that our work.
And there is another reason, namely that these venerable lords and
confrères of ours, the bishops of this province, not having a
metropolitan bishop,[18] with fraternal love, are ordering and pressing our insignificance to take action in their affairs as we do in our
own particular ones. Is that true, lord brothers?'

And those bishops replied: 'It is true.'

'Besides what the lord bishop our brother Adventius told you with
his own voice and on behalf of the rest of his and our brothers the
venerable bishops, you can also pay heed to this as being the will of
God: our lord and king here present, in the part of the realm he has
held and holds up to now, has presided and presides over, and has

18 The see of Trier remained vacant following Theutgaud's death, above 867: 142.
See further below 870, n. 15.

profited and profits, us and our churches and the people committed to his care for their temporal and spiritual well-being. And now he has come with the Lord's guidance from there to this place, where you have come together by His inspiration and have commended yourselves freely to this king, by the inspiration of Him who caused all living things to come together without anyone forcing them, into Noah's ark, signifying the unity of the Church.

His father of holy memory the Lord Louis, pious and august emperor, was descended from Louis [Clovis] famous king of the Franks, who was converted through the catholic preaching of St Remigius the apostle of the Franks, and baptised along with 3,000 of the Franks, not counting children and women, on the vigil of holy Easter at the metropolis of Rheims, and anointed and consecrated king with chrism got from heaven, of which we still have some.[19] And from him St Arnulf was descended; and from his flesh the pious and august Louis drew his carnal origin.[20] This Emperor Louis was crowned emperor by the Roman Pope Stephen at Rheims before the altar of the holy Mother of God and ever-virgin Mary, and after subsequently being deprived of earthly power by a faction of certain men, he was given back to the said part of his realm by the unamimity of bishops and faithful people before the tomb of St Denis, outstanding martyr of the holy Church, and was restored to full power with the crown of the realm in this house before this altar of Stephen the protomartyr, whose name being interpreted means "crowned", through the priests of the lord by the acclamation of the faithful people.

We read in the sacred histories that kings when they obtained kingdoms placed on their heads the diadems of their separate kingdoms [cf. I Macc. 11:13]. For all these reasons, therefore, it seems to these venerable bishops not inappropriate, if it is pleasing to your unamimity, that in the possession of the realm from which you have freely gathered to him and commended yourselves to him, he should be crowned by priestly ministry before this altar and consecrated to the Lord by sacred unction. If this pleases you, make

19 This is the earliest reference to Rheims's claim to have preserved some of the oil used by Remigius. The story looks like Hincmar's invention.

20 The Carolingians' genealogy tracing their descent from Clovis via St Arnulf was apparently concocted at Metz in the mid-ninth century; Oexle 1967. In the next passage, Hincmar plays on the link between the name Stephen (meaning 'crowned') and the successive coronations of Louis the Pious in 816, *RFA* s.a., and 835, above: 32.

a noise together with your own voices.'

And when all shouted their agreement to this, the same bishop said:

'Let us therefore with one mind give thanks to God, singing, 'We praise thee O God.'

After this the king was crowned by the bishops with priestly benediction.

From Metz Charles went to Florenges[21] where he made arrangements about everything that seemed to him to require it. From there he went off to take exercise in the autumn-hunting in the forest of the Ardennes. His brother Louis managed to make peace with the Wends on some terms or other and sent his son[22] along with the *marchiones* of his territory to confirm this treaty. He himself stayed at Regensburg for he was in poor health.[23] He sent envoys to Charles, reminding him about the firm undertaking made between them and also about his share of the kingdom of the late King Lothar. Charles returned a suitable reply.

Meanwhile, Basil, whom Michael emperor of the Greeks had associated with him as co-emperor, slew Michael by a trick, and assumed sole rule. He had despatched his *patricius* to Bari with 400 ships to bring aid to Louis II against the Saracens, and also to receive from Louis his daughter, already betrothed to Basil, and to take her back to be joined with him in marriage. But something happened, and Louis decided not to give his daughter to the *patricius*, who therefore left for Corinth very angry.[24] Louis left off his siege of the Saracens and returned from the region of Benevento, whereupon those Saracens came out from Bari and pursued Louis's army from behind. They captured over 2,000 horses from his army, and with these horses they arranged themselves into two cavalry formations which they rode all the way to the church of St-Michael on Monte Gargano. They plundered the clergy of that church and many other people who had gathered there on pilgrimage, and then they made off back to Bari with great spoils. This deed threw the emperor, the pope, and the Romans into great confusion.

21 Near Thionville (dep. Moselle).
22 Charles the Fat.
23 According to *AF*, his life was despaired of.
24 The Byzantine envoy was Nicetas. Basil had murdered Michael III on the night of 23/24 September 867. The failure of these negotiations gave rise to an acrimonious correspondence; Folz 1969: 181-4; Grierson 1981: 891-6, 913-14.

Louis son of Louis king of Germany waged war along with the Saxons against the Wends who live near the Saxons. With great slaughter of men on both sides, he somehow managed to win, and got home successfully.[25]

Roland archbishop of Arles obtained the abbacy of St-Caesarius from the Emperor Louis and from Engelberga, at an appropriate price. Now the island of the Camargue was all of it extremely well-endowed: most of the abbey's lands lay there, and the Saracens used to have a trading-post [*portus*] on it. There Roland was constructing a fort, but it was made only of earth and the work was done in a great hurry. When he heard that the Saracens were coming he very stupidly took up his position inside this fort: when the Saracens landed at it, more than 300 of Roland's men were slain and he himself was taken prisoner by the Saracens, tied up, and carried off into their ships. It was settled that 150 lb of silver, 150 cloaks, 150 swords and 150 slaves would be paid for his ransom, in addition to the things given in a general agreement. Meanwhile the bishop died on 19 September on board a Saracen ship. But the Saracens craftily speeded up the arrangements for his ransom: they could stay there no longer, they said, so if his ransomers wanted to get Roland back, they would have to hurry up and hand over the ransom. This was done. Then the Saracens, after receiving the whole ransom, set the bishop up on his throne, clad in the priestly vestments he was wearing at the time of his capture, and as if to do him honour they carried him from the ships on to dry land. His ransomers came to congratulate him – and found him dead. In deepest sorrow, they bore him away and buried him on 22 September, in the tomb which he had prepared for himself.

Salomon chief of the Bretons made a peace with the Northmen on the Loire, and along with his Bretons harvested wine from his part of the county of Anjou.[26] Abbot Hugh and Gauzfrid,[27] with their men from beyond the Seine, fought with the Loire Northmen and slew about sixty of them. They also took prisoner a certain apostate monk who had abandoned Christendom and gone to live with the Northmen, and had been extremely dangerous to the Christians: they now had him beheaded.[28] Charles ordered that the *civitates* beyond the Seine, namely

25 *AF* 869: Louis the Younger fought the Sorbs.

26 Regino 874: 108 says that the Viking chief was Hasting and the price of peace was 500 cows.

27 Hugh, above 866: 136; Gauzfrid, above 866, n. 26.

28 Cf. the case of the 'apostate' Pippin II, above 864: 111. On the penalty for treason, see above 866: 134.

Le Mans and Tours, should be fortified by their inhabitants, so that they could provide defensive strongholds against the Northmen for the surrounding populations.[29] When the Northmen heard about this, they demanded a great sum of silver and quantities of corn, wine and livestock from the local inhabitants, as the price of a peace with them.

On 9 October, Charles at the *villa* of Douzy[30] learned that his wife Ermentrude had died on 6 October at St-Denis, and had been buried there. With Boso, son of the late Count Bivin, carrying this royal order to his mother and his aunt Theutberga, King Lothar's widow, the king quickly had Boso's sister Richildis brought to him and took her as his concubine. On account of this, he gave to Boso the abbacy of St-Maurice along with other *honores* and lands.[31] He himself, taking his concubine along with him, made all the speed he could to the palace at Aachen to receive into his power there, as they had asked him to do, the rest of the men of that area who had formerly been Lothar's. Charles gave notice that from there he would move to the palace of Gondreville at Martinmas [11 November], to receive those who would come to him from Provence and from northern Burgundy[32] But when he got to Aachen, he won no new supporters that he had not had before.

From there, as he had previously announced, he went to Gondreville, where he received the envoys of Pope Hadrian, Bishops Paul and Leo, bearing letters addressed to him and to the bishops and leading men of the realm who resided in those parts of the Gauls. In these letters the pope ordered that no person should invade the realm of the late King Lothar or the men who lived in it, nor stir them up, nor attempt to turn them to himself, since that realm belonged by hereditary right to the Emperor Louis, Hadrian's spiritual son, and it had passed to Louis after the said Lothar's death. Hadrian added that if anyone should presume to take such actions, not only would he be rebutted through the application of papal authority, but he would be tied by the

29 See Vercauteren 1935-36; France 1979: 181.

30 Dep. Ardennes, previously in Lothar's kingdom.

31 Boso's family lands lay in the Metz area; Hyam 1990: 156; Bouchard 1988. For his uncle Richard, see above 836, n. 2. His uncle Hubert had held the abbacy of St-Maurice, Agaune: for its strategic importance, above 860, n. 7. Another uncle, Boso, held a countship in Italy; above 862, n. 31. T. 355 dates Charles's *conjunctio* with Richildis to 12 October. For Boso's career, see Airlie 1985, ch. 5.

32 Gondreville, near Toul was an important royal residence in southern Lotharingia; cf. below 872: 180.

bonds of anathema, deprived of the name of Christianity, and placed utterly with the devil; and if any of the bishops should keep silent and flee from the author of such wicked temerity or should consent to such action by not resisting it, he should know that he would be deemed to deserve the name, not of shepherd, but of hireling; and because no sheep would now belong to him, consequently no pastoral dignities would belong to him either.[33] There came along with these bishops also an envoy from the Emperor Louis called Boderad,[34] who had also been sent to negotiate on these points. Charles dismissed the papal and imperial envoys. Then, deceived by the empty advice of false messengers who suggested to him that his brother Louis was near to death, he marched swiftly into Alsace to win over Hugh son of Liutfrid and Bernard son of Bernard,[35] which he duly did. Then he went to Aachen and celebrated Christmas there.[36]

870

From Aachen he went to the palace of Nijmegen to hold discussions with the Northman Roric, whom he bound to himself by a treaty.[1] On Septuagesima Day [22 January] he took as his wife Richildis, whom he had already betrothed to himself and dowered.[2] Contrary to all his hopes, he received envoys from his brother Louis king of Germany to tell him that if he did not leave Aachen as fast as possible and completely abandon the realm of the late Lothar, and if he did not allow Lothar's men to hold that kingdom in peace just as they had been holding it at the time of Lothar's death, then Louis would make war on

---

33 Hadrian was clearly acting at the behest of the Emperor Louis II. The envoys were the bishops of Piacenza and Sabina. The letters are *MGH Epp.* VI, nos. 16, 17, pp. 717-20. Charles was especially indignant at Hadrian's appeal to his lay magnates to disobey royal orders; see Nelson 1991.

34 Emperor Louis II's count of the palace; *MGH Capit.* II, nos. 220, 221, pp. 100, 104.

35 For Liutfrid, above 862, n. 25; for this Bernard, 868, n. 21. The location of Hugh and Bernard in Alsace suggests that they may have been supporting Lothar II's son Hugh above 867: 139.

36 This may well have been the occasion of the composition of the verses in the Codex Aureus of St-Emmeram, a manuscript presented to Charles; Dutton and Jeauneau 1983; and perhaps also of John the Scot's celebratory poem *Aulae sidereae*; Herren 1987.

1 Above 850: 69; 855: 81; and 867: 139; and cf. *AF* 850, 857. See Wood 1987: 43-4.

2 Above 869: 164 and n. 31.

him, with no possibility of drawing back. Envoys raced back and forth between them, until they got as far as exchanging solemn oaths as follows:

> Thus I promise on behalf of my lord (so-and-so): my lord (so-and-so) agrees to his brother (so-and-so)'s having such a share of the realm of King Lothar as they themselves or all their faithful men together shall between them find to be more just and more equitable. Nor will he deceive or defraud him in that share or in the realm which he held before through any deception or trickery, provided that his brother (so-and-so) shall keep to my lord inviolably on his side, as long as he shall live, that firm commitment and faithfulness which I have promised to (so-and-so) on behalf of my lord.[3]

After arranging this unsettled kind of settlement, Charles left Aachen and went by a single journey to Compiègne, where he spent Easter [24 March]. From there he moved in May to Attigny, where he received twelve envoys from his brother Louis. They came to discuss the division of Lothar's realm.[4] They were arrogant and elated both because of Louis's good health and because of his good fortune in having captured, by a mixture of deceit and victory in battle, the Wend Rastiz who had been his bitter enemy for such a long time and whom he now held imprisoned.[5] Louis's envoys therefore thought it less needful than they ought to have done that the oaths made between him and Charles should be properly kept. The projected division was tossed about hither and yon on many sides and in many ways, and sent by means of various envoys from one brother to the other, until in the end on Charles's suggestion it was agreed that they should meet together peacefully in the realm which, according to the oaths they had given, was to be divided between them. Thus on lines which they would determine with the consent and agreement of all their faithful men, they would divide that realm according to the oaths exchanged between them.

3 *MGH Capit.* II, no. 250, p. 192 names the envoys and oath-swearers: Charles's were Engelram and Theuderic, while two Count Adalelms and Bishop Odo of Beauvais witnessed for him. One Count Adalelm was count of Laon; Grierson 1937: 55. Bishop Odo (861-81) was now a leading counsellor of Charles; Grierson 1935.

4 Cf. the procedure in March 842; Nelson 1986a (1985): 219-20; and above 865, n. 9.

5 Above 866: 135; *AF* 870.

Meanwhile, after being attacked on many charges, but especially for insubordination to the royal power and disobedience towards his archbishop, Bishop Hincmar of Laon, in order to clear himself of these charges, offered before a synod of the bishops of ten provinces a brief document subscribed by his own hand, containing the following statement:

> I, Hincmar, bishop of the church of Laon, shall be faithful and obedient now and henceforth to the lord my superior[6] King Charles, according to my office, as a man ought to be to his superior and any bishop ought in rightness to be to his king, and I profess myself willing to obey as far as I know and can the privilege of Hincmar metropolitan of the province of the church of Rheims, according to the sacred canons and the decrees of the apostolic see promulgated in accordance with the sacred canons.

And he subscribed this.[7]

Carloman, son of King Charles and abbot of several monasteries, was alleged to have been disloyal to his father and to have been stirring up trouble against him. He was deprived of his abbacies and imprisoned at Senlis.[8]

Charles sent his envoys Bishop Odo of Beauvais and Counts Odo and Harduin[9] to his brother Louis at Frankfurt, to request a meeting fro the purpose of dividing up Lothar's realm. Charles made for Ponthion, where he received envoys from his brother telling him to proceed to Herstal, while Louis would come to Meersen, and at the beginning of August they would hold talks at the mid-way point between those two places. Each of them was to bring to the talks no more than four

6 'Domnus senior meus.' The requirement that Bishop Hincmar swear this oath may well reflect Charles's suspicion of his complicity with Carloman, see below n. 8. The bishop swore his oath on 16 June at an assembly at Attigny; McKeon 1970: 411-18; McKeon 1978: 85-8, 105, 121, 127.

7 For the form of the bishop's oath, Odegaard 1945. Cf. Hincmar of Rheims's later objections to a similar oath, below 876, n. 7.

8 Carloman was arrested at the Attigny assembly on 18 June. His abbacies had been St-Médard, St-Amand, St-Arnulf Metz, St-Riquier and Lobbes. Cf. also above 868, n. 23. His rebellion, inspired by the new possibility of a Lotharingian kingdom, was more serious than Hincmar reveals in the *AB*; Nelson 1988b: 111-14.

9 Odo, above 870, n. 3; Count Odo may have been the brother-in-law of Louis the Stammerer, above 862, n. 13; 866, n. 3, and Harduin Odo's brother. Their counties are unknown, but probably lay in the area between the Seine and the Oise.

bishops, ten counsellors[10] and a further thirty men comprising *ministeriales* and vassals. On his way to Meersen Louis reached Flamersheim in the Ripuarian district. There he and some of his men fell from a second-storey room which had been built a long time ago and the beams had given way.[11] Louis was rather shaken, but soon recovered, and went on to Aachen. Envoys sped back and forth between those two brothers and kings, until finally they met together on 28 July at the place appointed for the discussions; and they made the following division of Lothar's realm between them:[12]

> This is the share that Louis accepted for himself: Cologne, Trier,[13] Utrecht, Strasbourg, Basel; the abbeys of Süsteren, Berg, Münster-eifel, Kessel, Cornelimünster, St-Maximin [Trier], Echternach, Oeren [Trier], St-Gangulf, Faverney, Poligny, Luxeuil, Lure, Baume, Vellefaux, Moyenmoutier, St-Dié, Bonmoutier, Étival, Remiremont, Murbach, Münster-im-Gregorienthal, Maursmün-ster, Ebersheim, Honau, Maasmünster, Odilienberg, St-Stephen at Strasbourg, Ernstein, St-Ursus at Solothurn, Granfelden, Mouthier-Hautepierre, Jussan [Besançon], Vaucluse, Château-Chalon, Herbitzheim, the abbey at Aachen, Hohenkirche, and Augustkirche; the counties of Teisterbant, Betuwe, Hatterun, Maasgau below this district and also Maasgau above this district, the Liège area on this side [of the Meuse], the Aachen district, the Maastricht district, five counties in the Ripuarian region: Meiengau, Bitgau, Niedgau, lower Saargau, Bliesgau, the Saulnois, Albegau, the Saintois, Chaumont, Upper Saargau, the Ornois which Bernard[14] held, the Soulossois, the Bassigny, Elzgau, the Varais,

---

10 *Consiliarii.* For the significance of this term to denote the group of leading men at court, Keller 1967: 123-55; Nelson 1986a (1983a): 103 and n. 63.

11 Cf. *AF* 870: 71.

12 See map 2, and *MGH. Capit.* II, no. 251, p. 193. For detailed discussion, Nelson 1992.

13 Note that the share is first defined in terms of ecclesiastical provinces. The two metropolitan sees, both vacant in 869, were vital points of control. Despite Charles's attempts to get Hilduin (above 864: 113 and n. 7) installed at Cologne late that year, Louis the German's candidate Willebert became archbishop in January 870; *AX* 871: 29, Regino 870: 99-100. But Charles was successful in having his candidate Bertulf, nephew of Adventius of Metz, consecrated at Trier; Regino 869: 98. Note that Hincmar in the *AB* mentions neither appointment.

14 To be identified as Bernard son of Bernard; cf. above 869: 165 and n. 35, implying that Lothar II in 868/9 had given him part of the Ornois, perhaps hoping to enlist his support for the bastard Hugh.

Escoens, Amous, Baselgau, two counties in Alsace, and in Frisia two-thirds of the realm that Lothar held. On top of this share, we have added this extra portion for the sake of keeping peace and affection: the *civitas* of Metz with the abbey of SS-Peter and Martin, and the county of the Moselle region, with all the *villae* therein, both those in demesne and those held by vassals, then from the Ardennes[15] along the River Ourthe from its source between Bellaing and Thommen and as it flows down to the Meuse, and along the road that runs straight into the Bitgau, according to what the envoys of both of us kings together may determine more justly, except that the eastern part of the county of Condroz which is across the Ourthe is to go to Louis; and the abbeys of Prüm and Stavelot with all their *villae*, both those in demesne and those held by vassals.

This is the share of Lothar's kingdom which Charles accepted for himself: Lyons, Besançon, Vienne, Tongres, Toul, Verdun, Cambrai, Viviers, Uzès; the abbeys of Montfaucon, St-Mihiel, Calmoustier, St-Mary at Besançon, St-Martin also at Besançon, St-Eugendus, St-Marcel [Chalon], St-Laurence at Liège, Senone, Nivelles, Maubeuge, Lobbes, St-Géry [Cambrai], St-Saulve, Crespin, Fosse, Maroilles, Honnecourt, St-Servatius [Maastricht], Malines, Lierre, Soigny, Antoing, Condé, Meerbeck, Dickelvenne, Leuze, Chaumont, St-Mary at Dinant, Aldeneik, Andenne, Walers, and Hautmont; the county of Toxandria, four counties in Brabant, Cambrésis, Hainaut, Lomme, four counties in the Hesbaye, Upper Maasgau on this side of the Meuse, Lower Maasgau on this side, the county of Liège which lies on this side of the Meuse and belongs to Viset, Scarponne, Verdun, the Dormois, Arlon, two counties in the Woëvre district, Mouzon, Mézières, Condroz, then from the Ardennes along the River Ourthe from its source between Bellaing and Thommen, and as it flows down from that part into the Meuse, and along the road that runs straight from this part of the west into the Bitgau, according to whatever our envoys may determine more justly; Toul, the other part of the Ornois which Theutmar[16] held, Bar-le-Duc, Portois, the Sermorens district, Lyons, Vienne, Viviers, Uzès; and the third part of Frisia.

15 The following 'Ardennes' clause evidently caused special difficulty and the boundary here had to be left for later decision; Gorissen 1949.

16 Probably the count who was an oath-swearer on Lothar II's behalf in 865, above: 125.

Next day, 10 August, the two brothers met together, and after wishing each other well went their separate ways: Louis went back to Aachen, and Charles, who had given his wife instructions to meet him at Lestinnes, there distributed as he wished the part of Lothar's realm he had just acquired. From Lestinnes he went to Servais by way of the monastery of St-Quentin, and thence via Quierzy to Compiègne. He spent the autumn hunting-season in the forest of Cuise.

Louis had not given his doctors enough time to cure properly the wound caused by the injury he sustained in falling from the upper storey, as mentioned earlier. He had to have the rotting flesh cut out by these doctors, which meant that he was laid up at Aachen longer than he had hoped, and indeed his condition there was so nearly hopeless that he only just escaped death.

Still at Aachen, Louis received envoys from Pope Hadrian, namely the Cardinal-Bishops John and Peter, and John, a priest of the Roman Church, and also envoys from the Emperor Louis, namely Bishop Wibod [of Parma] and Count Bernard [of Verona], all of whom told him not to usurp the realm of his late nephew Lothar, for it now should belong to Lothar's brother the Emperor Louis.[17]

After speedily dismissing these envoys, Louis sent them on to his brother Charles, while he himself, when he had recovered somewhat, quickly went to Regensburg. Rastiz, chieftain of the Wends, had been betrayed through a trick by his own nephew, captured by Karlmann and held in prison for some time. Louis, after a death sentence had been passed, now ordered him to be blinded and put into a monastery.[18] Then he told his sons Louis and Charles to come to him. But at their mother's prompting, they felt that their father favoured Karlmann rather than themselves,[19] so they refused to come. Just before Lent began, Louis came to the assembly he had arranged to be held at

---

17 In effect this was a joint mission from Hadrian and the Emperor Louis. Hadrian continued to uphold Louis's claims to Lothar's kingdom; *MGH Epp.* VI, nos. 21, 22, pp. 724-6, 726-7. The sees of Bishops John and Peter are unknown. Bishop Wibod of Parma (857-95) was a leading counsellor of Louis II; Keller 1967: 221-2.

18 *AF* 870: 70, adding that Rastiz's nephew was called Zwentibold. Cf. above: 166. The blinding of Rastiz was carried out in November, after an assembly in Bavaria.

19 An alternative translation of this sentence would have Louis the German's wife Queen Emma inciting her husband to favour her first-born son Karlmann against the other two; Fried 1984: 8.

Frankfurt.[20] Envoys went between him and his sons, and thanks to their efforts, an agreement was reached: until the following May, the sons would be able to remain secure so far as their father was concerned, while they were to leave off the ravaging of the realm which they had begun and were to pass the time peacefully until that next assembly. When this affair had thus been settled, Louis returned to Regensburg.

Charles, after completing his autumn hunting, went to the monastery of St-Denis to celebrate the saint's feast day [9 October] there. On that very day, while mass was in progress, the pope's envoys arrived with letters addressed to Charles and to the bishops of his realm, forbidding him with terrible imprecations to touch the realm of the late Lothar which rightly belonged to Lothar's brother the emperor. Charles was angry. But at the request of the envoys and also of a few of his own faithful men, he released his son Carloman from custody in Senlis ordering him to stay with him.[21] He had the envoys of the pope and the emperor conducted as far as Rheims: there he got many of his faithful men to assemble from all sides and after staying there for eight days, he dismissed the envoys. Afterwards he sent his own envoys, namely Ansegis priest and abbot of St-Mihiel, and the layman Etharius,[22] to Rome with letters to the pope: he also sent a piece of cloth made from his own golden vestments, for the altar of St Peter, along with two gold crowns adorned with precious stones.

Charles himself moved to Lyons, where Carloman one night ran away from his father and reached the Belgic province.[23] Gathering around

20 This assembly took place in February 871; *AF*: 73. Hincmar was evidently writing up the 870 annal in mid-871, and entered a block of information on East Frankish affairs; as Meyer-Gebel 1987: 100-1, points out, this explanation of the 'misdating' of the Frankfurt assembly renders redundant the suggestion of L/G: 176, n. 3, that a marginal note had been incorporated into the text at the wrong place.

21 Hadrian II's support for Carloman, again at the behest of the Emperor Louis II, was expressed in *MGH Epp.* VI, no. 31, pp. 735-6. Hincmar does not make explicit his own role as a mediator between Charles and his son; Flodoard III, c. 26, pp. 543-4.

22 Ansegis, a former monk of the diocese of Rheims, had presumably been given the abbacy of St-Mihiel (dep. Meuse) in Lotharingia by Charles in 869/70. He was appointed archbishop of Sens in 871 on Wenilo's death; GC 12, *Instrumenta*: 11. Etharius (following the reading of manuscripts 'A' and 'P') can probably be identified as Itherius, Charles's deputy-count of the palace; cf. T. 375.

23 This final paragraph of the 870 annal was clearly written up early the following year; the account of Carloman's activities is reproduced in a letter of Hincmar's to the archbishop of Lyons, written in February 871, *PL* 126, cols. 277-8; Meyer-Gebel 1987: 100. The 'Belgic province' included the area of Mouzon and Toul in the ecclesiastical province of Trier; Nelson 1988b: 112.

him many accomplices and sons of Belial, he wrought such cruelty and devastation at Satan's instigation, that it could only be believed by those who actually saw and suffered that destruction. Charles was extremely angry, but did not turn aside from his planned campaign: he hastened on as fast as he could to besiege Vienne, where Gerald's wife Bertha was ensconced,[24] while Gerald himself was waiting in another stronghold. During this siege, the surrounding regions were greatly devastated. Charles laid clever plans, and won over a large part of the people in Vienne. Realising this, Bertha sent word to Gerald who came to Vienne and handed the *civitas* over to Charles. The king entered it on Christmas Eve and celebrated Christmas there.

871

Charles, having got Vienne firmly under his control, forced Gerald to give him hostages for his other strongholds which were now to be handed over to royal *missi*. He gave Gerald three ships and let him withdraw from Vienne down the Rhône with his wife and his movable property.[1] Then Charles handed over Vienne to Boso his wife's brother,[2] while he himself sped away as fast as he could to St-Denis, by way of Auxerre and Sens.

Carloman, when he knew of his father's movements, went with his accomplices to Mouzon and laid waste that stronghold together with the surrounding *villae*. He then sent four envoys to his father with a spurious offer: he was willing, he said, to come to him without any *honores*, trusting only to his father's good faith, and to make satisfaction to God and to him for all the wrongs he had committed, only on condition that Charles would deal mercifully with those who were with him, so that their lives would be spared. But Carloman did not leave off, even the least bit, from the evildoing he had begun. Charles then sent Abbot Gauzlin and Count Baldwin, Carloman's brother-in-

---

24 For Gerald, above 856, n. 13, 861, nn. 13, 16 and 17. Gerald's wife Bertha was a daughter of Hugh of Tours, above 830, n. 5. Gerald had been on good terms with Charles in 868, T. 309, and was still in favour in July 870, T. 342. The reasons why Charles decided to oust him are unknown; but the ambitions of Boso may well have played a part; see below, 871. Gerald and Bertha had no surviving son.

1 Nothing more is known of Gerald's fate.

2 Above 869, n. 31.

law,[3] back to his son Carloman, along with two of the latter's envoys, but keeping the other two with him, to tell him a suitable time when he might come to his father in safety, if he wished to do so. Carloman deceitfully pretended he was going to come to his father, but while sending him other envoys who made impossible demands, went himself to the Toul region.

Charles sought a judgement on those who had stolen away his son, a deacon as he was, and a minister of Holy Church handed over to the Lord by his father, and had committed so many outrages and crimes and acts of devastation in his realm.[4] When a death-sentence had been passed on them Charles ordered all their property to be confiscated and squadrons were detailed to drive Carloman and his accomplices out of the realm. Then Charles sought an episcopal judgement on them; and since the Apostle has commanded: 'Do not even eat with such men' [I Cor. 5: 11], the bishops in whose dioceses those men had committed such great crimes excommunicated them according to the sacred canons, and sent letters, as the sacred rules prescribe, to the other bishops to report what they had done. But Charles decided that a judgement must be sought on Carloman from the bishops of the province of Sens, because he was a deacon of the Sens diocese,[5] and because he had perjured himself on solemn oaths he had given on two occasions, as his father took care to make known in a public declaration to all who were present, and had committed such great crimes of rebellion and infidelity against his father and such atrocities in his realm.

Then Charles returned to St-Denis at the beginning of Lent [1 March] and stayed there until Easter [15 April], which he also celebrated there.

---

3 Gauzlin, above 858, n. 6; he had received the abbacy of St-Amand, lost by Carloman in 870, and was also abbot of St-Germain-des-Prés. Baldwin, 862, n. 2, 863, n. 9. See Nelson 1988b: 136, n. 31.

4 Carloman's supporters included counts Goslin and Conrad; late in 870 and early in 871, Hincmar wrote to Counts Engelram, Goslin and Adalelm, conveying the king's instructions to mobilise troops against Carloman, but at the same time advocating joint efforts at conciliation; Flodoard III, c. 26, p. 543. Charles hoped to use these counts as go-betweens with Carloman. But Engelram fell from favour in 871 or early 872, presumably because he had gone over to Carloman: Grierson 1939: 309, n. 4. Hincmar himself clearly favoured conciliation: in the *AB* he is evidently not telling all he knows.

5 Carloman had been ordained deacon by Bishop Hildegar of Meaux, in the province of Sens; Hincmar Ep. 55, *PL* 126, col. 277.

Carloman, hotly pursued by the troops sent after him by his father, crossed the Jura Mountains, and went on with the evil deeds he had begun in the region of the Belgic provinces and of Gaul.

Hincmar, bishop of Laon in name only, an exceptionally arrogant man, rebelled against his king contrary to the truth of the Gospel and to apostolic and ecclesiastical authority. Without showing respect for anyone he raged against the neighbouring clergy and laity and those committed to him and scorned to pay any attention to his metropolitan when, as the rules lay down, he warned him about his behaviour. He roused the king, his archbishop, and the bishops of the whole realm to such fury against him that the king summoned a synod to meet at Douzy in August, to pass judgement there on Hincmar's depravities.[6]

King Charles, at the request of his nephews, his brother Louis's sons Louis [the Younger] and Charles [the Fat], travelled by way of Verdun to meet and talk with them.[7] Then he returned to the synod at Douzy.

Meanwhile Abbot Hugh of St-Martin and Gauzfrid,[8] with other men from beyond the Seine, launched an ill-considered attack on the island in the Loire where the Northmen had their base camp. Hugh and Gauzfrid suffered very heavy losses and barely managed to escape, leaving many dead.

[Bishop] Hincmar came to the synod in the end, but in a most arrogant fashion. There a petition was presented by King Charles following the ecclesiastical rules, and Hincmar, having been accused and convicted on clearly proven charges according to the statutory procedures, received the statutory sentence of deposition. All this is contained in the official records of the synod, as sent by the synod itself to the apostolic see through the venerable Bishop Actard who had been present at it.[9]

Charles's nephews now came to him at Douzy and asked him to reconcile them and their father. Envoys also came to Charles from his brother Louis asking him to come and hold talks with him near the township of Maastrict. Charles went along, taking with him his

6 Above 868, nn. 16, 17, 25; 870, n. 6; McKeon 1978: 132-46.

7 Above 870: 170-1.

8 Hugh and Gauzfrid, above 869: 163.

9 The Council of Douzy was attended by eight archbishops and twenty-one bishops. Hincmar of Rheims had a large hand in the *acta*, Mansi XVI, 569-678; Nelson 1991. For Actard, above 868, n. 7.

nephews' envoys to act as mouthpieces for them in explaining what they wanted from their father. There King Charles gave an audience to envoys sent from his own son Carloman, with his brother Louis acting as a go-between.[10] As before, Charles invited his son to return to him on condition that he abandoned his wicked ways, but the invitation produced no response at all. Louis and Charles stayed at their discussions for some time but made little or no progress, so at the beginning of September they parted from each other and returned to their own lands. Louis made for Regensburg, because he had suffered extremely heavy losses at the hands of the nephew of Rastiz who had succeeded him in the Wendish chiefaincy. Wendish attacks had been so severe that Louis had lost his *markiones* with a large force of his men, and also suffered disastrous losses of the territory he had gained in the years preceding.[11]

Charles for his part went by way of Lestinnes towards his *villa* of Orville where he planned to hunt. But on the way there he received envoys from a number of people in Italy, inviting him to go there: his nephew Louis, they said, along with his wife and daughter, had been slain in Benevento by the Beneventans.[12] Charles thereupon moved by way of Rheims to Besançon, where Carloman, hearing that his father was coming in pursuit of him, came to him at last, on the advice of his own men, with a show of humility. His father received him and ordered him to stay with him: when he had a chance to go to the Belgic province to speak with his faithful men there, Charles said, he would decide with their counsel what *honores* he ought to grant to Carloman. Louis king of Germany also reacted to the news of the death of his nephew the Emperor Louis: he dispatched his son Charles [the Fat] to the territory he held beyond the Jura Mountains, to bind as many men as he could to his allegiance by solemn oaths, and this young Charles duly did.[13]

Charles was still at Besançon when the envoys he had sent on ahead to Italy came back with the news that the Emperor Louis was alive after all and in good health. This is what had happened: Adalgis had

10 For the Maastricht meeting, *AF* 871 and n. 6. Charles and Louis the German were both exploiting their nephews' grievances.

11 Above 870, n. 18. *AF* 871 report a heavy defeat of Karlmann and the Bavarians by Zwentibold.

12 The rumour was false: for what had really happened, see below.

13 The dispatch of Charles the Fat to the region around Orbe is not mentioned in the *AF*.

conspired with other Beneventans against the emperor, because the
emperor at his wife's instigation had been planning to sent Adalgis
into permanent exile.[14] Adalgis in turn had planned a night-attack on
him, but the emperor along with his wife and those of his men he had
with him went up into a high and very well-fortified tower, where he
and his men defended themselves for three whole days. Finally the
bishop of Benevento got the Beneventans to agree to terms: the
emperor was to give them solemn oaths, and in return they would let
him go, safe and sound. The emperor, his wife and daughter, and all
the men he had with him then swore that they would never in any way
seek any vengeance at all for what had just happened nor take any
reprisal, whether in person or through anyone else, for the crime
committed against him; nor would the emperor ever enter Beneventan
territory with an army. So Louis got away, and journeyed by way of
Spoleto towards Ravenna. He sent word to Pope Hadrian to come and
meet him *en route* to absolve him and his men of the solemn oath they
had just sworn. Meanwhile Lambert with the other Lambert began to
suspect that the emperor believed them responsible for what had been
done to him, so they abandoned him and made their way to the
Benevento region, because Adalgis was in league with them.[15] Sending
his wife to Ravenna where he had arranged to hold his next assembly,
the emperor set off in pursuit of the two Lamberts. He gave orders for
all the leading men of the realm of Italy to join his wife at Ravenna to
discuss the issues he had put on the agenda, until he returned from his
expedition. But the emperor could not catch the men he pursued, so he
set about returning to Ravenna as planned.

Now Charles, having heard all about the episode in which he had
thought the Emperor Louis had been killed, and learning that in fact
he was still alive, left Besançon and travelled by a direct route, via
Ponthion and Attigny, all the way to Servais. There he held an
assembly with his cousellors, and on their advice he again consigned
Carloman to prison at Senlis, while Carloman's accomplices he ordered
to be bound by a solemn oath of fidelity, each of them in his own

---

14 Adalgis was duke of Benevento; Erchampert cc. 20, 29-38, pp. 242, 245-9, with
   the assertion, p. 247, that the Beneventans rebelled because 'the Gauls had
   begun to persecute them'. For the credibility of the Empress Engelberga's
   alleged role, Odegaard 1951: 79.

15 One Lambert (grandson of the Lambert who had been Lothar I's supporter,
   above 834, n. 7, 837, n. 5) was *marchio* of Spoleto (c. 860–c. 879), the other,
   Lambert the Bald, was count of Camerino; Hlawitschka 1960: 59-60, 214. For
   South Italian politics at this period, Wickham 1981: 62-3, 153-5.

county; and Charles allowed them to live in his kingdom on condition
that each received a lord, whomever he wished, from amongst the
king's faithful men, and that each expressed his willingness to live in
peace.[16] Then from Servais he went to Compiègne and spent Christmas
there.

872

On 19 January Charles left Compiègne and went to Moustier-sur-
Sambre[1] to hold talks with the Northmen Roric and Rodulf.[2] He returned to Compiègne at the beginning of Lent [13 February], and on
the Saturday before Palm Sunday [22 March], he reached St-Denis
where he celebrated Easter [30 March]. After Easter he set out for St-
Maurice to meet the Empress Engelberga, in accordance with the
suggestion he had made to her through his envoys. But then he found
out for certain that Engelberga was going to Trento in May to speak
with King Louis of Germany; so he turned back from his planned
journey and returned to Servais. There Adalard[3] came to him on behalf
of his brother Louis: Charles was requested to come to speak with his
brother Louis near Maastricht, when Louis had returned to Aachen
from Regensburg after sending an army with his son Karlmann
against the Wends.

To his son Louis Charles now assigned his wife's brother Boso as his
chamberlain and master of the door-keepers; he granted Boso the
honores of Count Gerald of Bourges[4] and sent him to Aquitaine along
with Bernard and the other Bernard, the *markio*, entrusting to him the
administration of that realm.[5] To Count Bernard of Toulouse, after

---

16 No capitulary survives from this assembly. But there are echoes of its terms in
the Capitulary of Quierzy, below 873, n. 2.

1 For this identification, Dierkens 1985: 65-70, 329.

2 Above 870, n. 1. Charles's aim was probably to forestall the alliance of these
warlords with Carloman; Nelson 1988b: 113.

3 This Adalard was perhaps the son of the ex-seneschal; Lot 1970a (1908b): 606-
7; or else his nephew; L/G: 185, n. 4. But it may be the ex-seneschal himself.
He had been deprived of his honours in Charles's kingdom in 865, above: 129,
and returned to his lands in the Middle Kingdom in the Moselle region which
now belonged to Louis the German. Cf. below 873, n. 11.

4 Above 868: 143, and n. 18. Nothing further is known of this Gerald.

5 This reorganisation of the sub-kingdom of Aquitaine reaffirmed Louis the
Stammerer's subordination to his father's authority, perhaps because Charles
feared that his eldest son might give support to his brother Carloman. Hence

G

solemn oaths had been sworn, Charles granted Carcassonne and the Razès, and sent him back to Toulouse.

Louis king of Germany summoned to him his sons Louis and Charles and to induce them to be reconciled with Karlmann he caused oaths to be sworn to them insincerely. But no less insincerely did those sons and their men give solemn oaths to Louis. Their father's real wish was that those sons should join their brother Karlmann in a compaign against the Wends, but he could not get them to agree. Still, he sent along with Karlmann as large an army as he could muster, while he himself, as mentioned earlier, went to speak with Engelberga at Trento. He secretly agreed to give up that part of Lothar's realm which he had received at Charles's expense, neglecting now the oaths sealed between them, and without the consent or even knowledge of the men of the late Lothar who had commended themselves to him. Thus there were now made between Louis and Engelberga mutual oaths different from, and indeed contrary to, those earlier oaths he had exchanged with his brother.[6] When all this was settled, Engelberga sent her envoy to Charles, asking him to take up an earlier suggestion and come to meet her at St-Maurice. But Charles, who knew all about what had gone on between her and his brother, refused to go there, instead sending her his envoys. They returned from her without anything definite to report.

Pope Hadrian, following out the intentions of his predecessor Nicholas, dispatched his envoys, Donatus bishop of Ostia, Stephen bishop of Nepi and Marinus, a deacon of the holy Roman Church, to Constantinople to the Emperor Basil and his sons the Augusti Constantine and Leo.[7] With these envoys there also travelled Anastasius, librarian of the Roman see, a man learned in both languages, that is, in Greek and in Latin.[8] A synod was summoned, termed by those who attended it the Eighth Oecumenical Council, and

---

too the establishment of Boso in Aquitaine. For Count Bernard of Toulouse, above 868, n. 19. Hincmar characteristically applies the title *marchio* to Bernard of Gothia, above 865, n. 3; 868, n. 20. The third Bernard, distinguished here by his lack of a title, can be identified as Bernard son of the tyrant Bernard. Perhaps now or shortly after, he was given the now-vacant countship of the Auvergne. Hincmar implies that until now he had recovered no countship in Charles's kingdom.

6 There is no mention of this Trento meeting in *AF*, or in any other source.

7 For Basil, now sole emperor, above 869: 162 and n. 24. Hadrian was keen to concert military operations against the Saracens in southern Italy.

8 Above 868, n. 9. Anastasius had been restored to Hadrian's favour in 869. For Hincmar's correspondence with him, see Nelson 1991.

there they calmed the schism that had arisen over the deposition of Ignatius and the ordination of Photius: Photius was anathematised and Ignatius reinstated. In this synod, they also passed decrees concerning the necessity of images, decrees different from what the orthodox teachers had previously laid down. In order to get the approval of the pope, who gave his assent to their desire that images be adored, they passed certain decrees that were contrary both to the ancient canons and, indeed, to their own synod, as anyone who reads the records of that synod will find clearly revealed.[9]

On the Eve of Pentecost, the Emperor Louis came to Rome, and was crowned next day [18 May] by Pope Hadrian.[10] Then after Mass had been celebrated, Louis wearing his crown rode with the pope in solemn procession to the Lateran palace. Afterwards, having mustered his army, he left Rome and again made for the region of Benevento. The magnates of Italy hated Engelberga because of her high-handedness, so they pressed the emperor to accept the daughter of Winigis[11] in her place, and got him to agree to send an envoy to Engelberga telling her to stay in Italy and not to follow him south but to wait until he came back again to Italy. Engelberga, however, paid not the slightest attention to these instructions, but hastened after Louis. Meanwhile she sent Bishop Wibod[12] to Charles to show, so she said, her feelings of true friendship; she thought Charles did not know about the agreements made between herself and Louis king of Germany.

Wibod presented himself to Charles at Pontailler,[13] where Charles had gone to sort out affairs in Burgundy. There he received the news that Bernard, nicknamed 'the Calf', had been killed by men of Bernard, son of Bernard; and his *honores* were given to that second Bernard.[14] But

9 Though the Eighth Oecumenical Council had ended in February 870; Dvornik 1948: 145-58, Hincmar seems to have first learned of its decrees via papal legates at Gondreville in November 872, below: 180. See Meyer-Gebel 1987: 81.

10 For this ritual as a 'confirmatory coronation', see Brühl 1962: 279-80.

11 Winigis was count of Siena; Hlawitschka 1960: 68. Hincmar's is the sole evidence for this episode.

12 Above 870: 170.

13 Identified as Pontailler (dep. Côte-d'Or) by Lot 1970a (1904b): 569-75.

14 Despite attempts by Dhondt 1948: 305-16 and Bouchard 1986 to identify 'Bernard the Calf' as Count Bernard of Toulouse, it seems clear from the context of this passage that this Bernard, and his *honores*, belong in Burgundy; Calmette 1951: 105-8. 'The Calf' is best identified as a man hitherto unmentioned by Hincmar in the *AB*: either a brother of Count Eccard of Autun, referred to in Eccard's will (876) as deceased; Levillain 1937b: 360-1, 374-80

Charles returned from Burgundy to Gondreville to hold the assembly he had already summoned there for the beginning of September.[15] After staying there for a short while and making all the arrangements that seemed to him necessary, he went off to hunt in the Ardennes.

In October he came by boat down the Meuse to Maastrict and held talks with the Northmen Roric and Rodulf who had come up the river to meet him. He gave a gracious reception to Roric who had proved loyal to him, but Rodulf he dismissed empty-handed, because he had been plotting acts of treachery and pitching his demands too high. Charles prepared his faithful men for defence against Rodulf's treacherous attacks.[16] Then he rode back by way of Attigny to the monastery of St-Médard where he spent Christmas.

Pope Hadrian died, and on 14 December, John, archdeacon of the Roman Church, was installed in his place.[17]

873[1]

Now there were many in Charles's realm who expected that Carloman would wreak still further evils in the holy Church of God and in the other realms in which Charles discharged the office of a king. Therefore with the advice of his faithful men and according to the custom of his predecessors and his ancestors, Charles promulgated laws relevant to the peace of the Church and the internal strengthening of the realm, and he decreed that all were to obey them.[2] He also

(though the identification was renounced by Levillain 1946, and Levillain 1948: 35), or another kinsman of Eccard. Bernard son of the tyrant Bernard would have had an hereditary claim to *honores* in Burgundy (not necessarily including the countship, as Wollasch 1957b: 187-8 observes) once held by his elder brother William; Nithard III, 2. Since 'the Calf' and the son of the tyrant Bernard were close kinsmen, the killing in 872 can be seen as part of a family dispute over property.

15 On 9 September, Charles received oaths from bishops and lay magnates to help him 'to gain what God shall grant you hereafter': probably a reference to the kingdom of Italy; *MGH Capit.* II, no. 277, pp. 341-2.

16 Above 872, n. 2. Nelson 1988b: 113 suggests that Rodulf had intrigued with Carloman.

17 John VIII (872-82). John clearly meant to support Charles's claims to the imperial title; Kelly 1986: 110.

1 Two recent attempts to analyse the structure of this annal are Meyer-Gebel 1987: 86-8, and Nelson 1988b.

2 Quierzy, 4 January 873, *MGH Capit.* II, no. 278, pp. 342-7: among measures promulgated were (i) that former rebels would be forgiven provided they made

gave orders that the bishops of his realm were to assemble at Senlis
where Carloman still was, so that they might carry out their episcopal
responsibility concerning him, in accordance with the sacred canons
from which, as Pope Leo says, they are 'not permitted to depart
through any negligence or any presumption'.[3] The bishops did what
had to be done: they deposed Carloman from all ecclesiastical rank,
according to the sacred rules, and left him only the communion of a
layman.

When this had been done, the ancient cunning Enemy incited
Carloman and his accomplices to exploit another argument, namely,
that because he no longer held any ecclesiastical orders he could be all
the more free to assume the title and power of a king, and because by
the bishops' judgement he had lost his clerical rank, he could all the
more readily abandon his ecclesiastical way of life. So it came about
that following his deposition, his former accomplices began to rally to
him again more enthusiastically than ever and to seduce into joining
him as many others as they could, so that, as soon as they got the
chance, they might snatch him away from the prison where he was
being held, and set him up as their king. It was therefore necessary to
bring out again into the open all those charges on which he had not
been judged by the bishops, and according to what was laid down in
the sacred laws[4] he was condemned to death for his crimes. So that he
might have time and opportunity for doing penance, however, yet not
have the power to commit the still worse offences he was planning, the
death sentence was commuted, by the public assent of all present, to a
sentence of blinding.[5] This was in order that the pernicious hope in
him on the part of those who hated peace might be deceived so far as
he was concerned, and the church of God and the Christian religion in
Charles's realm might not be disturbed by deadly sedition, in addition
to the attacks of the pagans.

amends and remained loyal in future; (ii) malefactors were threatened with
outlawry and confiscation of their allods ; and (iii) counts were to arrest and put
to the ordeal men and women suspected of witchcraft.

3 Leo I, Ep. 14, *PL* 54, col. 672. The *acta* of the Synod of Senlis are lost, but its
 five decrees were also concerned with presenting Charles's case against
 Carloman; Mansi XVII, col. 282.

4 *Sacrae leges*: a reference to Roman law which punished treason by death.

5 Blinding as a commutation for capital punishment in treason cases was a
 Byzantine practice imported into the West in the sixth and seventh centuries;
 McCormick 1986: 313, 334. Hincmar of Laon was also blinded, allegedly by
 Boso; *AV* 878: 43; *MGH Epp.* VI, p. 95. Hincmar of Rheims does not mention
 this.

King Louis of Germany came before Christmas to the palace of
Frankfurt, where he celebrated Christmas and gave notice that his
assembly would be held there at the beginning of February.[6] He gave
orders that his sons Louis and Charles with his other faithful men were
to attend this meeting, and also the men of the late Lothar's kingdom
who had commended themselves to him. While Louis waited there, the
Devil in the guise of an Angel of light came to his son Charles and told
him that his father, who was trying to ruin him for the sake of his
brother Karlmann, had offended God and would soon lose his
kingdom, and that God had arranged that that kingdom was to be held
by none other than Charles, and that he would have it very soon.
Charles was terror-stricken because the apparition clung to the house
where he was staying. He went into a church but the Devil followed
him in and said to him again: 'Why are you frightened and why do you
run away? If I who foretell to you what is soon to happen had not come
from God, I would not be able to follow you into this house of the
Lord.' By these and other smooth arguments, the Devil persuaded him
to receive from his hand the communion God had sent him. Charles
did so, and passing inside his mouth, Satan entered him.[7] Charles then
came to his father, and was sitting in council with his brothers and the
other faithful men, both bishops and laymen, when he leapt up,
suddenly possessed, and said that he wished to abandon the world and
would not touch his wife in carnal intercourse. Taking his sword from
his belt he let it fall to the ground. As he tried to undo his sword-belt
and take off his princely clothing he began to shake violently. He was
held firm by the bishops and other men, and with his father much
distressed and all present thunderstruck, he was led into a church.
Archbishop Liutbert[8] put on his priestly vestments and began to sing
mass. When he got as far as the Gospel, Charles began to shout out
with great cries in his native language,'Woe, woe', like that over and
over again, until the whole Mass was finished. His father handed him
over to the bishops and other faithful men, and ordered him to be led
about from one sacred place of holy martyrs to another, so that their
merits and prayers might free him from the demon and he might be
able by God's mercy to recover his sanity. Then he planned to send
Charles to Rome, but various other affairs intervened and the idea of
this journey was given up.

6 *AF*: 873.

7 For discussion of the theological significance of this account, Nelson 1988b:
    129-30.

8 Of Mainz (863-89), a strong supporter of Louis the German.

Emperor Louis of Italy was residing at Capua now that Lambert the Bald was dead.[9] The *patricius* of the emperor of the Greeks arrived with an army at the *civitas* of Otranto to bring help to the Beneventans, who now promised to pay him the tribute they had given until then to the emperors of Francia. Louis found there was no other way to win back Adalgis's adherence but to ask Pope John, who had baptised Adalgis's son, to come to him in the Campagna and reconcile Adalgis with him. Louis wanted it to look as if he was receiving Adalgis in response to an appeal from the vicar of St Peter.[10] He had sworn that he would never leave those parts until he had captured Adalgis, but this was something which in fact he was incapable of achieving by any act of military prowess.

Charles announced that the host would go in the direction of Brittany, so that the Northmen occupying Angers could not surmise that they were going to attack that region, in which case they might have fled away to other places where they could not be so tightly hemmed in. While he was going towards Brittany, and actually on the march, news came to Charles that as a result of the scheming of his brother King Louis of Germany, the now-blind Carloman had been taken away from the monastery of Corbie by some of his former supporters with the connivance of two false monks, and brought to Louis in order to harm Charles's interests, despite the effors of Adalard to intervene and prevent this.[11] Charles was not greatly upset by this news, but proceeded on the campaign he had begun.

The Northmen, after ravaging various towns, rasing fortresses to the ground, burning churches and monasteries and turning cultivated land into a desert, had for some time now been established in Angers. Charles now besieged this *civitas* with the host he had got together, and surrounded it with a very strong enclosing earthwork, while Salomon, duke of the Bretons, stayed in position on the other side of the River Mayenne with his army of Bretons to be ready to help Charles.[12] During the time that King Charles was engaged in this

9 Above 871: 176.

10 On Louis II's alliances with the Byzantines and with John VIII, Partner 1976: 66-7. Charters show the emperor at Capua in May.

11 This seems to be the last appearance in the sources of Adalard the seneschal. Louis the German's involvement in Carloman's escape may have something to do with Corbie's close connections with Korvey in Saxony. Cf. the escape of Charles son of Pippin, above 854, n. 10. Adalard may have been trying to balance the interests of Louis and Charles; cf. above 872, n. 3.

12 Regino's account, 873: 105-7, credits Salomon with the idea of diverting the

siege, Salomon sent to him his son, whose name was Wicon, together with the leading men of the Bretons, and Wicon commended himself to Charles and in the presence of his own faithful men swore him an oath of fidelity.[13]

Meanwhile the Northman Rodulf, who had inflicted many evils on Charles's realm, was slain in the realm of Louis with 500 and more of his accomplices.[14] Charles got reliable news of this as he remained in his position near Angers.

A swarm of locusts poured itself throughout Germany, the Gauls and especially Spain: it was so large, it could be compared with the plague of Egypt.[15]

King Louis of Germany was making arrangements to hold an assembly at Metz, when he got word that if he did not send help very quickly indeed to his son Karlmann on the Wendish frontier, he would never see him again. Immediately Louis turned round and made for Regensburg.[16] He entrusted the blind Carloman to Archbishop Liutbert to be looked after in the monastery of St-Alban at Mainz, thereby making very clear his strong disapproval of all the evil deeds which that Carloman had committed against the holy Church of God, against the Christian people and against his own father, whenever and wherever he had had the chance. Louis reached Regensburg, and through his envoys he won over as opportunities arose the various groups of Wends who were organised under different chiefs. He received the envoys who had been sent to deceive him by those people called the Bohemians: then he flung them into prison.

Charles carried on manfully and energetically his siege of the Northmen right round the *civitas* of Angers. He cowed them so

river Mayenne and so securing the Vikings' capitulation. Werner 1959a argues that Regino himself was at Angers in 873, and that notes left there by Regino underlie a tenth-century account of the episode written at Angers. But Schleidgen 1977 shows that this account depends on Regino. It is not clear that Regino's version of events should be preferred to Hincmar's, therefore; see below, nn. 13, 17.

13 Wicon's acknowledgement of Charles's overlordship may well have reflected Salomon's difficulties in Brittany; Smith 1992. It certainly fitted with Charles's developing ideas of imperial rulership; Nelson 1989b.

14 Cf. above 872, n. 16. *AF* date Rodulf's attack on Frisia to June. His defeat occurred near Dokkum; *AF* n. 10.

15 This plague is mentioned by *AF*: 78; *AX*: 33; *AV*: 40; and Regino: 105. See Nelson 1988b: 122, 123.

16 *AF* date the Metz assembly to August. Though *AF* mention no stay by Louis the German at Regensburg before November, he was probably there in mid-September; Dümmler 1887(ii): 371.

thoroughly that their chiefs came to him and commended themselves to him, swore exactly the solemn oaths he ordered, and handed over as many, and as important, hostages as he demanded.[17] The conditions imposed were, that on the day appointed, they should leave Angers and never again as long as they lived either wreak devastation in Charles's realm or agree to others' doing so. They requested to be allowed to stay until February on an island in the Loire, and to hold a market there; and, in February, they agreed, those of them who had by then been baptised and wished thenceforth to hold truly to the Christian religion would come and submit to Charles, those still pagan but willing to become Christian would be baptised under conditions to be arranged by Charles, but the rest would depart from his realm, never more, as stated above, to return to it with evil intent.

After all this, Charles together with the bishops and people, with the greatest demonstration of religious fervour, restored to their rightful places with rich offerings the bodies of SS Albinus and Licinius which had been disinterred from their graves for fear of the Northmen. So, when the Northmen had been thrown out of Angers and hostages had been received, Charles left there in October and travelling by way of the *civitas* of Le Mans and the town [*oppidum*] of Évreux, and passing close by the new fort at Pîtres he arrived at Amiens at the beginning of November. From there he went to hunt at his *villa* of Orville and in the surrounding district, and thus reached St-Vaast where he celebrated Christmas.

874

A long, hard winter, with such a tremendous amount of snow that no one could remember seeing anything like it.[1]

Charles held a meeting with his counsellors on the feast of the Purification of St Mary [2 February] at the monastery of St-Quentin. He then spent Lent at St-Denis and celebrated Easter [11 April] there. He also held a general assembly at the *villa* of Douzy on 13 June, and received his annual gifts. From there he moved to Compiègne by

17 The content and structure of Hincmar's account make it likely that he was with Charles at the siege of Angers. Charles's ability to secure the hostages he wanted confirms his success. *AV*: 40 condemn the agreement but mention Charles's receipt of hostages. Regino: 106 says the Vikings also gave Charles a lot of money.
1 Also noted in *AF* 874.

way of Attigny and the other usual staging-posts.[2]

The long summer produced a drying-up of the grass and a poor harvest.

Various conflicting reports had been arriving about Salomon chief of the Bretons, some saying that he was ill, some that he was dead. At Compiègne Charles got definite news of his death.[3] It came about like this: a rebellion was mounted against him by the Breton magnates Pascwethen, Guorhwant,[4] and Wicon son of Ruilin[5] and also some *Franci homines* to whom Salomon had been extremely oppressive.5 After they had captured Salomon's son Wicon and thrown him into prison, Salomon fled to Poher and went into a little monastery from which he hoped to be able to make his escape.[6] But he was surrounded and caught by his own people; and because no Breton might inflict any bodily harm on him, he was handed over to the *Franci homines*, Fulcoald and the rest, who blinded him so savagely that he was found dead next day.[7] Thus did Salomon receive his just deserts: he was the man who had turned on his own lord Erispoë[8] and slain him as he fled from his attacker into a church, even as he was crying out to the Lord on the altar.

Lous king of Germany sent his son Charles [the Fat], with other envoys, to his brother Charles, with the request that the two kings might hold discussions together by the Moselle. Charles was on his

---

2 *Mansionatica*: important evidence for the organisation of the king's itinerary, perhaps still using staging-posts at c. 20-km. intervals along Roman roads; Brühl 1968: 65-7.

3 28 June.

4 Pascwethen, above 867: 139; further information on his career, Davies 1990: 107. Guorhwant was perhaps Erispoë's son-in-law; Davies 1988: 21.

5 The term *Franci homines* here probably has the meaning of free tenants owing special military services. These men, or their ancestors, may have been settled on the Breton March by Carolingian rulers. By the 860s, they represented the local squirearchy of western Neustria who had been put under Salomon's control by the treaty of 867 (above: 140) and made to perform military service for him. The alliance of Breton and Frankish opponents proved fatal for Salomon. See further Smith 1992.

6 The Poher region is in western Brittany (dep. Finistère); Davies 1990: 99. Was the monastery Landévennec? (The identification as Plélan, Salomon's foundation near Rennes, Waitz 1883: 125, n. 6, cannot be right.)

7 Fulcoald's name suggests that he may have been a kinsman of Ingelger count of Angers; cf. Werner 1958: 277 for the name-element Fulc-. For blinding as a penalty, see above 873, n. 5.

8 Above 857: 85.

way to this meeting when he went down with dysentery and thus detained, was unable to appear at the meeting as arranged. The discussions between Louis and Charles were therefore held near the Meuse at Herstal about the beginning of December.[9] Charles returned from this meeting by way of St-Quentin and celebrated Christmas at Compiègne, while Louis spent it at Aachen and from there crossed the Rhine and returned to his palace at Frankfurt.

875

About the beginning of Lent [9 February] Charles came to St-Denis and he celebrated Easter [27 March] there. Richildis his wife gave birth prematurely to a baby boy on the night of 22 March. After being baptised the baby soon died. Richildis stayed at St-Denis until the days of her cleansing after childbirth were completed. Charles meanwhile moved to Bezu-Saint-Éloi,[1] came back to St-Denis to celebrate the litanies before Ascension Day [5 May], and then moved to Compiègne where he arrived on the Eve of Pentecost [14 May].

In May Louis king of Germany held his assembly at Tribur but failing to complete at it the business he had intended, he gave notice that another assembly would be held in August at the same place.[2]

In August Charles came to Douzy near the Ardennes, and there he learned for certain that his nephew Louis emperor of Italy had died.[3] At this news he moved rapidly from Douzy to Ponthion, where he gave orders for his counsellors[4] in those parts, those of them he could influence, to come to meet him, and he got help for his journey from as many as he could. From Ponthion he moved to Langres and waited for the men he had already picked to take with him to Italy. He sent his wife Richildis back to Servais by way of Rheims, and he sent his son Louis to that part of his realm which he had gained after the death of his nephew Lothar as a result of the agreement with his brother

9 The mission of Charles the Fat and the subsequent talks between his father and Charles the Bald must have centred on the Italian succession; *AF* 874, with nn. 10, 12, locating the talks between Louis and Charles at St-Lambert Liège.

1 Dep. Eure, 35 km. south-west of Beauvais. Charles stayed at this palace again in 876; T. 406, 407.

2 *AF*: 875.

3 At Brescia on 12 August. *AF* add that Louis II was buried at San-Ambrogio, Milan.

4 Cf. 870, n. 10.

Louis.[5] Then at the beginning of September he began his journey, and travelling by way of the monastery of St-Maurice, he crossed the *Mons Iovis* pass and entered Italy.

His brother Louis king of Germany sent his son Charles [the Fat] to Italy to put up opposition to his brother, but King Charles forced him to take flight and leave Italy altogether. Then Louis sent another son, Karlmann, to Italy, with as many men as he could muster to offer resistance to his [Louis's] brother.[6] King Charles got wind of this and advanced to meet him with a superior force. Karlmann, realising that he was incapable of resisting his uncle, came to talk with him and to sue for peace; and when oaths had been solemnly exchanged, he went back to his own country.

Engelram, Charles's former chamberlain and administrator of the fisc, had been thrown out of his *honores* and dismissed from Charles's favour through the influence of Queen Richildis.[7] He now persuaded Louis [the German] to march with his son and namesake Louis and a large army as far as Attigny.[8] On the orders of Queen Richildis the magnates of Charles's realm steeled themselves with solemn oaths to resist Louis, but instead of holding to their purpose they ravaged Charles's realm on their own account and devastated it in just the way an enemy would do. Louis and his army likewise ravaged that realm. Louis spent Christmas at Attigny, having bribed the magnates.[9] Then, after laying

5 Richildis was in effect being left as regent. Louis the Stammerer was sent to hold the part of Lotharingia acquired by his father in 870. Charles evidently feared an invasion from the east.

6 For the suggestion that Louis II had given Louis the German an undertaking on Karlmann's succession, see *AF* 875, n. 3. Hincmar's account implies the considerable extent of Charles's support in Italy. His nephew *Marchio* Berengar of Friuli supported Karlmann, however. Berengar's mother Gisèle was Charles the Bald's only full sibling; his father was Eberhard *marchio* of Friuli (for this marriage, Nelson 1990c: 152). Berengar became king of Italy in 887, and emperor in 915. He was killed in 924.

7 Above 871, n. 4.

8 According to *AF* 875, Louis's aim was 'to force Charles to leave Italy'.

9 Hincmar in this passage is disingenuous. In his *de Fide Servanda* ('Keeping Faith'), *PL* 125, cols. 963-84, a circular letter to the bishops and lay magnates of the Rheims province, he combined lukewarm counsels of loyalty with scathing criticisms of Charles attributed to others, in effect making the case for capitulation to Louis the German. Hincmar's real reason for hostility to Charles at this time is not stated in the *AB*: Charles had taken with him to Italy Archbishop Ansegis of Sens (above 870, n. 22) in order to have him appointed papal vicar north of the Alps; *PL* 126, col. 660. The church of Rheims suffered badly from the events of winter 875-76. Louis the German's men 'ravaged all they could find', *AF* 875. The important *villa* of Neuilly, recently restored to

waste Charles's realm, he withdrew along with certain of the counts of Charles's realm who had gone over to him.[10] Travelling by way of Trier he reached the palace of Frankfurt on the other side of the Rhine, and there he passed Lent and celebrated Easter [15 April]. He also got news that his wife Emma had died soon after Christmas at the palace of Regensburg.[11]

Some of the leading men of Italy did not come over to Charles,[12] but he received the submission of most of them, and on the invitation of Pope John he arrived at Rome.[13] There on 14 December he was received by the pope with great ceremony in the church of St-Peter, and

876

on Christmas Day, after making an offering of many precious gifts to St Peter, he was anointed and crowned emperor and was accorded the title of Emperor of the Romans.[1] He left Rome on 5 January, and returned to Pavia where he held his assembly.[2] Boso, his wife's brother, was set up as duke of that land and invested with a ducal crown.[3] Then

the church of Rheims by Charles, was granted by Richildis and Louis the Stammerer to local magnates, and recovered only when Charles returned from Italy in 876; Hincmar, *de Villa Noviliaco*, PL 125, col. 1124.

10 Only Engelram can be identified. Other defectors may have been former supporters of Carloman, above 871, n. 4.

11 On 31 January. She was buried at St-Emmeram, Regensburg. She had been Charles's maternal aunt, a sister of the Empress Judith.

12 One leading Italian who seems not to have come over to Charles was Berengar of Friuli, above 875, n. 6, whom Andreas of Bergamo, p. 230, names as a supporter of Charles the Fat. For other likely opponents of Charles the Bald, see below 878, n. 6. Suppo and Arding, cousins of the Empress Engelberga, supported Charles the Bald; *MGH Capit.* II, no. 220, pp. 99-100.

13 Cf. above 875, n. 6. According to *AF* 875, Charles dispensed lavish bribes to win support in Italy. Andreas, pp. 229-30, makes no such allegation.

1 The date was chosen to evoke the coronation of Charlemagne exactly seventy-five years before. The gifts to St Peter probably included the *cathedra Petri* (above 869, n. 16) and the Bible of San Paolo; Nees 1990: 343-4.

2 For the record of Charles's election, his oath, and the oaths of the Italian *fideles*, *MGH Capit.* II, nos. 220, 221, pp. 98-104. Present at Pavia were the archbishop of Milan, seventeen bishops, and twelve counts from the kingdom of Italy. Hincmar in the *AB* makes no mention of the appointment by Pope John VIII on 2 January 876 of Ansegis as papal vicar north of the Alps; *PL* 126, col. 660.

3 For Boso's career, above 869, n. 31; 871: 172; 872: 177; 873, n. 5. He subscribed Capit. 220 (previous note) as 'famous duke, chief minister of the sacred palace and imperial *missus*', thus becoming viceroy of Italy. His marriage to the only child of the Emperor Louis II was probably now arranged by Charles, despite

leaving in Italy Boso and those colleagues whom the duke himself chose, Charles went back by way of the *Mons Iovis* pass and the monastery of St-Maurice, and stiffened his pace so as to be able to celebrate Easter at St-Denis. Hearing of her husband's approach, Richildis, who had been staying at Servais, on 6 March set out quickly to meet him. Travelling at the greatest possible speed by way of Rheims, Châlons and Langres, on 16 March she reached a place called Vernierfontaine on the other side of Besançon.

The emperor then moved north with her by way of the cities of Besançon, Langres, Châlons and Rheims and the palace of Compiègne and reached St-Denis to celebrate Easter [15 April]. There he summoned the papal legates John bishop of Toscanella, John bishop of Arezzo and Ansegis archbishop of Sens, and on the pope's authority and their advice and his own decree he summoned a synod to meet in the July following at Ponthion. He went there by way of Rheims⁴ and Châlons.

After the emperor had left Italy and returned to Francia, Boso, through the intrigues of Berengar son of Eberhard, made a wicked plot and married the daughter of the late Emperor Louis, Ermengard, who was already living with him.⁵

On 20 June, in the eighth Indiction, the Lord Emperor Charles, in a gilded robe and clad in Frankish costume, came with the legates of the apostolic see into the synod where the bishops and other clergy were all clothed in their ecclesiastical vestments. The whole interior of the building and the seats were covered in fine cloths, and in the very heart of the synod in full view of the imperial throne the Holy Gospels were placed on a lectern. The chanters sang the antiphon 'Hear us O Lord' with the verses and 'Gloria', and after the 'Kyrie eleison' and a prayer said by John bishop of Toscanella, the Lord Emperor took his

---

what Hincmar implies in the *AB*; see next note. According to *AF* 878, Boso poisoned his first wife before abducting Louis II's daughter. Regino 877(!): 113 says that Charles conferred the title of king on Boso 'so that he [Charles] would be seen to be an overlord of kings in the style of the emperors of old'.

4 It may well have been during this visit that Charles held an assembly at which, with his magnates' consent, he designated his son Louis the Stammerer heir to the realm. Hincmar refers to this assembly elsewhere and was present at it himself, but is silent in the *AB*; Bautier 1978: xx.

5 Hincmar suggests that Boso married without Charles's consent. But Regino 877 (for 876): 113 more plausibly credits Charles with the initiative here. Perhaps Boso was trying to win over Berengar (above 875, n. 6) as a 'colleague'.

seat in the synod.[6]

John bishop of Toscanella read out the letters sent by the pope, including, notably, a letter concerning the primacy of Ansegis archbishop of Sens: he was to enjoy the post of papal deputy in the Gauls and Germanies in the summoning of a synod or in performing other functions, whenever the needs of the Church should require it; the decrees of the apostolic see were to be made known to the bishops through his agency, and whatever action was taken, as and when necessary, was to be reported back to the apostolic see through an account sent by him; more important and difficult cases were to be referred at his discretion to the apostolic see for its decision and explanation.[7] When the bishops asked permission to read this letter, which was after all addressed to them, the emperor would not consent, but demanded what response they would give to these papal orders.

Their reply was that, saving the rights and privileges of the various metropolitans,[8] they would obey Pope John's commands, following the sacred canons and the decrees of the pontiffs of the Roman see promulgated in accordance with those sacred canons. The emperor and the papal legates tried very hard to get the archbishops to reply that they would be obedient concerning Ansegis's primacy exactly in the terms the pope had used in his letter, without any reservations. But the emperor failed to extort from them any reply other than that given above. Only Frotar archbishop of Bordeaux, who had moved from Bordeaux to Poitiers and from there to Bourges through royal favour but against the canonical rules, through sheer sycophancy gave the

6 For the proceedings at Ponthion, see *MGH Capit.* II, no. 279, pp. 347-53: the oaths sworn at Pavia (above, n. 2) were repeated by the men of Francia, Burgundy, Aquitaine, Septimania, Neustria and Provence, the string of provinces indicating an imperial realm. Charles did not repeat his oath, however. Hincmar in the *AB* says nothing about his dispute with Charles over the oath required of him; for Hincmar's letter of protest, *PL* 125, cols. 1125-8, and see Odegaard 1945a; Devisse 1976: II, 815-17. The Synod of Ponthion was attended by seven archbishops, forty-two bishops and five abbots (lay participants, though certainly present, are not listed). For the imperial seal Charles now used, inscribed 'Renovatio imperii Romani et Francorum', see Schramm 1968(ii): 132; Folz 1969: 32-3.

7 For Ansegis's vicariate, above 876, n. 2. Hincmar had not opposed Lothar I's attempt to have *him* made papal vicar in 847, Löwe 1972: 520; Devisse 1976(ii): 810-14.

8 In June 876, Hincmar had written a short treatise *de Iure Metropolitanorum* (*The Rights of Metropolitans*); *PL* 126, cols. 189-210.

emperor the answer he knew would please him.[9]

Then the emperor was angry, and said that the lord pope had committed to him the task of representing the apostolic see before the synod, and he was going to apply himself to carrying out what the pope had commanded. He took the rolled-up letter, and together with John of Toscanella and John of Arezzo handed it over to Ansegis. Then he ordered a portable chair to be placed next to John of Toscanella (who was seated on his right) and so above all the bishops of his realm this side of the Alps, and he commanded Ansegis to take precedence over all those who had been ordained before he had, and to sit on that chair. The archbishop of Rheims protested, in the hearing of everyone present, that this action contravened the sacred rules.[10] But the emperor remained firm in his decision, and though the bishops begged that they might be allowed at least to take a copy of the letter that had been sent to them, they failed completely to get what they asked for. Then the synod was dissolved for that day.

On the 21st of the same month, the bishops assembled again. At this meeting letters sent by the lord pope to the laity were read out; and there was also read out the formal statement of the election of the lord emperor by the bishops and other men of the realm of Italy, and also the decrees which Charles had issued in the palace at Ticino[11] and had commanded were to be observed by all, and which he now ordered the bishops on this side of the Alps to confirm. Thus the synod was dissolved for that day.

On 4 July the bishops assembled without the emperor and disputes were heard concerning the priests of various dioceses who were appealing to the pope's legates.[12] Thus the synod was dissolved for that day.

On the fifth of the same month, the bishops assembled again and the emperor, taking his seat in the synod, gave audience to the envoys of his brother Louis, namely Archbishop Willibert of Cologne[13] and

9 Above, 868, n. 3. Frotar had been made bishop of Poitiers some time before 876 (L/G: 142, n. 3), and had just been appointed archbishop of Bourges (succeeding Wulfad) in 876, with special permission from the pope.

10 Seating arrangements expressed seniority, hence the reason for Hincmar's indignation; cf. Fichtenau 1984: 32-4.

11 I.e. Pavia. See above n. 2.

12 One such case concerned a priest called Adelgaud, *MGH Capit.* II, no. 279 (F), p. 350.

13 Above, 870, n. 13. Charles and his bishops had maintained their objections to Willebert's election for several years; McKeon 1978: 261-2.

Counts Adalard and Meingaud,[14] through whom Louis demanded a
share of the realm of the Emperor Louis, son of their brother Lothar,
as he claimed was his due according to hereditary right and as had
been guaranteed to him by solemn oath.[15] Then John of Toscanella
read out a letter from Pope John addressed to the bishops of Louis's
realm, and he gave a copy to Archbishop Willibert to deliver to those
bishops. The synod was then dissolved for that day.

On 10 July the bishops assembled and at about the ninth hour more
envoys from the lord pope arrived, namely Bishop Leo [of Sabina], the
papal *apocrisiarius* and also the pope's nephew, and Peter bishop of
Fossombrone, who brought letters to the emperor and the empress
and papal greeting to the bishops. The synod was then dissolved for
that day.

On 11 July, when the bishops had assembled, a letter from the pope
was read out concerning the condemnation of Bishop Formosus and of
Gregory the papal *nomenclator* and of their supporters.[16] Then the gifts
sent by the pope were formally presented to the emperor: outstanding
among these were a sceptre and a golden staff. The pope also sent gifts
to the empress: fine robes and armills encrusted with gems. The synod
was then dissolved for that day.

On 14 July the bishops assembled, and the emperor sent in the pope's
deputies to rebuke still more harshly the archbishops and the other
bishops who the day before had not complied with the emperor's
command. But the reproaches were stifled when a reasonable explanation in conformity with the canons was given to the emperor. Then on
the emperor's orders, the letter concerning Ansegis's primacy was
again read out by John of Toscanella, and when he had finished he
again demanded a reply from the bishops. The archbishops one by one
replied that they were willing to obey the pope's decrees in accordance
with the rules, just as their predecessors had obeyed his predecessors.
This reply of the archbishops was more readily forthcoming now than
it had been in the presence of the emperor.

14 Adalard was count of Metz, above 872, n. 3, and cf. *AF* 880, n. 11. Meingaud
   was count of the Wormsgau; L/G: 203, n. 2, and had close kinsmen in Charles's
   kingdom.

15 Above 875, n. 6.

16 See Partner 1976: 68-9. Formosus had been Hadrian's envoy, above 869, n. 8.
   In February 876 at Pavia, papal envoys accused Formosus of plotting with a
   faction of Roman nobles against John VIII. Formosus and his allies were
   condemned by a Roman synod in April; cf. *MGH Epp.* VII, pp. 326-9 for John's
   lurid denunciations of his opponents' sexual misdemeanours.

After many disputed cases had been aired concerning the priests of various dioceses who were appealing to the pope's legates, the statement of Frotar archbishop of Bordeaux was read out again: he declared that he was unable to remain in his *civitas* because of the insecurity caused by the pagans and he sought permission to take possession of the metropolitan see of Bourges. The bishops did not unanimously agree to his request.[17] The papal legates gave orders for the bishops to assemble on 16 July.

That morning about the ninth hour the emperor entered, clad in the Greek fashion and wearing his crown,[18] led by the papal legates clad in the Roman fashion and by the bishops wearing their ecclesiastical vestments, with everything else arranged as it had been on the first day when the synod began. Again, as on that earlier occasion, the antiphon 'Hear us Lord' was sung, with the verses and the 'Gloria' following the 'Kyrie eleison', and after Bishop Leo had said the prayer, everyone was seated. Then John of Arezzo read out a document that lacked both sense and authority, and after that Bishop Odo of Beauvais read out certain statements that had been dictated by the papal legates, and by Ansegis and Odo himself, which were mutually inconsistent, totally unhelpful, and lacking in both sense and authority and therefore are not reproduced here.[19] Then an interrogation was started again concerning Ansegis's primacy, but after both the emperor and the papal legates had made many complaints against the bishops, Ansegis gained at this last session of the synod precisely the same as he had on the first day.[20]

After this Peter bishop of Fossombrone and John of Toscanella went into the emperor's private apartments and brought out before the synod the Empress Richildis wearing her crown. As she stood beside the emperor, everyone rose to his feet, each standing in position according to his rank. Then Bishop Leo and Bishop John of Toscanella began the *Laudes*, and when these had been duly performed for the lord

---

17 Hincmar means that he did not agree. Nevertheless Frotar's transfer to Bourges went through.

18 Charles's 'Greek' (Byzantine) garb expressed his new claims to imperial status. Cf. the hostile reaction of *AF* 876.

19 For Odo's *capitula*, *MGH Capit.* II, no. 279 (G), pp. 351-2: what Hincmar objected to was c. 7's acknowledgement of Ansegis's primacy.

20 Hincmar's suggestion that Ansegis's primacy was not accepted at Ponthion is a piece of wishful thinking. He himself maintained his objections; but the rest of the assembled clergy accepted the imperial and papal decision.

pope and the lord emperor and the empress[21] and all the rest, according to custom, Bishop Leo of Sabina said a prayer, and the synod was finally dissolved.

After this the emperor presented the papal envoys Leo and Peter with gifts and sent them back to Rome, and with them Ansegis archbishop of Sens and Adalgar bishop of Autun.[22]

Meanwhile a group of Northmen were baptised by Hugh the abbot and *marchio*, and consequently were presented to the emperor. He bestowed gifts on them and sent them back to their own people, but afterwards, like typical Northmen, they lived according to the pagan custom just as before.

On 28 July the emperor moved from Ponthion and on 30 July reached Châlons, where he stayed until 13 August suffering from some kind of illness. He moved to Rheims in the August and from there proceeded by the direct route to Servais. On 28 August he dispatched the papal legates, John and the other John along with Bishop Odo and other envoys of his own, to his brother Louis and his sons and the bishops and magnates of his realm. These envoys were already on their way when news reached the emperor at Quierzy that King Louis had died at the palace of Frankfurt on 28 August and been buried on 29 August in the monastery of St-Nazarius.[23] Now the emperor sent out his envoys to the magnates of his late brother's realm, and moved from Quierzy as far as the *villa* of Stenay.[24] His plan was to get to Metz and receive the bishops and magnates of his late brother's realm who would come to him there. But he suddenly changed his mind and went to Aachen and from there to Cologne,[25] with the papal legates going

21 This ritual was an important statement of Richildis's position as empress, and of her prosepctive offspring (she was four months pregnant) as imperial heir. The *Laudes* were liturgical acclamations introduced by the Carolingians; Kantorowicz 1946.

22 Adalgar, a former royal notary who accompanied Charles to Rome in 875-76, had just been made bishop of Autun (877-93), and soon after also received the nearby abbey of Flavigny.

23 Lorsch, in Franconia, some 55 km. south of Frankfurt.

24 Charles was at Quierzy on 4 September (T. 412). Stenay is equidistant from Rheims and Metz.

25 Charles's aim, according to *AF* 876, was to acquire the enclave of Louis the German's kingdom that lay west of the Rhine. This area around Mainz, Worms and Speyer included important royal lands, and its acquisition had been especially important for Louis the German between 840 and 843; Nelson 1986a (1985): 219-20 and n. 109. Charles had shown in 870 that he appreciated the importance of control over Cologne, above 870, n. 13.

along with him.

While all the men in his retinue plundered as they went, without any respect for God, Northmen, with about 100 of their large ships which our people call *bargae*, sailed into the Seine estuary on 16 September. News of this reached the emperor at Cologne, but he made no change on this account in the plans he had already begun to put into effect. His nephew Louis the Younger came up to meet him across on the other bank of the Rhine with the Saxons and Thuringians, and he sent envoys to his uncle the emperor to beg his favour. His request was refused and when he and his counts then sought mercy from the Lord with fastings and litanies, the emperor's men jeered at them.

Louis son of King Louis then set up a Judgement of God before all his troops: ten men were put to ordeal of hot water, ten men to the ordeal of hot iron and ten men to the ordeal of cold water.[26] Then everyone prayed God to declare in this Judgement if it was more right that Louis should have the share of the realm left to him by his father, specifically that part which his father had acquired as a result of his agreement with his brother Charles, with Charles's consent and solemn oath.[27] All those put to the ordeal were unharmed. Then Louis with his men crossed the Rhine and got to the fort at Andernach.[28]

When news of this move reached Charles, he sent the empress Richildis, now pregnant again, with Abbot Hilduin and Bishop Franco[29] to Herstal. Charles in full array advanced along the bank of the Rhine against his nephew, meanwhile sending envoys on ahead to ask Louis to send some of his counsellors to meet with Charles's counsellors to negotiate peace terms. Louis received this suggestion with humble acquiescence: he felt secure in the knowledge that no armed attack might be made on him until such negotiations were completed.

On 7 October the emperor, having already given his squadrons their orders, got up during the night, and raising the standards, tried to launch a surprise attack on his nephew and those with him, moving along rough and narrow tracks that were more like trackless places. When he arrived close by Andernach, his men and horses were tired

26 Hincmar is the only source for these proceedings.

27 The reference is to the Second Treaty of Meersen in 870, above: 168.

28 On the west bank of the Rhine some 60 km. upstream from Cologne.

29 Abbot Hilduin of St-Bertin, above 870, n. 13, was Charles's librarian in 874 (T. 370) and acquired the abbacy of St-Mihiel (dep. Meuse) in 875; Bishop Franco of Liège (855-901) was an old associate of Hilduin, *AX* 870, and a key figure in northern Lotharingia.

out by the extreme difficulty of this route as well as by the rain which
had drenched them all night.

Now, all of a sudden, Louis and his men got word that the emperor
was coming upon them with a mighty army.[30] Louis and those with
him held their position directly opposite Charles. The emperor's
battalions charged, but Louis and his men resisted bravely. The
emperor's whole army turned tail and in its flight fell back on the
emperor. He himself with a few companions only just managed to
escape. Many who might have got away were prevented from doing so,
because the emperor's baggage and that of the others with him, and
also the traders and shield-sellers who followed the imperial army, all
clogged the narrow road and so blocked the escape route for the
fleeing soldiers. In this battle were slain Counts Raganar[31] and Jerome
and many others. On the battlefield itself and in the neighbouring
forest there were taken prisoner Bishop Ottulf [of Troyes], Abbot
Gauzlin,[32] Counts Aledramn,[33] Adalard,[34] Bernard[35] and Everwin and a
great many others. Louis's army seized all the baggage and all the
goods the traders were carrying. Thus was fulfilled the word of the
prophet saying: 'You who plunder, shall you yourself not be plundered?' [Isa. 33: 1]. Everything which those plunderers who were
with the emperor had, and even they themselves, now became the
plunder of someone else. So total were the losses that those who did
manage to escape on horseback possessed, instead of spoils, only their
own skins. The rest were stripped of all they had by the local peasants:
they had to cover their private parts by wrapping themselves in grass
and straw, and those whom their pursuers did not want to kill fled
naked away. 'And there was delivered a very great blow' [I Reg. 4: 10]
against a people of plunderers.

30 The warning came from Archbishop Willebert of Cologne; *AF* 876. Lacking
   the advantage of surprise, Charles's position was weak from the start.
   Hincmar's account of the battle can be compared with those of *AF*, and *AV*: 41.
   Regino 876: 112 cites *Ps.* xxxiii: 17, suggesting the importance of cavalry in
   this battle.
31 Regino: 112 says that Reginar was Charles's standard-bearer.
32 Charles's archchancellor; above 871, n. 3.
33 Count Aledramn (II) of Troyes, son of Count Aledramn, above 848, n. 7; 849,
   n. 9; 850, n. 2; Lot 1970a (1906), (1907): 582-90.
34 A Burgundian noble who served as a *missus* by 875, and was count of the palace
   probably by 876: Werner 1967: 432-3. Adalard's daughter was now Charles's
   daughter-in-law, below 877, n. 13; 878, n. 14.
35 Either Count Bernard of Gothia or Count Bernard of the Auvergne; see above
   872: 178 and n. 5. (Count Bernard of Toulouse was dead by 876.)

Richildis learned on 9 October that the emperor himself and his whole army had been put to flight. She hastily left Herstal and as she fled, during the night that followed at cock-crow she gave birth to a boy there on the road.[36] Her trusted servant carried the baby on ahead of her and fled until he brought him to Anthénay.[37] On the evening of 9 October the emperor reached the monastery of St-Lambert [Liège]. There Franco and Abbot Hilduin, leaving Richildis, rejoined Charles on 10 October, and stayed with him until following Richildis he arrived at Anthénay. From there he went on to Douzy, but returned to Anthénay to announce that he would hold his assembly at Samoussy on the fifteenth day after Martinmas [27 November].

Louis son of the late King Louis left Andernach and by way of Sinzig went back to Aachen where he stayed for three days. Then he went to meet his brother Charles [the Fat] at Koblenz. After holding talks together, Charles, a sick man, went off in the direction of Metz and from there into Alemannia, while Louis made his way across the Rhine. Their brother Karlmann came neither to them nor to his uncle Charles as he had asked him to do: Karlmann was fully engaged in fighting the Wends.[38]

The Emperor Charles sent Conrad[39] and others of his leading men to the Northmen who had come into the Seine, with instructions to make a treaty with them on whatever terms they could, and to report back to him at the planned assembly.

The Lord Emperor Charles came to his assembly at Samoussy, as arranged, and there he received men from the part of the late Lothar's realm which Charles's brother Louis had acquired by their mutual arrangement. These men had come over to Charles following his flight from Andernach. To some of them he gave whole abbeys intact; to others he granted benefices from the abbey-lands of Marchiennes which he had divided up;[40] and then he gave them permission to leave.

---

36 The baby must have been two months premature; see above n. 4.

37 About 25 km. south-west of Rheims.

38 According to *AF* 876, the three brothers met in November at Ries (in Franconia) and divided their father's kingdom: Karlmann got Bavaria, Louis the Younger Franconia and Saxony, and Charles the Fat Alemannia. See *AF* 866, n. 1.

39 Son of Charles's uncle Rudolf, above 866, n. 2 and probably a former supporter of Carloman, above: 173, n. 4. Here Hincmar does not give him the title of count.

40 For the abbey of Marchiennes, see Dierkens 1987: 110 and n. 159. The charter

He placed squadrons to form a defensive line along the Seine against the Northmen. Then he arrived at the *villa* of *Virziniacum*,[41] where he became gravely ill with a fever – so ill that his life was despaired of.[42] There he celebrated Christmas.

877

He recovered and went by way of Quierzy to Compiègne. While he was staying there, his baby son fell ill. He was the child to whom Richildis had given birth on the road before she could reach Anthénay. He was baptised with the name of Charles, with his uncle Boso standing godfather.[1] Then he died and was carried to St-Denis to be buried there.[2]

The Emperor Charles passed Lent and celebrated Easter [7 April] at Compiègne, where he received Pope John's envoys, Peter bishop of Fossombrone and another Peter, bishop of Sinigaglia. Through these envoys, Pope John summoned Charles both by word and by letter to come and rescue the Holy Roman Church, as he had promised, and defend it against the pagans who threatened it.[3]

At the beginning of May, Charles summoned to Compiègne the bishops of the province of Rheims and of the other provinces, and in the presence of himself and of the papal envoys he had the church which he had build as his palace chapel consecrated with great pomp by all those bishops.[4]

creating a conventual *mensa*, that is, earmarking certain lands for the community and implicitly leaving the rest to be exploited by the 'lord' (i.e. Charles), was granted only in 877 (T. 435), evidently ratifying earlier arrangements.

41 Perhaps Verzenay near Rheims, or Versigny near Laon.

42 This was Charles's second bout of illness in 876 (see also above: 195). Decour 1972 suggests that he had contracted malaria in Italy in 875-76. But note that he had been seriously ill in 874 (above: 187).

1 Boso had not been at Andernach (*Recueil Provence* XVbis shows him in Provence in mid-October); but he was clearly still high in Charles's favour. Cf. above 876, nn. 3 and 4.

2 For Charles the Bald's devotion to St Denis, see Brown 1989: 330-409.

3 John VIII was trying once again to organise defence against the Saracens; Engreen 1945; Partner 1976: 69-70.

4 The foundation-charter of St-Mary Compiègne (T. 415, dated 5 May) shows exceptionally lavish patronage appropriate to a new capital, and explicitly makes Compiègne a substitute for Aachen; Riché 1981; Schneidmüller 1979: 101-5; Falkenstein 1981: 33-45, 85-6. See also McKitterick 1990: 332 and n. 37.

From there he went to hold his general assembly at the beginning of July at Quierzy. There he laid down in a series of *capitula* how his son Louis, with his faithful men and the magnates of the realm, was to rule the realm of Francia until he himself should return from Rome.[5] He also made arrangements for how the tribute should be levied from that part of the realm of Francia which he held before Lothar's death, and also from Burgundy: from every manse in demesne one *solidus*; from every free manse 4 *denarii* from the lord's rent and 4 *denarii* from the tenant's assets; from every unfree manse 2 *denarii* from the lord's rent and 2 *denarii* from the tenant's assets; and every bishop to receive from each priest in his diocese, according to what each could afford, between 5 *solidi* maximum and 4 *denarii* minimum, and to hand this over to special *missi dominici*. Amounts were also taken from the treasuries of the churches in proportion to the quantity held in each place, to pay off this tribute. The total amount of tribute raised was 5,000 lb according to weight.[6] Those bishops and others too who lived across the Seine in Neustria, took measures to raise a tribute everywhere they could to pay the Northmen on the Loire according to what they demanded.

Now the lord emperor went from Quierzy to Compiègne, and thence by way of Soissons to Rheims. Then he continued his journey by way of Châlons and Ponthion and Langres, and, accompanied by his wife and a huge supply of gold and silver and horses and other movables, he left Francia and made for Italy. Crossing the Jura he reached Orbe, where he met Bishop Adalgar[7] whom he had dispatched to Rome the previous February to take part in the synod summoned by Pope John.

5 These arrangements are contained in the Capitulary of Quierzy (mid-June), *MGH Capit.* II, no. 281, pp. 355-61. The most famous clause provides that counts and royal vassals who die while their sons are in Italy with Charles are to be succeeded by those sons. In fact hereditary succession to such *honores* seems to have been normal at this period. More significant are (i) the clauses entrenching Charles's political control and denying freedom of manoeuvre to Louis the Stammerer: in c. 15, Charles listed the men who were to be with Louis 'assiduously', in effect to supervise him in Charles's absence; in c. 25, three bishops were given the job of keeping constant touch with Charles; in cc. 32, 33, Louis was given strictly limited hunting rights in Charles's forests in Francia; and (ii) the clause providing that if Charles came home safely, then Louis would be sent to Italy to be crowned king (c. 13); this opened up new possibilities for the succession in Francia and Aquitaine.

6 Cf. the arrangements of 866, above: 130. Note that those of 877 were to cover Burgundy as well as Francia; and that there was a substantial increase in landlords' contributions as compared with 866. The capitulary record, *MGH Capit.* II, no. 280, p. 354, shows that measures agreed at Compiègne were subsequently reconsidered and re-enacted at Quierzy.

7 Above, 876, n. 21.

Adalgar brought a copy of the decrees of this synod to the emperor, by way of a large gift. The gist of the synodal decrees, after many and varied praises of the emperor, was as follows: Charles's election and promotion to the imperial sceptres celebrated at Rome the previous year was to remain firm and settled from then on, now and forever, and if anyone should try to disturb or spoil these arrangements, of whatever order or rank or calling he might be, he was to be bound by anathema for all time until he might be brought to make amends, and the enacters or inciters of any such intent, if they were clerics, were to be deposed, or if laymen or monks, to be struck by perpetual anathema, so that this decision should everywhere prevail, since the work of the synod held the previous year at Ponthion had been of no help at Andernach.[8] Adalgar also informed the emperor, amongst other things, that Pope John would come to Pavia to meet him. Charles therefore sent on ahead Odacer, his notary of the second bureau,[9] Count Goiramn, and Pippin and Herbert,[10] to make arrangements for meeting all the pope's needs.

Charles himself hastened on his way and met the pope at Vercelli, and having been received with the greatest honour, went on together with the pope to Pavia. There they heard the news beyond any doubt that Karlmann, son of Charles's late brother Louis, was on his way to attack them with a huge body of troops.[11] So they left Pavia and moved to Tortona where Richildis was consecrated empress by Pope John. Then Richildis fled back towards Maurienne,[12] taking the treasure with her.

The emperor stayed for a while in those parts in the company of Pope John. He awaited the arrival of the leading men of his realm, Abbot Hugh, Boso, Count Bernard of Auvergne, and the other Bernard, *markio* of Gothia, all of whom he had ordered to come with him to Italy. But they had conspired and formed a plot against him together

---

8 This last phrase is an ironic Hincmarian comment on the synods of Rome and Ponthion. In this annal, Hincmar was writing with hindsight; Meyer-Gebel 1987: 101.

9 On this notary of Charles, and this passage as evidence for a reorganisation of the chancery, Tessier 1955: 85-7.

10 Pippin and Herbert were sons of Pippin the son of Bernard king of Italy (Nithard II, 3, and see Nelson 1986a (1985): 215). Hincmar does not call either a count. Nothing is known of them until 877; Charles was perhaps showing favour to hitherto obscure young kinsmen because of their grandfather's links with Italy. After Charles's death, Pippin is documented as count of Senlis, Herbert as count of Vermandois; Grierson 1939: 89-90.

11 Cf. *AF* 877 and n. 2.

12 Just across the Mont Cenis pass.

with the other leading men of the realm, with a few exceptions, and also the bishops.[13] When Charles realised that Abbot Hugh and the rest were not going to appear, and when he and Pope John heard news that Karlmann was getting close, the emperor took flight, following in Richildis's footsteps, while Pope John sped back to Rome as fast as he could. He carried with him on the emperor's behalf an image of the Saviour fixed to the cross: it was made out of a large amount of gold and adorned with precious stones, and Charles now sent it to St Peter the Apostle.

Karlmann heard false news that the emperor and Pope John were on their way to attack him with a huge body of troops, and he too now fled along the route by which he had come.[14] Thus did God with his usual mercy bring that conflict to nought.

Charles, stricken by fever, drank a powder which his Jewish doctor Zedechias, whom he loved and trusted all too much, had given him to cure his sickness. But he had drunk a poison for which there was no antidote. Carried by bearers, he crossed the Mont Cenis pass and reached a place called Brios.[15] There he sent for Richildis who was at Maurienne, and asked her to come to him, which she did. On 6 October, the eleventh day after he had drunk the poison, he died in a wretched little hut. His attendants opened him up, took out his intestines, poured in such wine and aromatics as they had, put the body on a bier and set off to carry him to St-Denis where he had asked to be buried. But because of the stench they could carry him no further, so they put him in a barrel which they smeared with pitch inside and outside and encased in hides, but even this did nothing to get rid of the smell. Only with difficulty did they manage to reach Nantua, a little monastery in the archdiocese of Lyons, and there they committed the

13 Hincmar is the only source for this conspiracy. He may oversimplify here, as he does below, 203 and n. 19. For possible reasons for the disaffection of Boso, above n. 5. Hincmar does not reveal in the *AB* the recent remarriage of Louis the Stammerer at his father's insistence. Charles's favour to the new bride's Burgundian kin, especially her father Adalard, above 876, n. 34; Nelson 1990a: 38-9, may well have upset the previous distribution of patronage. None of the conspirators named by Hincmar had his power-base in Francia proper.

14 Only Hincmar mentions Karlmann's flight; cf. the silence of *AF* 877: 90, strongly biased in Karlmann's favour. The *marchiones* of Spoleto and Tuscany, longstanding aggressors against the papal state, seem to have supported Karlmann; *AF* 878, n. 4. Again, Hincmar in the 877 annal is writing retrospectively: Karlmann fell seriously ill in November and withdrew from Italy.

15 Probably Briançon.

body, with its barrel, to the earth.[16]

Karlmann, so ill that he was almost dead, was carried back home in a litter. After that he lay sick for a whole year, his life despaired of by many.[17]

Louis [the Stammerer] was at the *villa* of Orville[18] when he heard the news of his father's death. He won over as many men as he could, granting them abbacies, countships and *villae* according to what each demanded. Then he travelled by way of Quierzy and Compiègne to Ver, intending to reach St-Denis to bury his father there. But he heard that his father had already been buried. He also heard that the leading men of his realm, abbots and counts alike, were outraged by his granting out *honores* to certain people without their consent, and had therefore formed a plot against him.[19] He returned to Compiègne, while the magnates, together with Richildis, ravaging everything in their path, came to the convent of Avenay and fixed Mont-Aimé [20] as their meeting place, and from there sent their envoys to Louis. Louis also sent his envoys to them, and after messengers had run back and forth between them, the outcome was that Richildis and those magnates were to come to him at Compiègne and they named their own meeting-point at Le Chêne-Herbelot in the forest of Cuise. On the Feast of St Andrew [30 November] Richildis came to Louis at Compiègne, and brought him the official command by which his father, just before his death, had handed over the realm to him; she also brought the sword known as the sword of St Peter, with which she was to invest him with the realm; she brought too the royal robes and crown and a sceptre made of gold and precious stones.[21] Then after

16 Nantua, some 40 km. west of Geneva. Regino 877: 113, says that his body was transferred 'after a few years' to St-Denis. Charles had made arrangements for his own burial there (T. 240, 247, 379). For his tomb at St-Denis in the twelfth century, see L/G: 217, n. 1.

17 He was back in Bavaria by early December; *AF* 877.

18 Bautier 1978: xxiv identifies this as Orville on the Oise, near Quierzy.

19 The grants included that of the abbacy of St-Denis to Gauzlin, and perhaps that of the countship of Paris to Conrad son of Rudolf (above 876, n. 39). Theuderic may also have been made chamberlain now; cf. below 878, n. 21. In November, Hincmar, hoping to recover a position of influence, wrote Louis an *Instructio*, *PL* 125, cols. 983-90, advising him to be a peacemaker, to choose good counsellors, and specifically 'to send quickly to Abbot Hugh, Abbot Gauzlin, Boso, Conrad, Bernard [of the Auvergne] and Bernard [of Gothia]', to seek a meeting with all together. But these men, far from presenting a united opposition to Louis, were split into rival factions led by Hugh on the one hand, Gauzlin on the other; Oexle 1969: 200-2.

20 Dep. Marne. For Avenay, above 864, n. 32.

more envoys had sped to and fro between Louis and the magnates of the realm, and *honores* had been agreed to all who sought them, on 8 December with the consent of all, bishops, abbots and all the rest of the magnates who were present, Louis was consecrated and crowned king by Archbishop Hincmar of Rheims.[22] The bishops commended themselves and their churches to him for due defence and the preservation of their canonical privileges, promising that they would be faithful to him with counsel and aid as far as they might know or be able to, and according to their office. The lay abbots and magnates of the realm and royal vassals commended themselves to him and promised fidelity to him with a solemn oath, according to custom.[23]

When King Louis, son of the Emperor Charles, was crowned at Compiègne, the bishops put the following request to him:[24]

> We request of you that you grant to us that you will preserve to each his canonical privilege and due law and justice concerning ourselves and the churches committed to us, according to the first clause which at Quierzy recently the lord emperor your father announced would be preserved by himself and by you (and Gauzlin read this out),[25] with the consent of his and your faithful men and of the legates of the apostolic see, just as a king in his kingdom ought in justice to show to each bishop and to the church committed to him.

Louis for his part made the following promise to the bishops:

> I promise and grant you that I shall preserve canonical privilege and due law and justice to each of you and to the churches committed to you, according to the first point which at Quierzy

21 Richildis's role as custodian of the regalia enhanced her political importance at this point. With 'the sword of St Peter', Charles the Bald was apparently claiming to transmit the empire to his son.

22 The *ordo* composed by Hincmar for this occasion, *MGH Capit.* II, no. 303 , pp. 461-2. For its later influence, Nelson 1986a (1971): 252.

23 For the distinct forms of the episcopal commendation and the laymen's oaths, Nelson 1986a (1977a): 154.

24 The episcopal *petitio* and royal *promissio*, *MGH Capit.* II, no. 283, pp. 363-5, would remain in later royal inaugurations. For the context in earlier commitments of Charles the Bald, especially that of Coulaines, Nelson 1986a (1977a): 152.

25 Above, n. 5. The *capitulum* quoted below was the preamble to the Quierzy capitulary. For Gauzlin's reading-out of these *capitula*, *MGH Capit.* II, no. 282, pp. 361-2.

recently the lord emperor my father announced he would preserve (and Gauzlin read it out), with the consent of his and our faithful men and of the legates of the apostolic see, and that I will offer protection so far as I am able, with God's help, just as a king in his kingdom is bound to show to each bishop and to the church committed to him.

This is the capitulary-clause referred to:

Concerning the honour and worship of God and of the holy churches which through God's plan are set under the command and protection of our rule, we decree, through the Lord's mediation, that, just as in the time of our lord father of blessed memory they were cultivated and honoured and made great with possessions, those which have been honoured and endowed through our generosity should be preserved in their integrity; also the priests and servants of God should have ecclesiastical strength and due privileges, according to the authority which must be revered; and the power of the prince, the efforts of exalted persons, and the officials of the state should hasten to help them in all things, in reasonable and just fashion, so that they may be able to carry out the tasks of their office in a suitable way. And let our son preserve the above-mentioned in a like manner, with God's help.

The commendation of Bishop Ansegis[26] and of the other bishops who were present at Compiègne when they blessed Louis, son of the Emperor Charles was as follows:

I commend myself to you, along with the church committed to me, to preserve due law and justice and to offer defence, just as a king ought by just judgement to preserve and offer to a bishop and to his church.

Their profession was the following:

I, so-and-so, profess thus: from this day and henceforth, I shall be a faithful man and helper in my faith and my priesthood to this my lord and my king Louis, son of Charles and Ermentrude, with aid and counsel, as far as I know and can and according to my office, as a bishop rightly owes to his lord.

26 Above 876, nn. 2, 6 and 19.

In response to the above request of the bishops, King Louis professed to the bishops the following, and gave them with his own hand this same text of his grant, at Compiègne in the year of our Lord's incarnation 877, on 30 November:[27]

I, Louis, constituted king by the mercy of our Lord God and by the election of the people, promise, with the Church of God as witness, to all orders, namely those of the bishops, of priests, of monks, of canons and of nuns, that I will preserve for them the rules in their entirety as written by the fathers and strengthened by apostolic attestations, from this time on and for the future. I promise, furthermore, that I shall preserve their laws and statutes to the people which, by God's mercy, has been committed to me to rule, for the common counsel of our faithful men, according to what the emperors and kings my predecessors established by their actions and decreed were to be held and observed absolutely, without any violation. Therefore I, Louis, through love of righteousness and justice, reading over this my freely-given promise, have confirmed it with my own hand.

878

King Louis celebrated Christmas in the monastery of St-Médard at Soissons. From there, he moved to the *villa* at Orville; and he celebrated Easter in the monastery of St-Denis. Hugh, the abbot and *markio*,[1] persuaded him to go west of the Seine, firstly, to help Hugh against the Northmen, and secondly, because the sons of Gauzfrid[2] had seized the stronghold and *honores* of the son of the late Count Odo,[3] and because Imino, brother of the *Markio* Bernard,[4] had seized Évreux and was causing widespread devastation in those parts, and even had

---

27 L/G: 221, n. 1, assuming an error in the date, emend to '12 December' ('II idus decembris' instead of 'II kal. decembris'). But the emendation is needless: this royal commitment was indeed given on 30 November, before the consecration; Nelson 1986a (1977a): 152 and n. 3.

1 Above, 871, n. 8; 876: 195; 877: 203 and n. 19.

2 Above 861, n. 9; 866, n. 26; 869, n. 27; 871, n. 8.

3 This Odo was the son of Harduin and brother of Louis the Stammerer's repudiated wife Ansgard; above 862, n. 13; 866, n. 3; 870, n. 9; 877, n. 13. The date of Odo's death is unknown. See also Levillain 1937a: 174–7.

the audacity to ravage the lands of Eiricus,[5] behaving the way the Northmen do.

Louis reached Tours, and became so ill that they despaired of his life. But by the Lord's mercy he recovered a little. Gauzfrid, through the influence of some of the royal counsellors who were friends of his, presented himself to Louis, bringing his sons with him. These were the terms they agreed on: Gauzfrid's sons should give up to King Louis the stronghold and *honores* they had wrongfully occupied, and then were to hold them thereafter by royal grant. Then Gauzfrid brought a group of Bretons over to the king's allegiance. But they behaved in the end the way Bretons always do.

Pope John was raging against Counts Lambert and Adalbert:[6] he had excommunicated them in most fearsome fashion because they had plundered his *villae* and his *civitas*. He left Rome and voyaged by ship to Arles where he arrived on the holy day of Pentecost [11 May]. He sent his envoys to Count Boso,[7] and with his help reached Lyons. From there he sent messengers to King Louis at Tours, asking him to come and meet him at whatever place might suit the king. So Louis sent certain bishops to meet the pope and asked him to come as far as Troyes. He ordered funds to be given to the pope there by the bishops of his realm. Louis joined the pope at Troyes on 1 September: he had not been able to get there sooner because of being so ill.

Meanwhile Pope John held a general synod with the bishops of the

---

4 For *Marchio* Bernard of Gothia, above 872, n. 5. His brother can probably be identified with the Emeno who served as Charles the Bald's count of the palace in the early 870s; T. 375, and cf. Auzias 1937: 537. *Marchio* Bernard's father had held *honores* in the lower Loire region, and his maternal grandfather was Rorgo count of Maine, above 865: 122 and n. 3.

5 Though L/G: 222. n. 5 emend *Eiricum* to *Uticum*, that is, the monastery of St-Evroult (dep. Orne), some 55 km. south-west of Évreux, I follow the suggestion of Werner 1960: 104, n. 70, that the reference here is to the region (perhaps the county of Dreux) controlled by a magnate called Eiricus, who was a kinsman of Theuderic, below, n. 21.

6 For Lambert, above 871, n. 15. Adalbert *marchio* of Tuscany (834–86) was his brother-in-law; John VIII, Ep. 87, *MGH Epp.* V, p. 82. Their attacks on papal territory, which stymied John VIII's efforts to organise a coalition against the Saracens, were probably also mounted to help Karlmann's cause in Italy; *AF* 878: 91 and n. 4.

7 Against the argument that John VIII was already considering Boso as his candidate for emperor; Fried 1976 shows that the pope consistently supported Louis the Stammerer and intended to crown him emperor. The pope wrote to Boso partly because of previous contacts between them in Italy, but mainly because Boso controlled the Rhône valley.

Gallic and Belgic provinces. He had a report read out before the synod concerning the way he had excommunicated Lambert and Adalbert and also Formosus and the *nomenclator* Gregory. The pope sought the consent of the bishops in respect of these excommunications. Therefore the bishops present requested that, just as the pope had had the excommunication which he had issued recounted in the synod by the reading-out of a written document, so he would give them permission to accord him their consent by means of a written document. When Pope John gave this permission, the bishops thus presented to him in the synod next day the following diploma:[8]

Lord John, most holy and most reverend father of fathers, pope of the catholic and apostolic Church, namely the holy first see of Rome: we, the servants and disciples of your authority, the bishops of the Gallic and Belgic provinces, share your pain over the things that evil men and ministers of the devil have committed against our holy mother and teacher of all churches, adding to the wounds of your griefs. Weeping with you in your woe, we share your grief, and we carry out the judgement of your authority, which, by the privilege of the Blessed Peter and of the apostolic see, according to the sacred canons founded by the spirit of God and consecrated by the authority of the whole world, and according to the decrees of the pontiffs your predecessors of that same holy Roman see, you have issued against those evil men and their accomplices whom we by our decision, our voice and our unanimity and by the authority of the Holy Spirit, by whose grace we have been ordained in the episcopal order, are slaying with the sword of the Spirit which is the word of God. That is to say, those whom you have excommunicated, as we have said above, we hold to be excommunicated; those whom you have cast out from the Church, we cast out; those whom you have anathematised, we judge to be anathematised; and those whom your authority and the apostolic see accepts as giving satisfaction according to the rules, we shall accept. But, as in sacred history we read concerning the plague justly visited on the Egyptians by God that 'there was not a house in which a dead boy did not lie' [Exod. 12: 30], and there was no one to comfort another since everyone had in his own house something over which to grieve, so we in our churches too grieve over the grievous. Therefore with all humility of mind we beg you to help us with your

8 This episcopal *démarche* was evidently written by Hincmar himself; L/G: 224, n. 2.

authority, requesting you to issue an order, backed by your
authority, telling us what action we ought to take concerning those
who wrongfully seize our churches, so that, fortified with the
censure of the apostolic see and henceforth made more vigorous and
more zealous, we may be strengthened, if God brings us aid, to
persist in our agreed sentence against perverse stealers and
ravagers of ecclesiastical lands and movables[9] and against despisers
of the sacred episcopal office; so that they, having been handed over
to Satan, according to the voice of the outstanding preacher and the
promulgation of your authority, may be saved in spirit on the day
of our Lord Jesus Christ.

The excommunication of the Apostolic John and of the other bishops
present at Troyes, concerning those who wrongfully seize ecclesiastical property was as follows:

Concerning those who wrongfully seize (forsooth!) ecclesiastical
property, whom the sacred canons, founded by the spirit of God and
consecrated by the reverence of the whole world, and the decrees of
the pontiffs of the apostolic see have determined should be placed
under anathema until they give satisfaction according to the rules;
and also concerning plunderers, whom the Apostle (with Christ
speaking in him) affirms can have no part in the kingdom of God
and forbids to take food with any Christian person so long as they
persist in that crime [I Cor. 5: 11; 6: 10]: we decree through the
strength of Christ and by the judgement of the Holy Spirit that if
they do not restore to their churches those goods which any
wrongful appropriators whosoever have unjustly seized and give
satisfaction according to the rules before 1 November next, they
shall be deemed removed from the communion of the body and
blood of Christ until the restitution of the churches' property and
due satisfaction be given. Those who scorn the Church's excommunication and the sacred episcopal ministry, having been warned
according to evangelic and apostolic authority by the bishops whose
concern that is, if they do not come to their senses and give
satisfaction according to the rules, are to remain knotted by the
bond of anathema until satisfaction be given. If they die persisting
in that obduracy, their memory is not to be kept at the sacred altar
among the faithful dead, according to the saying of the apostle and

9 Hincmar's anxieties over this perennial problem had recently been expressed in
letters of protest to Count Bernard of Toulouse, Flodoard III, 26, p. 543.

H

evangelist John: 'And is it a sin unto death? Concerning that, I do not say that anyone may pray'.[10] For a 'sin unto death' means: persisting in sin until death. And the sacred canons of the ancient fathers have decreed by the inspiration of the Holy Spirit concerning those who voluntarily bring death on themselves and who are punished for their crimes, that their bodies should not be carried to burial with hymns and psalms.[11] Following their decrees, we have decreed by the judgement of the Holy Spirit the things specified above concerning those who attack and wrongfully seize the lands and movables of churches, unless they come to their senses, as the blessed Gregory said when he decreed that 'such men are not Christians and I and all the catholic bishops, indeed the universal Church, anathematize them'. Farewell.

Pope John ordered this diploma to be drawn up for the excommunications he issued, and he confirmed it with his own hand and had it subscribed by all the bishops in the synod. Then, on his orders, there were read out in the synod the canons of the Council of Sardica, and the decrees of Pope Leo concerning bishops who change their sees, and the African canons to the effect that such transfers of bishops from one see to another should not be made, any more than rebaptisms or reordinations can be. This latter point referred to the case of Bishop Frotar of Bordeaux who was said to have jumped from Bordeaux to Poitiers and thence to the see of Bourges.[12]

Louis was crowned by Pope John on 7 September.[13] He invited the pope to his palace and regaled him sumptuously. Then he and his wife sent him back into Troyes loaded with many gifts; after this Louis sent messengers to ask the pope to crown his wife as queen, but he failed to get the pope's agreement.[14] In the assembly of bishops, Bishops

---

10 The citation is from *I Ep. Joh.* v. 16. Given the importance attached by some lay persons to liturgical commemoration, the threat to deny it to spoliators of church property was a serious one.

11 The reference is to c. 16 of the Second Council of Braga (563) Mansi IX, col. 779, denying Christian burial to suicides. The threat to extend this to spoliators of church property was another attempt at deterrence.

12 Above 876, nn. 8, 16.

13 The *ordo* used by Pope John, Schramm 1934: 142-3. Brühl 1962: 280-1 considers this a special confirmatory coronation.

14 Presumably the reason was the repudiation of Louis's first wife, and the grouping of political interests around her sons; above 877, n. 13. Hincmar himself seems to have supported them. The second wife was called Adelaide; above 197, n. 34.

Frotar and Adalgar presented to Pope John the order by which Louis's father had handed on the realm to him, and they requested the pope on Louis's behalf to confirm that order by issuing a privilege. Then Pope John produced a document purporting to be an order issued by the Emperor Charles to the effect that the abbey of St-Denis should be given to the Roman Church. A number of people thought that this document had in fact been put together on the advice of those bishops above-mentioned and of the other counsellors of King Louis, with the aim of providing reasonable grounds for the pope's taking that abbey away from Gauzlin and holding it himself. Pope John declared that if King Louis wished him to issue a privilege about the order whereby Louis's father had handed on the realm, then Louis should confirm, by an order of his own, his father's order about St-Denis. This proposal was never put into effect: it was a case of faction and not of good sense.[15]

Then on 10 September, King Louis was forced into action by the demands of some of the magnates. He came to the house where the pope was staying, spoke with him on friendly terms, and went back with him to the bishops' assembly, which was being held in a hall right next to the pope's residence. Hugh, son of Lothar [II],[16] and Imino[17] and their accomplices were excommunicated as a result of pressure exerted by certain bishops with the king's backing. After this, Pope John declared that Hedenulf, who had been ordained bishop by his authority, should hold his see and carry out his episcopal duties, while the blinded Hincmar should, if he wished, chant the Mass and have a share of the revenues of the see of Laon. When Hedenulf put a request to the pope to release him from that see, saying that he was ill and wanted to enter a monastery, he could not get his way. On the contrary, the pope ordered him, with the agreement of the king and of the bishops who supported Hincmar [the former bishop], to hold his see and to carry out his episcopal duties.[18] When Hincmar's supporters

15 *Factio et non ratio.* Behind Adalgar and Frotar in the faction opposed to Gauzlin were Abbot Hugh and Boso; Werner 1979: 419-20. Hincmar here sounds sympathetic to Gauzlin.

16 Above 869, n. 34. Hugh, unmentioned in the sources since 869, had probably continued to have supporters.

17 Above n. 4.

18 Hedenulf had succeeded the deposed and blinded Hincmar at Laon; above 873, n. 5, and McKeon 1978: 162-3. Hincmar of Rheims naturally had a strong interest in keeping Hedenulf in post. The blind Hincmar now presented Pope John with a dossier of his grievances against his uncle, *Libellus reclamationis*, PL 124, col. 1071.

heard what Pope John had said, namely that Hincmar, though blinded, could if he wished chant the Mass, and that the king had given his agreement to Hincmar's receiving a share in the episcopal revenues of Laon, the bishops of other provinces and also the metropolitans of other regions unexpectedly, and without having any orders from the pope, led Hincmar, clad in his priestly robes, into the papal presence; and from there, chanting, they brought him away and led him into the church and had him give the sign of blessing over the people. With that, the synod was brought to a close.

Next day, King Louis came to Boso's house at his invitation, with some of the magnates who were his counsellors. Regaled and treated with great honour by Boso and by Boso's wife, the king arranged a marriage between Boso's daughter and his own son Carloman;[19] and on the advice of those same counsellors of his, he distributed the *honores* of Bernard *markio* of Gothia amongst Theuderic the chamberlain,[20] Bernard count of the Auvergne,[21] and others for whom this had been secretly arranged.

Pope John left Troyes and reached Chalon. Travelling on from there by way of Maurienne, he entered Italy by the Mont Cenis pass, escorted on his way by Boso and his wife.

King Louis returned from Troyes to Compiègne where he heard a report from the envoys whom he had sent to his cousin Louis [the Younger] to arrange a peace between them. Thereupon he and some of his counsellors came to Herstal. The meeting between Louis and his cousin took place at Meersen on 1 November and a peace was confirmed between them by both sides. They fixed a further meeting for the following Feast of the Purification of Holy Mary [2 February

19 Boso married the Emperor Louis II's daughter Ermengard less than three years before, above 876, n. 3, so any daughter of theirs must have been tiny. Or was this a daughter of Boso's first marriage (above 876, n. 3)? Carloman, second son of Louis the Stammerer by Ansgard, was perhaps aged thirteen in 878; Werner 1967, family-tree.

20 One of Charles the Bald's faithful men left in Francia in 877 to help Louis the Stammerer; Capit. of Quierzy, c. 15, above 877, n. 5. Theuderic was probably made chamberlain by Louis at the time of his accession, above 877, n. 18, though he may already have held that office under Charles the Bald. Theuderic can be identified as a brother of Count Eccard of Autun (d. 876/7); Levillain 1937: 381-7, Lot 1970a (1941): 673, and had evidently been granted the countship of Autun by Louis the Stammerer; see below 879: 216. *Markio* Bernard of Gothia had been punished, presumably for his part in his brother's insurrection (above 878: 206) by the loss of at least some of his *honores*, and had retaliated by seizing Autun; below 879: 215.

21 Above 872, nn. 5 and 14; 876, n. 35

879]: Louis, son of Charles, was to come to Gondreville, and Louis, son of Louis [the German], to some place in the vicinity that suited him. At this assembly, anyway, they agreed, with the consent of their faithful men, that the following things would be observed between them:[22]

The agreement made between the glorious king Louis, son of the Emperor Charles, and the other Louis, son of King Louis, at the place called Fouron, on 1 November, with the favour and consent of them and of the faithful men of both, in the year of the Lord's Incarnation 878, in the eleventh Indiction.

King Louis, son of Charles, made this statement:

'We wish that the kingdom should remain divided just as it was divided between my father Charles and your father Louis. And if any one of our faithful men holds anything wrongfully, let him yield it up on our command. Further, concerning the realm which Emperor Louis of Italy held, because no division of it has yet been made, let whoever now holds it continue to do so until, by God's will, we can meet again with our faithful men from both sides, and discover and determine whatever seems to us better and more just in this matter. But concerning the kingdom of Italy, because no reasonable settlement exists at present, let all men know that we have demanded and are demanding our share of that kingdom, and with God's help we shall go on demanding it.'

Next day, the following things were settled:

'1. Because the firmness of our friendship-alliance and union could not be established up to now, because certain things have hampered us, may such friendship now remain between us henceforth, with God's help, from pure heart and good conscience and faith unfeigned, that no-one may covet or steal away from his fellow-ruler his life, kingdom or faithful men or anything pertaining to the well-being, prosperity and honour of the kingdom.

22 The meeting took place near Meersen at Fouron (modern Belgium, prov. Liège), just half-way between Aachen and Herstal, entailing an equal journey for both parties. Hincmar probably produced the text of the *conventio* (cf. *MGH Capit.* II, no. 246, p. 168) for which the *AB* are the sole source; note especially his interest in c. 7, below: 215. Both Louis the Younger and Louis the Stammerer were concerned to secure a stake in the Italian succession, at the expense of Karlmann and Charles the Fat; for Louis the Younger, see *AF* 877, n. 6. Fried 1984: 19 argues that this *conventio* signalled a new form of Carolingian diplomacy: each king represented an independent entity, 'their unity now no longer that of the Frankish empire, but that of the church'.

2. If the pagans or false Christians rise up against one of us in his kingdom, each of us should help his fellow-ruler wherever the latter thinks necessary and wherever he himself reasonably can, either in person or through his faithful men, with counsel and aid, as best he can.

3. If I survive you, I shall help your son Louis who is still a child, and whomsoever other sons the Lord may grant you, with counsel and aid, as best I can, so that they may be able to hold their father's kingdom peacefully and by hereditary right. If you survive me, however, I in my turn request you to help with counsel and aid, as best you can, my sons Louis and Carloman, and any others whom divine generosity may wish to grant me, so that they can hold their father's kingdom in peace.

4. If any whisperers and disparagers, envious of our peace and unable to bear the realm's being peaceful, wish to sow quarrels and contentions and discords between us, let none of us receive such a man nor willingly accept him, unless perhaps the intention is to bring such a man to answer for himself before both of us and all our faithful men. But if the man should refuse to do this, let him have no kind of association with any of us, but let us all, acting together, cast him away from us as a liar and a fraud and someone who wants to sow discords between brothers, so that no one from henceforth may dare to bring such falsehoods to our ears.

5. Acting together, we shall send our envoys as speedily as possible to the glorious kings Karlmann and Charles [the Fat] to invite them to the assembly which we have fixed for 6 February and to request them urgently not to delay coming; and if they are willing to come, in accordance with our wishes, let us with the Lord's assistance join together in fellowship in accordance with the will of God and for the salvation of Holy Church and our common honour and the advantage and well-being of the Christian people committed to us, so that from now on we may be as one, and wish to be one in Him who is One, and all say and do as one, as the Apostle says, and let there be no divisions amongst us.

6. If, however, Karlmann and Charles, or their envoys, summoned at our urgent request, should delay coming to the assembly abovementioned, we shall certainly be there, according to what we have decided, and shall not fail to unite in every way possible according to God's will, unless by chance such an inescapable commitment

arises as to make that quite impossible, and if that should happen,
let the one concerned ensure that his fellow-ruler finds out in good
time, so that our friendship may therefore not be lessened or
changed until, by the Lord's will, it can be fully confirmed at a
suitable time.

7. Concerning the lands of churches, in whosesoever kingdom the
Mother-Church may be (and this is to apply both to bishoprics and
abbeys): the rectors of those churches are to have possession of the
lands without any opposition. If any wrongdoing is committed
there by anyone at all, let the one in whose kingdom these lands lie
make the wrongdoer pay the legal penalty for it.

8. Because the peace and quiet of the realm keep being shaken by
rootless men who lack respect for anything and behave like tyrants,
it is our will that, to whomsoever of us such a man may come to
evade giving an account of what he has done and paying the penalty
for it, no one of us should receive or keep him for any purpose,
unless he be brought to right reason and due emendation. If he tries
to evade right reason, we shall all pursue him together, into
whosesoever kingdom he comes, until he is either brought to reason
or expelled and blotted out of the realm.

9. It is our will that those who have deservedly lost their own lands
in our kingdom shall be so judged as it was found right they should
be judged in the times of our predecessors: that is, those who claim
they have lost their lands unjustly should come into our presence
and judgement should there be given them, as is just, and they
should get what is their own.'

When all this had been said, Louis, son of Louis, returned to his own
lands, and Louis, son of Charles, came through the Ardennes

879

to Longlier where he celebrated Christmas. After staying for a while
in the Ardennes, he set off again and reached Ponthion around the
Feast of the Purification of Holy Mary [2 February]. Then he went on
to Troyes, because he wanted to get to the region of Autun in order
to suppress the rebellion of the *Markio* Bernard.[1] But his illness grew
worse (it was said that he had been poisoned) and he could journey no

1 Bernard of Gothia, above 878: 212 and n. 21.

further. So he sent his son and namesake Louis to Autun, committing
him to the guardianship[2] of Bernard, count of the Auvergne.[3] With his
son he sent to Autun Abbot Hugh, and Boso, as well as the Bernard
just mentioned, and he also sent Theoderic there with his men to make
good Theuderic's claim to that countship, which the king had
previously granted him.[4] As for King Louis himself, travelling by way
of the convent of Jouarre, he reached Compiègne only with great
difficulty. He realised that he was about to die; he therefore dispatched
Bishop Odo of Beauvais and Count Albuin to his son Louis with the
crown and sword and the rest of the regalia, and he sent orders to the
men who were with his son to have him consecrated and crowned
king.[5] Louis died on Good Friday, 10 April, in the evening, and was
buried next day, Easter Saturday, in the church of Holy Mary.[6]

When Odo and Albuin got news that the king was dead, they handed
over the regalia they were carrying to Theuderic the chamberlain and
hastily retraced their steps. But the men with the king's son, when
they learned of the child's father's death, told the magnates in those
parts to assemble at Meaux to meet them and there discuss what
should be done next. An agreement was reached between Boso and
Theuderic, with Abbot Hugh acting as mediator, whereby Boso was to
have the county of Autun and Theuderic by way of exchange was to
have the abbacies which Boso had held in those parts.[7]

At this point, Abbot Gauzlin, remembering the double-dealing and the
wrongs he had suffered from his rivals for some time previously,[8]
began to think about ways of revenging himself on those who opposed
him. He counted on the friendly relationships he had formed with King
Louis [the Younger] of Germany and his wife and with the magnates
of that country, when he had been taken east of the Rhine after being

2 *Baiulatio*: cf. above 861, n. 13.

3 For his interests in the Autunois, above 872, n. 14.

4 Above 878, n. 21.

5 Odo, above 870, n. 3; Albuin may be the man who as a youth had been among
  the following of Charles of Aquitaine, above 864, n. 4. There is no information
  on his career meanwhile. Note that Queen Adelaide was not entrusted with
  custody of the regalia, perhaps because of her questionable marital status,
  above 878, n. 15.

6 Charles the Bald's palatine chapel, above 877, n. 4. Meyer-Gebel 1987: 102
  suggests that Hincmar wrote up the whole of Louis the Stammerer's reign (i.e.
  from 877 up to this point) at one go.

7 In 877, Boso had been the patron of the abbey of St-Martin Autun (T. 444).

8 Above 878, n. 16. It is clear from the critical comments in the rest of this annal
  that Hincmar was no longer in alliance with Gauzlin.

captured at the battle of Andernach.[9] He found an ally in Count Conrad of Paris,[10] whom he misled with false hopes about gaining enormous power, spelling out some clever ideas about how he might exploit it.

Before the men who were with the king's son could come to the planned assembly at Meaux, Gauzlin and Conrad moved quickly to summon as many bishops and abbots and magnates as they could to an assembly at the point where the River Thérain flows into the Oise. Their pretext was that because the king was dead, they ought to meet to discuss what was best for the kingdom and for maintaining peace within it. They persuaded those who did come to their assembly to invite King Louis [the Younger] of Germany into this kingdom, and promised them that by grants from him they would now get whatever *honores* they had not been able to acquire before, and, they said, there would be no doubt about it. They sent messengers to that Louis and his wife, asking them to come with all possible speed to Metz:[11] there, they said, they would be able to bring to him all the bishops, abbots and magnates of this kingdom. So they went by way of Servais and along the Aisne, ravaging and plundering as they went, until they reached Verdun, while Louis came to Metz. Then they sent messengers to him again, asking him to come on to Verdun, for, they said, it would be easier to bring the magnates of this kingdom to him there. Louis now therefore advanced to Verdun, with his army committing so many atrocities of all kinds that their crimes seemed to outdo those of the pagans.

When Hugh, Boso and Theuderic, and their followers, heard what Gauzlin and Conrad and their accomplices were plotting, they sent Bishop Walter of Orléans and Counts Goiramn and Ansger[12] to Louis [the Younger] at Verdun. Their orders were, to offer him that part of the kingdom of Lothar [II] which Charles had received after negotiations with his brother Louis [the German], father of this Louis [the

9 Above 876: 197.

10 Above 876, n. 39. Conrad may also have already had connections with the East Frankish court; above 871, n. 4; 875, n. 10.

11 The venue, and the invitation to Queen Liutgard, suggest that a royal consecration was envisaged.

12 Walter of Orléans (868/9–c.891) was an ally of Abbot Hugh, *AV* 879: 45; Goiramn, above 877: 201; Ansger is identified by L/G: 237, n. 2 with the patron of Montiéramey (dep. Aube) in the charter of Carloman no. 81, pp. 214–15. The ensuing negotiations with Louis the Younger are mentioned by *AV* and by Regino, but not by *AF*.

Younger], and the plan was that this Louis, once he had gained that part of the realm, would return to his own kingdom and agree to let the rest of Charles's kingdom, which Louis [the Stammerer] had held, pass to the latter's sons. Louis [the Younger] and his men accepted this offer and they rejected with contempt Gauzlin, Conrad and their accomplices. After receiving the part of the kingdom he had been offered, Louis returned to his palace at Frankfurt.[13] When his wife heard what had happened, though, she was furious: she declared that he would have got the whole kingdom if she had gone with him!

It was to this queen that Gauzlin and Conrad now fled in desperation, complaining that they had been deceived.[14] Then messengers came to them, bringing assurances on Louis's behalf and other men sent by way of hostages. So Gauzlin and Conrad returned to their supporters, ravaging and pillaging *en route* wherever they could reach, and told them that Louis would indeed come with a large army just as soon as he could, but that he was unable to do so for the moment because he had got news from a reliable source that his brother Karlmann had been stricken by paralysis and was near death, and that Arnulf, Karlmann's son by a concubine, had occupied part of his kingdom.[15] It was clear that Louis ought to make for that area rapidly. That was what he did; he calmed down the trouble in those parts as far as he could and then returned to his wife.

When Abbot Hugh and the other magnates who had aligned themselves with Louis [III] and Carloman [II], the sons of their late lord Louis [the Stammerer], heard that Louis [the Younger] was coming westwards into that region with his wife, they despatched certain bishops, Ansegis [of Sens] and others, to the monastery of Ferrières and there they had the young Louis and Carloman consecrated and crowned kings.[16]

---

13 This agreement was confirmed in February 880 at Ribemont; below: 220.

14 Hincmar is the only source for Gauzlin's and Conrad's appeal to Queen Liutgard. It was this which led to a second invasion by Louis the Younger early in 880, below: 220.

15 Karlmann had never recovered from the illness that struck him down over a year before, above 877: 203. Arnulf, his son by a noble concubine Liutswind (*MGH DD Arnulfi* nos. 87, 136, pp. 128-30, 203-5, and Regino 880: 116), was already ruling Bavaria during his father's illness, *AF* 879, n. 4. He later became king of East Francia (887-99) and emperor (896).

16 The date was in September; Werner 1979: 428, n. 107. The *ordo* used by Ansegis of Sens is unknown, but may have been the 'Erdmann' *Ordo*, Schramm 1968 (ii) (1934): 216-19.

Meanwhile Boso's wife had kept on goading him into action. She declared that, as the daughter of the emperor of Italy and the one-time fiancée of the emperor of Greece, she had no wish to go on living unless she could make her husband a king.[17] So Boso persuaded the bishops of those parts to anoint and crown him king. He had partly browbeaten them by threats and partly won them over because they were greedy for the abbeys and estates he promised them, and which he afterwards gave them.[18]

Hugh, the son of Lothar [II] by Waldrada, gathered a large force of brigands and tried to gain possession of his father's kingdom.[19]

Charles [the Fat], son of the late King Louis of Germany, marched into Lombardy and seized that kingdom. Before he crossed the *Mons Jovis* pass, Louis [III] and Carloman [II] went to have talks with him at Orbe.[20] When he had gone on into Lombardy and they had returned from their journey, news reached them that the Northmen on the Loire were ravaging those parts, travelling about overland. Louis and Carloman marched immediately into that area and met up with them on St Andrew's Day [30 November]. They slew many of them and drowned many too in the River Vienne, and by God's will the army of the Franks came home safe and victorious.

17 Above, 869: 162; 876, n. 3; 878, n. 20.

18 According to Regino 879: 114, Boso despised the sons of Louis the Stammerer as 'of inferior birth' (*degeneres*). Boso's intention was to claim the whole West Frankish kingdom; Bautier 1973. See Nelson 1990d: 21-2. Regino distinguishes between the elective assembly of Mantaille, near Vienne, on 15 October (*MGH Capit.* II, no. 284, pp. 365-6) and the ensuing consecration by Archbishop Aurelian at Lyons. See Schramm 1968(ii): 257-66.

19 Above 878, n. 17. Cf. *AF* 879: n. 8. Despite Hincmar's dismissive language, Hugh evidently had much support. *AV* 879: 45 shows Hugh with a substantial band of followers mounting resistance to Vikings in Brabant; Bund 1979: 447-8.

20 Louis and Carloman renounced their claims in western Lotharingia in Charles's favour, below 882, n. 3, and also presumably relinquished their father's claims in Italy, above 878, n. 23. In a letter written late in 879 to Charles the Fat, Hincmar proposed that Charles adopt one of the two young sons of Louis the Stammerer in order to avert a division of the West Frankish kingdom; Flodoard III, c. 24, p. 537; Devisse 1976: 982-3. There is no hint of this in the *AB*.

880

Louis [the Younger] king of Germany together with his wife came from Aachen into these parts, and got as far as Douzy. There Gauzlin and Conrad went to meet them, but many of their accomplices had already withdrawn their support and were no longer with them. From Douzy, Louis and his wife went on to Attigny, and from there to Ercry, finally reaching Ribemont. They realised that Gauzlin and Conrad were incapable of delivering what they had promised, and therefore that what both the king and his wife had hoped for was quite unobtainable. So they made a friendship-treaty with the sons of Louis [the Stammerer], fixed a future assembly for June at Gondreville, and went back to their own country.[1] While on his way there Louis [the Younger] came upon some Northmen, and, with the Lord's help, his army slew most of them.[2] But Louis suffered serious losses of his faithful men in Saxony through the attacks of the Northmen there.[3]

The sons of the late King Louis [the Stammerer] returned to Amiens, and divided their father's kingdom between them along the following lines decided on by their faithful men: Louis was to have what was left of his father's kingdom of Francia, and also Neustria, while Carloman was to have Burgundy and Aquitaine, with their marches.[4] Each of the magnates commended himself to one of the two kings – namely the one in whose share of the kingdom the magnate in question held *honores*.

From Amiens the two kings returned to Compiègne and celebrated Easter [3 April] there. Then they went by way of Rheims and Châlons

---

1 The Treaty of Ribemont (dep. Aisne), near St-Quentin, confirmed the handing-over to Louis the Younger of the western part of Lotharingia, acquired by Charles the Bald in 870. The date was February; *AV* 880: 46. *AV* also reveal the rivalry between Hugh and Gauzlin. For the meeting at Gondreville which Charles the Fat was also to attend, below: 221.

2 The battle took place at Thiméon (modern Belgium, prov. Hainaut); *AF* 880, adding that Louis the Younger's bastard son Hugh was killed; *AV* 880: 46-7 signal Abbot Hugh's part in the battle. Hincmar made no reference in his 879 annal to the arrival in Francia of this new Viking force from England; cf. *AV* 879: 44. Hincmar's omissions and lack of details for the last years of his annals, especially 880-82, could well imply that he was writing up these events from memory at Épernay in 882; Meyer-Gebel 1987: 102-3.

3 This severe defeat occurred on 2 February, and among the slain was Queen's Liutgard's brother Duke Bruno; *AF* 880.

4 For similar details on the division at Amiens, *AV* 880: 47. Werner 1979: 431-3 stresses the role of rival factions around Hugh (supporting Carloman) and Gauzlin (supporting Louis III).

to meet their cousins at the assembly fixed for mid-June at Gondreville. Louis [the Younger] was prevented by illness from coming to this assembly, but sent envoys on his behalf. Charles [the Fat] arrived there after coming back from Lombardy.[5] It was decided by common consent at this assembly that the two kings who were sons of the late Louis [the Stammerer] should return to Attigny with a contingent of troops supplied by King Louis of Germany, and launch an attach on Hugh son of Lothar [II]. When they got there, they did not find Hugh, but they attacked Hugh's brother-in-law Theutbald and after many men had been killed in the battle they put him to flight.[6]

From there the two kings, with the host drawn from their kingdoms and also the troops supplied by King Louis of Germany, set off from Troyes in July and marched into Burgundy against Boso,[7] and King Charles [the Fat] was to join them there with his army. They had previously left a force based at Ghent to guard the kingdom against the Northmen.[8] In the course of this campaign, they drove Boso's men out of the stronghold [castrum] of Mâcon and captured the fortress [castellum] itself, and handed it over, along with the county, to Bernard nicknamed 'Hairy-paws'.[9] Charles, Louis and Carloman then advanced to besiege Vienne. Boso had left his wife and daughter there

---

5 Hincmar wrote to Charles the Fat at about this time asking him to pick suitable tutors for his young cousins Louis and Carloman, PL 125, cols. 989-94.

6 Cf. AF 880, dating this battle to August, and crediting the victory to East Frankish troops under Counts Henry and Adalard; AV 880: 47. The legitimate Carolingians of the east and west took joint action to eliminate Hugh, son of Lothar II and Waldrada. Theutbald was the son of Hubert, above 860, n. 7, and hence a nephew of Theutberga. Theutbald's marriage to Hugh's sister may have indicated an end to the conflict between the supporters of Theutberga and Waldrada, in the interests of reviving the Middle Kingdom.

7 Above 879.

8 AV: 48 add that King Louis (III) had put this force under Abbot Gauzlin, and that an unsuccessful campaign against the Vikings ended in early October.

9 The nickname implies foxiness; Malbos 1964. Though this is the first (and only) time it is so called, Bernard son of the tyrant Bernard, count of the Auvergne, seems to be meant; above 878, n. 22. Note that Hincmar's way of identifying persons in the AB is not consistent, and that the last few annals show peculiar traits; above n. 2. Count Bernard of the Auvergne, last referred to as the appointed guardian of the young Louis III, above 879: 216 and n. 3, was well-placed to develop his interests in Burgundy. After his death in 886, Mâcon seems to have been held by his son; Dhondt 1948: 296, against the suggestion of Levillain 1946: 169-202 that this Bernard was the marchio of Gothia, on the grounds that AF 880 show a Bernard defending Mâcon on Boso's behalf, and surrendering when the town was stormed. Levillain's argument that AB 880 and AF 880 referred to the same Bernard is unconvincing: the Marchio Bernard, last mentioned in the AB as in rebellion

with a large part of his troops, while he himself fled into a mountain-ous region.[10] But at this point Charles, who had promised to besiege Vienne along with his cousins, suddenly abandoned the siege, and after exchanging certain mutual oaths with them, went off to Italy.[11] He reached Rome and secured his own consecration as emperor by Pope John on Christmas Day.[12]

881

While Carloman with his men stayed to put down Boso's revolt, his brother Louis went back to a part of his kingdom to fight the Northmen[1] who, laying waste everything as they passed, had captured the monastery of Corbie, the *civitas* of Amiens, and other holy places.[2] A good number of the Northmen had been slain, and others put to flight, when Louis himself together with his men fled in their turn, though no one was even pursuing them. Thus was manifested a divine judgement, for what had been done by the Northmen obviously came about by divine, not human, power.[3] When Northmen yet again attacked part of his kingdom, this same Louis once more advanced to meet them with as many men as he could muster. Urged by some of his advisers, he constructed a fortress of wood at a place called Étrun, but it turned out to have been built more for the protection of pagans than for the help of Christians, for even King Louis himself could find no one to whom he could entrust the fortress's defence.[4] He returned from there ...

> against Louis the Stammerer, above 878: 212 and n. 21, 879: 215, had presumably made terms with Boso, leaving Autun (above 879: 216) in exchange for Mâcon, after Boso's usurpation. The pair then made common cause in 880 against the sons of Louis the Stammerer and their supporters.
>
> 10 Cf. *AV* 880: 47: 'Boso fortified himself very strongly inside the town.'
>
> 11 *AV* add that after his departure, the siege of Vienne had to be lifted. Hincmar omits this; but his attitude to Charles the Fat here and later turns cool.
>
> 12 This is wrong: Charles the Fat was consecrated on 12 February 881; Brühl 1962: 325.
>
> 1 *AV* 881: 49 add that Louis spent Christmas (880) at Compiègne.
>
> 2 *AV* add that this happened in February.
>
> 3 The battle of Saucourt-en-Vimeu, on 3 August, is strangely depicted by Hincmar as a defeat. Cf. *AV* 881: 50; *AF* 881; and especially Regino 883 (!): 120, describing a major victory. The Old High German poem the *Ludwigslied* celebrates Saucourt; Fouracre 1985; Yeandle 1989.
>
> 4 The fortress (*castellum*) at Étrun (dep. Nord), near Cambrai, was intended to block the Vikings' route inland via the river Scheldt. *AV* 881: 51 also record the building of this fort, but without Hincmar's critical comments. L/G: 245, n. 1

882

... and spent Christmas at Compiègne, and Easter [8 April] too. There he heard the news that his cousin Louis [the Younger], son of Louis king of Germany, after living with no benefit to himself or to the church or to his kingdom, had yielded to death.[1] Magnates from that part of the dead king's kingdom which had been given to Louis [III, of the West Franks] as a lease[2] now came to this Louis wanting to commend themselves to him so that he would give his approval to their holding what the father and grandfather of those kings had approved. On the advice of his magnates, however, Louis refused to receive them into his commendation because of the oaths that had been exchanged between himself and Charles [the Fat].[3] But he did assign a squadron of troops specifically to help them against the Northmen. He put Count Theuderic[4] in command of this force. The king himself went over the Seine because he wanted to receive the chiefs of the Bretons and make war on the Northmen.[5] He got as far as Tours, and there he became seriously ill. He was carried on a litter to the monastery of St-Denis, and in August he died and was buried there.[6]

The magnates of the kingdom sent a swift messenger to Carloman asking him to leave the troops who were besieging Vienne and trying

observe that Cambrai lay in the kingdom of Louis the Younger by the terms of Ribemont, above 880: 220. Louis the Younger may have envisaged some kind of imperial overlordship on lines sketched by Charles the Bald; cf. Fried 1984: 15-17. Louis III may thus have exercised delegated power in western Lotharingia; see below 882, n. 2.

1 Louis the Younger died on 20 January. (His only legitimate son, Louis, above: 214, had died in 879; Regino 882:119.) The news must surely have reached Louis III before Easter; Hincmar's sequence is blurred.

2 This passage implies some kind of lease-back arrangement between Louis the Younger and Louis III, following Ribemont; cf. above 881, n. 4.

3 Above 879: 219 and n. 20.

4 Above 878: 212; 879: 216.

5 Cf. *AV* 882: 52, adding that the chief of these Vikings was called 'Alstingus', and that he gave Louis III an undertaking to quit the Loire. See below: 224 and n. 11 and cf. above 163, n. 26.

6 According to *AV* 882: 52, Louis III died on 5 August of internal injuries incurred as follows: 'because he was a young man, he was pursuing a girl, the daughter of a man called Germund, and when she fled into her father's house, the king seated on his horse pursued her for a joke and bashed his shoulders very hard on the upper part of the doorway and his chest on the saddle of his horse'.

to put down Boso's revolt.[7] The magnates said he should make haste to come to them as fast as he could, since they had made all their military preparations for a campaign against the Northmen who had burned the cities of Cologne and Trier and their adjacent monasteries and had got control of the monasteries of St-Lambert at Liège, Prüm and Inden and even the palace at Aachen and all the monasteries of the neighbouring dioceses, that is, of Tongres, Arras and Cambrai and part of the diocese of Rheims, much of which they had burned, including the fortress of Mouzon.[8] They had also slain Bishop Wala of Metz and put his companions to flight;[9] Wala was bearing arms and fighting, contrary to sacred authority and the episcopal office. The magnates, anyway, were ready to receive Carloman and commmend themselves to him, which they then did. While he was occupied with preparations for this campaign, Carloman got news in September from a trustworthy source that Vienne had been captured but that Richard, Boso's brother, had then taken Boso's wife and daughter away with him to his county of Autun.[10] Carloman also learned that the Northman Asting and his accomplices had left the Loire and made for the coastal regions[11]

Charles [the Fat], who had the title of emperor, marched against the Northmen with a large army and advanced right up to their fortification. Once he had got there, however, his courage failed him. Through the intervention of certain men, he managed to reach an agreement with Godefrid and his men on the following terms: namely,

7 Cf. above 880, n. 11. The siege had been restarted by Carloman in 881; L/G: 244, n. 1.

8 Hincmar here conflates the events of 881 and 882. *AF* and Regino date the burning of Cologne and the sack of the monasteries and of Aachen to 881, the burning of Trier to 5 April 882. See L/G: 247, n. 2.

9 Cf. *AF* (Meginhard's Continuation) 882. The Vikings moved from Trier towards Metz, were confronted at Remich on the Moselle by Bishop Wala, Archbishop Bertulf of Trier (above 870, n. 13) and Count Adalard of Metz (above 872, n. 3), whom they put to flight, and they then sacked Metz; Vogel 1906: 287.

10 This is the first appearance of Richard, later duke of Burgundy. He had presumably been given control of Autun by Boso; cf. above 880, n. 9. It was no doubt after the fall of Vienne that Boso fled to the mountains, as recorded by Hincmar above 880: 222.

11 Above n. 5. By 'coastal regions' Hincmar means the coast of Francia between Frisia and the Seine, where other Viking forces were now active. The later career of Hasting (Asting, Alstingus, Haesten) can be traced in 890-92 in Francia and in 892-93 in England; Amory 1979; Keynes and Lapidge 1983: 114-16.

that Godefrid would be baptised, and would then receive Frisia and the other regions that Roric had held.[12] To Sigfrid and Gorm and their accomplices he gave several thousand pounds of silver and gold which he had seized from the treasury of St-Stephen at Metz and from the resting-places of other saints, and he gave them permission to stay so that they could go on ravaging a part of his cousin's kingdom as they had before.[13] To Hugh the son of Lothar [II] he handed over the ecclesiastical property of the see of Metz for him to lay waste[14] – lands which the sacred canons command should be reserved for any future bishop.

Engelberga, widow of Louis [II] king of Italy, had been brought by the emperor over the Alps into Alemannia. At her own request he now sent her back with Bishop Liutward of Vercelli to Pope John in Rome.[15] At the same time, Charles drew back from the Northmen towards Worms where he planned to hold his assembly on 1 November. Abbot Hugh came to this assembly, bringing some of his followers along with him. Their request was that Charles should restore to Carloman, as he himself had promised to do, that part of the kingdom which Carloman's brother Louis [III] had received as a lease.[16] But Hugh secured no firm commitment, while Charles's absence brought the utmost harm to this kingdom, since Carloman lacked the resources to mount resistance to the Northmen once certain magnates of his kingdom withdrew from offering him help.[17] This was the reason that the Northmen came as far as the neighbourhood of the

---

12 Above 872: 177 and 180. This Godefrid (Gotfrid) was a kinsman (?son) of the Godefrid who came to terms with Charles the Bald, above 853: 75; Wood 1987: 44. *AV* 882: 52, and Regino 882: 120 add that Charles the Fat gave Godefrid Gisèle, daughter of Lothar II and Waldrada, in marriage.

13 Cf. *AF* 882 (Regensburg Continuator): 108. Sigfrid led the attack on Paris in 886; L/G: 248-9, n. 2.

14 L/G: 249, n. 1 suggest that this was the price exacted from the emperor by Hugh for agreement to his sister's marriage to Godefrid. Cf. *AF* 883 (Meginhard's Continuation): 100, describing an alliance between Hugh and Godefrid, with no mention of Charles the Fat.

15 Engelberga, held captive by Charles the Fat to prevent her intriguing on Boso's behalf, had appealed to John VIII to secure her release; Odegaard 1951: 92-3.

16 Above n. 2.

17 The reference is probably to Gauzlin and Conrad; Werner 1979: 454 with n. 189. Hincmar does not mention the Vikings' previous movements reported by *AV* 882: 53: in October, the Vikings fortified their camp at Condé (dep. Nord) while Carloman and his men encamped at Barleux (dep. Somme). The Vikings then moved south and crossed the Oise to reach the neighbourhood of Laon.

fortress of Laon, and ravaged and burned all the fortresses in the surrounding area. They planned to move to Rheims and from there to come back by way of Soissons and Noyon and storm the fortress mentioned above and bring the kingdom under their control. Bishop Hincmar[18] found out for certain that this was their plan: since the fighting-men in the command of the see of Rheims were away with Carloman, he only just managed to escape by night, taking with him the body of Remigius and the treasures of the church of Rheims. His physical weakness meant that he had to be carried in a portable chair. While the canons, monks and nuns scattered in every direction, he fled across the Marne and only just managed to reach a *villa* called Épernay. A band of Northmen now went on ahead of the main force and got right up to the gates of Rheims. They ravaged everything they could find outside the *civitas*, and burned a number of small *villae*. But Rheims itself, though defended neither by a wall nor by any human hand, was defended by the power of God and by the merits of the saints, so that the Northmen could not get into it.

When Carloman heard of the Northmen's coming, he attacked them with as many men as he could muster. A large number of those Northmen who were carrying off booty were slain and many of them were drowned in the Aisne. Most important of all, Carloman prised their plunder out of those Northmen who were trying to rejoin their companions after the attack on Rheims. The main host of the Northmen, greater in terms of both size and strength, barricaded themselves up at a *villa* called Avaux. Carloman's men could not attack them there without grave danger to themselves, so as evening drew on they cautiously drew back and took up their posts in nearby *villae*. But the Northmen got out of Avaux as soon as the moon gave them enough light, and they went back again on the route by which they had come.[19]

18 The author refers to himself.

19 *AV* 882: 53 present Avaux (dep. Ardennes) as a Frankish victory (though adding that it 'did not crush the Vikings'), and confirm that the Vikings on their way back 'to Condé to their ships' were attacked and defeated by Carloman and Abbot Hugh near Condé. Hincmar probably died, on 23 December, at Épernay, before the news of this Frankish success reached him; Werner 1979: 453, n. 186.

BIBLIOGRAPHY

Primary sources

A Narrative, annalistic and biographical texts

N.B. included here are only sources cited more than once in the notes to the *Annals of St-Bertin*.

1 *Annals of St-Bertin (Annales Bertiniani).*
See Introduction.

2 *Annals of Angoulême (Annales Engolismenses)*
Ed. O. Holder-Egger, *MGH SS* XVI (Hanover, 1859), p. 486. Very brief annals written at Angoulême in Aquitaine during the ninth century.

3 *Annals of Fontanelle (Annales Fontanellenses; Chronicle of St-Wandrille)*
Ed. (with French translation) by J. Laporte, Société de l'histoire de Normandie 15 sér. (Rouen and Paris, 1951). Brief annals produced at the monastery of Fontanelle (also known as St-Wandrille) near Rouen from 840 to 856.

4 *Annals of Fulda (Annales Fuldenses)*
Ed. F. Kurze, *MGH SRG* (Hanover, 1891). The main annalistic work in the East Frankish kingdom, from 830 to 901; written at Mainz. English translation by T. Reuter forthcoming in the companion volume of *Ninth-century histories.*

5 *Annals of St-Vaast (Annales Vedastini)*
Ed. B. von Simson, *MGH SRG* (Hanover, 1909). Annals written at the monastery of St-Vaast, Arras, from 873 to 900. English translation by S. Coupland forthcoming in the MUP series.

6 *Annals of Xanten (Annales Xantenses)*
Ed. B. von Simson, *MGH SRG* (Hanover, 1909). Written in the lower Rhine area (probably Ghent, then Cologne, rather than Xanten). Draws on *RFA* down to 811; then a fuller, and independent, account from 832 to 873. English translation by S. Coupland forthcoming in the MUP series.

7 Astronomer, *Vita Hludovici Pii*
Ed. G. Pertz, *MGH SS* II (Berlin, 1829), pp. 607-48. Anonymous biography of Louis the Pious, written shortly after 840. A new *MGH* edition by E. Tremp is forthcoming. English translation by Cabaniss, 1961.

8 Flodoard, *Historia Remensis Ecclesiae*
Ed. I. Heller and G. Waitz, *MGH SS* XIII (Hanover, 1881). History of his church written by a Rheims cleric c. 960, using rich archival materials, and

including summaries of letters of Archbishop Hincmar. See Introduction:
11-12.

9 Nithard, *Historiarum Libri IV (Four Books of Histories)*
   Ed. P. Lauer, Nithard, *Histoire des Fils de Louis le Pieux* (Paris, 1926).
   Contemporary history, covering 814 to 843, written by participant
   observer. English translation Scholz, 1970.

10 Regino of Prüm, *Chronicon*
   Ed. F. Kurze, *MGH SRG* (Hanover, 1890). Universal chronicle which
   becomes fairly full annals from c. 850, written up at Trier in 909, and
   particularly well-informed on Lotharingia.

11 *Royal Frankish Annals (Annales Regni Francorum)*
   Ed. F. Kurze, *MGH SRG* (Hanover, 1895). English translation Scholz,
   1970. See Introduction: 4-5.

12 Thegan, *Gesta Hludowici imperatoris*
   Ed. G. Pertz, *MGH SS* II (Berlin, 1829), pp. 585-604. Biography of Louis
   the Pious written in 837 by Trier cleric. A new *MGH* edition by E. Tremp
   is forthcoming.

B Other sources

(i) Letters

1 Hincmar of Rheims, *Epistolae*
   Ed. E. Perels, *MGH Epp.* VIII(i) (Berlin, 1939), 206 letters and summaries
   (via Flodoard) covering the period from 845 down to 868; for letters from
   869 to 882, *PL* 126. The second *MGH* volume is forthcoming.

2 Lupus of Ferrières, *Epistolae*
   Ed. L. Levillain, Loup de Ferrières, *Correspondance*, 2 vols. (Paris, 1927-35),
   with French translation. New ed. by P. Marshall (Leipzig, 1984). English
   translation by G. W. Regenos, *The Letters of Lupus of Ferrières* (The Hague,
   1966). Collection of 133 letters, spanning the period c. 830 to c. 862. (All
   citations in *AB* notes use Levillain's numbering.)

3 Papal correspondence
   Letters of Leo IV, ed. A. de Hirsch-Gereuth, *MGH Epp.* V (Berlin, 1899);
   Nicholas I and Hadrian II, ed. E. Perels, *MGH Epp.* VI (Berlin, 1925); John
   VIII, ed. E. Caspar, *MGH Epp.* VII (Berlin, 1928).

4 Eulogius of Toledo, *Epistolae*
   Ed. *PL* 115, cols. 841-52. Three letters of archbishop of Toledo martyred
   at Cordoba in 859.

(ii) Capitularies and conciliar decrees
Note: Capitularies are legislative and administrative documents drawn up
under headings (*capitula*) and formally promulgated at Carolingian assemblies.
Ecclesiastical councils issued legislation in the form of canons.

1 *Capitularia regum Francorum*
   Ed. A. Boretius and V. Krause, *MGH Capit.* II (Hanover, 1897). Edition of

the capitularies of Charles the Bald, decrees emanating from meetings between ninth-century Carolingian rulers and from church councils, and other related documents.

2 *Die Konzilien der karolingischen Teilreiches 843-859*
Ed. W. Hartmann, *MGH Concilia* III (Hanover, 1984). Fine modern edition with discussion of the texts, their sources and contexts.

(iii) Royal charters

1 *Receuil des Actes de Charles II le Chauve, roi de France*
Ed. G. Tessier, 3 vols. (Paris, 1943-55). Edition of 354 complete royal charters (with 68 mentions of lost charters also noted), also with a few letters and judgements.

2 *Die Urkunden Lothars I und Lothars II*
Ed. T. Schieffer, *MGH Diplomata Karolinorum* III (Berlin, 1966). Edition of 145 complete charters of Lothar I (with 50 further mentions of lost charters), and 39 charters of Lothar II (with 11 further mentions of lost charters).

3 *Receuil des Actes de Pépin I et Pépin II, rois d'Aquitaine*
Ed. L. Levillain (Paris, 1926). Edition of 43 charters (mostly complete) of Pippin I, and 13 of Pippin II; with very full introduction and commentary.

(iv) *Translationes* and *miracula*

Note: A *translatio* is an account of the carrying-away of a saint's body to escape attack. Descriptions of the saint's miracles are often associated with *translationes*.

1 Anonymous, *Translatio Sancti Germani Parisiensis*
Ed. in *Analecta Bollandiana* 2 (1883), pp. 69-98. *Translatio* with *miracula*, including an account of the Viking attack on St-Germain-des-Prés, Paris, in 845. Written up at St-Germain before 851. Translation by D. Bullough, *The Vikings at Paris*, forthcoming in the MUP series.

2 Ermentarius, *De translationibus et miraculis Sancti Philiberti Libri II*
Ed. R. Poupardin, *Monuments de l'histoire des abbayes de Saint-Philibert* (Paris, 1905). An account of the travels of the community of St-Philibert, Noirmoutier, following Viking attack in 836, to Saumur, Cunauld and then Messay (Poitou). Written up in stages in c. 855 and 863. Translated by D. Herlihy,1970.

3 Aimoin of St-Germain-des-Prés, *Translatio* of George, Aurelius et Nathalie
Ed. *PL* 115, cols. 939-60.
Translatio of saints martyred at Cordoba in the early 850s, to St-Germain in 859. Written up at St-Germain c. 875.

4 Aimoin of St-Germain-des-Prés, *Translatio* of Saint Vincent
Ed. *PL* 126, cols. 1011-24.
Translatio of Cordoban martyr to the monastery of Castres near Albi. Written up c. 875.

5 Aimoin of St-Germain-des-Prés, *Miracula Sancti Germani*
Ed. *PL* 126, cols. 1027-50.
Revised version, with additional miracles, of *miracula* of St Germain of
Paris. Written up c. 875.

6 Adrevald of Fleury, *Miracula Sancti Benedicti*
Ed. *PL* 124, cols. 909-48; extracts ed. O. Holder-Egger, MGH SS XV
(Hanover, 1887), pp. 474-97.
Written up at St-Benoît, Fleury, c. 870. Contains historical material for the
period from Charlemagne onwards.

7 Heiric of Auxerre, *De Miraculis Sancti Germani Episcopi Autissiodorensis
Libri II*
Ed. *PL* 124, cols. 1207-70. Written up at St-Germain, Auxerre in later
860s. Book II includes miracles from the 850s.

(v) Collections of episcopal lives and deeds *(gesta)*:

1 *Liber Pontificalis*
Ed. L. Duchesne (revised C. Vogel), 3 vols. (Paris, 1955-57). Papal
biographies, continued up to 870 (the pontificate of Hadrian II) (The
English translation by R. Davis, *The Book of Pontiffs* (Liverpool, 1989) only
goes down to 715, but has a valuable introduction.) No English translation
exists for the ninth-century lives.

2 *Gesta episcoporum Autissiodorensium*
Ed. P. Labbe, *Bibliotheca nova manuscriptorum* 1 (Paris, 1657), pp. 411-626,
extracts ed. G. Waitz, *MGH SS* XIII, pp. 393-400. Deeds of the Bishops of
Auxerre, written up in 870s at request of Bishop Wala (872-79) by two
Auxerre clerics.

3 Agnellus of Ravenna, *Liber Pontificalis Ecclesiae Ravennatis*
Ed. O. Holder-Egger, *MGH SRL* (Hanover, 1878), pp. 265-391. Biographies of archbishops of Ravenna written up by local cleric. Earlier part
written in 830s, then covers pontificate of Archbishop George (817-46).

(vi) Miscellaneous works

1 Ermold the Black (Ermoldus Nigellus), *In Honorem Hludowici Pii*
Ed. E. Faral, *Ermold le Noir. Poème sur Louis le Pieux* (Paris, 1964), with
French translation. Extracts in English translation in Godman 1985.
Panegyric verse biography.written in 827/828 by an Aquitanian cleric.

2 Einhard, *Vita Karoli Magni*
Ed. O. Holder-Egger, *MGH SRG* (Hanover, 1911). English translation L.
Thorpe, *Two Lives of Charlemagne* (Harmondsworth, 1969). Biography of
Charlemagne written in the reign of Louis the Pious, probably in the early
830s by former confidant of the emperor.

3 Dhuoda, *Liber Manualis*
Ed. with French translation by P. Riché (Paris, 1975). Handbook of
spiritual instruction written in 841-43 by Frankish noblewoman for her
son.

4 Walahfrid Strabo, *Carmina*

Ed. E. Dümmler, *MGH Poet. Lat.* II (Berlin, 1884), pp. 259-423. Selected extracts translated in Godman 1985. Poems, many of them written at Louis the Pious's court in the 820s and 830s.

5 Paschasius Radbertus, *Epitaphium Arsenii*

Ed. E. Dümmler, *Abhandlungen der kaiserlichen Akademie der Wissenschaften zu Berlin, phil.-hist. Klasse*, 1900. English translation by Cabaniss 1967. Life of Abbot Wala of Corbie in dialogue-form. Written up in the mid-850s.

6 Hildegar of Meaux, *Vita et miracula Sancti Faronis*

Extracts ed. B. Krusch, *MGH SSRM V* (Hanover, 1910), pp. 171-203. Life of seventh-century bishop of Meaux written by Bishop Hildegar (c. 856-873/6) not long after the Viking attack on Meaux in 862.

7 Ado of Vienne, *Chronicon*

Extracts ed. G. Pertz, *MGH SS* II (Hanover, 1829), pp. 315-23. World history, written c. 870 by archbishop of Vienne (860-75). Brief section covering ninth century is written from Lotharingian standpoint.

8 Rimbert, *Vita Anskarii*

Ed. G. Waitz, *MGH SRG* (Hanover, 1884). English translation by C. H. Robinson, *Askar, the Apostle of the North* (London, 1921). Life of Anskar, missionary to the Danes and bishop of Hamburg-Bremen. Written c. 875 by Anskar's pupil and successor.

9 Andreas of Bergamo, *Historia*

Ed. G. Waitz, *MGH SRL* (Hanover, 1878), pp. 220-30. Written soon after 877. Brief continuation of Paul the Deacon's *History of the Lombards* down to Andreas's own time, with north Italian focus.

10 Erchampert of Monte Cassino, *Historia Langobardorum Beneventanorum*

Ed. G. Waitz, *MGH SRL* (Hanover, 1878), pp. 231-64. History of Lombards in Benevento. Written c. 890 at Capua where the monks of Monte Cassino had fled after Arab attack in 885.

11 *Anglo-Saxon Chronicle*

Ed. C. Plummer, 2 vols. (Oxford, 1892-99); translated G. N. Garmonsway (London, 1972).

12 *Annals of Ulster*

Ed. S. MacAirt and G. MacNiocaill (Dublin, 1983).

13 *Chronique de Nantes*

Ed. R. Merlet (Paris, 1896).

14 *Gesta Sanctorum Rotonensium* and *Vita Conuuoionis*

Ed. with English translation, *The Monks of Redon*, by C. Brett (Woodbridge, 1989).

(vii) Works of Hincmar of Rheims

1 *De Divortio Lotharii regis et Tetbergae reginae, PL* 125, cols. 619-772.

2 *De Ecclesiis et Capellis*, ed. M. Stratmann, *MGH Fontes* (Hanover, 1990).
3 *De ordine palatii*, ed. T. Gross and R. Schieffer, *MGH Fontes* (Hanover, 1980).
4 *Instructio ad Ludovicum Balbum regem*, ed. PL 125, cols. 983-90.
5 *Opera*, ed. PL 125.

Secondary works

Airlie, S. 1985. 'The Political Behaviour of Secular Magnates in Francia, 829-879', Oxford University D.Phil. thesis.

Airlie, S. 1990. 'Bonds of power and bonds of association in the court circle of Louis the Pious', in Godman and Collins ed., *Charlemagne's Heir*, pp. 191-204.

Amory, F. 1979. 'The Viking Hasting in Franco-Scandinavian legend', in M. I. King and W. S. Stevens eds., *Saints, Scholars and Heroes. Studies in Medieval Culture presented to C. W. Jones*, 2 vols., Collegeville, Minnesota, ii, pp. 265-86.

Angenendt, A. 1984. *Kaiserherrschaft und Königstaufe*. Arbeiten zur Frühmittelalterforschung 15, Berlin and New York.

Auerbach, E. 1965. *Literary Language and its Public in Late Latin Antiquity and in the Middle Ages*, London.

Auzias, L. 1937. *L'Aquitaine carolingienne*, Toulouse and Paris.

Baldwin, J. 1970. *Christianity through the Thirteenth Century*. New York.

Bautier, R.-H. 1973. 'Aux origines du royaume de Provence. De la sédition avortée de Boson à la royauté légitime de Louis', *Provence Historique 23*, pp. 41-68.

Bautier, R.-H. 1978. Introduction to *Receuil des Actes de Louis II le Bègue, Louis III et Carloman II rois de France, 877-884*, Paris.

Bishop, J. 1985. 'Bishops as marital advisors in the ninth century', in Kirshner and Wemple eds., *Women of the Medieval World*, pp. 54-84.

Bloch, M. 1961. *Feudal Society*, London.

Blumenkranz, B. 1960. *Juifs et chrétiens dans le monde occidental, 430-1096*, Paris and The Hague.

Borgolte, M. 1987. *Die Grafen Alemanniens im merowingischer und karolingischer Zeit*, Sigmaringen.

Bouchard, C. 1981. 'The origins of the French nobility: a reassessment', *American Historical Review* 86, pp. 501-52.

Bouchard, C. 1986. 'Family structure and family consciousness among the aristocracy in the ninth to eleventh centuries', *Francia* 14, pp. 639-58.

Bouchard, C. 1988. The Bosonids or rising to power in the late Carolingian age', *French Historical Studies* 15, pp. 407-31.

Bouquet, M. 1749-52. *Receuil des historiens des Gaules et de la France*, vols. VI, VII and VIII, Paris.

Boussard, J. 1968. 'Les destinés de la Neustrie du ixe au xie siècle', *CCM* 11, pp. 15-28.

Braunfels, W. ed. 1965-7. *Karl der Grosse. Lebenswerk und Nachleben*, 5 vols., Düsseldorf.

Brown, G. 1989. 'Politics and Patronage at the Abbey of St-Denis (814-98): the rise of a Royal Patron Saint', Oxford University D.Phil. thesis.

Brühl, C.-R. 1962. 'Fränkischer Krönungsbrauch', *HZ* 194, pp. 265-326.

Brühl, C.-R. 1968. *Fodrum, Gistum, Servitium Regis*, Cologne.

Brühl, C.-R. 1975. *Palatium und Civitas Studien zur Profantopographie spätantike Civitates vom 3. bis zum 13. Jht*, vol. I, Gallien, Cologne and Vienna.

Brühl, C.-R. 1988. 'The problem of continuity of Roman *civitates* in Gaul', in Hodges and Hobley eds., *The Rebirth of Towns*, pp. 43-6.

Brunner, H. 1928. *Deutsche Rechtsgeschichte*, vol.II, 2nd edn, Leipzig and Munich.

Brunner, K. 1979. *Oppositionelle Gruppen im Karolingerreich*, Vienna.

Bullough, D. 1962. '"Baiuli" in the Carolingian *regnum Langobardorum* and the career of Abbot Waldo (+813)', *EHR* 77, pp. 625-37.

Bullough, D. 1985. '*Albuinus deliciosus Karoli regis:* Alcuin of York and the shaping of the early Carolingian court', in L. Fenske, W. Rösener and T. Zotz eds., *Institutionen, Kultur und Gesellschaft im Mittelatter. Festschrift für J. Fleckenstein*, Sigmaringen, pp. 73-92.

Bund, K. 1979. *Thronsturz und Herrscherabsetzung im Frühmittelalter*, Bonn.

Cabaniss, A. 1952-53. 'Bodo-Eleazar, a famous Jewish convert', *Jewish Quarterly Review n.s.* 43, pp. 313-28.

Cabaniss, A. 1961. *Son of Charlemagne: a Contemporary Life of Louis the Pious*, Syracuse, New York.

Calmette, J. 1901. *La diplomatie carolingienne*, Paris.

Calmette, J. 1917. 'Le siège de Toulouse par les normands en 864 et les circonstances qui s'y rattachent', *AM* 19-20, pp. 153-74.

Calmette, J. 1951. 'Les comtes Bernard sous Charles le Chauve: état actuel d'une énigme historique', in *Mélanges d'histoire du moyen age dédiés à la mémoire de Louis Halphen*, Paris, pp. 103-9.

Campbell, J. 1989. 'The sale of land and the economics of power in early England: problems and possibilities', *Haskins Society Journal* 1, pp. 23-37.

Canard, M. 1966. 'Byzantium and the Muslim world', *CMH* IV, pp. 697-736.

Chadwick, H. 1967.*The Early Church*, Harmondsworth.

Chédeville, A. and Guillotel, H. 1984. *La Bretagne des saints et des rois, Ve-Xe siècle*, Rennes.

Classen, P. 1963. 'Die Verträge von Verdun und Coulaines, 843, als politische Grundlagen des westfränkischen Reiches', *HZ* 196, pp. 1-35.

Classen, P. 1972. 'Karl der Grosse und der Thronfolge im Frankenreich', *Festschrift für H. Heimpel*, 3 vols., Göttingen, iii, pp. 109-34.

Claude, D. 1960. *Topographie und Verfassung der Städte Bourges und Poitiers bis in das 11 Jhdt.*, Lübeck and Hamburg.

Claussen, M. 1990. 'Carolingian spirituality and the *Liber Manualis* of Dhuoda', *SCH* 27, pp. 43-52.

Collins, R. 1983. *Early Medieval Spain*, London.

Collins, R. 1986. *The Basques*, Oxford.

Collins, R. 1990a. 'Charles the Bald and Wilfred the Hairy', in Gibson and Nelson ed., *Charles the Bald*, pp. 169-88.

Collins, R. 1990b. 'Pippin I and the Kingdom of Aquitaine', in Godman and Collins eds., *Charlemagne's Heir*, pp. 363-89.

Coupland, S. 1987. 'Charles the Bald and the defence of the West Frankish Kingdom against the Viking Invasions, 840-877', Cambridge University Ph.D. thesis.

Coupland, S. 1988. 'Dorestad in the ninth century: the numismatic evidence', *Jaarboek voor Munt- en Penningkunde* 75, pp. 5-26.

Coupland, S. 1990. 'Money and coinage under Louis the Pious', *Francia* 17, pp. 40-1.

Coupland, S. 1991. 'The early coinage of Charles the Bald', *Numismatic Chronicle* (forthcoming).

Coupland, S. and Nelson, J. L. 1988. 'The Vikings on the Continent', *History Today*, December, pp. 12-19.

Cousin, L. 1683. *Histoire de l'Empire d'Occident*, Paris.

d'Abadal, R. 1980. *Els Primers Comtes Catalans*, 3rd edn, Barcelona.

Davies, W. 1988. *Small Worlds*, London.

Davies, W. 1990. 'Charles the Bald and Brittany', in Gibson and Nelson eds., *Charles the Bald*, pp. 98-114.

Davis, R. H. C. 1987. 'Domesday Book: Continental Parallels', in J. Holt ed., *Domesday Studies*, Woodbridge, pp. 15-40.

Dearden, B. 1989. 'Charles the Bald's fortified bridge at Pîtres (Seine): recent archaeological investigations', *Anglo-Norman Studies 11*, pp. 107-11.

Dearden, B. 1990. 'Pont-de-l'Arche or Pîtres? a location and archaeomagnetic dating for Charles the Bald's fortifications on the Seine', *Antiquity* 64, pp. 567-71.

Decour, P. 1972. 'Le paludisme provoque la mort de Lothaire II et de Charles le Chauve', *Archives Internationales Cl. Bernard no. 2*, pp. 13-26.

Delogu, P. 1968a. 'L'istituzione comitale nell'Italia Carolingia', *BISI* 79, pp. 53-114.

Delogu, P. 1968b. 'Strutture politiche e ideologia nel regno di Ludovico II', *BISI* 80, pp. 137-89.

Deshaines, A. 1871. *Les Annales de Saint-Bertin et de Saint-Vaast*, Paris.

Despy, G. and Verhulst, A. eds. 1986. *La fortune historiographique des thèses d'Henri Pirenne*, Brussels.

Devisse, J. 1975, 1976. *Hincmar, archevêque de Reims, 845-882*, 3 vols., Geneva.

Devos, P., 1967. 'Anastasius the Librarian', *NCE I*, pp. 480-1.

Devroey, J.-P. 1985. 'Réflexions sur l'économie des premiers temps carolingiens (768-877): grands domaines et action politique entre Seine et Rhin', *Francia* 13, pp. 475-88.

D'Haenens, A. 1970. *Les invasions normandes. Une catastrophe?*, Paris.

Dhondt, J. 1948. *Études sur la naissance des principautés territoriales en France (IXe - Xe siècles)*, Bruges.

Dierkens, A. 1985. *Abbayes et chapîtres entre Sambre et Meuse (VIIe-IXe siècles)*, Sigmaringen.

Doehaerd, R. 1971. *The Early Middle Ages in the West. Economy and Society*, Amsterdam, New York and Oxford.

Dubois, J. ed. 1965. *Le Martyrologe d'Usuard. Texte et Commentaire*, Brussels.

Dubois, J. and Renaud, G. eds. 1984. *Le Martyrologe d'Adon*, Paris.

Duby, G. 1974. *The Early Growth of the European Economy*, London.

Du Chesne, F. 1641. *Historiae Francorum Scriptores*, 3 vols., Paris.

Duchesne, L. 1910. *Fastes Épiscopaux de l'ancienne Gaule*, 3 vols., Paris.

Duchesne, L. ed. 1955. *Liber Pontificalis*, revd ed., 3 vols., Paris.

Dümmler, E. 1887-88. *Geschichte des ostfränkischen Reiches*, 3 vols., Leipzig.

Duparc, P. 1951. 'Les cluses et la frontière des Alpes', *BEC* 109, pp. 5-31.

Dutton, P. and Jeauneau, E. 1983. 'The verses of the "Codex Aureus" of St Emmeram', *Studi Medievali* 3rd. ser. 24, pp 75-120.

Dvornik, F. 1948. *The Photian Schism*, Oxford.

Dvornik, F. 1966. 'Constantinople and Rome', *CMH IV*, pp. 431-72.

Ehlers, J. 1976. 'Karolingische Tradition und frühes Nationalbewusstsein in Frankreich', *Francia* 4, pp. 213-35.

Eiten, G. 1907. *Das Unterkönigtum im Reiche der Merovinger und Karolinger*, Heidelberg.

Engreen, F. E. 1945. 'Pope John VIII and the Arabs', *Speculum* 20, pp. 318-30.

Enright, M. J. 1979. 'Charles the Bald and Æthelwulf of Wessex: the alliance of 856 and strategies of royal succession', *Journal of Medieval History* 5, pp. 291-302.

Falkenstein, L. 1981. *Karl der Große und die Entstehung des Aachener Marienstiftes*, Paderborn.

Felten, F. 1980. *Abte und Laienäbte im Frankenreich. Studie zum Verhältnis Staat und Kirche im früheren Mittelalter*, Stuttgart.

Fichtenau, H. 1984. *Lebensordnungen des 10. Jahrhundert*, Stuttgart.

Folz, R. 1969. *The Concept of Empire*, London.

Fossier, R. 1981. 'Les tendances de l'économie: stagnation ou croissance?',*SS Spoleto* 27, pp. 261-90.

Fossier, R. 1986. 'L'économie du haut moyen âge entre Loire et Rhin', in Despy and Verhulst eds, *La fortune historiographique des thèses d'Henri Pirenne*, pp. 51-9.

Fouracre, P. 1985. 'The context of the OHG *Ludwigslied*', *Medium Ævum* 54, pp. 87-103.

France, J. 1979. 'La guerre dans la France féodale', *Revue Belge d'Histoire Militaire* 23, pp. 177-98.

France, J. 1985. 'The military history of the Carolingian period', *Revue Belge d'Histoire Militaire* 26, pp. 81-99.

Fried, J. 1976. 'Boso von Vienne oder Ludwig der Stammler? Der Kaiserkandidat Johannes VIII', *DA* 32, pp. 193-208.

Fried, J. 1984. *König Ludwig der Jüngere in seiner Zeit*, Lorsch.

Fried, J. 1990. 'Ludwig der Fromme, das Papsttum und die fränkische Kirche', in Godman and Collins eds., *Charlemagne's Heir*, pp. 231-73.

Fuhrmann, H. 1958. 'Eine im Original erhaltene Propagandaschrift des Erzbischofs Gunthar von Köln (865)', *Archiv für Diplomatik, Schriftsgeschichte, Siegel- und Wappenkunde* 4, pp. 1-51.

Fuhrmann, H. 1972-74. *Einfluß und Verbreitung der pseudoisidorischen Fälschungen*, Schriften der MGH 24, 3 vols., Munich.

Fuhrmann, H. 1990. 'Fälscher unter sich: zum Streit zwischen Hinkmar von Reims und Hinkmar von Laon', in Gibson and Nelson eds., *Charles the Bald*, pp. 224-34.

Ganshof, F. L. 1949. 'Notes critiques sur les *"Annales Bertiniani"*', in *Mélanges dédiés à la mémoire de F. Grat*, 2 vols., Paris, ii, pp. 159-74.

Ganshof, F. L. 1956. 'Zur Entstehungsgeschichte und Bedeutung des Vertrags von Verdun (843)', *DA* 12, pp. 313-30, translated in Ganshof 1971.

Ganshof, F. L. 1970. 'L'historiographie dans la monarchie franque sous les Mérovingiens et les Carolingiens', *SS Spoleto* 17 (ii), pp. 631-85.

Ganshof, F. L. 1971. *The Carolingians and the Frankish Monarchy*, London.

Ganz, D. 1979. Review of Devisse 1975-76, *Revue Belge de Philologie et d'Histoire* 57, pp. 711-18.

Ganz, D. 1990a. 'The debate on Predestination', in Gibson and Nelson eds., *Charles the Bald*, pp. 283-302.

Ganz, D. 1990b. *Corbie in the Carolingian Renaissance*, Sigmaringen.

Gerberding, R. 1987. *The rise of the Carolingians and the Liber Historiae Francorum*, Oxford.

Gibson, M. T. and Nelson, J. L. eds. 1990. *Charles the Bald. Court and Kingdom*, 2nd rev edn, London.

Gillingham, J. 1990. 'Ademar of Chabannes and the history of Aquitaine in the reign of Charles the Bald', in Gibson and Nelson eds, *Charles the Bald*, pp. 41-51.

Gillmor, C. 1988. 'War on the rivers: Viking numbers and mobility on the Seine and Loire, 841-886', *Viator 19*, pp. 79-109.

Gillmor, C. 1989. 'The logistics of fortified bridge building on the Seine under Charles the Bald', *Anglo-Norman Studies* 11, pp. 87-106.

Godman, P. 1985. *Poetry of the Carolingian Renaissance*, London.

Godman, P. 1987. *Poets and Emperors*, Oxford.

Godman, P. and Collins, R. 1990. *Charlemagne's Heir. New Perspectives on the Reign of Louis the Pious*, Oxford.

Goffart, W. 1966. *The Le Mans Forgeries*, Cambridge, Mass.

Goffart, W. 1988. *Narrators of Barbarian History*, Princeton.

Gorissen, P. 1949. 'Encore la clause ardennaise du traité de Meersen', *MA 55*, pp. 1-4.

Grat, F., Vielliard, J. and Clémencet, S. eds. 1964. *Les Annales de Saint Bertin*, Paris.

Grégoire, H. 1966. 'The Amorians and Macedonians, 842-1025', *CMH* IV, pp. 105-52.

Grierson, P. 1934. 'Hugues de S.-Bertin: était-il archichapelain de Charles le Chauve?', *MA* 44, pp. 241-51.

Grierson, P. 1935. 'Eudes de Beauvais', *MA* 45, pp. 161-98.

Grierson, P. 1937. 'The early abbots of St-Bavo's of Ghent', *RB* 49, pp. 29-61.

Grierson, P. 1939. 'Les origines des comtés d'Amiens, Valois et Vexin', *MA* 49, pp. 81-123.

Grierson, P. 1940. 'Abbot Fulco and the date of the *Gesta abbatum Fontanellensium*', *EHR* 55, pp. 275-84.

Grierson, P. 1965. 'Money and coinage under Charlemagne', in W. Braunfels ed., *Karl der Grosse*, vol. I, pp. 501-36, reprinted in Grierson 1979.

Grierson, P. 1979. *Dark Age Numismatics*, London.

Grierson, P. 1981. 'The Carolingian Empire in the eyes of Byzantium', *SS Spoleto* 27 (ii), pp. 885-918.

Grierson, P. 1990. 'The *Gratia Dei Rex* coinage of Charles the Bald', in Gibson and Nelson eds., *Charles the Bald*, pp. 52-64.

Guillotel, H. 1975-16. 'L'action de Charles le Chauve vis-à-vis de la Bretagne, 843-851', *Mémoires de la Société d'Histoire et d'Archéologie de la Bretagne* 53, pp. 5-32.

Guizot, F. 1824. *Collection des Mémoires relatifs à l' Histoire de France*, Paris.

Halphen, L. 1977. *Charlemagne and the Carolingian Empire*, Amsterdam, New York and London.

Harrison, K. 1976. *The Framework of Anglo-Saxon History to A.D. 900*, Cambridge.

Hartmann, W. ed. 1984. *MGH Concilia III. Die Konzilien der karolingischen eilreiche 843-859*, Hanover.

Hartmann, W. 1989. *Die Synoden der Karolingerzeit im Frankenreich und in Italien, 843-859*, Paderborn.

Hassall, J. and Hill, D. 1970. 'Pont-de-l'Arche: Frankish influence on the West Saxon **burh**?', *Archaeological Journal* 197, pp. 188-95.

Hay, D. 1977. *Annalists and Historians*, London.

Hendy, M.F. 1988. 'From public to private: the western barbarian coinages as a mirror of the disintegration of late Roman state structures', *Viator 19*, pp. 29-78.

Hennebicque, R. 1981. 'Structures familiales et politiques au IXe siècle: un groupe familial de l'aristocratie franque', *RH 265*, pp. 289-333.

Herlihy, D. 1970. *The History of Feudalism*, New York.

Herren, M. 1987, 'Eriugena's "Aulae sidereae", the "Codex Aureus", and the palatine church of St. Mary at Compiègne', *Studi Medievali* 3rd ser. 28, pp. 593-608.

Herrin, J. 1988. *The Formation of Christendom*, Princeton.

Hill, D. 1988. 'Unity and diversity - a framework for the study of European towns', in Hodges and Hobley eds., *The Rebirth of Towns*, pp.8-15.

Hlawitschka, E. 1960. *Franken, Alemannen, Bayern und Burgunder in Oberitalien 774-962*, Freiburg.

Hodges, R. 1990a. *Dark ˙Age Economics*, 2nd edn, London.

Hodges, R. 1990b. 'Trade and market origins in the ninth century: relations between England and the Continent', in Gibson and Nelson ed., *Charles the Bald*, pp. 203-23.

Hodges, R. and Hobley, B. eds. 1988. *The Rebirth of Towns in the West AD 700-1050*, London.

Hoffmann, H. 1958. *Untersuchungen zur karolingischen Annalistik*, Bonn.

Hyam, J. 1990. 'Ermentrude and Richildis', in Gibson and Nelson eds., *Charles the Bald*, pp. 154-68.

Jacob, A. 1972. 'Une lettre de Charles le Chauve au clergé de Ravenne', *RHE* 67, pp. 402-22.

James, E. 1982. *The Origins of France*, London.

Jarnut, J. 1985. 'Die frühmittelalterliche Jagd unter rechts- und sozialgeschichtlichen Aspekten', *SS Spoleto* 31(ii), pp. 765-808.

Jarnut, J. 1990. 'Ludwig der Fromme, Lothar I. und das *Regnum Italiae*', in Godman and Collins eds., *Charlemagne's Heir*, pp. 349-62.

Joranson, E. 1923. *The Danegeld in France*, Rock Island, Illinois.

Kantorowicz, E.H. 1946. *Laudes Regiae. A Study in Liturgical Acclamations and Medieval Ruler Worship*, Berkeley, California.

Keller, H. 1967. 'Zur Struktur des Königsherrschaft im karolingischen und nachkarolingischen Italien. Der "consiliarius regis" in den italienischen Königsdiplomen des 9. und 10. Jhdts.', *Quellen und Forschungen aus Italienischen Archiven und Bibliotheken* 47, pp. 123-223.

Kelly, J. 1986. *The Oxford Dictionary of Popes*, Oxford.

Keynes, S. and Lapidge, M. 1983, *Alfred the Great. Asser's Life of Alfred and Other Contemporary Sources*, Harmondsworth.

Kienast, W., 1968. *Studien über die französischen Volksstamme des Frühmittelalters*, Stuttgart.

Konecny, S. 1976. *Die Frauen des karolingischen Königshauses*, Vienna.

Kottje, R. 1988. 'Kirchliches Recht und päpstlicher Autoritätsanspruch. Zu den Auseinandersetzungen über die Ehe Lothars II', in Mordek, H. ed., *Aus Kirche und Reich: Studien zu Theologie, Politik und Recht im Mittelalter. Festschrift für F. Kempf*, Sigmaringen, pp. 97-103.

Kurze, F. 1881. Introduction to *Annales Fuldenses*, MGH SSRG, Hanover.

Kurze, F. 1895. Introduction to *Annales regni Francorum*, MGH SSRG, Hanover.

Lair, J. 1897. 'Les Normands dans l'île d'Oscelle', *Mémoires de la société historique et archéologique de Pontoise et du Vexin* 20, pp. 9-40.

Lebecq, S. 1989. 'La Neustrie et la mer', in H. Atsma ed., *La Neustrie*, Beiheft der *Francia* 16/1, pp. 405-40.

Le Goff, J. 1969. *Les intellectuels au moyen age*, Paris.

Le Maître, P. 1980. 'L'oeuvre d'Aldric du Mans et sa signification', *Francia* 8, pp. 43-64.

Lesne, E. 1910-1943. *Histoire de la propriété ecclésiastique en France*, 6 vols., Lille.

Levillain, L. 1903. 'Le sacre de Charles le Chauve à Orléans', *BEC* 64, pp. 31-53.

Levillain, L. 1926. Introduction to *Receuil de Actes de Pépin I et Pépin II rois d'Aquitaine (814-848)*, Paris.

Levillain, L. 1937a. 'Essai sur le comte Eudes, fils de Harduin et de Guérinbourg, 845-871', *MA* 46, 47, pp. 153-82, 233-71.

Levillain, L. 1937b. 'Les Nibelungen historiques et leurs alliances de famille', *AM* 49, pp. 337-407.

Levillain, L. 1938. 'Les Nibelungen historiques et leurs alliances de famille' (suite), *AM* 50, pp. 5-52.

Levillain, L. 1939. Review of Auzias 1937, *MA* 49, pp. 131-46.

Levillain, L. 1941. 'Les comtes de Paris à l'époque franque', *MA* 50, pp. 137-205.

Levillain, L. 1946. 'De quelques personnages nommés Bernard dans les Annales d'Hincmar', in *Mélanges dédiés à la mémoire de Félix Grat*, 2 vols., Paris, i, pp. 169-202.

Levillain, L. 1947. 'Les personnages du nom de Bernard dans la seconde moitié du IXe siècle', *MA* 53, pp. 197-242.

Levillain, L. 1948. 'Les personnages du nom de Bernard dans la seconde moitié du IXe siècle' (suite), *MA* 54, pp. 1-35.

Levillain, L. 1964. Introduction and notes to Grat, F. *et al.* eds., *Annales de Saint-Bertin*.

Leyser, K.J. 1979. *Rule and Conflict in an Early Medieval Society: Ottonian Saxony*, London.

Lot, F. 1902. 'Une année du règne de Charles le Chauve: année 866', *MA* 15, pp. 394-438, reprinted in Lot 1970a, pp. 415-60.

Lot, F. 1904a. 'Le Pont de Pitres, *MA* 2nd sér. 18, pp. 1-27, reprinted in Lot 1970a pp. 535-61.

Lot, F. 1904b. 'Pons Liadi', *MA* 2nd sér. 18, pp. 127-39, reprinted in Lot 1970a, pp. 569-78.

Lot, F. 1906. 'Aleran comte de Troyes', MA 19, pp. 199-204, reprinted in Lot 1970a, pp. 582-7.

Lot, F. 1908a. 'La grande invasion normande de 856-862', *BEC* 69, pp. 5-62, reprinted in Lot 1970a, pp. 713-70.

Lot, F. 1908b. 'Note sur le sénéchal Alard', *MA* 2nd sér. 12, pp. 185-201, reprinted in Lot 1970a, pp. 591-607.

Lot, F. 1915. 'La Loire, l'Aquitaine et la Seine de 862 à 866: Robert le Fort', *BEC* 76, pp. 473-510, reprinted in Lot 1970a, pp. 781-818.

Lot, F. 1924. 'Les tributs aux normands et l'église de France au IXe siècle', *BEC* 85, pp. 58-78, reprinted in Lot 1973, pp. 699-719.

Lot, F. 1941. 'I: Les comtes d'Auvergne entre 846 et 877. II. Les comtes d'Autun entre 864 et 878', *BEC* 102, pp. 282-91, reprinted in Lot 1970a, pp. 664-73.

Lot, F. 1968, 1970a, 1973. *Receuil des travaux historiques*, 3 vols., Geneva and Paris.

Lot, F. 1970a. 'Roric. Ses incursions', in *Receuil* ii, pp. 678-85.

Lot, F. 1970b. 'Godfred et Sidroc sur la Seine', in *Receuil* ii, pp. 686-90.

Lot, F. 1970c. 'Sidroc sur la Loire', in *Receuil* ii, pp. 691-704.

Lot, F. and Halphen, L. 1909. *Le règne de Charles le Chauve, i. 840-851*, Paris.

Louis, R. 1946. *Girard, comte de Vienne (...819-877)*, 3 vols., Auxerre.

Löwe, H. 1951. 'Studien zu den *Annales Xantenses'*, *DA* 8, pp. 59-99.

Löwe, H. 1967. 'Die Geschichtsschreibung der ausgehenden Karolingerzeit', *DA* 23, pp. 1-30.

Löwe, H. 1972. 'Hinkmar von Reims under der Apokrisiar', in *Festschrift für H. Heimpel*, 3 vols., Göttingen, iii, pp. 197-225.

Löwe, H. 1988. Die Apostasie des Pfalzdiakons Bodo (838) und das Judentum der Chasaren', in G. Althoff, D. Geuenich, O.G. Oexle and J. Wollasch eds., *Person und Gemeinschaft im Mittelalter. Festschrift für K. Schmid*, Sigmaringen, pp.157-69.

Loyn, H and Percival, J. 1975. *The Reign of Charlemagne*, London.

McCormick, M. 1975. *Les 'Annales' du haut moyen age*, Typologie des sources du haut moyen âge occidental 14, Turnhout.

McCormick, M. 1984. 'The liturgy of war in the early Middle Ages: crises, litanies and the Carolingian monarchy', *Viator* 15, pp. 1-23.

McCormick, M. 1986. *Eternal Victory. Triumphal Rulership in Late Antiquity, Byzantium and the Early Medieval West*, Cambridge.

McKeon, P. 1970. 'Le Concile d'Attigny', *MA* 80, pp. 401-25.

McKeon, P. 1974a. 'The Carolingian Councils of Savonnières (859) and Tusey (860) and their background', *RB* 84, pp. 75-110.

McKeon, P. 1974b. 'Archbishop Ebbo of Rheims', *Church History* 43, pp. 437-47.

McKeon, P. 1978. *Hincmar of Laon and Carolingian Politics*, Urbana, Chicago and London.

McKitterick, R. 1977. *The Frankish Church and the Carolingian Reforms*, London.

McKitterick, R. 1980. 'Charles the Bald and his library: the patronage of learning', *EHR* 95, pp. 28-47.

McKitterick, R. 1983. *The Frankish Kingdoms under the Carolingians*, London.

McKitterick, R. 1989. *The Carolingians and the Written Word*, Cambridge.

McKitterick, R. 1990. 'The palace school of Charles the Bald', in Gibson and Nelson eds., *Charles the Bald*, pp. 326-39.

Magnou-Nortier, E. 1976. *Foi et fidelité. Recherches sur l'évolution des liens personnels chez les Francs du VIIe au IXe siècle*, Toulouse.

Malbos, L. 1964. 'Du surnom de Plantevelue', *MA* 70, pp. 5-11.

Malbos, L. 1966. 'L'annaliste royal sous Louis le Pieux', *MA* 72, pp. 225-33.

Malbos, L. 1970. 'La capture de Bernard de Septimanie', *MA* 76, pp. 7-13.

Mansi, J.-D. 1757-98. *Sacrorum Conciliorum Nova et Amplissima Collectio*, 31 vols.,Venice.

Marenbon, J. 1981. 'Wulfad, Charles the Bald and John Scottus Eriugena', in Gibson and Nelson eds., *Charles the Bald*, 1st edn, pp. 375-83.

J

Marenbon, J. 1990. 'John Scottus and Carolingian Theology: from the *De Praedestinatione*, its background and its critics, to the *Periphyseon*', in Gibson and Nelson eds., *Charles the Bald*, 2nd edn, pp. 303-25.

Martindale, J. 1977. 'The French aristocracy in the early Middle Ages: a reappraisal', *Past and Present* 75, pp. 5-45.

Martindale, J. 1985. 'The kingdom of Aquitaine and the dissolution of the Carolingian fisc', *Francia* 11, pp. 131-91.

Martindale, J. 1990a. 'Charles the Bald and the government of the kingdom of Aquitaine', in Gibson and Nelson eds., *Charles the Bald*, pp. 115-38.

Martindale, J. 1990. 'The nun Immena and the foundation of the abbey of Beaulieu: a woman's prospects in the Carolingian church', *SCH* 27, pp. 27-42.

Metcalf, D.M. 1990. 'A sketch of the currency in the time of Charles the Bald', in Gibson and Nelson eds., *Charles the Bald*, ppp. 65-97.

'Metcalf, D.M. and Northover. J.P. 1989, 'Coinage alloys from the time of Offa and Charlemagne to c. 864', *Numismatic Chronicle* 159, pp. 101-20.

Metz, W. 1960. *Das karolingische Reichsgut. Eine verfassungs- und verwaltungsgeschichtliche Untersuchung*, Berlin.

Meyer-Gebel, M. 1987. 'Zur annalistischen Arbeitsweise Hinkmars von Reims', *Francia* 15, pp. 75-108.

Morrison, K .F. 1964. *The Two Kingdoms. Ecclesiology in Carolingian Poliiical Thought*, Princeton.

Muratori, L. A., 1723-51. *Rerum Italicarum Scriptores*, 24 vols., Milan.

Musset, L. 1965. *Les invasions. Il. Le second assaut contre l'Europe chrétienne (Vlle-Xle siècle)*, Paris.

Mütherich, F. 1971. 'Der Elfenbeinschmück des Thrones', in M. Maccarrone *et* al eds., *La Cattedra lignea di S. Pietro in Vaticano*, Atti della Pontificia Accademia Romana de Archeologia, ser. iii, Memorie X, Vatican City, pp. 253-73.

Mütherich, F. and Gaehde, J.E. 1977. *Carolingian Painting*, London.

Nees, L. 1990. 'Charles the Bald and the *Cathedra Petri*', in Gibson and Nelson eds., *Charles the Bald*, pp. 340-7.

Nelson, J. L. 1971. 'National synods, kingship as office and royal anointing: an early medieval syndrome', *SCH* 7, pp. 41-59, reprinted in Nelson 1986a, pp. 239-57.

Nelson, J. L. 1977a. 'Kingship, law and liturgy in the political thought of Hincmar of Rheims', *EHR* 92, pp. 241-79, reprinted in Nelson 1986a, pp. 133-72.

Nelson, J .L. 1977b. 'Inauguration Rituals', in P.H. Sawyer and I.N. Wood eds., *Early Medieval Kingship*, Leeds, pp. 50-71, reprinted in Nelson 1986a, pp. 283-308.

Nelson, J. L. 1979. 'Charles the Bald and the Church in town and countryside', *SCH* 16, pp. 103-18, reprinted in Nelson 1986a, pp. 75-90.

Nelson, J. L. 1980. 'The earliest surviving royal *Ordo:* some liturgical and historical aspects', in B. Tierney and P. Linehan eds., *Authority and Power. Studies in Medieval Law and Government presented to Walter Ullmann*, Cambridge, pp. 29-48, reprinted in Nelson 1986a, pp. 341-60.

Nelson, J. L. 1983a. 'Legislation and consensus in the reign of Charles the Bald', in P. Wormald ed., *Ideal and Reality. Studies in Frankish and Anglo-Saxon Society presented to J.M. Wallace-Hadrill*, Oxford, pp. 202-27, reprinted in Nelson 1986a, pp. 91-116.

Nelson, J. L. 1983b. 'The church's military service in the ninth century: a contemporary comparative view?', *SCH* 20, pp. 15-30, reprinted in Nelson 1986a, pp. 117-32.

Nelson, J. L. 1985. 'Public *Histories* and private history in the work of Nithard', *Speculum* 60, pp. 251-93, reprinted in Nelson 1986a, pp. 195-238.

Nelson, J. L. 1986a. *Politics and Ritual in Early Medieval Europe*, London.

Nelson, J. L. 1986b. '"A king across the sea": Alfred in Continental perspective', *Transactions of the Royal Historical Society* 36, pp. 45-68.

Nelson, J. L. 1986c. 'Dispute settlement in Carolingian West Francia', in W. Davies and P. Fouracre eds., *The Settlement of Disputes in Early Medieval Europe*, Cambridge, pp. 45-64.

Nelson, J. L. 1987. 'Carolingian royal ritual', in D. Cannadine and S. Price eds., *Rituals of Royalty. Power and Ceremonial in Traditional Societies*, Cambridge, pp. 137-80.

Nelson, J. L. 1988a. 'Kingship and empire', in J. H. Burns ed., *The Cambridge History of Medieval Political Thought*, Cambridge, pp. 211-51.

Nelson, J. L. 1988b. 'A tale of two princes: politics, text and ideology in a Carolingian annal', *Studies in Medieval and Renaissance History* 10, pp. 105-41.

Nelson, J.L. 1989a. 'Ninth-century knighthood: the evidence of Nithard', in C. Harper-Bill, C. Holdsworth and J. L. Nelson eds., *Studies in Medieval History presented to R. Allen Brown*, Woodbridge, pp. 255-66.

Nelson, J. L. 1989b. 'Translating images of authority: the Christian Roman emperors in the Carolingian world', in M.M. Mackenzie and C. Roueché eds., *Images of Authority. Papers presented to Joyce Reynolds on the occasion of her 70th birthday*, Cambridge, pp. 194-205.

Nelson, J. L. 1990a. 'The reign of Charles the Bald: a survey', in Gibson and Nelson eds., *Charles the Bald*, pp. 1-22.

Nelson, J. L. 1990b. 'The Annals of St Bertin', in Gibson and Nelson eds., *Charles the Bald*, pp. 23-40.

Nelson, J. L. 1990c. 'The last years of Louis the Pious', in Godman and Collins eds., *Charlemagne's Heir*, pp. 147-60.

Nelson, J. L. 1990d. 'Hincmar of Reims on king-making: the evidence of the Annals of St. Bertin', in J.M. Bak ed., *Coronations*, Berkeley and Los Angeles, pp. 16-34.

Nelson, J. L. 1990e. 'Perceptions du pouvoir chez les historiennes du haut moyen-âge', in M. Rouche and J. Heuclin eds., *La femme au moyen âge*, Maubeuge, pp. 75-85.

Nelson, J. L. 1991. 'Not bishops' bailiffs but lords of the earth', in D. Wood ed., *The Church and Sovereignty. Essays in Honour of Michael Wilks*, Oxford.

Nelson, J. L. 1992. *Charles the Bald*, London, forthcoming.

Nicol, D. M. 1967. 'The Byzantine view of Western Europe', *Greek, Roman and Byzantine Studies* 8, pp. 315-39.

Nineham, D. 1989. 'Gottschalk of Orbais', *JEccH* 40, pp. 1-18.

Obolensky, D. 1966. 'The Empire and its Northern neighbours', *CMH* IV, pp. 473-518.

Odegaard, C. 1941. 'Carolingian oaths of fidelity', *Speculum* 16, pp. 284-96.

Odegaard, C. 1945a. ' The concept of royal power in Carolingian oaths of fidelity', *Speculum* 20, pp. 279-89.

Odegaard, C. 1945b. *Vassi and Fideles in the Carolingian Empire*, Cambridge, Mass.

Odegaard, C. 1951. 'The Empress Engelberge', *Speculum* 26, pp. 77-103.

Oexle, O.G. 1967. 'Die Karolinger und die Stadt des heilige Arnulf', *FMS* 1, pp. 250-364.

Oexle, O.G. 1969. 'Bischof Ebroin von Poitiers und seine Verwandten', *FMS* 3, pp. 138-210.

Parisot, R. 1899. *Le royaume de Lorraine sous les Carolingiens, 843-923*, Paris.

Partner, P. 1976. *The Lands of St. Peter*, London.

Penndorf, U. 1975. *Das Problem der 'Reichseinheitsidee nach der Teilung von Verdun*, Munich.

Pertz, G. 1826. ed. *Annales Bertiniani*, in *MGH SSI*, Hanover.

Poly, J.-P. 1976. *La Provence et la société féodale (879-1166)*, Paris.

Poupardin, R. 1905. 'Notes carolingiennes. Un nouveau manuscrit des *Annales de Saint-Bertin*', *BEC* 66, pp. 390-400.

Poupardin, R. 1907. *Les institutions politiques et administratives des principautés lombardes*, Paris.

Prinz, J. 1965. 'Ein unbekanntes Aktenstück zum Ehestreit König Lothars II', *DA* 21, pp. 249-63.

Prinz, J. 1977. 'Der Feldzug Karls des Kahlen an dem Rhein im September 876', *DA* 33, pp. 543-5.

Rau, R. 1957?. *Quellen zur karolingischen Reichsgeschichte*, vol. II, Berlin.

Reuter, T. ed. 1978. *The Medieval Nobility*, Amsterdam and New York.

Reuter, T. 1985. 'Plunder and tribute in the Carolingian Empire', *Transactions of the Royal Historical Society* 35, pp. 75-94.

Reuter, T. 1990. 'The end of Carolingian military expansion', in Godman and

Collins eds., *Charlemagne's Heir*, pp. 391-405.

Richard, A. 1893. 'Observations sur les mines d'argent et l'atelier monétaire de Melle sous les Carolingiens', *Revue Nunismatique* 3rd sér.11, pp. 194-225.

Riché, P. 1975. Introduction to Riché ed. *Dhuoda. Manuel pour mon fils*, Paris.

Riché, P. 1977. 'Charles le Chauve et la culture de son temps', in *Jean Scot Eriugène et l'histoire de la philosophie*, Colloques internationales du CNRS 561, Paris, pp. 37-46, reprinted in Riché 1981.

Riché, P. 1981. *Instruction et vie religieuse dans le haut moyen âge*, London.

Riché, P. 1983. *Les Carolingiens. Une famille qui fit l'Europe*, Paris.

Sanchez-Albornoz, C. 1969. 'El tercer rey de España', *Cuadernos de Historia de España* 49-50, pp. 5-49.

Sawyer, P. H. 1982. *Kings and Vikings*, London.

Sawyer, P. H. and Wood, I. N. eds. 1977. *Early Medieval Kingship*, Leeds.

Schieffer, R. 1979. 'Möglichkeiten und Grenzen der biographischen Darstellung frühmittelalterlichen Persönlichkeiten. Zu dem neuen Hinkmar-Buch von J. Devisse', *HZ* 229, pp. 85-95.

Schieffer, R. 1980. 'Arsenius', in *LM 1*, pp. 1054-5.

Schieffer, R. 1982. 'Ludwig der Fromme'. Zur Entstehung eines karolingischen Herrscherbeinamens', *FMS* 16, pp. 58-75.

Schieffer, R. 1986. 'Hinkmar von Reims', *Theologische Realenzyklopädie* 15, pp. 355-60.

Schieffer, R. 1990. 'Väter und Söhne im Karolingerhause', in *Beiträge zur Geschichte des Regnum Francorum*, Beihefte der *Francia*, Band 22, Paris, pp. 149-64.

Schieffer, T. 1960. 'Karl von Aquitanien', in L. Lenhart ed., *Universitas. Festschrift für A. Stohr*, 2 vols., Mainz, ii, pp. 42-54.

Schieffer, T. 1966. Introduction to *MGH Diplomata Karolingorum 3: Die Urkunden Lothars I und Lothars II*, Berlin and Zurich.

Schleidgen, W. 1977. *Die Überlieferungsgeschichte der Chronik des Regino von Prüm*, Mainz.

Schlesinger, W. 1965. 'Die Auflösung des Karlsreiches', in W. Braunfels ed., *Karl der Grosse*, 5 vols., Düsseldorf, vol. 1, pp. 792-857.

Schlesinger, W. 1965. 'Die Auflösung des Karlsreiches', in W. Braunfels ed., *Karl der Grosse*, 5 vols., Düsseldorf, vol. I, pp. 792-857.

Schlesinger, W. 1970. 'Zur Erhebung Karls des Kahlen zum König von Lothringen, 869 in Metz', in G. Dröge *et al.* eds., *Landschaft und Geschichte. Festschrift für F. Petri*, Bonn, pp. 173-98.

Schmid, K. 1968. 'Ein karolingischer Königseintrag im Gedenkbuch von Remiremont', *FMS* 2, pp. 96-134.

Schneidmüller, B. 1979. *Karolingische Tradition und frühes französisches Königtum. Untersuchungen zur Herrschaftslegitimation der westfränkisch-französischen Monarchie im 10. Jahrhundert*, Frankfurt.

Scholz, B. 1970. *Carolingian Chronicles*, Ann Arbor.

Schramm, P.E. 1934. 'Die Krönung bei den Westfranken', *Zeitschrift für Rechtsgeschichte* 54, Kanonistische Abteilung 23, pp. 117-242.

Schramm, P.E. 1954-56. *Herrschaftszeichen und Staatssymbolik*, Schriften der MGH 13, 3 vols., Stuttgart.

Schramm, P.E. 1960. *Der König von Frankreich. Das Wesen der Monarchie vom 9. zum 16. Jahrhundert*, 2 vols., 2nd edn, Darmstadt.

Schramm, P. E. 1968. *Kaiser, Könige und Päpste*, 4 vols., Stuttgart.

Simson, B. von. 1909. Introduction to *Annales Xantenses*, MGH SSRG, Hanover.

Smith, J. M. H. 1982. 'The archbishopric of Dol and the ecclesiastical politics of ninth-century Brittany', *SCH* 18, pp. 59-70.

Smith, J. M. H. 1985. 'Carolingian Brittany', Oxford University D.Phil. thesis.

Smith, J. M. H. 1992. *Province and Empire. Brittany and the Carolingians*, Cambridge.

Smyth, A. P. 1977. *Scandinavian Kings in the British Isles 850-880*, Oxford.

Spufford, P. 1988. *Money and its Use in Medieval Europe*, Cambridge.

Stafford, P. 1981. 'The king's wife in Wessex', *Past and Present* 91, pp. 5-27.

Stafford, P. 1990. 'Charles the Bald, Judith and England', in Gibson and Nelson eds., *Charles the Bald*, pp. 139-53.

Staubach, N. 1982. *Das Herrscherbild Karls des Kahlen. Formen und Funktionen monarchischer Repräsentation im früheren Mittelalter*, Münster.

Stevenson, W. ed. 1904. *Asser, Gesta Ælfredi Regis*, Oxford.

Stratmann, M. ed. 1990. *Hincmar, Collectio de Ecclesiis et Capellis*, MGH Fontes 14, Hanover.

Sullivan, R. E. 1955. 'The papacy and missionary activity in the early middle ages', *Medieval Studies* 17, pp. 46-106.

Tabacco, G. 1989. *The Struggle for Power in Medieval Italy*, Cambridge.

Tessier, G. 1955. Introduction to *Receuil des Actes de Charles II le Chauve*, vol. iii, Paris.

Ullmann, W. 1972 *A Short History of the Papacy in the Middle Ages*, London.

Van Caenegem, R. C., and Ganshof, F. L. 1978. *Guide to the Sources of Medieval History*, Amsterdam and New York.

Van Es, W.A. and Verwers, W. J. H. 1980. *Excavations at Dorestad 1: The Harbour, Hoogstraat 1*, Nederlandse Oudheden no. 9, Amersfoort.

Vercauteren, F. 1935-36. 'Comment s'est-on défendu au IXe siècle dans l'empire franc contre les invasions normandes?', *Annales du XXXe congrès de la fédération archéologique et historique de Belgique*, pp. 117-32.

Verhulst, A. 1989. 'The origins of towns in the Low Countries and the Pirenne Thesis', *Past and Present* 122, pp. 3-35.

Verwers, W. J. H. 1988. Dorestad: a Carolingian town?', in Hodges and Hobley eds., *The Rebirth of Towns*, pp. 52-6.

Vlasto, A. P. 1970. *The Entry of the Slavs into Christendom*, Cambridge.

Vogel, W. 1906. *Die Normannen und das fränkische Reich bis zur Gründung der Normandie (799-911)*, Heidelberg.

Waitz, G. ed. 1883. *Annales Bertiniani, MGH SSRG*, Hanover.

Wallace-Hadrill, J. M. 1960. *The Fourth Book of the Chronicle of Fredegar with its continuations*, Oxford.

Wallace-Hadrill, J. M. 1971. *Early Germanic Kingship in England and on the Continent*, Oxford.

Wallace-Hadrill, J. M. 1975. 'The Vikings in Francia', Reading.

Wallace-Hadrill, J. M. 1976. *Early Medieval History*, Oxford.

Wallace-Hadrill, J. M. 1978. 'A Carolingian Renaissance Prince: the Emperor Charles the Bald', *Proceedings of the British Academy* 64, pp. 155-84.

Wallace-Hadrill, J. M. 1981. 'History in the mind of Archbishop Hincmar', in J. M. Wallace-Hadrill and R. H. C. Davies eds., *The Writing of History in the Middle Ages. Essays presented to R. W. Southern*, Oxford, pp. 43-70.

Wallace-Hadrill, J. M. 1983. *The Frankish Church*, Oxford.

Ward, E. 1990. 'Caesar's wife: the career of the Empress Judith, 819-29', in Godman and Collins eds., *Charlemagne's Heir*, pp. 205-27.

Wattenbach, W., Levison, W. and Löwe, H. 1952-73. *Deutschlands Geschichtsquellen im Mittelalter*, 5 vols.

Weinrich, L. 1963. *Wala. Graf, Monch und Rebell*, Hamburg.

Wemple, S .F. 1981. *Women in Frankish Society*, Philadelphia.

Werner, K. F. 1958. 'Untersuchungen zur Frühzeit des französischen Fürstentums (9.-10. Jht.), I-III', *WaG* 18, pp. 256-89.

Werner, K. F. 1959a. 'Zur Arbeitsweise Reginos von Prüm', *WaG 19*, pp. 96-116.

Werner, K. F. 1959b. 'Untersuchungen zur Frühzeit des französischen Fürstentums (9.-10. Jht.), IV', *WaG 19*, pp. 146-93.

Werner, K. F. 1960. 'Untersuchungen zur Frühzeit des französischen Fürstentums (9.-10. Jht.), V-VI', *WaG 20*, pp. 87-119.

Werner, K .F. 1965. 'Bedeutende Adelsfamilien im Reiche Karls des Grossen', in W. Braunfels ed., *Karl der Grosse*, vol. I, pp. 83-142.

Werner, K. F. 1967. 'Die Nachkommen Karls des Grossen', in W. Braunfels ed., *Karl der Grosse*, vol. IV, pp. 403-79.

Werner, K. F. 1975. 'La date de naissance de Charlemagne', *Bulletin de la Société nationale des Antiquaires de France pour 1972*, Paris, pp. 116-42.

Werner, K. F. 1978. 'Important noble families in the kingdom of Charle-magne', in T. Reuter ed., *The Medieval Nobility*, pp. 137-202.

Werner, K. F. 1979a. 'Gauzlin von Saint-Denis und die westfränkische Reichsteilung von Amiens (880)', *DA* 35, pp. 395-462.

Werner, K .F. 1979b. *Structures politiques du monde franc (VIe - XIIe siècles)*, London.

Werner, K. F. 1980. '*Missus-marchio-comes:* entre l'administration centrale et l'administration locale de l'empire carolingien', in W. Paravicini and K.F. Werner eds., *Histoire comparée de l'administration (IVe-XVIlle siècle)*, Beihefte der *Francia* 9, Munich, pp. 191-239.

Werner, K. F. 1990. '*Hludovicus Augustus:* Gouverner l'empire chrétien - idées et réalités', in Godman and Collins eds., *Charlemagne's Heir*, pp. 3-124.

Wickham, C. 1981. *Early Medieval Italy*, London.

Wickham, C. 1990. 'European forests in the early Middle Ages: landscape and land clearance', *SS Spoleto* 37, pp. 479-548.

Wolfram, H. 1987. *Die Geburt Mitteleuropas*, Vienna and Berlin.

Wollasch, J. 1957a. 'Das *Patrimonium Beati Germani* in Auxerre', in G. Tellenbach ed., *Studien und Vorarbeiten zur Geschichte des großfrankischen und frühdeutschen Adels*, Freiburg, pp.185-224.

Wollasch, J. 1957b. 'Eine adlige Familie des frühen Mittelalters, ihr Selbstverständnis und ihre Wirklichkeit', *Archiv für Kulturgeschichte* 39, pp. 150-88.

Wollasch, J. 1959. 'Königtum, Adel und Kloster im Berry während des 10. Jhdt.', in G. Tellenbach ed., *Neue Forschungen über Cluny und die Cluniacenser*, Freiburg, pp. 20-49.

Wood, I. N. 1987. 'Christians and pagans in ninth-century Scandinavia', in B. Sawyer, P. Sawyer and I. Wood eds., *The Christianization of Scandinavia*, Alingsås, pp. 36-67.

Wormald, P. 1982. 'The Ninth Century', in J. Campbell ed., *The Anglo-Saxons*, Oxford.

Yeandle, D. N. 1989. The *Ludwigslied:* King, Church and Context', in J. Flood and D. N. Yeandle eds., '*mit regulu bituungan'. Neue Arbeiten zur althochdeutschen Poesie und Sprache*, Göppingen.

INDEX

Notes: (i) Homonyms are listed thus: clerical personnel precede lay, lay persons are ordered chronologically, and generational seniority is followed within families. (ii) An asterisk indicates that a person can be found on one of the genealogical tables. (iii) Places in modern France are identified by *département*; other places by region and country.

Aachen (Nordrhein-Westfalen, Germany) 4, 5, 7, 21, 22, 24, 26, 28, 29, 30, 33, 35, 36, 38, 48, 51, 52, 53 n.3, 164, 165, 166, 168, 170, 177, 187, 195, 198, 220, 224 and n.8; synod of (860) 92 n.1

'Abd al-Rahman II, amir of Cordoba 64 and n.1, 66 n.7, 75

Abodrites, *see* Obodrites

accola 130 and n. 5

Aclea (unidentified, England) 69 n. 6

Actard, bishop of Nantes 140 and n. 11, 141, 142, 144, 145, 174

Adalard, abbot of St-Bertin 88 n. 13

Adalard, seneschal, then count of Tours, then count in Lotharingia 23 n. 5, 30 n. 9, 54–5 and n. 12, 56 n. 5, 67 n. 1, 95 and n. 5, 96, 128 and nn. 17, 18, 129, 177 and n. 3, 183 and n. 11

Adalard, count of Metz, ?son of Adalard the seneschal 177 and n. 3, 193 and n. 14, 224 n. 9

Adalard, count of the palace 197 and n. 34, 202 n. 13

Adalbert, *marchio* of Tuscany 207 and n. 6, 208

Adalelm, count in West Francia 166 n. 3, 173 n. 4

Adalelm, count of Laon 166 n. 3

Adalgar, bishop of Autun 195 and n. 22, 200–1, 211

Adalgar, count in Francia 35, 40

Adalgis, *dux* of Benevento 175–6, 183

Adalgrim, Roman 149

Adelaide, daughter of Count Hugh of Tours, wife of Count Conrad 117 n. 3, 144 n. 1

Adelaide*, queen, second wife of Louis the Stammerer 197 n. 34, 202 n. 13, 210 and n. 14, 216 n. 5

Adelgaud, priest 192 n. 12

adnuntiatio (nes) 70 n. 3; 103 and n. 29

Ado, archbishop of Vienne 125 and n. 11, 134

Ado, priest at Rome 149

Adventius, bishop of Metz 96 and n. 17, 117 n. 14, 125, 144, 157 and n. 15, 158, 159, 160, 168 n. 13

Æthelbald*, king of West Saxons 86, 97

Æthelwulf*, king of West Saxons 15, 42–3, 59 n. 22, 80, 83, 86

Africa 54, 90, 154 n. 6

African Council, *see* Carthage, Council of (418)

Agius, bishop of Orléans 79

Aimoin, monk of St-Germain-des-Prés, Paris 16, 229–30

Aisne, river 217, 226

Albegau, region, eastern France 168

Albinus, saint, at Angers 185

Albuin, Frankish noble 112 and n. 4, 216 n. 5

Albuin, count 216

Aldeneik, monastery (Limburg, Belgium) 169

Aldo, bishop of Limoges 134 and n. 23

Aldric, bishop of Le Mans 26 n. 6, 27 n. 3

Aledramn (I), count of Barcelona and the Spanish March 66 n. 7, 68 n. 9, 69 and n. 2, 197 n. 33

Aledramn, count of Troyes, son of Aledramn (I) 197 n. 33

Alemans, Alemannia 21 n. 4, 24, 25, 28, 39, 41, 45, 51, 123, 127, 198, 225

Alfred, king of West Saxons viii, 4